CARPENTRY ESTIMATING

By W.P. Jackson

Includes inside the back cover:

A 3½" high density disk with all the labor estimate tables in the book plus an estimating program for Windows™. The carpentry estimating worksheets on pages 295 to 314 are also on the disk in formats that work with Word, Excel, WordPerfect, and MS Works for Windows™.

Craftsman Book Company

6058 Corte del Cedro / P.O. Box 6500 / Carlsbad, CA 92018

Library of Congress Cataloging-in-Publication Data

Jackson, W.P.
    Carpentry estimating / by W.P. Jackson
      p. cm.
    Reprint of the 1987 ed. with a new computer disk and instructions for the disk.
    Includes index.
    ISBN 0-934041-98-9
    1. Carpentry--Estimates.   2. House construction--Estimates.
  I. Title.
TH5615.J33   1994   94-7835
694--dc2   CIP

Fourth printing 1997

Contents

Estimating Construction Costs

This book was written to help you make fast, accurate carpentry estimates. Read and understand what's written here and you'll be able to estimate the carpentry work on nearly any job. You'll compile reliable, professional estimates without the mistakes that others often make.

If you've never estimated a carpentry job before, picking up this manual is a good first step. I'll get you started off right, learning correct procedures and picking up good habits that can last you a lifetime.

If you've been preparing carpentry estimates for years, you already know much of what I'm going to explain. But even experienced professional carpentry estimators will find in this book new ways to save time and improve accuracy.

It takes some figuring to assemble a carpentry estimate. But don't worry. Even if math wasn't your best subject in high school, you'll have no trouble following my explanations. The right way to estimate any job is the simplest way. Eliminate mistakes by shortening calculations to the barest minimum. The less math, the less likely a math error. That's why I recommend using the multiplying tables you'll see throughout this book. They'll make your estimating faster and eliminate the most common errors.

I'll also emphasize good record keeping. The best carpentry estimators are great record keepers. They prepare neat, tidy, systematic estimates that are easy to read and easier to check. They have a permanent file with all the estimates they've done for the last several years. And right beside each estimate is a list of the actual job costs if their company did the work that was estimated. They refer to this cost file again and again when compiling estimates because they know there's no substitute for experience. No price authority, no published cost data, no rule of thumb, no best guess can beat your own cost records for accuracy. The cost of work done today by your crews, on your jobs, under your supervision and at your labor rates is the best predictor of costs on your next job. That's the truth now and always will be, no matter how estimates are compiled and no matter what type of job you're figuring.

If you don't have a good file of carpentry cost records, don't be concerned. I'm going to give you the figures I've used for many years. But these aren't your costs. They're *my* costs. Yours will be different. My estimates are based on my costs. Yours have to be based on your costs. That's why making and saving good cost records is so important. No one can do it for you. You have to do it yourself.

Start with the Plans

We're not going to do a detailed labor and material take-off in this chapter. That comes in the chapters that follow. Instead, this chapter will cover some important preliminaries: what to do when you get a set of plans, figuring your "labor burden," including all your costs in every estimate, how much to add for profit, setting up a good cost recording system, and using the cost data you compile.

Since nearly every estimate you make will begin with a review of the plans and specifications, that's where this chapter will start.

This isn't a book on plan reading. I'm not going to explain every line you see on a set of prints. But don't assume that plan reading isn't important. It is. In fact, it's the foundation on which all carpentry estimating skills are built. If you aren't comfortable working with plans, spend a few hours with a book that explains plan reading in detail. Several good books are available. At the back of this manual you'll find references that can help sharpen your plan reading skills.

When I get a new set of plans and specifications, I like to begin by developing a mental picture of the proposed building. Once I have the big picture, the details will make more sense. Sometimes the architect will help you get the big picture by including a drawing of the finished building in the prints. This is called a *perspective drawing*. Perspectives are done in ink or water color and show the finished building in its intended surroundings. While in no sense a true working drawing, perspectives make it easier to understand the plans and can save an expensive mistake — like leaving the entire second story off your estimate!

If you don't have a perspective drawing, spend a little more time leafing through the plan sheets until you have a mental picture of the finished structure.

Reading the Floor Plans and Elevations

The working drawings will include all the floor plans, elevation views, cross sections, schedules and detail drawings needed to frame and finish the building. The plans are sure to include floor plans and elevations. The detail drawings and sectional views provide information on items that may not be clear on floor plans and elevations. If detail drawings and cross sections aren't included, you'll usually find the additional information you need in the specifications.

A floor plan (sometimes called a *plan view*) shows what the building would look like if a horizontal line were cut through the walls, windows, and doors and the roof were lifted off. It shows the exact position of those openings. Elevations depict the sides of buildings and show the heights of doors and windows, the height of the roof and other information that isn't on the floor plan.

A sectional drawing is like a floor plan. It's a cutaway view of some part of the building. Sectionals show what materials are to be used or what dimensions are to be followed when that information wouldn't be clear on a floor plan or elevation.

No matter how good the plans may be, you'll probably have at least a few questions after you've studied them. Construction is just too complex to expect an architect to think of everything before work begins. Even the most professional architects can forget something or leave some point unclear. That's when you have to visualize what's needed and use some judgment. If the plans are so poor that it's impossible to bid the job with a reasonable degree of certainty, stop work until you get better guidance. Don't waste the owner's or architect's time asking ridiculous questions.

Many of your questions will be answered if you simply picture yourself inside the house or structure represented. Compare the rooms with others you have built or are familiar with. Study the heights. Compare the various dimensions with those you consider ideal for similar purposes.

Nearly every set of plans you get will include written specifications that have detailed information on materials and installation procedures. Putting all this written information on the floor plans and elevations would make the drawings too cluttered. But don't assume that the specifications are any less important than the plans. They're not. To understand the plans, you have to read the specs. And don't assume that everything on carpentry will be covered in Section 6, Carpentry. For example, carpentry work such as framing supports for HVAC (heating, ventilating and air conditioning) equipment may be found in Section 15, Mechanical.

Once you've given all the drawings and specifications a quick pass and have an overview of the job, the next step is to study each sheet in detail.

Take a Closer Look

When you get the various plans, elevations, and details from the architect, they're probably bound on one edge. The order of the plans in that pack is usually based on the preference of the architect. Some architects place the elevation first, then the floor plans and the details. Others start with a site plan, followed by the basement plan, floor plans and elevations, then the sections, details and schedules.

On a larger project the plans will include a *plot plan*. This shows the position of all buildings on the lot and all site improvements that surround those buildings: sewer, gas and water lines, direction of connections, walks, drives, fences and parking area.

The order you follow when reading these plans depends on your experience and preference. The only important point is to observe some logical, consistent procedure and stick to it. Don't get into the habit of jumping from one sheet to another, reading a little here, a little there. If you do, you'll probably end up forgetting several important items.

The Basement Plan

I start with the basement plan, if there is one, because I like to work from the bottom to the top. That's how the building will go up. And it's also the order I'll follow when estimating the job. True, I have to refer to other plans and elevations to figure the entire basement, but the basement plan is my starting point.

The first thing you'll notice about the basement plan is that the two parallel foundation lines form a somewhat irregular rectangle. The outer line represents the outside of the foundation and the exterior wall of the building. The inner line represents the inside line of foundation. Figures written parallel to the foundation lines give the length of each wall section. The total of all sections should match overall wall length. If these totals don't agree, either there's an error somewhere or something is missing. By comparing lengths on several plan sheets and scaling off dimensions where figures are obviously wrong, you can usually get the measurements needed without calling the architect. If you can't figure out what's required, don't guess. Call the architect or owner and get the answer.

Studying the foundation walls further, you should notice the footings. If they're not shown on the basement plan — because of possible confusion with other lines — find this information on one of the other drawings. Note the relation of the grade to the top of the foundation wall. Note the basement finish, if any. Then look in the specifications to confirm what you find. Note any special items in the basement such as laundry room, drainage outlets, layouts for heating and air conditioning equipment, fuel storage, closets, or special platforms. Examine in detail the placement of supporting columns or special piers.

The height of the foundations above ground and style of any basement windows will usually be found on the elevations.

The First Floor Plan

Study the first floor plan the same way you studied the basement plan. Note the details in each room: dimensions, special cabinet work, closets and so on. If bookcases, china closets, stairways or other finish carpentry items are indicated, look for detail drawings on other sheets in a larger scale.

Windows will be shown by two parallel lines. Check them for location and style. Note whether they're grouped, mullion, or triple. You may have to refer to the elevation for this. Then look at the doors: number, position, and swing. If the swing results in a clash between sets of doors, you may want to suggest that the swing of one door be changed. Note the kitchen cabinets and all shelving.

Next, examine the stairs. Risers, steps, platforms or special construction deserve your close attention. Is the staircase a "box flight" between two walls or is it open on one side or both (requiring posts, rails and balusters)? Make mental notes on the stairs leading down to the basement. Is it a single flight with a straight run or will turns and landings be needed?

Next, study any porches on this first floor plan. Refer to the elevation to discover which lines represent steps, posts, etc. You may find large scale drawings for the front porch or any deck area.

The Second Floor Plan

Next, go to the second floor plan, if any. Here you'll find the same outline as the first floor, except where dotted lines indicate a variation from the first floor extension. Again, check the partitions, doors and windows, just as you did on the first floor plan.

Note carefully any special construction on the second floor. Compare what you see with work you've done previously on similar jobs. That will help you visualize what's required and suggest how the work should be done.

Be alert for conflicts with other trades: How will your framing fit around drain and vent lines? What conflicts can be expected with the heating contractor? What supports will the electrical contractor require?

Continue your examination of the plans to the roof, including cornices, ridges, and so on. All the information needed to build every part of the structure should be on the plans, in notes attached to the plans, or in the specifications. If, after making your examination, something is still unclear, call the architect for clarification.

The Elevations

Next, look at the front, rear and side elevations. Each depicts what you would see when standing directly in front of that side. The elevations show door and window heights, their widths and style, the shape of the roof, its slope, the style of cornice, porches, balustrades, and outside trim. Notes on the drawings should indicate the materials used for wall and roof coverings.

Larger scale detail drawings may be included to show the style and construction of such things as cornices, porches, or bay windows. Additional scale sections through a wall or roof may indicate the size of joists, rafters, or molding.

This preliminary reading of the plans may take an experienced estimator only a few minutes. But it's important. It gives you a picture of the entire building. It helps you understand the parts so you can make an accurate take-off of the whole.

Examine the Site

On a larger job or if you're going to do any of the excavation or formwork, you'll probably want to visit the site. That's the best way to determine soil conditions, slope of the lot, storage space available, access problems and the availability of power and water.

On smaller jobs, such as remodeling and repair work, a visit to the site is essential. There's no other way to be sure what has to be replaced and what can be used in the existing structure.

If the site is in the city, it may be so congested and cramped that there's no room to unload a stack of lumber or set up a cutting area. That can drive your costs up considerably. So visit the site — it pays.

Before Estimating Begins

My advice is to avoid estimating under time pressure. Of course, every experienced carpentry estimator has prepared a rush bid. General contractors sometimes demand it. A heavy estimating workload may require it. And homeowners always seem to be in a hurry to know *how much it's going to cost*. It's hard to convince anyone that a rush bid has to be higher than a bid prepared when there's ample time to consider all the ways of reducing building expense. But it's true.

Rush bids are bad business. They usually have an error. If the mistake is in your favor, the owner or general contractor will ignore your bid. If it's in the owner's or general contractor's favor, you may need legal assistance to get out of the contract.

If you're backed into a corner and have to give some figure, offer a ballpark estimate based on cost per square foot of floor. Figure the square feet of floor on a similar building that has a known cost for framing and finish carpentry. Divide the square foot total into the known cost. Then multiply that square foot cost by the square feet in the building you're asked to estimate. That figure may satisfy your client. But make it clear that the figure is only a ballpark estimate. The actual bid will take more time.

Getting Organized

Earlier in this chapter I mentioned how important good organization and established procedures are to experienced estimators. My advice is to follow the same order on every estimate when making a material and labor take-off. I try to follow the order of construction: foundation forms, sill, floor joists, floor sheathing, wall framing, and so on, right up to the ridgeboard and then the finish carpentry. Your system may be different. That doesn't matter. What does matter is that you follow the same logical procedure on every estimate.

Why follow the same system every time? That's easy. Every estimator's biggest mistake is omitting some important item. You can underestimate or overestimate the cost of every item by 10% or even 20% on most jobs and still come out O.K. If you're lucky, the mistakes will balance out — the underestimates equaling the overestimates. But the estimate on anything you forget is always zero. That's a 100% miss! It doesn't take many of those to wipe out your profit.

How do you avoid missing an important item? Using checklists is one good way. Most estimators use written checklists to be sure everything is included in the estimate. But an old ''pro'' will tell you that his best checklist is the one he carries around in his head. That's the *procedure* he (or she) follows on every estimate. He looks for forming first on every estimate. When all the formwork is tabulated, he goes on to sills. Going through the complete mental checklist in the same order on every estimate practically guarantees that every cost has been considered.

When taking off quantities, always make up the list of materials in the same order, preferably the order in which materials will be used. Follow a set routine to reduce the chance of leaving something out.

More Organization

Every estimator needs good cost records — copies of completed estimates and summaries of actual job costs. Collect these in a file or notebook. Probably the most convenient and practical book for this purpose is a three-ring 8½'' x 11'' binder. The advantage of a loose-leaf notebook is that it keeps all current estimates together. Yet you can remove an estimate at any time and take it with you without being burdened with the entire book. Also, any page can be removed and replaced when the plans change or when new work is added.

Each section of the estimate should be kept separate as far as possible. A summary sheet at the end will show the totals from each section. If you find an error or when changes are made, only the section or sections affected and the summary sheet have to be changed.

You may want to develop your own estimating forms or copy the forms included in this book. No matter what form you use, each estimate should be assigned a sequential number. Several sheets will be needed for each estimate, but all sheets of an estimate should bear the same estimate number. The first page of each estimate should show the estimate number, sheet number, address or lot number, owner, architect, date of bid, closing date, and the names of the people who prepared and checked the estimate.

When your book is full, or as estimates are rejected, remove the unneeded estimates and file them in numerical order in a drawer or file box. An index in your file or in the estimate binder itself will simplify locating the cost data you're looking for.

This estimating file will become the most valuable and most used set of documents in your office. The time required to shingle a roof, the manhours needed to frame 100 linear feet of partition, time for laying flooring, setting doors or installing trim should be recorded and filed for ready reference.

This cost data is essential when estimating, of course. But it also has other applications. Suppose your cost data shows that a double flight 6-foot wide stairway with railing took 40 manhours. On the current job a similar stairway was estimated at 40 manhours but took 52 manhours. You'll want to know what made this job more difficult or why the crew assigned took so much more time.

When estimating manhours, always keep in mind the season of the year when the work is to be done. A framing crew will work faster on a warm sunny day than when the cold is stiffening their hands and interfering with movement.

I usually estimate that temperatures below freezing will increase framing manhours about 10%. But when it gets really cold, there's so much wasted time that I'd rather not have a framing crew on the job at all. Here's my rule of thumb: If the temperature isn't at least 10 degrees and rising by 8 A.M., I give my crew the day off. To any Californians reading this book, this may seem absurd, but for those of us who build where we get some real weather, it's a factor you must consider.

If you don't have cost records that show how weather affects productivity on your jobs, use Figure 1-1. It was compiled by the National Association of Home Builders Foundation from a survey of 2,500 home builders in all parts of the country. The percentages show the additional time needed to do the work listed during the three worst weather months of the year.

Still More Organization

The Construction Specification Institute (CSI) has developed a construction classification system that is now accepted throughout the industry. Specifications for nearly all large jobs and most smaller jobs follow the CSI order. The CSI index places all construction into one of 16 major headings. See Figure 1-2. Carpentry falls under Section 6. Each major heading has subheads. Subheads for carpentry (called ''Wood and Plastic'') are shown in Figure 1-3.

The chapters that follow explain how to estimate all the rough and finish carpentry you're likely to find in a construction project. Regardless of the type of work involved, the estimating method is the same: Picture in your mind how the work will be performed. Consider the time required, the materials needed and the equipment necessary to perform each step. Most important, don't leave anything out! Experienced carpentry estimators know how important it is to include every cost item in every estimate.

Your ''Labor Burden''

Even after all the labor, material and equipment costs have been totaled, you haven't found the full cost yet. The ''labor burden'' will *add* between 25% and 30% to the labor cost. This means that for every dollar of payroll, you'll have to pay an additional 25 to 30 cents in taxes and insurance to government agencies and insurance companies.

Type of Building Activity	North	Mid South	Deep South	West			
				Mountain	Desert	North Coast	South Coast
Lot layout	5	4	3	10	2	7	3
Form footings	8	8	8	9	--	15	8
Form foundation walls	9	9	8	15	3	15	9
Strip foundation walls	4	3	2	12	3	6	4
Decking	6	8	12	5	2	6	4
Rough framing	8	8	10	9	3	5	9
Roofing	8	10	10	10	2	16	6
Install windows and doors	4	2	4	6	2	5	5
Exterior siding	10	8	6	10	2	10	8
Hang drywall	3	3	4	6	2	5	6
Finish drywall	5	8	12	12	--	9	10

The numbers show the additional average percentage of time needed to do each job during the three worst weather months.

Figure 1-1
How weather affects productivity

Many carpentry contractors routinely add 25% to their estimated labor cost to cover taxes and insurance. Here's a breakdown of where the "labor burden" comes from:

Unemployment insurance— All states levy an unemployment insurance tax on employers. This tax is based on total payroll for each calendar quarter and will vary with your history of unemployment claims. It may be as little as 1% or as much as 4% of payroll. You'll pay this tax monthly and file a state unemployment tax return quarterly.

The federal government also levies an unemployment insurance tax (FUTA). The tax has been about 0.8% of payroll up to a maximum per employee as established by law. This tax must be paid quarterly to a Federal Reserve Bank with Federal Tax Deposit Form 508. In January you file Form 940, showing all FUTA deposits made for the previous year, and pay any additional tax due.

Social Security and Medicare— The federal government also collects Social Security and Medicare (FICA) taxes. As an employer, your share is about 7.5% of payroll on earnings up to an annual maximum per employee as set by law. Requirements vary, but you'll probably pay this tax several times a month. Deposits have to be made to a Federal Reserve Bank with Federal Tax Deposit Form 501. Every three months you'll file the Employer's Quarterly Federal Tax Return, Form 941, showing the FICA deposits made. These deposits must also include the *employee's* share of FICA tax and all income tax withheld from employee paychecks.

Workers' Comp— All states require that employers have Workers' Compensation Insurance to cover their employees in the event of job-related injury. Heavy penalties are

General Requirements 1
Fees
Temporary Utilities
Equipment
Site Work 2
Demolition
Earthwork
Piles
Caissons
Shoring
Piping
Paving
Fencing
Irrigation
Landscaping
Marine Work
Concrete 3
Formwork
Reinforcement
Job Cast Concrete
Finishes
Precast Concrete
Tilt-Up
Masonry 4
Clay Brick
Concrete Block
Stone
Metals 5
Structural Steel
Decking
Building Frames
Fabrications
Wood and Plastic 6
Rough Carpentry
Rough Hardware
Finish Carpentry
Thermal and Moisture Protection 7
Insulation
Shingles
Preformed Siding
Membrane Roofing
Sheet Metal
Doors and Windows 8
Metal Doors
Wood Doors
Special Doors
Store Fronts
Metal Windows
Hardware
Glazing

Finishes 9
Lathing and Furring
Plastering
Metal Studs
Gypsum Wallboard
Tile
Terrazzo
Suspended Ceilings
Wood Flooring
Resilient Flooring
Carpeting
Painting
Specialties 10
Chalkboards
Compartments
Identifying Devices
Partitions
Toilet Accessories
Equipment 11
Banks
Ecclesiastical
Food Service
Athletic
Furnishings 12
Cabinets
Fabrics
Seating
Special Construction 13
Conveying Systems 14
Elevators
Material Handling Systems
Mechanical 15
Piping
Plumbing Equipment
Plumbing Fixtures
Fire Protection
Heat Generators
Cooling Systems
Heating and Cooling
Air Moving Equipment
Duct Work
Electrical 16
Power Transmission
Switchgear
Conduit
Wire
Cable
Raceways
Lighting Fixtures

Figure 1-2
CSI Construction Index

Division 6 - Wood and Plastic			
Number	Title	Number	Title
06050	**Fasteners and Supports**	**06170**	**Prefabricated Structural Wood**
		—80	Glue-laminated construction
		—81	Glue-laminated structural units
06100	**Rough Carpentry**	—82	Glue-laminated decking
—10	Framing and sheathing	—90	Wood trusses
—11	Light wooden structures framing	—92	Fabricated wood trusses
—12	Preassembled components		
—13	Sheathing	**06200**	**Finish Carpentry**
—14	Diaphragms	—20	Millwork
—20	Structural plywood	—40	Laminated plastic
—25	Wood decking		
—26	Fiberboard decking		
—27	Fiber underlayment	**06300**	**Wood Treatment**
—28	Asbestos cement panels	—10	Pressure treated lumber
		—11	Preservative treated lumber
		—12	Fire retardant treated lumber
06130	**Heavy Timber Construction**		
—31	Timber trusses	**06400**	**Architectural Woodwork**
—32	Mill-framed structures	—10	Cabinetwork
—33	Pole construction	—11	Wood cabinets: Unfinished
—34	Trestles	—20	Paneling
		—21	Hardwood plywood paneling
		—22	Softwood plywood paneling
06150	**Wood-Metal Systems**	—30	Stairwork
—51	Wood chord metal joists	—31	Wood stairs and railings

Figure 1-3
CSI carpentry subheads

imposed on employers who fail to provide the required coverage. The cost of "workers' comp" insurance is taken as a percentage of payroll and is based on the type of work each employee performs. Clerical and office workers have a very low rate — they're not very likely to get hurt on the job. Your cost may be only a fraction of 1% of payroll. But hazardous occupations such as roofing carry a very high rate — usually at least 25% of payroll. The rate for most construction trades is between 5% and 10%. Carpentry is usually 8% to 10% of base pay. The actual cost will vary from year to year, depending on how many claims are filed. Your insurance carrier can quote the current cost of coverage.

Liability insurance— Every contractor should maintain liability insurance to protect the business from a lawsuit if there's an accident. Liability insurance is also based on total payroll. The cost of coverage will vary by location, the liability limits needed, and your history of claims. But here's a rule of thumb that will be useful when estimating costs: Allow 5% of payroll for a comprehensive general liability policy, truck, auto and equipment floaters, fidelity bonds and umbrella liability coverage. Your insurance agent will quote the exact cost based on the coverage you need.

Here's a summary of the typical "contractor's burden"—

State Unemployment: 4.0%
Federal Unemployment (FUTA):   0.8%

Social Security (FICA):   7.5%
Worker's Compensation: 10.0%
Liability Insurance: 5.0%

If you think that there's any way to cut corners on these taxes, you're mistaken. They have to be paid if you have employees and intend to stay in business. Both your state and the federal government have very effective ways to enforce payment of these taxes — and they apply heavy penalties against contractors who ignore the law.

That's why this labor burden has to be part of every estimate you make. If your labor burden is 25% and your wage cost for carpentry will be $1,000 on a job, your labor cost will be $1,250 — $1,000 for wages and benefits and $250 for taxes and insurance.

Overhead

Of course, wages, materials, taxes and insurance aren't your only costs on a job. Most of the rest is generally called *overhead*. It comes in two categories — direct and indirect.

Direct Overhead

There are many costs which the contractor must bear that are not associated with any particular trade or phase of construction, but are the direct result of taking on a particular job. These costs are usually called *direct overhead* and can be thought of as administrative costs. Here are some common expenses that are generally included under direct overhead:

- Fire insurance
- Surety bonds
- Building permit
- Sidewalk permit
- Job phone
- Water
- Electricity
- Sewer connection
- Timekeeper
- Watchman
- Temporary office
- Repairs to adjoining property

You can probably think of many more direct overhead items. Some carpentry contractors include in direct overhead the cost of supervision and other nonproductive labor such as the cost of estimating the job. The time you spend on each job should be charged against that job. These are very real costs and must be included somewhere in the estimate. Since they are incurred as a result of taking each particular job, they can be properly included under direct overhead.

Indirect Overhead

After everything is figured, there are certain expenses you must bear in conducting your business, but which cannot be charged directly against any single job. For example, office rent and utilities, telephone, office staff, small tools, office insurance, printing, your car, postage, advertising, and countless other items. These are indirect overhead expenses.

Some carpentry contractors favor assigning the week's indirect overhead cost to the jobs that are in progress that week. For example, if you are doing two jobs of about the same size during a given week, each would bear one-half the indirect overhead cost for that week. Multiply weekly indirect overhead cost by the expected job duration to estimate indirect overhead cost for that project.

Some contractors load indirect overhead cost on each productive manhour. For example, if indirect overhead is $1,000 a month and your carpenters work 1,000 manhours a month, the cost per manhour for indirect overhead would be $1. Other carpentry contractors figure indirect overhead as a percentage of each bid. If contract volume averages $50,000 per month and indirect overhead is $2,500 per month, indirect overhead is 5%. I've even heard of contractors who have reduced indirect overhead expense to a cost per thousand board feet of lumber used.

Any of these systems is good if it works. Keep a record of your indirect overhead and develop some method of dividing this cost among your jobs. Most important, don't forget to include this cost in your bid. Direct and indirect overhead together will be more than 10% of the estimated job cost for most carpentry contractors. This 10% will make the difference between a profit and a loss on many of your jobs.

Contingency and Escalation

Most carpentry contractors add a small amount to their bid to allow for problems that can't be forecast before work begins. Construction is seldom done faster than planned. Most surprises will increase the cost, not decrease it. The right amount to add for contingencies such as overtime, low productivity or poor scheduling depends on the contractor and the job. For most carpentry, 2% may be enough. Remodeling or repair work requires a larger allowance because it's harder to anticipate what's needed before work begins. Finally, if the plans are poorly drawn or unclear, the contingency allowance may have to be much higher.

Escalation covers increases in cost of labor, materials and equipment between the time the bid is submitted and the time work is actually done and paid for. Even if you're sure of the price of 1,000 board feet of framing lumber when making up the estimate, it may be hard to predict what that lumber will cost when it's actually bought from the yard. Lumber and plywood prices can change rapidly. Prices for materials such as wallboard, concrete and nails change much more slowly. If you can't get firm quotes that are good for several weeks, it's good practice to either allow some amount for escalation or exclude price increases from your bid.

Profit

The profit is the contractor's return on his investment in the contracting business. It isn't the owner's wage. Profit is what's left after all expenses (including the owner's wage) are paid. The business owner's income should be charged either to indirect overhead (when managing the business), to direct overhead (when supervising the work or estimating a job), or as a labor cost (when driving nails).

At the end of each year the profit earned should provide a reasonable return on money invested in the business (after the owner has drawn a reasonable wage). Profit should be 10% to 20% of the *tangible net worth* of your business. The tangible net worth is the value of everything the business owns less what the business owes and less any intangible items such as goodwill.

A carpentry contractor with only a truck, table saw, some tools and a few hundred dollars in working capital may have a tangible net worth of about $10,000. Any profit he shows, after taking a reasonable wage, will very likely be used to buy more equipment and increase his working capital. Still, he should include enough profit in each job to provide a 10% to 20% annual return on his $10,000 investment. That's $1,000 to $2,000 for the year.

Think of profit as interest on the money invested in equipment, office, inventory, work in progress and everything else associated with running a carpentry contracting business.

How much then, should you include in an estimate for profit? You'll hear contractors claim a 20% profit margin on some jobs. That's pretty high if it means that 20% is left after all costs (including the owner's wage) are covered. Some builders may operate efficiently enough to earn a 20% profit, but they're the exception. The contractor who boasts about a 20% profit probably means he has 20% left after paying for field labor, materials and equipment. A good portion of the 20% that's left has to go toward overhead and the owner's wage. That isn't profit at all. A profit is what remains after *all* costs are considered, including overhead and the owner's wage.

What, then, is a realistic profit in the true sense? Dun and Bradstreet, the national credit reporting organization, has compiled figures on construction contractors for many years. They report the average profit after taxes for all contractors sampled to be consistently between 1.2% and 1.5% of gross receipts. This includes many contractors who reported losses or became insolvent. A 1.5% profit, even after taxes, is a fairly slim profit.

Not many contractors, especially contractors on residential projects, include only a 1% or 2% profit in their bids. On extremely large projects such as highways, power plants or airports, a contractor may include only 1% for profit — especially on a "cost plus" contract where risk of a loss is nearly eliminated.

Residential carpentry, especially remodeling and repair work, should carry a much higher profit margin because jobs are smaller and the risk of loss is larger. Probably 8% to 10% profit is a reasonable expectation on most jobs. Profit on small jobs or remodeling work may be as much as 25%.

Of course, there is more to "profit" than just how much profit you would like to earn. Competition will usually limit the profit you can include in an estimate. If you include too much profit, you'll be underbid on work you would like to have. If you have enough work to stay busy and are asked to bid more, consider increasing the profit margin by a few percent.

When work is scarce, many carpentry contractors take work at little or no profit just to keep their best crews busy (and themselves in the carpentry contracting business). That's making the best of a bad situation. But it isn't a disaster if the bid you submit really does cover all your costs.

To summarize, there is no single profit figure that fits all situations. For most carpentry work, an 8% to 10% profit is reasonable. A contractor who has all the work he needs and wants and is asked to bid on more work may feel that a 15% profit isn't excessive.

Figure 1-4 shows how profit is figured into the bid. Note that a profit of 8% of the job cost is only 7.3% of the total contract price.

Checking Estimates

Your estimate isn't complete just because the bid price has been computed. Now the checking should begin. Every estimate you submit should be checked with the same care as the estimator used in preparing it. The best system is to have two estimators prepare estimates for the same job without comparing their figures until the work is done. You won't have enough time for that on most jobs. But, as a minimum, have someone check all price extensions and total all cost columns.

I've never met an estimator who doesn't make mistakes — and you won't either. There are going to be errors in your estimates. Plan on it! Challenge whoever checks your work to find a significant mistake. Create an incentive to find errors before they become a major loss.

Checking is easier when you follow a consistent order, when your handwriting is clear and when you show all the computations used to arrive at totals. If you're making estimates on the back of an envelope in hieroglyphics that only a cryptographer could decipher, checking is nearly impossible.

The most common errors will fall into four categories. Watch out for these:

1) Errors in addition, multiplication, division, and misplaced decimal points.

2) Errors in transcribing numbers from one sheet to another.

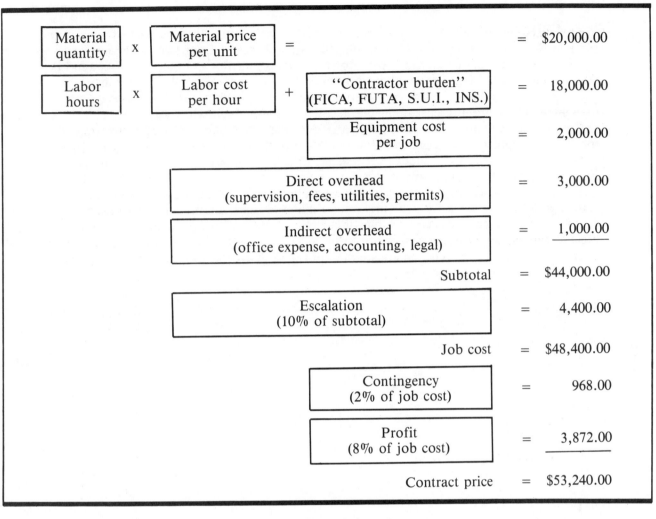

Material quantity	x Material price per unit =	= $20,000.00
Labor hours	x Labor cost per hour + "Contractor burden" (FICA, FUTA, S.U.I., INS.)	= 18,000.00
	Equipment cost per job	= 2,000.00
	Direct overhead (supervision, fees, utilities, permits)	= 3,000.00
	Indirect overhead (office expense, accounting, legal)	= 1,000.00
	Subtotal	= $44,000.00
	Escalation (10% of subtotal)	= 4,400.00
	Job cost	= $48,400.00
	Contingency (2% of job cost)	= 968.00
	Profit (8% of job cost)	= 3,872.00
	Contract price	= $53,240.00

Figure 1-4
Figuring overhead and profit on a bid

3) Missing an item — material, labor, equipment, or overhead. Develop and use a good checklist to avoid careless omissions.

4) Forgetting to include an installation cost for every material item.

Controlling Costs

Once your bid is accepted, the next step is to do the work — at the costs you estimated and with the profit you predicted. It's a nice pat on the back when estimated costs equal actual costs. But remember that it's possible to earn a second and third profit on every job. The first profit is the profit you estimated. The second comes from reducing costs by careful purchasing and good supervision. The third profit is what you learn from comparing estimated and actual costs. Where were the estimating mistakes? What should you do differently on the next job? Don't miss this opportunity to record and control actual expenses.

All three profits require good cost-keeping — recording what's spent on each part of the job. A carpentry contractor who has little or no payroll and personally watches every part of every job may need only a very simple cost-keeping system: A file for paid material bills on each job and a few notes on how many manhours were spent doing each task. But a larger carpentry business needs a better system for recording and controlling costs.

The cost-keeping system you use should record what's spent on each part of every job: the board feet of lumber used for framing, the square feet of floor and linear feet of wall framed, and the manhours needed to frame walls and floor. Your records should be detailed enough to identify the labor and material cost for forms, sills, floor joists, sheathing, wall framing, ceiling joists, roof framing, windows, doors, and finish carpentry. These are unit cost items you'll use again and again when estimating.

Comparing estimated unit costs and actual unit costs will help you find estimating mistakes, of course. A comparison should also uncover waste of materials, poor supervision, marginally productive carpenters, time lost waiting for supplies or tools, poor planning, excess labor and padded payrolls.

The job supervisor should consider the estimate to be a job budget. It should be a challenge to do the work with the manhours, materials and equipment listed in the estimate. If there are mistakes in the estimate, the supervisor is not to blame if it can't be met. It's the supervisor's responsibility to bring any estimating errors to your attention as soon as they're noticed. The supervisor should try to deliver a finished job for the cost you estimated.

Estimating Rough Carpentry

A good working knowledge of lumber and plywood grades and uses is important to every carpentry estimator. That's the reason for this chapter. But if you've been working as a carpenter for several years, you probably already know a lot about the materials you use. You probably know what lumber and plywood grades mean and how the various grades should be used. And you probably have no trouble converting lumber quantities to board foot measure. If that's true, consider skipping this chapter. But if you think a little review may be in order, keep reading.

Here's a quick way to test yourself on what's in this chapter: Answer the 15 questions that follow. A score of 12 or more correct answers means you can move right on to Chapter 3. Fewer than 12 right means it's probably worth your time to review the information here. The answers are at the end of this chapter. Circle either *True* or *False* after each question.

1) A dry 2 x 4 measures 1½'' by 3½''. A 10-foot length of dry 2 x 4 has 4.375 board feet of lumber.   **True   False**

2) An 8-foot length of 1/2'' x 6'' siding has 2 board feet of lumber.   **True   False**

3) Framing lumber marked *Standard* or *STD&BTR* is better quality than lumber marked *Construction* or *CONST*.   **True   False**

4) Lumber marked *B&BTR* must be at least 25% ''better'' grade.   **True   False**

5) Stress-graded lumber is tested for strength by equipment designed to evaluate its load-carrying capacity.   **True   False**

6) A Douglas Fir 2 x 4 carrying the grade *Construction* will probably have more knots, checks or splits than a Southern Pine 2 x 4 with the same grade stamp.   **True   False**

7) Any lumber marked *Structural* is going to have a higher bending strength than *Construction* grade lumber.   **True   False**

8) Studs stamped *PET* indicate that the material should be used for the particular purpose of wall framing only.   **True   False**

9) Lumber inspectors realize that there is no reliable way to predict the load-carrying capacity of lumber from the way it looks.   **True   False**

10) Lumber grading rules are designed so that *Standard & Better* lumber from one tree will have about the same strength as *Standard & Better* lumber from another tree.   **True   False**

11) Lumber from the hybrid Hem-Fir tree can replace Douglas Fir in many residential applications.   **True   False**

12) *Select* grade boards are selected for strength, graded by number, and are particularly suitable for concrete forms and floor sheathing.   **True   False**

13) Appearance grade and engineered grade plywood are usually stamped with an "identification index" which tells you the maximum support spacing for floor and wall sheathing.   **True   False**

14) Though plywood sheathing can be applied either vertically or horizontally, vertical application offers a better base for shingle siding.   **True   False**

15) Appearance grade plywood is stamped with a letter that indicates the quality of the front and back surface. A-A grade shows that the front and back face are highest quality.   **True   False**

When you've answered all 15 questions, turn to the end of this chapter and find out how many you missed.

Lumber Basics

If you've decided to continue with this chapter, let's get started with the essentials. Estimators usually have two headings for carpentry work: rough carpentry and finish carpentry. Rough carpentry includes all the framing and sheathing. Finish carpentry takes in trim, molding, baseboard, flooring, stairs, windows, doors, siding, cabinets and shelves. Hardware items like handles and locksets are usually included in finish carpentry, except in a commercial job, where it would probably be listed under a separate heading. Whether it's rough carpentry or finish carpentry, finding the right grade and species for each part of the job is your responsibility. If you base your estimate on lumber that's better than needed, you'll be underbid. If you use lumber that won't pass inspection, you'll end up wasting time and money reframing the job.

You don't need to be a lumber expert, of course, to estimate carpentry. But every carpentry estimator needs a working knowledge of lumber and plywood grades and uses. This chapter covers enough of the basics to keep you out of trouble, both when calculating board footage and selecting the right grades.

Standard sizes and lengths have been established for all construction lumber. Lumber that's 5" and larger in its smallest dimension is sold as timber. Lumber less than 5" in the smallest dimension is called *dimension lumber*. Boards are usually 1" thick and from 2" to 12" wide. If they're surfaced or dressed on one side, the width will be about 7/8". When surfaced on two sides, the width will be about 25/32" or 13/16". Note that boards less than 1" thick are figured as though they were 1" thick — each nominal square foot is considered to be one board foot. That's why the tongue and groove (T&G) siding you buy is called *1 x 4, 1 x 6* or *1 x 8,* even though it measures only about 5/8" thick.

Nominal size	Actual size	
	Unseasoned	**Dry**
1" x 4"	25/32" x 3-9/16"	¾" x 3½"
1" x 6"	25/32" x 5-5/8"	¾" x 5½"
1" x 8"	25/32" x 7-1/2"	¾" x 7¼"
1" x 10"	25/32" x 9½"	¾" x 9¼"
1" x 12"	25/32" x 11-1/2"	¾" x 11¼"
2" x 4"	1-9/16" x 3-9/16"	1½" x 3½"
2" x 6"	1-9/16" x 5-5/8"	1½" x 5½"
2" x 8"	1-9/16" x 7-1/2"	1½" x 7¼"
2" x 10"	1-9/16" x 9-1/2"	1½" x 9¼"
2" x 12"	1-9/16" x 11-1/2"	1½" x 11¼"
3" thickness	2-9/16"	2½"
4" thickness	3-9/16"	3½"
6" thickness	5-5/8"	5½"
8" thickness	7-1/2"	7¼"
10" thickness	9-1/2"	9¼"
12" thickness	11-1/2"	11¼"
14" thickness	13-1/2"	13¼"
16" thickness	15-1/2"	15¼"

Widths for lumber 3" to 16" thick are the same as widths of 1" and 2" lumber.

Figure 2-1
Nominal and actual sizes for lumber

Framing lumber is also sold by its nominal dimensions rather than its actual measurements. For example, note from Figure 2-1 that a dry 2 x 4 is actually 1½" by 3½".

Obviously, better grades of lumber cost more than lesser grades. Select grades are used for finish carpentry where the surface will be exposed after construction is complete. Common grades usually cost less because they have more blemishes and imperfections. When buying select grades, the costs decline from A grade, which is the best, to D grade, which is the cheapest. In the common grades, costs decrease as the numbers increase: 1, 2 and 3.

The cost of lumber is higher for thick and wide planks than for thin and narrow ones. Lengths longer than 16 or 20 feet may require special orders. Unless you request otherwise, the yard will usually quote lumber prices for random lengths to 20 feet. Longer pieces and specified lengths will cost more.

Lumber is sold by the board foot. A nominal 1 x 12 board that's 12 inches long has one board foot. A nominal 2 x 6 that's 12 inches long also has one board foot. The term is abbreviated *BF*. Here's a quick way to figure the number of board feet in any length of lumber: Write the nominal dimension (width and thickness in inches, length in feet) over 12 in the form of a fraction. Then reduce the fraction to get the board footage. For example, figure the board feet in a joist 2 x 8 x 16' long:

$$\frac{2 \times 8 \times 16}{12} = \frac{256}{12} = 21\text{-}1/3 \text{ BF}$$

When figuring more than one piece, simply multiply the board footage in one piece by the number of pieces. For example, if there are 40 joists 2 x 8 x 16', the number of board feet would be:

$$\frac{40 \times 2 \times 8 \times 16}{12} = 853 \text{ BF}$$

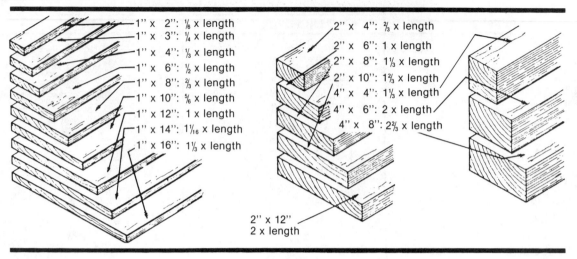

Figure 2-2
Illustration of board foot conversions

Notice that every linear foot of 2 x 8 has 1⅓ BF, every linear foot of a 2 x 6 has 1 BF and every linear foot of 2 x 4 has 2/3 BF. Use the formula given above for figuring board footage to verify that this is true.

Figure 2-2 may help you visualize these relationships. Using the numbers in Figure 2-2, find the board feet in a piece 1 x 8 x 18'. You'll see that 1 x 8 lumber has 2/3 BF per linear foot. Multiply 18 by 2/3 to find 12 BF.

Your yard will usually quote framing lumber prices in thousands of board feet, abbreviated *MBF*. To convert the MBF cost to BF, divide by 1,000. For example, to find the cost of 40 pieces of 2 x 4 x 18' at $500.00 per MBF:

$$\frac{40 \times 2 \times 4 \times 18}{12} = 480 \times \frac{500}{1000} = \$240$$

Let's figure a job the other way around. Suppose you know 2½ MBF of 2 x 6 x 20' were ordered for the job. How many pieces will the yard deliver? First, figure the BF in each piece:

$$\frac{2 \times 6 \times 20}{12} = 20 \text{ BF}$$

If there are 20 BF in each piece, 2,500 board feet will have 2,500 divided by 20, or 125 pieces.

Smaller size lumber is sometimes figured in linear feet. Suppose an estimate calls for 135 board feet of 1 x 3 cross bridging. You need to know how many linear feet that requires:

$$\frac{1 \times 3}{12} = 1/4 \text{ BF per linear foot}$$

If each linear foot has 1/4 BF, 135 board feet must be 4 times 135, or 540 linear feet.

Lumber dealers often price sheathing by the hundred linear feet (CLF). To convert linear feet to board feet, multiply the nominal dimensions by the length (in linear feet) and divide by 12. For example, let's assume that you placed an order for 380 linear feet

Lumber size (thickness and width)	Linear feet	x	Factor	=	Board feet
1" x 4"	*380*	x	.33333	=	*126.67*
1" x 6"		x	.50000	=	
1" x 8"		x	.66667	=	
1" x 10"		x	.83333	=	
1" x 12"		x	1.00000	=	
2" x 4"	*8*	x	.66667	=	*5.33*
2" x 6"	*8*	x	1.00000	=	*8.00*
2" x 8"		x	1.33333	=	
2" x 10"	*14*	x	1.66667	=	*23.33*
2" x 12"		x	2.00000	=	

Figure 2-3
Worksheet for converting linear feet to board feet

of 1 x 4 S4S. How many board feet is that? Here's the answer: One times 4 times 380 divided by 12 is 126.67.

We can simplify this computation by using multiplying factors. Look at Figure 2-3. It's a worksheet for converting linear feet to board feet. (You'll find a blank copy of all of the worksheets in this chapter in the back of the book.) The problem in the paragraph above is solved using the factor 0.33333. I think you'll find that using the factors in this table will save time and prevent mistakes. Figure 2-3 lists conversion factors for lumber ranging from 1 x 4 to 2 x 12.

Look up the nominal dimensions in the first column. Enter the linear feet on that line in the second column. Multiply the number of linear feet by the factor to find the board feet. In our example, the factor for 1 x 4 lumber is 0.33333. Multiply that by 380 to get 126.67 board feet.

Use the factors in Figure 2-3 to calculate the board feet for other lumber sizes. Figure 2-3 shows sample calculations for 1 x 4, 2 x 4, 2 x 6 and 2 x 10 lumber.

Converting Board Feet to Linear Feet

What if your measurements are in board feet, but the lumber is priced in linear feet? To convert board feet to linear feet, multiply the board feet by 12 and divide by the nominal dimensions. For example, how many linear feet are there in 1,280 board feet of 2 x 4 lumber? 1,280 times 12 divided by (2 times 4) equals 1,920 linear feet. That's one way to do it. There's a better way.

Figure 2-4 shows conversion factors from board feet to linear feet. Find the nominal dimensions of the lumber in the first column. In the next column enter the number of board feet. Now multiply the number of board feet by the factor to find the number of linear feet. Our example was 1,280 BF of 2 x 4 lumber. Multiply 1,280 by the factor, 1.5

Lumber size (thickness and width)	Board feet	x	Factor	=	Linear feet
1" x 4"	12667	x	3.00	=	380
1" x 6"	140	x	2.00	=	280
1" x 8"		x	1.50	=	
1" x 10"		x	1.20	=	
1" x 12"		x	1.00	=	
2" x 4"	1,280	x	1.50	=	1,920
2" x 6"		x	1.00	=	
2" x 8"		x	.75	=	
2" x 10"	23.33	x	.60	=	14
2" x 12"		x	.50	=	

Figure 2-4
Worksheet for converting board feet to linear feet

and you have 1,920 linear feet of lumber.

Our new formula for converting board feet to linear feet is: Multiply board feet by the factor to get the number of linear feet.

Most framing lumber is priced by the thousand board feet. Some dealers quote smaller quantities by the piece. You may find 2 x 10 joists, 16'0" long, priced at $8.80 each. What's the cost per MBF? The usual way to find the answer would be to convert linear feet to board feet, then divide the price by the number of board feet to find the cost per board foot. Then multiply that by 1,000 to find the cost per MBF: 2 times 10 times 16 feet divided by 12 would give you 26.67 board feet. Divide $8.80 by 26.67 to get $0.33 per board foot. Multiply that by 1,000 to find the answer: $330.00 per MBF.

Let's use the factor table in Figure 2-5 to find the price per MBF the easy way. Look down the first column until you find the lumber dimensions. Read across from left to right. In the next column enter the price per piece. Multiply the piece price by the factor to get the price per MBF. In our example, the factor for a 2 x 10 x 16' is 37.50. Multiply that by $8.80 to find the cost, $330.00 per MBF.

When framing lumber is sold by the piece rather than by the MBF, it's easier to compute the price for a small purchase. Here's an example: Let's say 2 x 4 x 8' studs are priced at $1.65 each. Joists measuring 2 x 6 x 14' cost $4.41 each, and 2 x 6 x 16' joists cost $5.04 each. Let's assume you need them in quantities of 400, 66 and 40. Here's how you calculate the total cost:

```
2 x 4 x  8:  400 @ $1.65  = $660.00
2 x 6 x 14:   66 @ $4.41  = $291.06
2 x 6 x 16:   40 @ $5.04  = $201.60
                            $1,152.66
```

Lumber size	Price per piece	x	Factor	=	Price per MBF	Lumber size	Price per piece	x	Factor	=	Price per MBF
2 x 4 x 8	$1.65	x	187.50	=	$309.38	2 x 8 x 14	$5.79	x	53.57142	=	$310.18
2 x 4 x 10	2.07	x	150.00	=	310.50	2 x 8 x 16	6.61	x	46.87501	=	309.84
2 x 4 x 12	2.48	x	125.00	=	310.00	2 x 8 x 18	7.68	x	41.66667	=	320.00
2 x 4 x 14	2.89	x	107.14290	=	309.64	2 x 8 x 20	8.53	x	37.50	=	319.88
2 x 4 x 16	3.36	x	93.74997	=	315.00	2 x 10 x 8	4.40	x	75.00	=	330.00
2 x 4 x 18	3.78	x	83.33333	=	315.00	2 x 10 x 10	5.50	x	60.00	=	330.00
2 x 4 x 20	4.20	x	75.00	=	315.00	2 x 10 x 12	6.60	x	50.00	=	330.00
2 x 6 x 8	2.52	x	125.00	=	315.00	2 x 10 x 14	7.70	x	42.85715	=	330.00
2 x 6 x 10	3.15	x	100.00	=	315.00	2 x 10 x 16	8.80	x	37.50	=	330.00
2 x 6 x 12	3.78	x	83.33333	=	315.00	2 x 10 x 18	10.20	x	33.33333	=	340.00
2 x 6 x 14	4.41	x	71.42857	=	315.00	2 x 10 x 20	11.33	x	30.00	=	339.90
2 x 6 x 16	5.04	x	62.50	=	315.00	2 x 12 x 8	6.72	x	62.50	=	420.00
2 x 6 x 18	5.76	x	55.55556	=	320.00	2 x 12 x 10	8.40	x	50.00	=	420.00
2 x 6 x 20	6.40	x	50.00	=	320.00	2 x 12 x 12	10.08	x	41.66667	=	420.00
2 x 8 x 8	3.31	x	93.74997	=	310.31	2 x 12 x 14	11.76	x	35.71429	=	420.00
2 x 8 x 10	4.13	x	75.00	=	309.75	2 x 12 x 16	13.44	x	31.25	=	420.00
2 x 8 x 12	4.96	x	62.50	=	310.00	2 x 12 x 18	15.12	x	27.77778	=	420.00
						2 x 12 x 20	16.80	x	25.00	=	420.00

Figure 2-5
Factors for converting price per piece to price per MBF

If lumber is priced by the MBF and you want to buy it by the piece, the cost calculation is more difficult. Assuming again that you are purchasing this lumber in quantities of 400, 66 and 40, the conventional math looks like this:

$$400 \times (2 \times 4 \times 8) \div (12 \times 1{,}000) \times \$309.38 = \$660.01$$
$$66 \times (2 \times 6 \times 14) \div (12 \times 1{,}000) \times \$315.00 = \$291.06$$
$$40 \times (2 \times 6 \times 16) \div (12 \times 1{,}000) \times \$315.00 = \$201.60$$

$$\$1{,}152.67$$

Lumber size	Number of pieces	x	Factor	x	Price per MBF	=	Cost of lumber
2 x 4 x 8	400	x	.00533	x	$309.38	=	$659.60
2 x 4 x 10	35	x	.00667	x	310.50	=	72.49
2 x 4 x 12	50	x	.0080	x	310.00	=	124.00
2 x 4 x 14	20	x	.00933	x	309.64	=	57.78
2 x 4 x 16	12	x	.01067	x	315.00	=	40.33
2 x 4 x 18	14	x	.0120	x	315.00	=	52.92
2 x 4 x 20	16	x	.01333	x	315.00	=	67.18
2 x 6 x 8	1	x	.0080	x	315.00	=	2.52
2 x 6 x 10	20	x	.0100	x	315.00	=	63.00
2 x 6 x 12	5	x	.0120	x	315.00	=	18.90
2 x 6 x 14	66	x	.0140	x	315.00	=	291.06
2 x 6 x 16	40	x	.0160	x	315.00	=	201.60
2 x 6 x 18	40	x	.0180	x	320.00	=	230.40
2 x 6 x 20	4	x	.0200	x	320.00	=	25.60
2 x 8 x 8	1	x	.01067	x	310.31	=	3.31
2 x 8 x 10	8	x	.01333	x	309.75	=	33.03
2 x 8 x 12	28	x	.0160	x	310.00	=	138.88
2 x 8 x 14	6	x	.01867	x	310.18	=	34.75
2 x 8 x 16	115	x	.02133	x	309.84	=	760.02
2 x 8 x 18	15	x	.0240	x	320.00	=	115.20
2 x 8 x 20	12	x	.02667	x	319.88	=	102.37
2 x 10 x 8	1	x	.01333	x	330.00	=	4.40
2 x 10 x 10	25	x	.01667	x	330.00	=	137.53
2 x 10 x 12	16	x	.0200	x	330.00	=	105.60

Figure 2-6
Factors for converting price per MBF into total cost

Lumber size	Number of pieces	x	Factor	x	Price per MBF	=	Cost of lumber
2 x 10 x 14	114	x	.02333	x	330.00	=	877.67
2 x 10 x 16	108	x	.02667	x	330.00	=	950.52
2 x 10 x 18	4	x	.0300	x	340.00	=	40.80
2 x 10 x 20	8	x	.03333	x	339.90	=	90.63
2 x 12 x 8	1	x	.0160	x	420.00	=	6.72
2 x 12 x 10	12	x	.0200	x	420.00	=	100.80
2 x 12 x 12	44	x	.0240	x	420.00	=	443.52
2 x 12 x 14	2	x	.0280	x	420.00	=	23.52
2 x 12 x 16	88	x	.0320	x	420.00	=	1,182.72
2 x 12 x 18	4	x	.0360	x	420.00	=	60.48
2 x 12 x 20	5	x	.0400	x	420.00	=	84.00

Figure 2-6 (continued)
Factors for converting price per MBF into total cost

Now look at Figure 2-6. Use these factors to simplify your calculations when lumber is priced by the MBF and you're buying it by the piece. Here's how:

Look down the first column until you find the lumber dimensions in our example. Let's look first at the 2 x 4 x 8' studs. In the next column enter the number of pieces (400). Multiply the number of pieces by the factor for 2 x 4 x 8' lumber (0.0053333) times the price per MBF ($309.38). This gives the total cost of $660.01.

Now calculate the 2 x 6 x 14' joists. Find the lumber dimensions in the first column. In the next column enter the number of pieces (66). Multiply the number of pieces by the factor for 2 x 6 x 14' lumber (0.014), times the price per MBF ($315.00). They'll cost $291.06.

Use the same procedure for the 2 x 6 x 16' joists. Find the dimensions, and enter the number of pieces. Then multiply the number of pieces by the factor times the price per MBF. The total cost is $201.60.

Listing Lumber Quantities

Your takeoff sheets should always show the board foot conversions. That makes checking your work much easier. Here's the information that will usually be on your takeoff sheet:

1) The number of pieces of each size
2) The thickness of the lumber
3) The width of each piece
4) The length of each piece
5) The grade of lumber
6) The kind of wood
7) Is it rough or surfaced?

Keep lumber for each part of the job separate. All lumber needed for floor framing should be listed together; all roof framing lumber should be together, and so on. Later you'll draw up a lumber list that shows the total 2 x 4's, 2 x 6's and 2 x 10's that are required.

Don't try to save paper! Crowding estimates causes mistakes. Leave plenty of room for totaling and making notes or changes. Follow some consistent sequence.

Here's a typical order of takeoff for a frame building. Under each category you list the number of pieces, dimensions, grade and description of the lumber needed to do the work.

Basement: Formwork, posts, girders.

Floors: Joists, bridging, subfloors, insulation, finish floors.

Outside wall framing: Sill, bottom and top plates, studs, door and window frames, ribbons, bracing, firestop, nails, sheathing, insulation.

Partitions: Bottom and top plates, studs, bracing, firestop, nails.

Roof framing: Plates (if separate from plates over studs), rafters, collar beams, bracing, roof boards, roofing felt, nails, insulation.

Outside wall covering: Building paper, sheathing, siding, shingles, furring, grounds and lath for stucco, nails.

Roof covering: Shingles or other covering and flashing.

Exterior trim: Water table, corner boards, cornice, molding, brackets, doors, windows, blinds and shutters, nails.

Porch work: Framing, subfloors, finish floors, columns, cornice, ceiling, brackets, rails, balusters, steps.

Rough interior work: Lath, grounds, wall or plaster board, rough stairs.

The Basics of Lumber Grades

Lumber comes in many grades and is cut from many species of trees. Selecting the right grade and species can make a big difference in your estimate. On most framing jobs, the lumber costs much more than the labor to install it.

Fortunately, it's fairly easy to know what lumber to use. Since 1970 nearly all major U.S. and Canadian mills have adopted a uniform lumber grading standard. The mills have made it easy to understand what grade marks mean. Now it's up to you.

Until 1970 the lumber mills had no uniform grading standard. There were about as many grades of lumber as there were mills. Worse, "Number 1" grade at one mill wasn't necessarily anything like "Number 1" grade at another mill.

If you only used lumber from one or two mills, that wasn't any problem. But if you bought lumber in another part of the country, you couldn't rely on the grade stamps unless you had a copy of that mill's grading rules.

All that has changed. Now nearly all lumber used in construction is graded under the American Softwood Lumber Standard PS 20-70. You can imagine how hard it was to develop a set of standards that could be used on every species of tree and by every mill in the U.S. and Canada. But the standard was adopted in 1970 and is used now by nearly all major mills and grading authorities.

Strength Table	
Lumber classification	**Bending strength ratio**
Light framing (2" to 4" thick, 4" wide)[1]	Pct.
Construction	34
Standard	19
Utility	9
Structural light framing (2" to 4" thick, 2" to 4" wide)	
Select structural	67
1	55
2	45
3	26
Studs (2" to 4" thick, 2" to 4" wide)	
Stud	26
Structural joists and planks (2" to 4" thick, 2" to 4" wide)	
Select structural	65
1	55
2	45
3	26
Appearance framing (2" to 4" thick, 2" to 4" wide)	
Appearance	55

[1]Widths narrower than 4" may vary in strength

Figure 2-7
Lumber bending strength ratios

PS 20-70 provides a national grading rule for dimension lumber — anything from 2 inches up to, but not including, 5 inches in nominal thickness. Nearly all lumber that size sold in the U.S. and Canada conforms to PS 20-70. Special products such as scaffold planks have been excepted from the rule.

Under PS 20-70, all construction lumber is placed in one of three categories: stress-graded, nonstress-graded, and appearance lumber. Stress-graded lumber is mostly framing lumber. Nonstress-graded lumber is mostly 1" boards. Appearance lumber is used mostly for siding and flooring where appearance is more important than strength.

Let's look closely at these three categories.

Stress-Graded Lumber

Almost all softwood lumber from 2" to 4" thick is stress graded under PS 20-70. Stress grading doesn't require that each piece actually be tested for strength. That would be mechanical stress grading and it's used only on key structural members. Most stress-graded lumber is visually graded. Someone inspects each piece and classifies it by the number and type of defects, such as knots and other imperfections.

For visually-graded lumber, a single set of grade names and descriptions is used throughout the United State and Canada. Other stress-graded products include timbers, posts, stringers, beams, decking and some boards.

Dimension lumber is the most common stress-graded item in lumber yards. Nearly all dimension lumber is 2" wide. Visually-graded dimension lumber is divided into five categories: Light Framing, Structural Framing, Studs, Structural Joists and Planks, and Appearance Framing. See Figure 2-7.

Most of the lumber you use is *Light Framing*. The grades are either Construction, Standard or Utility. These are the lower strength materials and are available up to 4" thick. The best Light Framing grade is Construction. Utility grade has the lowest strength.

Notice the "34" at the right of Construction grade in Figure 2-7. I'll explain what that column of percentages means shortly.

A grade mark "STD&BTR" means that the lumber was originally graded both Standard and Construction. That alone doesn't explain how much was Standard and how much was Construction grade. The mill's agreement with the original buyer probably makes that clear, but you have no way of telling the percentages specified. Even if you did know that at least 75% was Construction grade, the stack may have been broken and resorted before it reached your yard.

Structural Framing includes thicker material such as 2 x 6, 2 x 8, and 2 x 10. The grades are Select Structural, No. 1, No. 2, and No. 3. These grades are used where bending strength is critical. Rafters and trusses are common applications. Wider material would be used for posts, beams and stringers. Most structural lumber is graded in combinations such as No. 2&BTR or possibly No. 3&BTR.

Stud grade may be 2 x 2 to 4 x 4 and up to 10 feet long. Naturally, 2 x 4 is the most common dimension. Stud grade is usually identified "PET" which means it has been precision end trimmed to save end cutting waste.

Structural Joists and Planks and *Appearance Framing* are used less than other dimension lumber. Grades for Structural Joists and Planks are the same as for Structural Framing. Appearance Framing is available only as Appearance grade.

Strength of Lumber Grades

The column of percentages at the right in Figure 2-7 shows the bending strength ratio for visually-graded dimension lumber. The number indicates the percentage of strength compared to the average for a clear, straight-grained piece *of the same species*. Notice that Stud grade has less bending strength than Construction grade, but more than Standard or Utility. Notice also that the two Structural classes have very similar bending strength ratios.

PS 20-70 has established these classes, grade names and the minimum bending strength ratios. This strength ratio is your index of relative quality. Actual strength for any grade depends on the type of tree the lumber was cut from. That's why bending strength is given in a ratio. For example, Construction grade Douglas Fir will have a higher bending strength than Redwood of the same grade. But the strength ratio of both will be the same because grades compare the average of clear wood of the same species.

How does the lumber inspector decide whether a length of 2 x 4 is Construction, Standard or Utility? He does it by eye, comparing each piece with pictures in the lumber grading book that's published by each of the grading associations. Grades of lumber will have about the same appearance regardless of species. So Stud grade Southern Yellow Pine will have about the same number of knots, checks and other imperfections as Stud grade Fir. But the strength will be different because Fir and Pine have different bending strengths.

The National Grading Rule also establishes some limits on sizes of edge knots and other defects for lumber that is graded by a combination of mechanical and visual methods.

Grouping of Species

Species that have about the same bending strength and are very similar in appearance are usually grouped together in the grading rules. Properties assigned to the group may not apply to any single species in that group. The group is known by a unique name approved by the American Lumber Standards Committee.

You've probably heard the term *Hem-Fir* but probably don't know that Hem-Fir can be California Red Fir, Grand Fir, Noble Fir, Pacific Silver Fir, Shasta Fir, White Fir, or Western Hemlock. Figure 2-8 shows what the grade stamp might look like on a piece of

GRADE STAMP

Hem Fir

Figure 2-8
Lumber grade stamp

Hem-Fir lumber.

You will also see the term *Hem-Fir (Coast)* which is generally Hemlock produced in western Oregon, Washington or British Columbia. Hem-Fir (Inland) is generally White Fir grown in Northern California. These designations are the result of an informal understanding between producers and buyers rather than classes established by PS 20-70.

Another important group of species is sold under the S-P-F designation. This is Spruce, Pine and Fir grown in Canada. Southern Yellow Pine is a group of species grown from Texas to Virginia. Most Southern Yellow Pine is either Longleaf or Shortleaf Pine, Loblolly Pine or Slash Pine.

Each association that grades lumber has very precise definitions of the identities, properties and characteristics of individual species for each group. The seven major grading associations are shown in Figure 2-9. Each publishes reference materials about the lumber produced by association members and the grading rule book currently in use.

Your local yard doesn't stock every grade for every species, of course. No yard could do that. Some grades listed in most rule books aren't even produced. Most yards stock only the type of framing lumber that's most economical for your area. For example, if Douglas Fir is available locally, it would be foolish for your yard to stock Southern Pine. Smaller yards will offer only a few grades for whatever species they sell.

Here's an example. Joist and plank material is often sold as No. 2 and Better (2&BTR). If you need No. 1 grade material for joists or planks, you'll either have to place a special order or sort through a pile of No. 2 and Better to find the best of the lot. Larger yards usually carry several dry dimension grades along with clear, finish, and decking.

Nonstress-Graded Lumber
For most of this century, most lumber intended for general building purposes was not stress graded. This category of lumber has been referred to as *yard lumber*. Today, many former yard items have been given defined properties. So "yard" lumber doesn't mean what it used to.

Boards are the most common nonstress-graded construction lumber. Boards are usually sold as nominal 1″ thickness. The actual thickness will be less. Standard nominal widths are 2″, 3″, 4″, 6″, 8″, 10″, and 12″. Grades generally available in retail yards are No. 1, No. 2, and No. 3 (or Construction, Standard, and Utility). These will often be combined in grade groups. Boards are sold square edged, dressed and matched (tongued and grooved) or with a shiplapped joint. Boards formed by end-jointing shorter sections are common.

Boards are usually identified either as *selects* or *commons*. Selects are graded for appearance. Common grades are used in sheathing and for utility purposes. They are

Name and Address	Species Covered by Grading Rules
National Lumber Grades Authority P.O. Box 97 Ganges, B.C. Canada VOS IEO	Douglas-fir, Larch, Hem-fir, SPF (Spruce, Pine, Fir), Hem-tam, Western Cedar, Aspen
Northeastern Lumber Manufacturers Association, Inc. 13 South Street Glen Falls, New York 12801	Balsam Fir, Eastern White Pine, Red Pine, Eastern Hemlock, Black Spruce, White Spruce, Red Spruce, Pitch Pine, Tamarack, Jack Pine, Northern White Cedar
Northern Hardwood and Pine Manufacturers Association 305 E. Walnut Street Green Bay, Wisconsin 54301	Bigtooth Aspen, Quaking Aspen, Eastern White Pine, Red Pine, Jack Pine, Black Spruce, White Spruce, Red Spruce Balsam Fir, Eastern Hemlock, Tamarack
Redwood Inspection Service 617 Montgomery Street San Francisco, California 94111	Redwood
Southern Pine Inspection Bureau Box 846 Pensacola, Florida 32502	Longleaf Pine, Slash Pine, Shortleaf Pine, Loblolly Pine, Virginia Pine, Pond Pine, Pitch Pine
West Coast Lumber Inspection Bureau Box 25406 1750 SW. Skyline Boulevard Portland, Oregon 97225	Douglas-fir, Western Hemlock, Western Red cedar, Incense-cedar, Port-Orford-cedar, Alaska-cedar, Western True Firs, Mountain Hemlock, Sitka Spruce
Western Wood Products Association 700 Yeon Building Portland, Oregon 97204	Ponderosa Pine, Western White Pine, Douglas-fir, Sugar Pine, Western True Firs, Western Larch, Engelmann Spruce, Incense-cedar, Western Hemlock, Lodgepole Pine, Western Red cedar, Mountain Hemlock, Red Alder

Figure 2-9
Principal lumber grading associations

separated into three to five different grades, depending on the species and grading rule used. Grades are identified either by number (No. 1, No. 2) or by descriptive terms (Construction, Standard).

Unfortunately, there is no uniform system for identifying various species and grades of boards. First-grade boards are usually graded primarily for strength, but appearance is also considered. First-grade is used for siding, cornice, shelving, and paneling. Knots and knotholes will be larger and more frequent in the lower grades. Second- and third-grade boards are often used together for subfloors, roof and wall sheathing, and concrete forming. Fourth-grade boards have only adequate strength. They're used for roof and wall sheathing, subfloor, and concrete forms.

Grading of nonstress-grade lumber varies by species, product, and grading association. Lath, for example, is available generally in two grades, No. 1 and No. 2. The appropriate lumber grading rule book has complete descriptions of these products.

Appearance Lumber

Appearance lumber is nonstress-graded but it's in a separate category because looks are important in the grading process. This category includes most lumber worked to a pattern. Some appearance lumber comes prefinished to save the cost of finishing. The appearance category of lumber includes trim, siding, flooring, ceiling, paneling, casing, base, stepping, and finish boards.

Most appearance lumber grades are described by letters and combinations of letters (B&BTR, C&BTR, D) and are also known as select grades. Descriptive terms such as ''prime'' and ''clear'' are applied to some species. The letters FG (flat grain), VG (vertical grain), or MG (mixed grain) are an option for some appearance lumber products.

In Cedar and Redwood, there's a clear difference in color between heartwood and sapwood. Heartwood has high natural resistance to decay and will be identified as *heart*.

In some species, two or three appearance grades are available for some products. A typical example is casing and base in the grades of C&BTR and D. Other species are sold as B&BTR, C, C&BTR, and D. Although several grades may be described in grade rules, only one or two will be offered at your lumber yard.

Grade B&BTR allows a few small imperfections, mainly in the form of minor skips in finishing ("hit and miss"), small checks or stains due to seasoning. Depending on the species, small pitch areas and pin knots may be present. Since appearance grades are based on the quality of one face, the reverse side may be lower quality. Grade C&BTR is the combination most common in construction. It's used for high-quality interior and exterior trim, paneling and cabinet work, especially where a clear finish will be used. It's also used for flooring in homes, offices, and public buildings.

The number and size of flaws in the wood increases as the grades drop from B&BTR to D and E. Your only key to what the letters mean is the grade rule used by the producing mill. C is used for many of the same purposes as B&BTR. Grade D will have larger and more surface blemishes than C grade. But this may not detract from the appearance when painted. Grade D is used in finish construction for many of the same uses as C.

Redwood and Cedar have different grade designations. Grades such as Clear Heart, A, or B are used in Cedar: Clear All Heart, Clear, and Select are typical Redwood grades. Finish boards are usually a nominal 1" thick. When dressed on two sides, they measure about 3/4".

Lumber Siding

Beveled siding is ordinarily stocked only in White Pine, Ponderosa Pine, Western Red Cedar, Cypress, or Redwood. Drop siding, also known as rustic siding or barn siding, is usually stocked in the same species as beveled siding. Siding may be stocked as B&BTR, except in Cedar, where Clear, A, and B may be available. In Redwood, Clear All Heart and Clear are the usual designations. Vertical grain (VG) is sometimes a part of the grade designation. Drop siding sometimes is stocked also in sound knotted C and D grades of Southern Pine, Douglas Fir, and Hemlock. Drop siding may be dressed, matched, or shiplapped.

Flooring

Oak, Maple and harder softwood species such as Douglas Fir, Western Larch, and Southern Pine are used for flooring. Your lumber yard probably has at least one softwood and one hardwood flooring in stock. Flooring is usually nominal 1" thick dressed to 25/32" and 3" or 4" nominal width. Thicker flooring is available for heavy-duty floors both in hardwoods and softwoods. Thinner flooring is available in hardwoods, especially for recovering old floors.

Vertical and flat grain (also called quarter-sawed and plain-sawed respectively) flooring is manufactured from both softwoods and hardwoods. Vertical-grained flooring shrinks and swells less than flat-grained flooring and resists opening of joints better.

The chief grades of Maple are Clear No. 1 and No. 2. Quarter-sawed Oak comes in Clear and Select. Plain-sawed is available in Clear, Select and Number 1 common.

Shingles and Shakes

Shingles are sawn from Western Red Cedar, Northern White Cedar, and Redwood. The shingle grades are: Western Red Cedar, No. 1, No. 2, and No. 3; Northern White Cedar, Extra, Clear, 2nd Clear, Clear Wall, Utility; Redwood, No. 1, No. 2 VG, and No. 2 MG.

Shingles that are all heartwood resist decay better than shingles that contain sapwood. Edge-grained shingles are less likely to warp than flat-grained shingles. Thick-butted shingles and narrow shingles are also less likely to warp. The thickness of shingles may be described as 4/2 or 5/2¼, for example. This means that four shingles have 2" of butt thickness, or five shingles have 2¼" of butt thickness. Lengths may be 16", 18", or 24".

Shingles are usually packed four bundles to the square. A square of shingles will cover 100 square feet of roof area when applied at standard weather exposures.

Shakes are handsplit or handsplit and resawn from Western Red Cedar. There is only one grade: 100% clear, graded from the split face in the case of handsplit and resawn material. Handsplit shakes are graded from the best face. Shakes must be 100% heartwood, free of bark and sapwood. The standard thickness of shakes ranges from 3/8" to 1¼". Lengths are 18" and 24" and a 15" "starter-finish course" length.

Green and Dry Lumber

Timbers are usually surfaced while green, or unseasoned. It isn't economical to dry them for most purposes. Dimension lumber and boards may be sold as green or dry. The mill makes this choice. Green lumber is slightly wider and thicker than the same nominal dimension of dry lumber. For example, a nominal 2 x 4 measures 1½" by 3½" when dry and 1⁹⁄₁₆" by 3⁹⁄₁₆" when green. A piece of green lumber will shrink to approximately the standard dry sizes as it dries down to about 15% moisture content. The American Lumber Standard definition of "dry" is a moisture content of 19% or less. Many types of lumber are dried before surfacing and only dry sizes for these products are given in the standard.

Surfacing

Lumber can be produced either rough or surfaced (dressed). Rough lumber has marks left by the saw blade. It's usually larger in both thickness and width than the standard size. A rough-sawn surface is common in post and timber products. Because of surface roughness, grading of rough lumber can be difficult.

Surfaced lumber has been planed or sanded on one side (S1S), two sides (S2S), one edge (S1E), two edges (S2E), one edge (S1E), two edges (S2E), or combinations of sides and edges (S1S1E, S2S1E, S1S2E, or S4S).

Selecting the Right Lumber

By now you should feel comfortable with lumber grades and what the names mean. Of course, there's more to learn. The lumber grading books have it all and only cost a few dollars. Get the lumber grading rule for the grades you use most. But you don't have to be an expert. A little knowledge here goes a long way.

Figure 2-10 shows what grades should be used where in most common applications. Your building code or the job specifications may call for different grades, of course. But the table will be a good guide in most situations.

Selecting Plywood

For everything from subfloors to roof decks to siding and built-ins, plywood is usually the best choice. Plywood is an engineered product. But the natural wood is changed very little in the manufacturing process. When a log arrives at a plywood mill, it's peeled, placed in a giant lathe, and turned against a lathe knife. Every plywood panel is a built-up board made of dried layers of veneer. An odd number of layers is used for every panel so that the grain direction on the face and back run in the same direction.

Plywood, like lumber, carries a grade-mark which identifies the product and indicates the type of plywood — either indoor or outdoor. Letter grades N, A, B, C, D, refer to the quality of the face and back veneers. N is the highest veneer quality. A two-letter combination, such as A-C, indicates the quality of the panel face (A) and back (C).

Grades A-A, A-B, or A-D interior type sanded plywood are recommended for cabinet doors, furniture and built-ins. If the surface will be waxed, sealed, or varnished, you'll want A-A, A-B, or A-D grades. For exterior siding, interior paneling and ceilings, textured plywood panels are available in many different species, surfaces, and patterns. Textured plywood sidings are usually finished with stains. You'll also see MDO (Medium Density Overlaid) plywood used as siding. This grade has a smooth resin-treated fiber surface bonded to the panel face. It holds paint well.

Item	Grade
Wall framing	Stud
Sills on foundation walls or slab on ground	Utility
Sills on piers — built up[1]	No. 2
Joists, rafters, headers[2]	No. 2
Plates, caps, bucks	Utility
Ribbon boards, bracing, ridge boards (1")	No. 3
Collar beams	No. 3
Furring grounds (1")	No. 3
Subflooring, wall sheathing	No. 3
Roof sheathing (pitched)	No. 3
Roof decking (flat) — 1" or 2"	No. 2
Exposed decking — 3" or 4"	Dense Standard or Select DT&G Deck
Industrial decking — 3" or 4"	Commercial DT&G Deck
Heavy timber beams, posts, and columns (over 5" thick)[2]	No. 1

Finish

Moldings	Standard molding
Interior paneling — rustic	No. 2
— appearance	C and BTR
Shelving	No. 3

Exterior

Railings, rail posts	No. 1
Decking (bark side up)	No. 2
Trim, fascia, corner boards	No. 1

[1] For sills within 12" of ground, wood should have high natural durability, or be pressure preservative treated.

[2] Higher structural grades may be required by engineering design or building codes.

Figure 2-10
Lumber grades for construction

Plywood is available in both appearance and in engineering grades. Appearance grades are normally sanded. The grade-trademark on appearance grade plywood includes a group number that shows which of the more than 70 wood species was used in the plywood. See Figure 2-11. Since species vary in strength and stiffness, they have been classified into five groups. The strongest woods are in Group 1.

Engineered grades have an identification index which tells you the maximum support spacing. See Figure 2-12. The identification index is two numbers separated by a diagonal, such as 24/0 or 32/16. The number to the left of the diagonal is the maximum spacing of supports in inches when used as roof decking. The number to the right is the maximum support spacing for subflooring applications. Unsanded grades designated as *Structural I* and *Structural II* are recommended for heavy loads where strength is essential.

Most residential jobs will include plywood floor sheathing. The conventional floor has two layers of plywood — plywood sheathing as the subfloor and a separate layer of

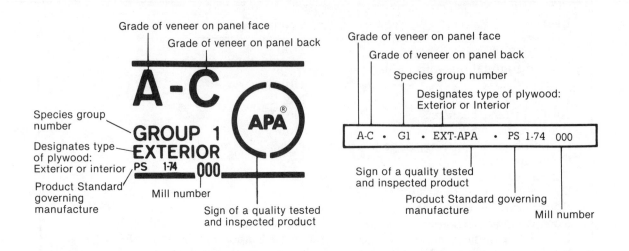

Figure 2-11
Grade-trademark for appearance grade plywood

Figure 2-12
Grade-trademark for engineered grade plywood

plywood as underlayment below vinyl or carpet. Underlayment eliminates swelling and buckling in the floor.

It's possible to use one layer of plywood as a combination subfloor and underlayment. Plywood called *2.4.1* serves both as a structural subfloor and as an excellent base for resilient floorings, carpeting, and for other nonstructural floorings. Plywood marked 2.4.1 is usually 1⅛'' thick and is usually laid over 2'' joists spaced 32'' on center, or 4'' girders spaced 48'' on center.

You'll also see glued plywood floor sheathing. The APA Glued Floor System uses both glue and nails to bond plywood to the joists. A glued floor will be stronger and less apt to squeak. The glue must be an elastomeric adhesive that meets performance specification AFC-01. It can be applied even when the air temperature is below freezing, and comes in cartridges that fit in standard caulking guns.

Plywood is also the most popular wall sheathing material. It covers large areas quickly and adds strength and rigidity, usually making bracing unnecessary. Plywood wall sheathing is installed either vertically or horizontally. But remember that horizontal application gives more stiffness under loads perpendicular to the surface. So, if you're going to be nailing siding such as shingles directly to the sheathing, apply the sheathing horizontally.

On some jobs you'll see plywood siding used directly over the studs without any other sheathing material. This is usually called *single wall* construction. Panels for single wall construction are known as "303 sidings" and have the maximum support spacing listed in the grade-trademark. A 303 siding, for example, stamped *303-24 in o.c.* can be applied vertically to studs 16" or 24" on center. Texture 1-11 siding is 5/8" thick and has 3/8"-wide vertical grooves spaced 2", 4", 6", or 8" on center. It's used vertically over studs spaced 16" on center.

All edges of panel siding should be backed with framing or blocking. To keep from staining the siding with rust marks from nails, use hot dip galvanized, aluminum, or other nonstaining nails. No extra corner bracing is needed with plywood panel siding.

Roof Sheathing

When using plywood roof sheathing, refer to the identification index for the maximum rafter spacing. For example, for a 24" span, plywood marked 24/0 will do the job. The identification index will appear on panels from 5/16" through 7/8" thick.

Your plan will show either open soffits or closed soffits on most jobs. For a roof deck over closed soffits, use C-D interior grade sheathing. To enclose the soffits, medium density overlaid (MDO) plywood is best because it holds paint better.

With open soffits, panels will be exposed at the overhang. Use Exterior type plywood and an Appearance grade on the lower (exposed) side. That gives a better finished appearance from below and makes it easier to apply a smooth coat of paint. You could also use textured plywood with the textured side down on an exposed soffit. Staining may be the only finish required.

Wood Panel Products

Besides softwood plywood, you'll see several other panel products. Some provide strength and stiffness. Others are primarily for finish, sound reduction or insulation.

Most of these products are partly or entirely wood-based — hardwood plywood, insulation board, hardboard, laminated paperboard, particleboard, and gypsum board. Insulation board, hardboard, and laminated paperboard are made of wood fibers which are laced together with a binder. Particleboard is made of wood particles bonded together with resin under heat and pressure. Gypsum board has a noncombustible gypsum core between faces of paper.

The insulation board-hardboard-paperboard group is usually known as building fiberboard. The names you'll see most often are the trade names Celotex, Insulite, Masonite, Beaverboard, and Homasote.

Oldest of the boards is insulation board, made in two categories — semi-rigid and rigid. Semi-rigid is a low-density product used as insulation and cushioning. The rigid type includes both the interior board used for walls and ceilings and the exterior board used for wall sheathing.

Hardboard is a grainless, smooth, hard product. It's used for siding, underlayment, and as prefinished wall panel.

Laminated paperboard serves as sheathing and other covering, but it's not used as much as the other building fiberboards.

Particleboards are often known by the kinds of particle used — flakeboard, chipboard, chipcore, or shavings board. Some of these boards are very stiff and durable. They can be used for subfloors and sheathing. Both hardboard and particleboard make good underlayment. Hardboard comes in 3' x 4' or 4' x 4' panels a little less than 1/4" thick. It's often used in remodeling to create an even, smooth surface over an existing, irregular floor. Particleboard comes in a 4' x 8' size, in a variety of thicknesses from 1/4" to 3/4". Special insulation boards are also used as underlayment for carpeting as a resilient, noise-deadening material.

Before figuring the underlayment, find out what's recommended for the final floor covering. You need to know about conditioning the underlayment, preparing the surface, panel arrangement, edge clearances to allow for shrinking and swelling, nailing, stapling or gluing, and possible filling and sanding. Do it right and avoid problems later.

Insulation board sheathing is available in three types — nail-base, intermediate density, and regular density. Nail-base has the most strength; regular density the least. Thickness is 1/2" in the first two types and 1/2" or 25/32" in the last. Wood and asbestos shingles can be applied directly to nail-base with annular-grooved nails. Regular density is least dense and the best insulator. The Federal Housing Administration recommends that all three types be applied vertically on the wall. These boards usually provide adequate racking resistance without corner bracing. But insulation board in 2' x 8' panels applied horizontally needs corner bracing.

Wrapping It Up

Having covered lumber, plywood and panel products, we've covered most of the materials a carpentry estimator has to deal with. But there's one item of unfinished business. I promised answers to the questions at the beginning of this chapter. All questions are false. If you answered "True" to no more than three, you're ready to start making take-offs. Go on to Chapter 3.

Estimating Footings and Foundations

Inferior construction, poor workmanship and shoddy materials never save money. Maintenance and repair costs will exceed by far any initial savings. This is true of all construction, but especially true of footings. *Never* skimp on the footing or foundation. *No building is any better than the foundation it sits on.*

This chapter covers both footings and foundations. Footings go in first, so we'll cover that subject first.

A footing is the base of the foundation wall or pier. It's usually concrete even if the foundation wall is masonry and will be wider than the foundation wall it supports. Some footings require no forms other than the natural soil that surround them. If so, no carpentry will be required. But if your estimate includes the foundation, footings will be part of that estimate.

Footings have to be strong enough to carry the entire building load for as long as the building stands. That's no easy task when you consider that the ground under the building will almost certainly shift and settle as the building ages. Any movement in the foundation can cause walls and ceilings to crack and door and window frames to wrack out of shape. Chimney and column footings have to support even heavier loads per square foot than sidewall footings. The footings you design and build should resist settling and provide good support for the life of the structure.

Soil conditions vary, of course. But normally you won't need a soil bearing analysis to design good footings for residential construction. When an architect draws the plans for a house, he should make footings appropriate for the site a part of the plan. Plans furnished with a factory-built house or stock plans from a house planning service usually show footings that will support the house under normal soil conditions. Your building code may require wider and deeper footings for unusual soil conditions. That's why some stock plans don't give any footing dimensions. They leave it up to you to follow the code.

Most codes require 12'' wide footings for single story residences, 15'' wide footings for two story residences and 18'' wide footings for three story residences. The minimum thickness of the footing will usually be 6'' for single story, 7 inches for two story and 8 inches for three story homes. Your code or the specifications may require more. If so, the plans should show the correct footing dimensions.

How deep should the footing be? Your code probably provides that it has to go below the undisturbed ground surface by a certain depth: 12 inches for single story, 18 inches for two story and 24 inches for three story. But you won't see many footings at 12 inches in most parts of the country.

As a practical matter, footing excavation has to go down to solid earth below the frost depth. This is probably much more than 12 inches. Ground moves and heaves as it freezes and thaws. Putting the footing below frost depth reduces the chance of movement in very cold weather. Your building department will identify the frost depth in your community.

Pouring footings on soft or wet soil or on fill will result in cracks in the foundation wall. And make sure you excavate below any roots or stumps you find. Organic matter under a footing will decay eventually, leaving the footing without any support in that area.

Generally, footings should be poured in monolithic concrete. That means all at one time. When poured all at once, there's no joint to allow cracking or uneven settling. But you can pour footings for a detached garage, porch or stoop separately from the main footings. If there are detached or isolated footings, don't overlook them when compiling your estimate.

Footing Cost Variables
It takes skill (and a little luck) to estimate footings accurately. That's true of most excavation. When you're moving soil, most surprises will increase costs rather than reduce them. Hard digging or rock will increase the manhours and may increase the cost of equipment. There's no sure way to anticipate all excavation costs. But eliminate as many unknowns as possible.

This book isn't about estimating excavation, but I'll offer some tips that most excavation contractors would probably endorse:

• Price the job by cubic yards removed, not by the linear feet of foundation. If you have to dig deeper to get down to firm soil, that extra expense shouldn't come out of your pocket.

• Walk the site before estimating the job. If you don't know what kind of soil to expect, dig a hole and find out.

• Note in your estimate that the excavation cost is based on sandy loam or light soil. Light clay or loose rock will cost 50% more, and tough clay or rock will be bid on a cost plus basis. Any de-watering will be extra.

• Watch out for lines under or through a footing that indicate conduit for water, sewer, electricity, gas, telephone or T.V. cable service. Conduit crossing under or through a foundation must be installed while you're preparing to pour the footing. Don't overlook this cost in your estimate.

• Sloping sites usually involve extra costs. Stepped footings on hillsides will increase costs three ways: excavation, forming and pouring. If the concrete truck can't pour directly into the footings, you'll need to add the cost of a pump rig and operator or include a front-end-loader in your estimate.

• It's more expensive to pour footings in cold weather. Add between 5% and 15% to labor costs and include the cost of protective measures to prevent freezing, if necessary. Cold weather doesn't have to stop construction, but pour the concrete as soon as possible after excavation and protect it against freezing until it's hardened. Concrete that freezes before setting may have to be removed and replaced.

• Calcium chloride, a water-absorbing chemical, is normally added to concrete to

Footing depth	12"	14"	16"	18"	Footing width 20"	22"	24"	26"	28"	30"
6"	.01852	.02160	.02469	.02778	.03086	.03395	.03704	.04012	.04321	.04630
7"	.02160	.02521	.02881	.03241	.03601	.03961	.04321	.04681	.05041	.05401
8"	.02469	.02881	.03292	.03704	.04115	.04527	.04938	.05350	.05761	.06173
9"	.02778	.03241	.03704	.04167	.04630	.05093	.05556	.06019	.06481	.06944
10"	.03086	.03601	.04115	.04630	.05144	.05658	.06173	.06687	.07202	.07716
11"	.03395	.03961	.04527	.05093	.05658	.06224	.06790	.07356	.07922	.08488
12"	.03704	.04321	.04938	.05556	.06173	.06790	.07407	.08025	.08642	.09259
13"	.04012	.04681	.05350	.06019	.06687	.07356	.08025	.08693	.09362	.10031
14"	.04321	.05041	.05761	.06481	.07202	.07922	.08642	.09362	.10082	.10802
15"	.04630	.05401	.06173	.06944	.07716	.08488	.09259	.10031	.10802	.11574

Figure 3-1
Factors for concrete and crushed stone

accelerate setting and reduce the time it's vulnerable to damage from freezing. But adding too much calcium chloride will weaken the concrete. In freezing weather, order concrete with 1% calcium chloride. That increases the cost about a dollar per cubic yard. In extreme temperatures, more may be required. The chapter on cold-weather building covers these adjustments in detail, plus other cold-weather tips. But note that some specifications and building codes set limits on the amount of calcium chloride you can use. That may make other protective measures necessary in very cold weather.

Layout
When excavation is complete, permanent corners for the foundation can be laid out. That's the start of footing work. Although a rough layout of the foundation was probably made before excavation and reference stakes were placed, you'll probably have to place the batterboards you plan to use.

The cost of laying out the foundation and house corners, including setting and leveling the forms and grade stakes to the correct footing elevation, will be between $120 and $220 on most residential jobs. That includes $20 to $40 for stakes and batterboards and $100 to $180 for labor. These figures are based on 1" lumber at $300 per MBF and layout labor at $25 per hour. Costs will be higher for homes with more than 10 corners and where no reference point is available on or near the site. Neither surveying nor brush clearing are included in these estimates.

Concrete Multiplication Factors

Many experienced contractors use multiplying factors to speed and simplify concrete calculations. Throughout this book I'll offer tables of multiplying factors and recommend that you at least try using them. If you haven't used multiplying factors to figure concrete, consider Figure 3-1, a table for concrete and crushed stone. Find the factor by reading down in the column that shows footing depth and across in the row that shows footing width. The number at the intersection of the appropriate row and column is the factor to use.

Here's an example. Assume you have a footing 8" deep by 16" wide and 65'4" long. How much concrete is needed? Follow the lines on the chart for an 8" footing depth and a 16" footing width. Where they intersect you'll find the factor, 0.03292. Multiply this by the linear feet of footing to find the cubic yards of concrete required. The calculation: 0.03292 times 65.33' equals 2.15 cubic yards. Note that this includes no waste and has no allowance for over-excavation or short delivery. You'll have to add whatever allowance you feel is necessary.

To estimate concrete for column or pier footings, multiply the factor for the width and depth of the footing by the length of the footing, then multiply that by the number of footings on the plan. If there are five column footings measuring 24'' wide, 12'' deep and 24'' long, multiply the factor (0.07407) times 2.0' times five (the number of footings). The answer is 0.74 cubic yards.

If the footings are wider than the width shown in the table in Figure 3-1 (as for a chimney footing), add two factors together and then multiply as before.

Example: A chimney footing will be 36'' wide, 6.0' long and 12'' deep. The footing width in Figure 3-1 only goes to 30'' wide. To find the factor for 36'', add together the factors for two widths that total 36'':

The factor for 20'' x 12'' is .06173
The factor for 16'' x 12'' is .04938

The factor for 36'' x 12'' is .11111

.11111 x 6.0' = .67 cubic yards

To check the answer, let's do the calculation the long way:

3.0' x 6.0' x 1.0' ÷ 27 = .67 cu. yd.

Estimating Concrete Quantities

Using the multiplying factors makes quantity calculations easy. But the quantity computed from the plans and the quantity that you'll actually use may be two different figures. Consider the following:

• Excavation for the footing usually will be wider than the specified footing width. (It should never be less than the specified width). You can set forms for the concrete very close to the true dimensions. But precision excavation usually isn't worth the time and effort. Some hand trimming is always required at corners and to remove loose dirt. That makes the excavation slightly oversize. Remember, you have to fill the entire excavated area with concrete. You can't stuff dirt back in the hole. That's sure to cause settling cracks — maybe even before you get paid.

• Excavation to the exact depth is also difficult. The depth of the concrete should never be less than the specified depth. If the excavation is more than the required depth, you have to fill the difference with concrete, not loose dirt.

• Some concrete will spill from the truck during unloading. And, if direct chuting isn't possible, from the wheelbarrows, loader bucket or pump. You may be able to salvage some of this concrete, but most will be wasted.

It's often cheaper to pay for a little extra concrete than it is to pay for partial loads. Seven and one-half cubic yards is usually considered a full load. Anything less will increase the cost per load. A one cubic yard load of concrete will probably cost more than two or three cubic yards delivered in a fully-loaded truck.

Most contractors order 5% to 10% more concrete than the plans call for. One convenient way to allow for waste is to "double count" the corners. Where two walls come to a corner, the first 6 or 8 inches at the corner could actually be counted in both walls. If you measure the length of both walls all the way to the end of the corner,

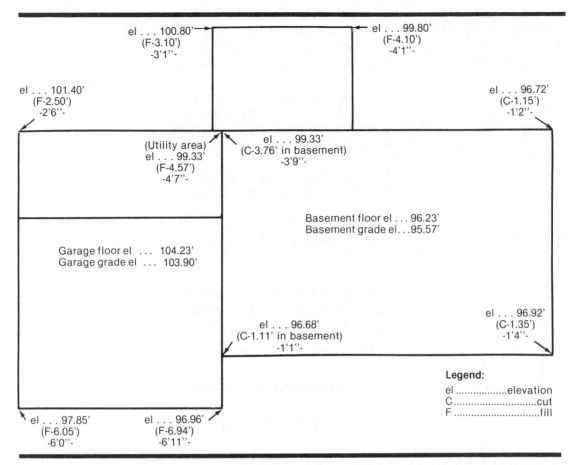

el . . . 100.80'
(F-3.10')
-3'1"-

el . . . 99.80'
(F-4.10')
-4'1"-

el . . . 101.40'
(F-2.50')
-2'6"-

el . . . 96.72'
(C-1.15')
-1'2"-

(Utility area)
el . . . 99.33'
(F-4.57')
-4'7"-

el . . . 99.33'
(C-3.76' in basement)
-3'9"-

Basement floor el . . . 96.23'
Basement grade el. . .95.57'

Garage floor el . . . 104.23'
Garage grade el . . . 103.90'

el . . . 96.68'
(C-1.11' in basement)
-1'1"-

el . . . 96.92'
(C-1.35')
-1'4"-

Legend:
el . . . . elevation
C . . . . cut
F . . . . fill

el . . . 97.85'
(F-6.05')
-6'0"-

el . . . 96.96'
(F-6.94')
-6'11"-

Figure 3-2
Foundation plan

you've counted that last 6 or 8 inches twice. This "double counting" allows a small percentage for waste. It may be enough to compensate for over-excavation and spillage.

Before estimating the concrete, examine the foundation plan for grade elevations to see what footings will be required. Figure 3-2 is the foundation plan for a house we're going to estimate. Figure 3-3 is a foundation footing detail.

Stepped Footings
When the plans include a stepped footing, extra concrete will be required. Where? In the vertical rise of the step. It's not apparent on the plan view. That makes it easy to overlook. Look at Figures 3-2 and 3-3. Let's do some calculations:

1)   In Figure 3-2, the basement grade elevation is shown as 95.57'. The grade elevation at the left back corner of the utility area is 101.40'. This is a rise of 5.83'. (101.40' less 95.57' equals 5.83', or 5'10".) The garage and utility area will require fill dirt, and the footing here will start from the present grade elevation.

2)   This job will have a concrete block foundation. Block will be 8" high. The footing has to have steps in multiples of 8" from the left front corner of the basement (adjacent to the garage area) around the perimeter of the front and left side of the garage, to the left back corner of the utility area. The sum of the vertical rise for these steps must be a multiple of 8". Since 5'10" is 70", which isn't a multiple of 8", increase it to 72".

Cubic yards of concrete needed for the vertical rise in the stepped footing will be the width of the footings (24") times the vertical thickness (6") times the vertical rise (72") times 2 (the front and back perimeters), divided by 27. Start your calculation by

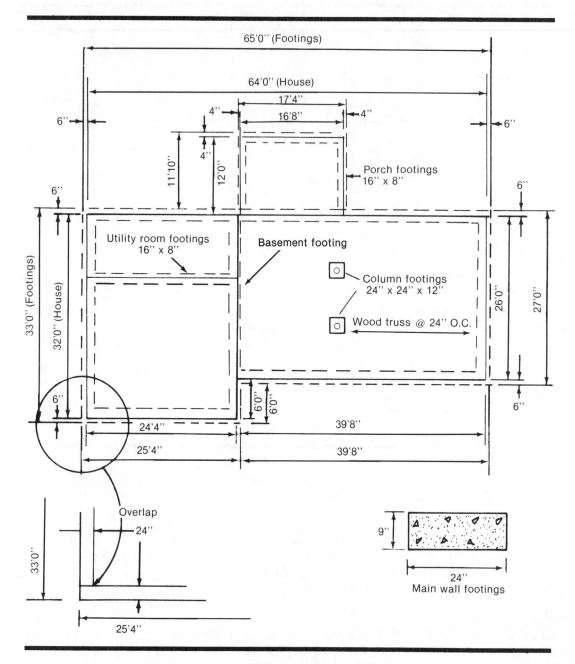

Figure 3-3
Foundation footing detail

converting all dimensions to decimals of a foot. To speed things up, refer to Figure 3-4, a chart of decimal equivalents. After conversion, the calculation looks like this:

$$2.0' \times .5' \times 6.0' \times 2 \div 27 = .44 \text{ cu. yd.}$$

It's quicker and easier to do the calculation using the factor from Figure 3-1. It looks like this:

$$.03704 \times 6.0' \times 2 = .44 \text{ cu. yd.}$$

4th	8th	0"	1"	2"	3"	4"	5"	6"	7"	8"	9"	10"	11"
0	0	.00	.08	.17	.25	.33	.42	.50	.58	.67	.75	.83	.92
	1	.01	.09	.18	.26	.34	.43	.51	.59	.68	.76	.84	.93
1	2	.02	.10	.19	.27	.35	.44	.52	.60	.69	.77	.85	.94
	3	.03	.11	.20	.28	.36	.45	.53	.61	.70	.78	.86	.95
2	4	.04	.13	.21	.29	.38	.46	.54	.63	.71	.79	.88	.96
	5	.05	.14	.22	.30	.39	.47	.55	.64	.72	.80	.89	.97
3	6	.06	.15	.23	.31	.40	.48	.56	.65	.73	.81	.90	.98
	7	.07	.16	.24	.32	.41	.49	.57	.66	.74	.82	.91	.99

Explanation: The first column designated "4th" is fourths of an inch, the second column designated "8th" is eighths of an inch. The remaining columns from 0" to 11" are full inches. Example, the decimal equivalent in hundredths of fractional parts of a foot for the following inches and fractional parts of an inch are:

5" is .42'; 6" is .50'; 9" is .75'.
5¼" is .44'; 6-3/8" is .53'; 9¾" is .81'.
7" is .58'; 7-1/8" is .59'; 7-7/8" is .66'.
0-1/8" is .01'; 0½" is .04'; 0¾" is .06'.

Figure 3-4
Decimal equivalents

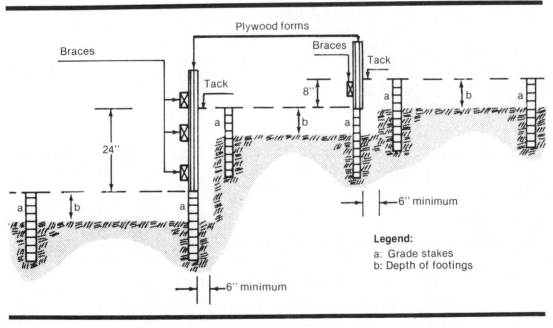

Figure 3-5
Construction of stepped footing forms

That isn't a lot of concrete — unless the truck has to make a special trip back to the job to deliver it. Then it will seem like plenty . . . and probably be the most expensive mud you'll pour all day.

Figure 3-5 shows formwork for the stepped footings. Figure 3-6 shows what the stepped footing should look like when complete. From these drawings you should be able to visualize how you'd excavate, form and pour concrete for these stepped footings.

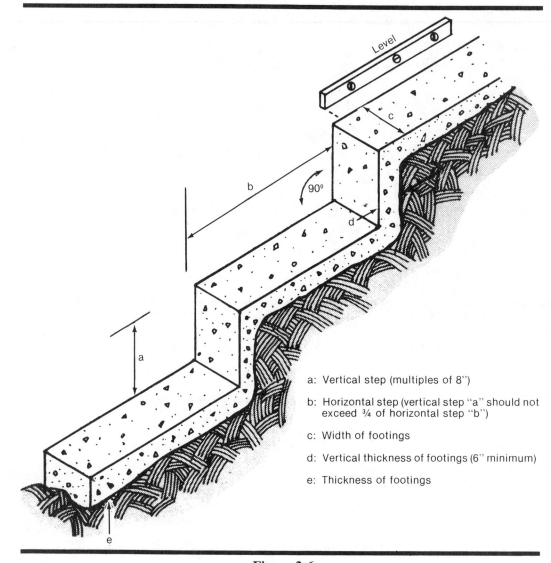

a: Vertical step (multiples of 8")

b: Horizontal step (vertical step "a" should not exceed ¾ of horizontal step "b")

c: Width of footings

d: Vertical thickness of footings (6" minimum)

e: Thickness of footings

Figure 3-6
Guidelines for stepped footings

The Main Footing

Now estimate the concrete you'll need for the main footing. The main wall footing is 24'' wide and 9'' deep. The total length of the main footings (disregarding the overlaps) as shown in Figure 3-3 is:

Left side, garage (33'0'') + basement (27'0'')	60'0''
Back	65'0''
Right side (27'0'' + 6'0'')	33'0''
Front	65'0''
Total linear feet	223'0''

So there are **223** linear feet of main footings. The calculation is:

$$223.0' \times 2.0' \times .75' \div 27 = 12.39 \text{ cu. yd.}$$

Again, look up the factor in Figure 3-1 to simplify the calculation. The factor for 24'' by 9'' is 0.05556.

$$.05556 \text{ x } 223.0' = 12.39 \text{ cu. yd.}$$

The Porch and Utility Area
The footings for the back porch and utility area are 16" x 8".

Back porch (11'10" + 17'4" + 11'10")	41'0"
Utility area	24'4"
Total linear feet	65'4"

We'll do this calculation both ways. First:

$$65.33' \text{ x } 1.33' \text{ x } .67' \div 27 = 2.16 \text{ cu. yd.}$$

Using the factor:

$$.03292 \text{ x } 65.33' = 2.15 \text{ cu. yd.}$$

Notice that the two calculations came out with slightly different answers. That's because the factor is carried out to five decimal places and the numbers in the first calculation were rounded off to two decimal places. *The multiplying factors in Figure 3-1 are more accurate.*

Column Footings
The plans show two column footings, each with dimensions of 24" x 24" x 12".

$$2.0' \text{ x } 2.0' \text{ x } 1.0' \text{ x } 2 \div 27 = .30 \text{ cu. yd.}$$

Using the multiplication factor:

$$.07407 \text{ x } 2.0' \text{ x } 2 = .30 \text{ cu. yd.}$$

Total Concrete for Footings
The total concrete required for the footings will be:

Main wall	12.39 cu. yd.
Porch and utility area	2.16 cu. yd.
Vertical rise in stepped footing	.44 cu. yd.
Column footings	.30 cu. yd.
Total	15.29 cu. yd.

Estimating Other Materials

Besides the concrete, the cost of the footings will include crushed stone, rebar and lumber. We'll take them one at a time.

Crushed Stone
When crushed stone is required for a footing, use Figure 3-1 to compute the cubic yards needed. The factors are the same as for concrete.

Let's say that you need 4" of crushed stone under a footing that's 196'0" long, 24" wide and 9" deep. Since the chart doesn't include a 4" depth, take the factor for 24" x 8" and halve it by multiplying by 0.5. The factor for 24" by 8" is 0.04938. Here's how it works:

.04938 (factor for 8" x 24") x .5 = .02469 (factor for 4" x 24")

Then multiply the new factor, (0.02469), by the total linear feet (196'0''). This gives you the cubic yards of crushed stone required:

.02469 x 196.0' = 4.84 cu. yd. crushed stone

Crushed stone is usually sold by the ton. To find the tons of crushed stone needed, multiply the cubic yards (4.84) by the tons in a cubic yard. Most crushed stone weighs about 2,700 pounds per cubic yard. So a cubic yard is 1.35 tons (2700 divided by 2000). Multiplying 4.84 cubic yards by 1.35 tons per cubic yard gives us 6.53 tons.

Rebar

Next, find the size and number of reinforcing rods to be placed in the footing. This information is probably in the wall section of the plans. Figure 3-7 shows a typical example. Your local building code may require more rebar, or soil conditions at the building may dictate it. If there's a conflict between the plans and the code, follow whichever requires more steel.

There are two ways of identifying the size of reinforcing rods. The first way is by their diameter in inches, such as 1/2''. The second is by number, such as number 4 rods. The bar numbers indicate the diameter in one-eighths of an inch (1/8''). Thus, number 4 rods are 4/8'', or 1/2'' in diameter. Number 3 rods are 3/8'' in diameter. If your dealer sells rebar by the ton, use Figure 3-8 to convert linear feet to weight.

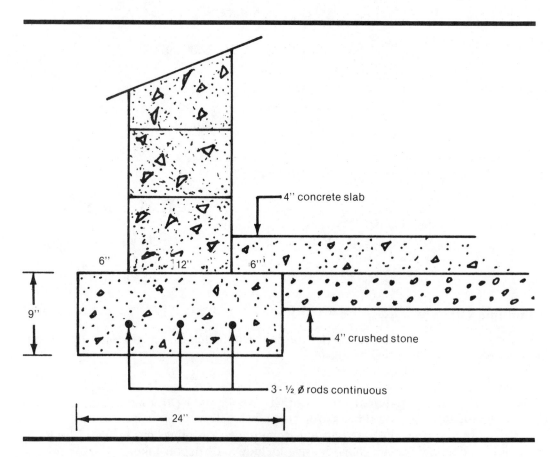

Figure 3-7
Continuous reinforcing rods in footings

Reinforcing rods

| Rod size | | Weight in |
Diameter in inches	Rod number	pounds per foot
1/4"	2	.167
3/8"	3	.376
1/2"	4	.668
5/8"	5	1.043
3/4"	6	1.502
7/8"	7	2.044
1"	8	2.670

Note: If the reinforcing rods are sold by weight, compute the total weight and cost as follows: 1) Multiply the total number of linear feet by the weight per foot. **Example:** The weight of 940 linear feet of ½" diameter rods is 627.92 pounds (940 x .668 = 627.92 lbs.) 2) Total weight (rounded off) multiplied by the rate = cost.

Figure 3-8
Table of rod numbers and weights

After computing the linear feet of reinforcing required, add 10% to allow for overlaps and waste. Each bar should overlap the rod it extends by a specific length. Usually this is expressed in bar diameters. For example, if the specifications or the code requires an overlap of 30 diameters, a 1/2" rod would overlap the rod it extends by 15 inches. Most codes require an overlap of at least 30 diameters.

Rebar usually comes in 20' lengths. To find the number of lengths required, divide the total by 20.

Here's how to compute the steel needed for the footing shown in Figure 3-3:

Perimeter of foundation

Left side [33'0" + 27'0"]	60'0"
Back	65'0"
Right side [27'0" + 6'0"]	33'0"
Front	65'0"
Utility room footing	24'4"
Back porch [11'10" + 17'4" + 11'10"]	41'0"
Column footing [2 x 24"]	4'0"
Vertical rise in steps	12'0"
Total	304'4"

According to Figure 3-7, three continuous rods run through the footings of this house. So the total linear feet of reinforcing rods will be:

3 x 304.33' (304'4")	912.99'
Grade stakes (see Figure 3-12)	58.33'
(30 stakes x 20" in length divided by 12)	
Subtotal	971.32'
Allow 5% for overlapping	+48.57'
Total	1,019.89'

1,019.89' divided by 20' = 50.99 or 51

You'll have to order 47 pieces of 1/2'' (No. 4) rods, or 940 linear feet.

Forming Lumber

Now let's figure the lumber needed for footing forms. Figures 3-9 and 3-10 show the footing forms both before and after excavation. We'll use 2 x 4 framing lumber. Note that stone fill under the concrete floor will be level with the top of the footing. See Figures 3-7 and 3-11.

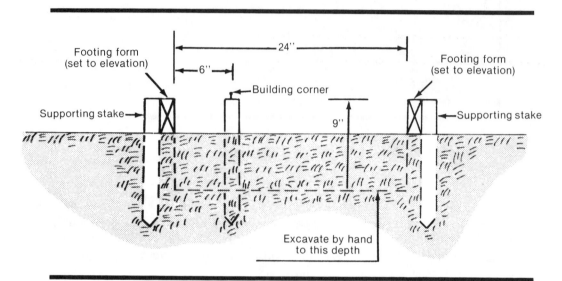

Figure 3-9
Forms for footing before excavation

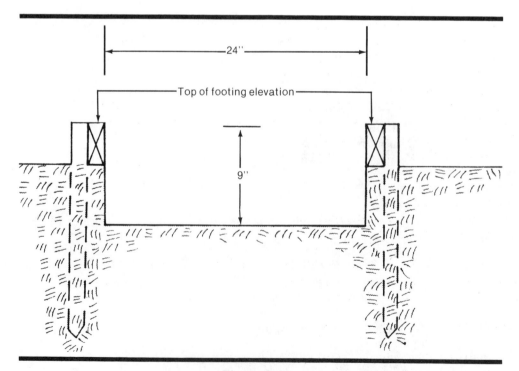

Figure 3-10
Forms for footing after excavation

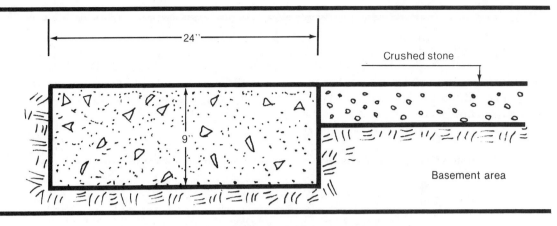

Figure 3-11
Crushed stone and footing

Calculate the perimeter of the basement footing from Figure 3-3:

Front	39'8"
Left side	27'0"
Back	39'8"
Right side	27'0"
Column footing (2 x 24" x 24")	16'0"
Total	148'16" (149'4")

149.33' (149'4") ÷ 12 = 12.44

So far you need thirteen 2 x 4's, 12' in length.

Next, estimate the lumber for supporting stakes and braces at the stepped footings around the garage and utility areas. You'll probably need longer bracing here, so plan to use 2 x 4's. That gives more stability than 1 x 4 stakes and braces. I would estimate 120 linear feet of 2 x 4. That's ten pieces 12' long, bringing our total to 23 pieces.

For the stepped footing, (Figure 3-5), figure two pieces of 1/2" x 4' x 8' C-D plywood. Include an allowance for wire to tie the rebars together and nails for the forms.

When you build forms for the footing, make sure the top of the forms are set at the calculated footing elevation. When there are no forms, as in Figure 3-12, drive a grade stake into the ground occasionally to show the correct finished height. The top of these grade stakes should be set to the footing elevation. A 20" length of rebar makes a good grade stake.

Note that I haven't assumed any salvage of form material. If you're careful, most of the forming lumber and some of the stakes and braces can be salvaged and used again, either on the same job if pouring will go on for several days, or on your next job. In some cases form material can be reused as bracing or backing on the same job. But if you plan to reuse form material, add extra time for disassembling and cleaning the forms.

Estimating Labor Costs

Estimating form material accurately is fairly easy. But estimating labor for forms requires more judgment. Here's why. No two jobs are really identical, even when done by the same crew and from a similar plan. Too many subtle factors influence

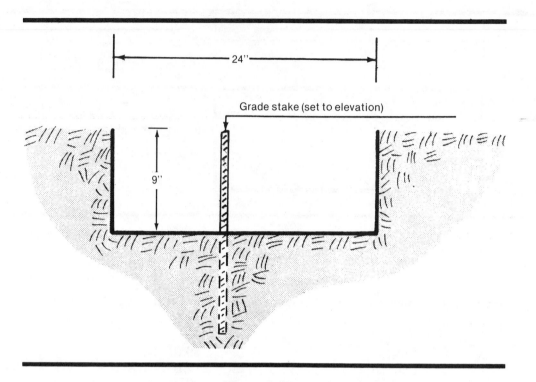

Figure 3-12
Grade stakes when forms are not used

productivity: the weather, the quality of supervision, what the building code, specifications and designer require, conflicts with other trades, the tools and equipment available, the skill of the craftsmen, how many hours of sleep your tradesmen got the night before, the incentive to complete the job, and much more. There's no single production rate that covers all jobs.

But you'll find that most jobs of about the same size and about the same complexity require about the same labor, give or take 10% or so. But some jobs will take much more time and others will take less. Only experience with your own jobs and crews can provide the judgment needed to spot a particularly difficult or a much easier job.

I include many manhour estimates in this book. Please don't assume that they're the only correct manhour estimates for carpentry. They're not. They're based on jobs I've estimated and completed. To the extent that your jobs, crews, supervision, specifications, building code, materials and equipment are like mine, the estimates will be useful. Where they aren't, the figures may be wrong.

Use my figures until you have more reliable data from your own jobs. And that brings me to the next important topic. How do you collect manhour data?

The Weekly Time Sheet
Make it a habit to collect manhour estimates from every job. I've found that the best way to do this is with a daily log and weekly payroll sheet. It takes only a few minutes a day to compile this information, and it can add thousands of dollars a year to your income. I've kept data like this for years and recommend it to any contractor who's serious about improving estimating accuracy.

Figure 3-13 shows a time sheet for labor used in laying out and setting the forms for footings. There's a blank form like Figure 3-13 in the back of this book. Use the information you gather from the time sheets to estimate future labor costs on similar jobs. Make notes on the completed time sheet describing any abnormal conditions.

Page _/_ of _/_ pages
Weekly Time Sheet

For period ending 8-21-XX

BROWN job

#	Name	Exemptions	Days AUGUST						Rate	Hours worked		Total earnings
			16 M	17 T	18 W	19 T	20 F	21 S		Reg.	Over-time	
1	D. White		X	X	3	8	8	X		19		
2	R. Kidd		X	X	3	8	8	X		19		
3	R. Farlow		X	X	3	8	8	X		19		
4												
5												
6												
7												
8												
9												
10												
11												
12												
13												
14												
15												
16												
17												
18												
19												
20												

Daily Log

Monday _____

Tuesday _____

Wednesday LAID OUT FOOTING _____

Thursday FORMS FOR FOOTING IN BASEMENT AREA. _____

Friday FORMS FOR FOOTING IN BASEMENT AREA. _____

Saturday _____

Figure 3-13
Weekly time sheet

Weekly Time Sheet

Page _1_ of _1_ pages

For period ending _8-28-XX_   _BROWN_ job

	Name	Exemptions	Days AUGUST						Rate	Hours worked		Total earnings
			23 M	24 T	25 W	26 T	27 F	28 S		Reg.	Over-time	
1	D. White		8	8	6	6½	2½	X		31		
2	R. Kidd		8	8	6	6½	2½	X		31		
3	R. Farlow		8	8	6	6½	X	X		28½		
4	H. Neel		X	X	X	6½	X	X		6½		
5												
6												
7												
8												
9												
10												
11												
12												
13												
14												
15												
16												
17												
18												
19												
20												

Daily Log

Monday _FORMS FOR STEPPED FOOTING IN GARAGE AREA._
Tuesday _FORMS FOR STEPPED FOOTING IN GARAGE AREA._
Wednesday _FINISHED STEPPED FOOTING -- READY FOR CONCRETE._
Thursday _POURED CONCRETE FOR FOOTING (14 CU. YDS.)_
Friday _STRIPPED FORMS FROM FOOTINGS._
Saturday _____

Figure 3-14
Weekly time sheet

A weekly time sheet from my file reminds me of a stepped footing job I had several years ago. I still remember it well. Usually a backhoe will excavate 75 to 100 cubic yards a day under normal conditions. I had a backhoe with a 24″ bucket take 5½ hours to excavate 6.4 cubic yards for the footing. Add an hour for travel time to and from the building site. On that job it took 6½ hours to excavate 6.4 cubic yards. That's less than one cubic yard per hour! Hand labor could have done it cheaper. Save information like that on your jobs to prevent expensive mistakes the next time a similar job comes along.

To compute the labor costs to form, hand excavate, pour concrete and strip the forms from the footings shown in Figure 3-3, follow these steps:

1)   Refer to the time sheets for a similar house you've built recently. We'll use Figures 3-13 and 3-14.

2)   The daily log at the bottom of these time sheets shows that work started on the forms on Thursday, August 19th and was completed on Wednesday, August 25th. The concrete was poured on Thursday the 26th. An extra man was used this day to help with the pour because some concrete had to be placed with wheelbarrows. On Friday the 27th, two men stripped the footing forms. It took 145 manhours to form, hand excavate, pour concrete and strip the forms for 14 cubic yards, including the stepped footing.

Worksheet for Manhour Factors

Figure 3-15 is a footing labor worksheet. Use it to help you compute the manhour factors to excavate, pour concrete and strip forms.

Take the total manhours from the weekly time sheets. For example, 145 manhours were needed for footings on the Brown job. Record this number on your worksheet. Then record the total cubic yards of concrete used on the job. For the Brown job it was 14 cubic yards. The total manhours (145) divided by cubic yards of concrete (14) gives you the manhours required per cubic yard of concrete (10.36). I'll call this the *manhour factor*.

To estimate manhours for footings on similar jobs in the future, multiply the manhour factor by the cubic yards of concrete. For example, assume your manhour factor is 10.36 and the estimated cubic yardage is 18. The total manhours required to do the footing work will be 186.48. Round this to 187 manhours.

To estimate labor costs for footings on future bids, multiply the total manhours (187) by the current hourly cost for labor (including taxes and insurance) to find the total labor cost for footing work. If the labor cost is $25.00 per hour, the labor cost for 187 manhours would be $4,675.00.

Cost Estimate Worksheet for Footings

Figure 3-16 is a completed cost estimate worksheet for footings. I've filled it out to show the estimate for the footings in this chapter. You'll find a blank form at the end of the book. Use it as a checklist for footing estimates. It brings together all the data needed to complete your estimate for footings.

Keeping good costs records will save you time and money. This means extra profit in your pocket.

Estimating Foundations

Now let's make a quick, accurate estimate for the concrete block foundation on this job. We'll use actual cost records and multiplying factor tables to calculate materials and labor quickly and easily.

When estimating foundations, you're not likely to forget the principal foundation materials such as crushed stone, concrete block, masonry cement, sand, parging materials and drain tile. But some other materials are easy to overlook. Let's examine each of these materials to see how they contribute to foundation costs.

Manhour factors for footings

Date: _____   _____Job

Formula

Total manhours divided by cubic yards concrete = manhour factor

Total manhours = _____

Cubic yards concrete = _____

Total manhours _____ divided by cubic yards concrete _____ = Manhour factor _____

Weather conditions: Good - Fair - Poor

Rock removal required: Yes - No

Wheelbarrows required: Yes - No

Formula to estimate manhours for future bids

Manhour factor multiplied by estimated cubic yards concrete = Total manhours

Manhour factor _____ x estimated cubic yards concrete _____ = Total manhours _____

Formula to estimate labor costs

Total manhours multiplied by rate per hour = Estimated cost

Total manhours _____ x Rate per hour $_____ = Estimated labor cost $_____

Figure 3-15
Manhour factors for footings

Crushed Stone
Crushed stone is usually sold by weight and priced by the ton. Occasionally it's sold by volume and priced by the cubic yard. Let's figure the quantity needed for a basement area 65'6'' by 32'6'' if 4'' of crushed stone go under the concrete slab. How many cubic yards of crushed stone will you need? How many tons of crushed stone should you order?

The mathematical formula for computing cubic yard requirements is:

Multiply the length in feet by the width in feet by the depth (thickness) in feet, then divide by 27.

Once again, you'll have to convert feet and inches into decimal feet before using the formula. Here's an example:

$$65.5' \text{ x } 32.5' \text{ x } .3333' \div 27 = 26.3 \text{ cu. yd.}$$

Cost Estimate Worksheet for Footings

Layout   ALLOW $ _100.00_

Concrete Quantity
   Regular footings:
      Size: _24"_ width x _9"_ depth x _196_ lin. ft. = _294_ cu. ft.
      Size: _16"_ width x _8"_ depth x _65'4"_ lin. ft. = _58.22_ cu. ft.
   Column footings: (*number* _2_)
      Size: _24"_ w x _12"_ d x _2_ lf x _2_ no. = _8_ cu. ft.
   Chimney footings: (*number* _NONE_)
      Size: _____ w x _____ d x _____ lf x _____ no. = _____ cu. ft.
   Vertical rise for stepped footings:
      Size: _24"_ w x _6"_ thickness x _12'_ height = _12_ cu. ft.
                        (6' FRONT +6' BACK)
   Other (specify):
      _____ _____ cu. ft.

   Total cubic feet _372.22_ divided by 27 = _13.79_ cubic yards
   Cost per cubic yard $ _45.75_ x _14_ cubic yards = $ _640.50_
   Total cost of concrete (test: _2500_ psi)

Other Material
   Reinforcing rods:
      Linear feet of _#4_ (size) reinforcing rod _940 LIN. FT._
      Cost per foot $ _25.60 ¢/LIN. FT.)_
      Total cost of reinforcing rods $ _240.64_

   Plywood forms:
      Quantity and size _2 PCS. - 1/2" x 4' x 8'_
      Total cost of forms $ _21.90_

   Framing lumber:
      Quantity and size _25 PCS. - 2" x 4" x 12'_
      Total cost of lumber $ _62.00_

   Cost of other material:
      ALLOW FOR TIE WIRE AND NAILS $ _10.00_
   Subtotal material cost: $ _975.04_
   Plus sales tax (% _4_): $ _39.00_
   Total material cost: $ _1,014.04_

Labor Cost
   Estimated cost of excavation: $ _180.00_ (MACHINE)
   Estimated cost to form and pour: (_145 MANHOURS x $25.00_) $ _3,625.00_
   Total labor cost: $ _3,805.00_

Total Cost of Footings: $ _4,919.04_

Figure 3-16
Cost estimate worksheet for footings

The formula for converting cubic yards to tons (assuming one cubic yard weighs 2,700 pounds) is:

Multiply the number of cubic yards times 2,700, then divide by 2,000.

26.3 cu. yd. x 2,700 lbs. ÷ 2,000 = 35.5 tons

For the 26.3 cubic yards, you need 35.5 tons of crushed stone.

Using a multiplying factor— Now let's do it the easy way. We'll do the same computation using a multiplying factor. Figure 3-17 is a worksheet for figuring crushed stone. It includes all the factors you need. Look down the first column until you see the correct thickness (4''). The next column to the right shows the factor (0.01235) you need. Multiply this factor by the area of the basement. (In our example, 65.5' times 32.5' equals 2,128.75 square feet.) This is the cubic yardage required.

.01235 x 2,128.75 sq. ft. = 26.3 cu. yd.

Thickness	Factor	Foundation area (square feet)		Cubic yards
3''	.00926	x	=	
3½''	.01080	x	=	
4''	.01235	x *2,128.75*	=	*26.3*
4½''	.01389	x *928*	=	*12.89*
5''	.01543	x	=	
5½''	.01698	x	=	
6''	.01852	x	=	

Cubic yards crushed stone multiplied by 1.35 = tons

Cubic yards crushed stone *26.3* x 1.35 = *35.5* tons crushed stone
(ORDER 36 TONS)

Figure 3-17
Worksheet and factors for crushed stone

You can also use a factor (1.35) to convert cubic yards to tons. The new formula is:

Cubic yards multiplied by 1.35 equals tons of crushed stone required.

26.3 cu. yd. x 1.35 = 35.5 tons

Both methods of calculation yield the same answer — 35.5 tons of crushed stone. We entered the calculation in Figure 3-17 to show you how to use the worksheet. Look in the back of this book for a blank copy of this worksheet. Run off a few copies for your use.

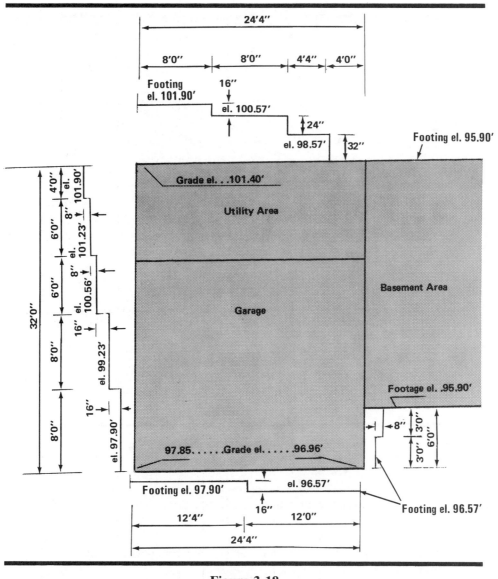

Figure 3-18
Layout of stepped footing

You can see how factor tables can make your estimates easier, quicker and more accurate. Any time you can reduce the number of computations, you reduce the chance of error.

Concrete Block
In many parts of the country, foundation walls are made from concrete block. Block is less expensive than forming and pouring solid concrete walls. But be cautious when estimating concrete block for a foundations. Remember the following points:

1) In crawl spaces, the undisturbed ground level should be at least 18 inches below the bottom of the floor joists, and 12 inches below the bottom of girders. When you have to provide access for maintenance and repair of mechanical equipment located in the underfloor space, the ground level should be not less than 24 inches below the floor joists.

2) On all foundation walls of hollow masonry, cap the blocks with 4 inches of solid masonry or concrete.

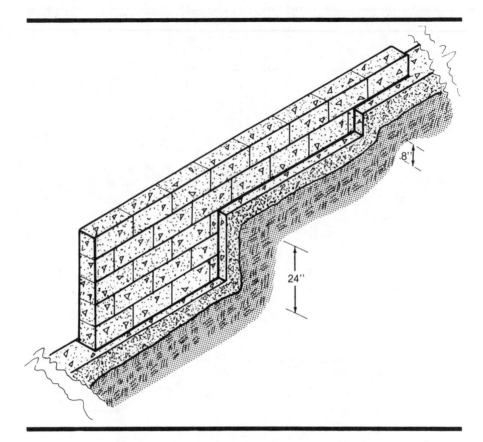

Figure 3-19
Blocks on stepped footing

3)   The top of the foundation wall must extend at least 6'' above the finished grade level.

4)   Block can be 6'' wide for single story homes. But two story homes require 8'' wide block, and three story homes require 10'' wide block.

Study the foundation plan, specifications and the plot plan showing the grade elevations before estimating masonry block for a foundation. The foundation plan shows the dimensions of the foundation and the basement, crawl space or both. It will show the height of the foundation walls, the size and location of the windows and doors, and the number and size of the piers and pilasters.

Use the plot plan showing grade elevations to calculate the stepped footings, if any are included in the job. Figure 3-18 shows a typical layout for stepped footings.

Estimating the quantity of masonry blocks is easy when the footing is horizontal around its entire perimeter. But stepped footings take a little more time. Figure 3-19 shows blocks laid on a stepped footing.

For a detailed explanation of how to estimate the masonry blocks for stepped footings, see another handbook by this author, *Estimating Home Building Costs.* You'll find an order form in the back of this book.

Masonry block sizing— The actual size of masonry blocks is less than the nominal size. The block plus one mortar joint (usually 3/8'') will equal the nominal size. Figure 3-20 shows the actual size and nominal size of the most common concrete block.

•   One regular or corner block plus one 3/8'' mortar joint totals 16'' in length.

Nominal size	Actual size
4" x 8" x 16"	$3\frac{5}{8}$" x $7\frac{5}{8}$" x $15\frac{5}{8}$"
8" x 8" x 16"	$7\frac{5}{8}$" x $7\frac{5}{8}$" x $15\frac{5}{8}$"
12" x 8" x 16"	$11\frac{5}{8}$" x $7\frac{5}{8}$" x $15\frac{5}{8}$"

The actual size of a 8" x 8" x 16" masonry block:

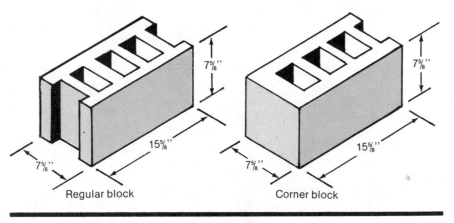

Figure 3-20
Nominal and actual sizes of concrete block

- One regular or corner block plus one 3/8" mortar joint totals 8" in height.

There's an easy formula for calculating the number of 16" blocks required per course:

Multiply the length of the wall in decimal feet by 0.75 (75%).

For example:
A wall 4'0" long will require three blocks per course.

$$4.0' \times .75 = 3 \text{ blocks}$$

A wall 39'8" in length will require 29.75 blocks per course.

$$39.67' \times .75 = 29.75 \text{ blocks}$$

To find the total number of each size of block needed for the foundation, multiply the total length of the foundation by 0.75 and by the number of courses of each size.

The basement area of a house foundation is 39'8" x 26'0". The plans show 12 courses of regular block plus one course of 4" x 8" x 16" solid blocks. There will be eight courses of 12" x 8" x 16" blocks, four courses of 8" x 8" x 16" blocks and one course of 4" x 8" x 16" solid blocks. The perimeter of the basement wall is 131'4".

$$39'8" + 26'0" \times 2 = 131'4"$$

Using the factor— You can use a factor to calculate the number of blocks required for the foundation wall in the basement. Figure 3-21 is a worksheet and factor table for 12" x 8" x 16", 8" x 8" x 16" and 4" x 8" x 16" blocks. Using these factors to compute

Factor	Foundation length (linear feet)		Number of courses	Number of blocks
.75	x	*131.33' (131'4")* x	*8*	= *787.98 (or 788)*

Computing number of blocks (12" x 8" x 16")

Factor	Foundation length (linear feet)		Number of courses	Number of blocks
.75	x	*131.33' (131'4")* x	*4*	= *393.99 (or 394)*

Computing number of blocks (8" x 8" x 16")

Factor	Foundation length (linear feet)		Number of courses	Number of blocks
.75	x	*131.33' (131'4")* x	*1*	= *98.5 (or 99)*

Computing number of blocks (4" x 8" x 16")

Factor	Foundation area (square feet)	Number of blocks
1.125	x *700.43*	= *787.98 (or 788)*

Computing number of blocks by square foot method
(blocks 8" in height x 16" in length)

Figure 3-21
Worksheet and factors for concrete block

the quantities on the worksheet, we find we need a total of 1,281 blocks.
    Note: *No allowance is made for the overlapping at the corners. The extra blocks will help compensate for the waste.*

There's another way to estimate blocks — the square foot method. You'll need 112.5 blocks (8" in height x 16" in length) per 100 square feet of wall space. Here's an example:
    Assume you're building a wall 25'0" long and 4'0" high. That's 100 square feet. Using the original formula, you calculate that you need 112.5 blocks:

$$25'0'' \text{ x } .75 \text{ x } 6 \text{ courses} = 112.5 \text{ blocks}$$

Divide the number of blocks needed by 100 to find the multiplying factor:

$$112.5 \div 100 = 1.125$$

So 1.125 blocks per square foot is the multiplying factor for blocks 8" high and 16" long.
    You'll find this factor in Figure 3-21. But remember, this square foot method only works for blocks 8" high and 16" long. Don't use the 1.125 factor to compute the quantity of 4" x 8" x 16" blocks.
    Use the factor to compute the number of 8"-high blocks you need:

12" x 8" x 16" blocks:

131.33' x 5.33' (8 courses) = 700 sq. ft.

700 sq. ft. x 1.125 = 787.5 blocks

8" x 8" x 16" blocks:

131.33' x 2.67' (4 courses) = 350.65 sq. ft.

350.65 sq. ft. x 1.125 = 394.48 blocks

Compare these answers with your answers from the worksheet (Figure 3-21). Either method gives you a fast, accurate estimate for foundation concrete blocks. Use the method that seems easier for you, but always compute 4" x 8" x 16", 8" x 8' x 16" and 12" x 8" x 16" blocks separately.

Also remember that some blocks will be broken during construction. Breakage varies from job to job and from one mason to another. Note the breakage and waste on each of your jobs. Then compute the average loss for each type of job. Add this to your quantity when estimating and ordering. My allowance is usually between 4% to 8% on most jobs and for most crews.

Masonry Cement and Sand
There's always a lot of waste in mortar. It can be as high as 25%. Cost records from previous jobs will give you an idea of how much waste to assume. Waste isn't the only variable. The quantity of mortar used also depends on mix consistency and the thickness of the mortar joints. The 3/8" joint is the most common, but it's not always used.

More mortar may be needed for some sizes and types of block. But the difference is so minor that it can probably be ignored on most jobs. The quantity of mortar and sand needed to lay 100 or 1,000 blocks will be about the same on 12" x 8" x 16" blocks as 8" x 8" x 16" and 4" x 8" x 16" combined.

Most estimating tables for mortar are calculated in cubic feet. For example, the table might tell you that you'll need 60 cubic feet of mortar to lay 1,000 masonry blocks. But you order cement by the bag and sand by the ton. How much cement and sand do you need to yield 60 cubic feet of mortar?

Figure 3-22 will help you compute the bags of cement and tons of sand required for the job. The factors will work for nearly all block sizes, since they include an allowance for some waste and for variation in the size of mortar joints.

Look at section A in Figure 3-22. The first factor (0.024) allows for limited waste. If you want a waste allowance of 25%, use the 0.03 factor.

For the job in Figure 3-21, we'll need to lay 1,281 concrete blocks. To find how many bags of cement to order, multiply the cement factor (we'll use 0.024) by the number of blocks (1,281). Order 31 bags of cement.

To find how many tons of sand you'll need, multiply the factor in Figure 3-22 B (0.003) by the number of blocks (1,281). Order four tons of sand.

Remember, it's cheaper to order sand by the truckload than in small quantities. If there will be brick chimney or other masonry work later, buy the sand by the truckload to save money.

Concrete Foundations
For foundation walls built of concrete, here's how to estimate the cost of forms. Suppose forms will use 4' x 8' plywood panels. Multiply the form area in square feet by the factor 0.03125 to get the number of pieces required. For 4' x 12' plywood panels, multiply the area in square feet by the factor 0.02083 to get the number of pieces required.

Factor	Number of blocks	Bags of masonry cement
.024	x *1,281*	= *30.74 (or 31)*
.03 (25% waste)	x	=

A Bags of masonry cement

Factor	Number of blocks	Tons of sand
.003	x *1,281*	= *3.84 (or 4)*

B Tons of sand

Figure 3-22
Worksheet and factors for masonry cement and sand

If you're using 1'' lumber instead of plywood, the calculation is a little different. Suppose we'll use 1 x 6 boards, surfaced on one side (S1S), braces, walers, stakes and tie wire. Look at Figure 3-23. If the foundation wall will be exposed, lay the boards with the smooth side in. That leaves the concrete with a smoother appearance. When the concrete wall is to be covered, place the forms with the rough side of the boards in. That way you can reuse the lumber for sheathing or subfloor. But clean off the loose concrete before nailing it in place.

Place the boards horizontally and hold them in place with stakes. The stakes can be any size as long as they're strong enough to hold the form in place until the concrete has set. I usually use 1-inch material. For a basement wall, use vertically-placed form studs instead of stakes. You can build a complete unit, then place it in position.

To strengthen the form, use braces and walers. A waler is a piece of lumber, usually 2 x 4, placed horizontally against the outside face of the stakes to hold the form true and straight. For an ordinary foundation, you only need one waler for each side of the concrete form. Use tie wires to keep the form from spreading while the concrete is being placed.

While not a part of the form itself, the bolts that are used to hold down the sill are usually figured at the same time as the form material.

We'll take the parts of the form one at a time:

Form boards— The height of the form is figured on the basis of 6-inch boards. For a 10-inch height, figure two boards; 16 inches, three boards; 24 inches, four boards, and so on.

Here's the rule:

To find the board feet of lumber for one wall of a form, multiply the height of the form, in 6-inch boards, by the length of the form. Add 1/5 for waste. Double it to find the amount of lumber needed for both forms.

For a house, the length of the form is the perimeter of the building. When figuring the perimeter, increase fractional parts of a foot to the next half or whole foot. For example, if a wall is 54'8'' long, figure it as 55'0''. And round up your answer to the next whole even number, since lumber is always cut to even foot lengths.

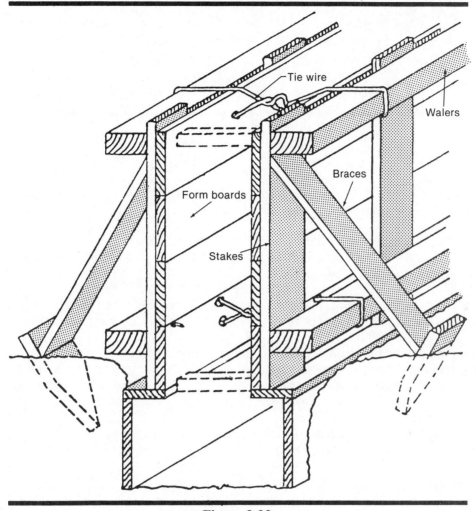

Figure 3-23
Section through concrete form

Stakes— There's no set rule on how many stakes you'll need. Common practice in some areas is to place them 2 feet on center. The length of the stake is the same as the height of the form plus a sufficient amount for the point. Here's the rule:

To find the number of stakes, divide the perimeter by the spacing of the stakes and add one. Then double the answer.

Form studs— The space between form studs depends on the height of the form. The form boards or plywood panels are nailed to the vertical studs. The size of the lumber also depends on the height of the form.

To find the number of studs, divide the perimeter by the spacing of the studs and add one. Double your answer for the other form.

This will give the number of uprights required. Each stud will be as long as the form is high. Multiply the number of studs by the length of each, then order that many linear feet of stock. Order lengths which will cut with the least waste.

Walers— A waler is a piece of 2 x 4 or 2 x 6 framing stock placed horizontally on the outside of a form against the form studs. The walers hold the studs true to a straight line, and give rigidity.

Size of wire	Weight per linear foot	Feet per pound
No. 11	.0387	25.82
No. 12	.0296	33.69
No. 13	.0223	44.98

Figure 3-24
Wire sizes and weights

Find the perimeter of the building and then double it, as each form will require a waler. Multiply the result by the number of walers.

Braces— You probably won't have to order material for braces, as there are usually enough odds and ends of lumber for this purpose. If not, you can cut 1 x 6 form boards to short lengths and split them to 1 x 3.

Tie wire— Tie wire is used to keep the forms from spreading when the concrete is poured. See Figure 3-23. It comes in flat rolls and is bought by the pound. For an average job, figure one roll.

Spacing of tie wires depends on the height of the forms and the thickness of the wall. About 4 feet apart horizontally and 2 feet apart vertically is standard. The length of each piece of wire will be twice the thickness of the wall, plus enough wire to go around each stake and waler. For an 8-inch wall, each piece should be at least 60 inches long.

Multiply the number of pieces of wire required by the length of each. Then multiply by the weight per foot of the size wire specified.

To change linear feet of wire to pounds, use Figure 3-24.

Wedge form ties— Wedge form ties are used for building concrete foundations out of 1 x 6 S1S form boards. These ties replace tie wires and usually save time because they tap into place very quickly. See Figure 3-25. The length of the ties depends on the thickness of the concrete wall.

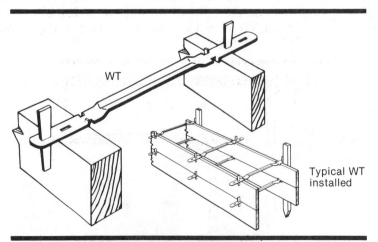

WT

Typical WT installed

Courtesy: Simpson Strong-Tie Co., Inc., San Leandro, CA

Figure 3-25
Wedge form tie

These ties are embedded in the concrete and are not recoverable. Order new ties for every new foundation job. After the forms are removed, break off the protruding ends of the ties with the twist of a pair of pliers or the claw of your hammer.

The height of the wall determines how many ties will be needed. Vertical spacing is usually every 12 inches. The illustration shows them placed on the top edge of each row of form boards. Horizontally, they're spaced 2 feet on center.

Divide the perimeter of the building by 2 to find the number of ties required horizontally. The height of the wall divided by the spacing of the ties, minus one, equals the number of ties required vertically. The number of horizontal ties times the number of vertical ties gives you the total ties to order.

Bolts— These bolts are used to tie the house to the foundation. See Figure 3-31. Your building code probably requires 1/2" diameter foundation bolts that go 10 inches into concrete or 15 inches into a masonry foundation. A nut and washer is needed above the plate on each washer. Maximum spacing is commonly 6 feet on center, but some codes allow 8' spacing. There must be at least two bolts in each bottom plate and neither may be more than 12" from the end of the piece. Plan placement of foundation bolts carefully to save time and trouble once framing gets started.

To estimate the number of anchor bolts for a foundation wall:

1) Divide the perimeter of the foundation wall by 8 (if you're using 8'0" spacing) or by 6 (for 6'0" spacing).

2) Add one bolt for each exterior and interior corner in the masonry wall.

3) Total the answers for the total number of anchor bolts required.

Here's an example:

The perimeter of a house foundation wall is 192'0". You'll use 8'0" spacing for the anchor bolts. Dividing 192.0' by 8 gives you 24 anchor bolts.

There are six exterior and interior corners. Adding 6 to 24 gives you a total of 30 anchor bolts needed for this foundation.

Nails— A 6d box nail is best for formwork. An average foundation will take 12 to 15 pounds of these box nails. Also order a few pounds of 8d box nails.

The point to remember in nailing is that the form must be straight, plumb and very rigid. If the nails are too long, more form material will be destroyed when the form is disassembled. Also, long nails will crack or chip the concrete. Avoid driving the nails too tight so they pull out more easily. And here's another tip for easy form removal. Let one board extend several inches beyond the corner, then nail a vertical cleat to the extension. This makes a corner that will hold tight but comes off easily. See Figure 3-26.

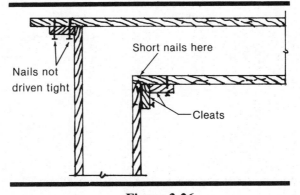

Figure 3-26
Typical form corner construction

Weekly Time Sheet

For period ending 3-12-XX   BROWN job

	Name	Exemptions	Days MARCH						Rate	Hours worked		Total earnings
			7 M	8 T	9 W	10 T	11 F	12 S		Reg.	Over-time	
1	D.L. White		8	8	6½	8	8	X		38½		
2	A.L. King		X	8	8	8	8	X		32		
3	T.E. King		X	X	8	8	8	X		24		
4	Holston Drywall, Inc.		X	X	X	✓	X	X		—		
5												
6												
7												
8												
9												
10												
11												
12												
13												
14												
15												
16												
17												
18												
19												
20												

Daily Log

Monday Started waterproofing foundation (8 manhours for parging)

Tuesday Finished 902 S.F. parging (8 manhours). Started bituminous coating (8 manhours)

Wednesday Finished 902 S.F. bituminous coating (6½ manhours). Drain tile around basement area (16 manhours)

Thursday Drywall. Outside trim.   106'

Friday Outside trim.

Saturday XXXX

Figure 3-27
Weekly time sheet

Spreaders— Spreaders are needed to keep concrete forms properly spaced. Use 1 x 1 pieces of wood cut to a length equal to the wall thickness. Spreaders are removed as the concrete is poured. Of course, spreaders aren't needed if ties are used. Metal ties act as both ties and spreaders. When these are used, the inside form doesn't have to be braced so securely. The metal tie holds the inside form in place the correct distance from the outside form.

Form oil— Specifications sometimes call for concrete forms to be oiled before the concrete is placed. This makes removal easier and leaves a more uniform surface. One gallon of oil will cover about 600 square feet of surface.

Multiply the total linear feet of wall by the height to find the square feet of area in one form. Double this for both forms. Divide by 600 to find the gallons of oil required.

Waterproofing

Parging

Foundation walls that enclose basements have to be waterproofed to prevent passage of moisture into the basement. One way to do this is to parge the foundation wall with 1/2 inch of masonry mortar. Then apply a bituminous coating. But even if the wall is parged, it's essential that moisture that collects at the base of the wall be channeled away from the building. Nearly all basements will show footing drain tile installed around the foundation. This keeps any standing water from penetrating the foundation wall.

Waterproofing can be done any time after foundation blocks have been laid and before backfilling around the foundation begins. Let's look at each of the materials you'll use for waterproofing.

Figure 3-27 is a weekly time sheet and daily log for the Brown job. The daily log shows that 1/2-inch parging is required for 902 square feet of foundation wall.

Cement

Figure 3-28 is a worksheet and factor table for parging. Multiply the factor (0.01848) by the square feet of foundation area to be parged (902). This gives us 16.67 bags of masonry cement. Add a 5% waste allowance for a total of 17.5, or 18 bags.

Sand

Use Figure 3-28, section B, to compute the sand required for parging. Multiply the factor (0.00231) by the square feet of the foundation area to be parged (902). This comes to 2.084 tons. Add a waste allowance of 5%. The total is 2.188 tons of sand. Include this quantity of sand in your order for any other sand you'll need for the job.

Bituminous Coating

Usually one gallon of bituminous coating will cover 100 square feet of wall. It's normally sold in five-gallon cans, so you'll need two five-gallon cans of bituminous coating for 902 square feet of foundation area.

Drain Tile

Drain tile relieves the hydrostatic pressure against the foundation wall and basement floor. Your code probably requires that tile discharge by gravity or by pump to an outfall, such as a drainage ditch or into a sump pit from which it can be pumped into a storm system. Drainage pipe can be either 4'' farm tile (12'' long), 4'' perforated bituminous fiber or 4'' perforated plastic (sold in 10' lengths). Place a minimum of 2 inches of crushed stone under the pipe and a minimum of 6 inches of crushed stone to cover it. Figure 3-29 shows typical foundation waterproofing.

Factor	Foundation area (square feet)	Bags of masonry cement
.01848	x *902*	= *16.67*

Bags of masonry cement		*16.67*
Add for waste (*5* %)		*.83*
Total		*17.50 or 18*

A Bags of masonry cement

Factor	Foundation area (square feet)	Tons of sand
.00231	x *902*	= *2.084*

Tons of sand		*2.084*
Add for waste (*5* %)		*.104*
Total		*2.188*

B Tons of sand

Figure 3-28
Worksheet and factors for parging cement and sand

Figure 3-30 is a worksheet for computing the cubic yards and tons of crushed stone required for foundation drain tile 18 inches wide and 12 inches deep. Assume that 4'' drain tile is surrounded with crushed stone. Multiply the factor (0.05232) by the linear feet of foundation drain tile. This gives you the cubic yards of stone (allowance is made for the 4'' drain tile). Multiply the number of cubic yards by 1.35 to get the tons of crushed stone required.

The calculation shown in Figure 3-30 is for the drain tile on the Brown job. Multiply the factor (0.05232) by the linear feet (106). This gives you 5.55 cubic yards of crushed stone. Then multiply 5.55 by 1.35. That's 7.49 tons of crushed stone. Order 8 tons.

Other Foundation Materials

Depending on the plan, you may have windows, doors, or other materials in the foundation you're estimating. Let's take them one at a time.

Basement Windows

Natural light and ventilation are essential in all basements. Most basement windows are metal and have a flange that fits into sash blocks the mason installs around the window opening. This lets the mason install a temporary window before placing the lintel above the window opening. When the interior walls of the basement are finished, you'll probably install the permanent window.

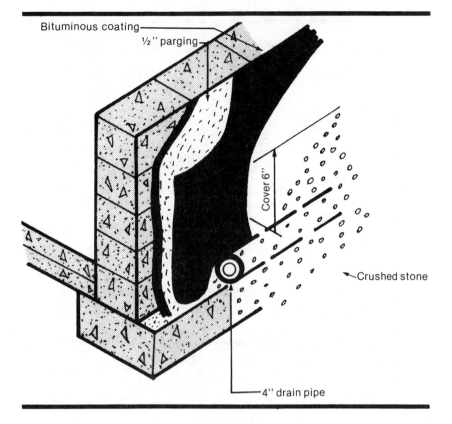

Figure 3-29
Foundation waterproofing

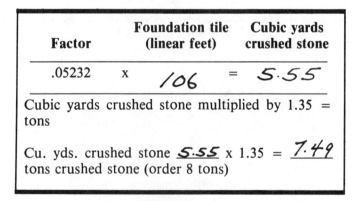

Factor	Foundation tile (linear feet)	Cubic yards crushed stone
.05232 x	*106* =	*5.55*

Cubic yards crushed stone multiplied by 1.35 = tons

Cu. yds. crushed stone *5.55* x 1.35 = *7.49* tons crushed stone (order 8 tons)

Figure 3-30
Worksheet and factors for drain tile

Foundation Vents

In basementless spaces (crawl spaces), provide at least four foundation wall ventilators, one located close to each corner of the space. Some codes require a net free vent area not less than 1/150 of the area of the crawl space. Other codes require 1½ square feet of vent for each 25 linear feet of foundation wall.

Here's an example based on crawl space area. A crawl space 30'0" x 40'0" has 1,200 square feet of space. Divide 1,200 by 150 to find that you need 8 square feet of ventilation for this area. If you're using 8" x 16" vents, you'll need nine of them. (Each vent is 0.89 square feet. Divide 8 by 0.89. That's 8.99, or 9 vents needed.)

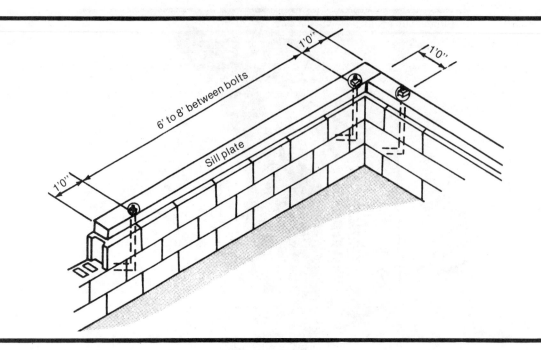

Figure 3-31
Spacing anchor bolts

Basement Doors
If there's a basement in the plan, it will probably include an outside entrance to and from the basement. The basement door should be a minimum of 2'8'' (32 inches) wide to accommodate most materials and supplies that will be moved to and from the basement. Crawl space homes require an opening at least 18'' x 24''. If mechanical equipment is installed in the crawl space, install an access opening large enough to permit removal and replacement of the equipment.

Lintels
The lintels for masonry blocks come in precast reinforced and flat steel forms. The type of lintel used depends on the load it will carry and the span of the opening it will cover. The plans and specifications should specify the type of lintel to use.

Beams
Beams or girders will be required on long spans or if unusually heavy loads are expected. Beams may be laminated, box beams, built-up beams, or steel. In residential construction, the only beams that are normally required in the foundation are the beams that support the floor system, and occasionally the opening for a garage door that leads to a basement area.

Column Posts
Look on the foundation plan for the number and size of column posts.

Miscellaneous Materials
Don't overlook any of these miscellaneous materials when estimating foundations.

Wall ties— If brick is to be used (in a chimney, for example) and if the brick starts below grade, wall ties will be needed in the foundation wall.

Polyethylene— Use this film to cover the ground surface above a crawl space. Cover masonry cement and other materials with polyethylene while you're storing them.

***Bucks for basement windows and doors*—** 2" x 4" or 2" x 6" framing lumber is the most common material used for bucks.

***Bolts*—** Use 1/2" x 6" bolts with nuts and washers to secure bucks to the masonry wall.

***Door frame for basement door*—** If a door frame is to be set before masonry blocks are laid, estimate the door frame here.

***Areaways*—** Windows and vents below grade will have to be protected by areaways.

***Dryer vents*—** If a laundry area will be in the basement, install the dryer vent during construction of the foundation.

***Mortar antifreeze*—** It may be required if block will be laid during cold weather.

***Termite protection*—** This can be metal shields or chemical treatment.

***Brushes for the bituminous coating*—** Order them if needed.

***Scaffold rental*—** Estimate the cost if needed.

Foundation Labor

Estimating foundation manhours isn't much easier than estimating footing manhours. But any kind of estimating is easier if you keep accurate labor records on each phase of the job. That's the most reliable guide available for your estimates.

Let's look at a quick, accurate way to make labor estimates for foundation work. We'll cover all the important foundation wall components: crushed stone, concrete block and parging.

Crushed Stone

When you need crushed stone under a concrete basement floor, do yourself a favor. Place and spread the stone before the foundation walls are set. The truck will be able to move in close to the foundation area, and the masons and carpenters will have a safer, drier working area. If the crushed stone isn't spread before the walls go up, you'll have to haul it to the basement in wheelbarrows later.

Once the crushed stone is delivered to the basement area, additional labor is required to spread it evenly and bring it to the correct elevation. Look at Figure 3-32. This is a weekly time sheet and daily log for the Brown job for the week ending September 4th. The daily log tells us that on Monday, three workers spent 13 manhours laying out the house corners and 8 manhours spreading gravel in the basement. On Tuesday, it took 4 manhours to finish spreading the stone. A total of 12 manhours were required to spread the 18 tons of stone.

Only 4 inches were required, but 4½ inches of crushed stone were spread. It's hard to spread exactly 4 inches, and you should never spread less than that on a surface that's been machine graded.

Figure 3-33 is a foundation labor worksheet. To compute the manhours required for spreading crushed stone under a basement area, use the formula shown in section A. Here's how:

Total the hours for foundation work on your weekly time sheet. Enter the total for crushed stone labor under total manhours in section A. In the next column, enter the tons of crushed stone required for the job. According to the weekly time sheet for the Brown job (Figure 3-32), it took 12 manhours to spread and level 18 tons of crushed stone.

Now divide the total manhours by the number of tons of crushed stone. This will give you the manhour factor. In our example, the total manhours (12) divided by the number of tons of crushed stone (18) gives us a manhour factor of 0.66667.

Weekly Time Sheet

Page____of____pages

For period ending ___9- 4- XX___   ___BROWN___ job

Name	Exemptions	Aug. 30 M	31 T	SEPT 1 W	2 T	3 F	4 S	Rate	Reg.	Over-time	Total earnings
1 D.L. White		7	X	X	X	X	X		7		
2 J.E. King		7	2	X	X	X	X		9		
3 W.R. Farlow		7	2	X	X	X	X		9		
4 W.C. Martin, Masonry Sub.		X	X	✓	X	✓	X		—		
5											
6											
7											
8											
9											
10											
11											
12											
13											
14											
15											
16											
17											
18											
19											
20											

Days header spans columns 30–4. *Hours worked* spans Reg./Over-time.

Daily Log

Monday __LAID out HOUSE CORNERS (13 MANHOURS). GRAVEL IN BASEMENT (8 MANHOURS).__
Tuesday __FINISHED GRAVEL IN BASEMENT AREA (4 MANHOURS). Total 18 tons of GRAVEL.__
Wednesday __STARTED laying blocks for FOUNDATIONS.__
Thursday __RAIN.__
Friday __Blocks for FOUNDATION.__
Saturday __X X X__

Figure 3-32
Weekly time sheet

Total manhours	÷	Tons of crushed stone	=	Manhour factor
12	÷	*18*	=	*.66667*

A Spreading crushed stone in basement area

Total manhours	÷	Foundation area (square feet)	=	Manhour factor
16	÷	*902*	=	*.01774*

B Parging foundation walls

Total manhours	÷	Foundation area (square feet)	=	Manhour factor
145,	÷	*902*	=	*.01608*

C Brushing on bituminous coating

Total manhours	÷	Foundation tile (linear feet)	=	Manhour factor
16	÷	*106*	=	*.15094*

D Installing drain tile

Figure 3-33
Foundation labor worksheet

Use this manhour factor when making future estimates. To find the labor for spreading crushed stone on a similar job, multiply the manhour factor from Figure 3-33 (0.66667) by the estimated number of tons of crushed stone. If your estimate shows 26 tons of crushed stone, then your manhour estimate for this job will be 17.33, or 18 manhours.

Now multiply the estimated manhours by the hourly cost of labor. This gives you the estimated labor cost for the job. For example, 18 manhours times $25.00 per hour gives an estimated labor cost of $450.00.

Concrete Block
Masonry contractors bid their work either by the job or by the block. If masonry work is done on contract, just enter the masonry subcontractor's name on your weekly time sheet. Use a check mark to indicate the days he worked. See Figure 3-32. If you use a masonry contractor, he will hire his own crew and will be responsible for their payroll records, taxes and insurance. If you hire masons and helpers by the hour, you have to pay the FICA tax, FUTA tax, withholding taxes, workers' compensation and liability insurance premiums. List their names and manhours on your weekly time sheets. Keep payroll records for each employee so you can file accurate quarterly and year-end reports.

Labor laying concrete block will vary with the size of block, the number of openings in the foundation walls, the height of the walls, the weather, and the skill and motivation of the tradesmen. Some masons can lay 200 or more blocks in one eight-hour shift. Others may average half this number. Whether it's better to pay by the hour or by the block depends on the expected productivity.

For example, assume one mason and his helper will earn $280.00 in one eight-hour shift when they're working by the hour. If the mason averages 200 blocks in this shift, the labor cost per block is $1.40. If he contracts to lay the block on a per-block fee (most masonry contracts are by the block), at a fee of $2.50 per block, you'll be better off with the hourly rate.

A good mason would rather get paid per block because he can make more money by working faster. One who knows he's not that fast will, naturally, prefer to be paid by the hour.

Parging
Let's look at the manhours required for waterproofing the 902 square feet of foundation wall for the Brown job. There are three parts to this job: parging mortar, bituminous coating, and drain tile.

Crushed stone fill under concrete slab:
_____ tons stone @ _____ = $_____

Masonry blocks:
_____ 12" x 8" x 16" @ _____ =   _____
_____ 8" x 8" x 16" @ _____ =   _____
_____ 4" x 8" x 16" @ _____ =   _____
_____ Total blocks $_____

Mortar and sand:
_____ bags masonry cement @ _____ $_____
_____ tons sand @ _____ =   _____
                                                                          $_____

Basement windows, foundation vents and basement doors:
_____ basement windows (size _____) @ _____ = $_____
_____ foundation vents (size _____) @ _____ =   _____
_____ basement doors (size _____) @ _____ =   _____
                                                                          $_____

Lintels, beams, column posts, anchor bolts, and reinforcing steel:
_____ lintels (size _____) @ _____ = $_____
_____ beams (size _____) @ _____ =   _____
(If necessary itemize on separate sheet and enter total cost here)
_____ column posts (size _____) @ _____ =   _____
_____ anchor bolts (size _____) @ _____ =   _____
_____ reinforcing steel (size _____) @ _____ =   _____
                                                                          $_____

Waterproofing and drain tile:
_____ bags masonry cement @ _____ = $_____
_____ tons sand @ _____ =   _____
_____ (5-gal. cans) bituminous coating @ _____ =   _____
_____ lin. ft. drain tile @ _____ =   _____
_____ ells @ _____ =   _____
_____ tons stone @ _____ =   _____
                                                                          $_____

Miscellaneous materials:
(Itemize on separate sheet and enter totals here)   _____
                              Cost of material $_____
                              Sales tax (_____%)   _____
                              Total cost of material   (1) $_____

Masonry labor:
_____ blocks @ _____ =   (2) $_____

Other labor:
(Itemize on separate sheet and enter totals here)   (3) $_____

(Add lines 1, 2 and 3 for total foundation cost) $_____

Figure 3-34
Foundation cost estimate worksheet

Mortar— Look again at Figure 3-27. The daily log shows that the waterproofing of the foundation began on Monday, March 7th. D.L. White worked 8 hours parging that day. On the following day, it took 8 manhours to finish parging. A total of 16 manhours was required to parge the wall.

To convert this information to a manhour factor, use Figure 3-33, section B. Divide the total manhours (16) by the foundation area in square feet (902). This gives a manhour factor of 0.01774. Use this manhour factor as a basis for future parging estimates. Here's how:

Let's say you're estimating the labor for 1/2-inch parging for 1,258 square feet of foundation wall. Multiply the factor (0.01774) by 1,258 square feet. The manhour estimate for the work will be 22.32, or 23 manhours.

Now multiply the number of manhours (23) by the hourly cost ($25.00). Your labor cost estimate for the job is $575.00.

Bituminous coating— Figure 3-27 indicates that work on bituminous coating began on Tuesday, March 8th. Workers spent 8 manhours on bituminous coating that day. On the following day, workers spent 6½ manhours finishing up the job. A total of 14½ manhours was required to apply bituminous coating on 902 square feet of foundation wall.

To convert this information to a manhour factor, use section C of Figure 3-33. Divide the total manhours (14.5) by the foundation area in square feet (902). This gives you a manhour factor of 0.01608. Use this factor as a basis for future bituminous coating estimates.

If you're estimating labor for the bituminous coating on a job with 1,258 square feet of foundation wall, multiply the factor (0.01608) by 1,258 square feet. The manhour estimate for the work will be 20.23, or 21 manhours.

Now multiply the number of manhours (21) by the hourly labor cost ($25.00). Your estimated labor cost for this job is $525.00.

Drain tile— The daily log shows that 16 manhours were spent installing 106 linear feet of drain tile around the basement foundation. Record this information on section D of the worksheet. Divide the total manhours (16) by the linear feet of the drain tile (106) to get the manhour factor (0.15094).

If you're estimating the labor on a job requiring 126 linear feet of drain tile, just multiply the factor (0.15094) by the linear feet (126) to get your manhour estimate. This job will require about 19 manhours.

Now multiply the number of manhours by the hourly cost ($25.00) to get the estimated cost of labor for the job.

Cost Estimate Worksheet for Foundations

Use Figure 3-34, the cost estimate worksheet for foundations, to bring together all foundation costs.

If you keep good cost records, turning out fast, accurate foundation estimates should become routine.

Estimating Floor Systems

With this chapter we begin to estimate the framing. This is the most expensive part of nearly any wood-frame building — about 12% to 15% of the cost of most homes and apartments when both labor and material are included. That's why your take-off and estimate have to be complete and accurate. A careless mistake can cost you more than the profit in most jobs. Get in the habit of working carefully so you avoid a major error. It's easier to prevent an error in the first place than it is to catch the mistake after it's happened. But never consider the estimate complete until every number has been checked and verified.

As in previous chapters, I'll recommend that you use tables of multiplying factors to speed up and simplify the estimate. True, the only completely accurate way to estimate floor systems is to count every stick and every nail. But if you can get nearly the same answer in a fraction of the time, why quibble over the last 10 board feet. It isn't worth the extra labor on your part. Even if you insist on counting every stick, consider using the tables in this chapter to check your figures. If your estimate and the table differ by more than about 10%, there's probably an error somewhere.

Remember the points made earlier: neatness and order are important parts of every cost estimate. Include all the calculations and make them easy to understand. If your estimates are like mine, there'll probably be several changes before work is complete. Every change will make the estimate harder and harder to read. It's nearly impossible to change an estimate that's illegible at the outset.

An estimate should follow a logical order. That makes it less likely that you'll omit some major cost. Visualize how the work will be done and make sure each step shows up on your estimate. Put a check mark through each item as it's read off the plans and listed on your spread sheet. When the estimate is complete, every carpentry item on the plans should be checked off.

On a longer estimate you'll probably have several pages of spread sheet and a summary sheet that brings all totals forward. If you transfer page totals to a summary sheet, put a check mark beside each page total as it's transferred to the summary. When complete, every page's total should be checked off.

The summary sheet can also serve as a lumber list when it's time to order materials.

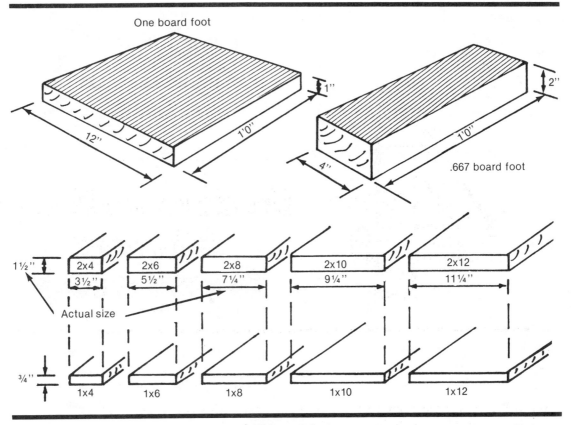

Figure 4-1
Nominal and actual lumber sizes

Consider reversing the order on the lumber list so the first items needed are on the top of the lumber pile. Otherwise your yard will probably deliver roof framing lumber on the top of the stack and mudsills at the bottom.

Beginning the Floor System Estimate

Most of the information needed to estimate a floor system will be in the wall section of the plans: the size of the sill plate, the size and spacing of the floor joists and the type and thickness of the subfloor. Some plans will also include girders.

On most jobs the entire floor frame will be softwood lumber. Occasionally steel beams will be used to span a long opening such as over a two-car garage.

In this and the following chapters you'll use the information from Chapter 2 on board foot calculations. You'll recall that a board foot of lumber is equivalent to the lumber in a piece 1'' thick by 12'' wide by 1'0'' long. That's the nominal size. Figure 4-1 will help you visualize how board footage is calculated, and compare nominal and actual sizes.

There are several common ways to abbreviate board foot measurements. In this book, I'm using *BF* for board feet, *MBF* for thousand board feet, *SF* for square feet and *LF* for linear feet.

We can simplify all board foot calculations by using the multiplying factors in Figure 4-2. It converts linear feet to board feet. (You'll find a blank copy of all of the worksheets in this chapter in the back of the book.) The worksheet lists the factors for converting linear feet to board feet for lumber ranging from 1 x 4 to 2 x 12.

Look up the nominal dimensions in the first column and enter the linear feet on that line in the second column. Multiply the number of linear feet by the factor for that size lumber to find the board feet. The factor for 1 x 4 lumber is 0.33333. If we need 380 linear feet of 1 x 4, multiply 380 by the factor to get 126.67 board feet.

Lumber size (thickness and width)	Linear feet	x	Factor	=	Board feet
1" x 4"	**380**	x	.33333	=	**126.67**
1" x 6"		x	.50000	=	
1" x 8"		x	.66667	=	
1" x 10"		x	.83333	=	
1" x 12"		x	1.00000	=	
2" x 4"	**8**	x	.66667	=	**5.33**
2" x 6"	**8**	x	1.00000	=	**8.00**
2" x 8"		x	1.33333	=	
2" x 10"	**14**	x	1.66667	=	**23.33**
2" x 12"		x	2.00000	=	

Figure 4-2
Worksheet for converting
linear feet to board feet

Lumber size (thickness and width)	Board feet	x	Factor	=	Linear feet
1" x 4"	**126.67**	x	3.00	=	**380**
1" x 6"	**140**	x	2.00	=	**280**
1" x 8"		x	1.50	=	
1" x 10"		x	1.20	=	
1" x 12"		x	1.00	=	
2" x 4"	**1,280**	x	1.50	=	**1,920**
2" x 6"		x	1.00	=	
2" x 8"		x	.75	=	
2" x 10"	**23.33**	x	.60	=	**14**
2" x 12"		x	.50	=	

Figure 4-3
Worksheet for converting
board feet to linear feet

Our formula for converting linear feet to board feet is:

Multiply the linear feet by the factor to get the number of board feet.

Use the factors in Figure 4-2 to calculate board footage for different lumber sizes. There are three more examples on Figure 4-2, using 2 x 4, 2 x 6 and 2 x 10 lumber.

Converting Board Feet to Linear Feet

What if your measurements are in board feet, but the lumber is priced by the linear foot? The conventional formula for converting board feet to linear feet is:

Multiply the board feet by 12 and divide by the nominal dimensions.

For example, how many linear feet are there in 1,280 board feet of 2 x 4 lumber?

$$1,280 \text{ BF} \times 12 \div (2 \times 4) = 1,920 \text{ LF}$$

Now let's do it the easy way. Figure 4-3 has a list of factors for converting board feet to linear feet. Find the nominal dimensions of the lumber in the first column. In the next column enter the number of board feet. Now multiply the number of board feet by the factor to find the number of linear feet. In our example, for 1,280 BF of 2 x 4 lumber, multiply 1,280 by the factor, 1.5. to get 1,920 linear feet of lumber.

Our new formula for converting board feet to linear feet is:

Multiply board feet by the factor to get the number of linear feet.

Usually, floor joists are priced by the thousand board feet. But some dealers sell joists by the piece. You may find 2 x 10 joists, 16'0" long, priced at $8.80 each. What's the cost per MBF? The conventional solution would be to convert linear feet to board feet,

Lumber size	Price per piece	x	Factor	=	Price per MBF	Lumber size	Price per piece	x	Factor	=	Price per MBF
2 x 4 x 8	$1.65	x	187.50	=	$309.38	2 x 8 x 14	$5.79	x	53.57142	=	$310.18
2 x 4 x 10	2.07	x	150.00	=	310.50	2 x 8 x 16	6.61	x	46.87501	=	309.84
2 x 4 x 12	2.48	x	125.00	=	310.00	2 x 8 x 18	7.68	x	41.66667	=	320.00
2 x 4 x 14	2.89	x	107.14290	=	309.64	2 x 8 x 20	8.53	x	37.50	=	319.88
2 x 4 x 16	3.36	x	93.74997	=	315.00	2 x 10 x 8	4.40	x	75.00	=	330.00
2 x 4 x 18	3.78	x	83.33333	=	315.00	2 x 10 x 10	5.50	x	60.00	=	330.00
2 x 4 x 20	4.20	x	75.00	=	315.00	2 x 10 x 12	6.60	x	50.00	=	330.00
2 x 6 x 8	2.52	x	125.00	=	315.00	2 x 10 x 14	7.70	x	42.85715	=	330.00
2 x 6 x 10	3.15	x	100.00	=	315.00	2 x 10 x 16	8.80	x	37.50	=	330.00
2 x 6 x 12	3.78	x	83.33333	=	315.00	2 x 10 x 18	10.20	x	33.33333	=	340.00
2 x 6 x 14	4.41	x	71.42857	=	315.00	2 x 10 x 20	11.33	x	30.00	=	339.90
2 x 6 x 16	5.04	x	62.50	=	315.00	2 x 12 x 8	6.72	x	62.50	=	420.00
2 x 6 x 18	5.76	x	55.55556	=	320.00	2 x 12 x 10	8.40	x	50.00	=	420.00
2 x 6 x 20	6.40	x	50.00	=	320.00	2 x 12 x 12	10.08	x	41.66667	=	420.00
2 x 8 x 8	3.31	x	93.74997	=	310.31	2 x 12 x 14	11.76	x	35.71429	=	420.00
2 x 8 x 10	4.13	x	75.00	=	309.75	2 x 12 x 16	13.44	x	31.25	=	420.00
2 x 8 x 12	4.96	x	62.50	=	310.00	2 x 12 x 18	15.12	x	27.77778	=	420.00
						2 x 12 x 20	16.80	x	25.00	=	420.00

Figure 4-4
Factors for converting piece price to MBF price

then divide the price by the number of board feet to find the cost per board foot. Multiply that by 1,000 to find the cost per MBF.

$$2" \times 10" \times 16' \div 12 = 26.67 \text{ BF}$$
$$\$8.80 \div 26.67 = \$.33 \text{ per BF}$$
$$\$.33 \times 1,000 = \$330.00 \text{ per MBF}$$

Now let's use the factor table in Figure 4-4 to find the price per MBF the easy way. Look down the first column until you find the lumber dimensions. Read across from left to right. In the next column enter the price per piece. Multiply the piece price by the factor to get the price per MBF. In our example, the factor for a 2 x 10 x 16' is 37.50. Multiply that by $8.80 to find the cost, $330.00 per MBF.

Lumber size	Number of pieces	x	Factor	x	Price per MBF	=	Cost of lumber
2 x 4 x 8	400	x	.00533	x	309.38	=	660.01
2 x 4 x 10	35	x	.00667	x	310.50	=	72.45
2 x 4 x 12	50	x	.0080	x	310.00	=	124.00
2 x 4 x 14	20	x	.00933	x	309.64	=	57.80
2 x 4 x 16	12	x	.01067	x	315.00	=	40.32
2 x 4 x 18	14	x	.0120	x	315.00	=	52.92
2 x 4 x 20	16	x	.01333	x	315.00	=	67.20
2 x 6 x 8	1	x	.0080	x	315.00	=	2.52
2 x 6 x 10	20	x	.0100	x	315.00	=	63.00
2 x 6 x 12	5	x	.0120	x	315.00	=	18.90
2 x 6 x 14	66	x	.0140	x	315.00	=	291.06
2 x 6 x 16	40	x	.0160	x	315.00	=	201.60
2 x 6 x 18	40	x	.0180	x	320.00	=	230.40
2 x 6 x 20	4	x	.0200	x	320.00	=	25.60
2 x 8 x 8	1	x	.01067	x	310.31	=	3.31
2 x 8 x 10	8	x	.01333	x	309.75	=	33.04
2 x 8 x 12	28	x	.0160	x	310.00	=	138.88

Lumber size	Number of piece	x	Factor	x	Price per MBF	=	Cost of lumber
2 x 8 x 14	6	x	.01867	x	310.18	=	34.74
2 x 8 x 16	115	x	.02133	x	309.84	=	760.14
2 x 8 x 18	15	x	.0240	x	320.00	=	115.20
2 x 8 x 20	12	x	.02667	x	319.88	=	102.36
2 x 10 x 8	1	x	.01333	x	330.00	=	4.40
2 x 10 x 10	25	x	.01667	x	330.00	=	137.50
2 x 10 x 12	16	x	.0200	x	330.00	=	105.60
2 x 10 x 14	114	x	.02333	x	330.00	=	877.80
2 x 10 x 16	108	x	.02667	x	330.00	=	950.40
2 x 10 x 18	4	x	.0300	x	340.00	=	40.80
2 x 10 x 20	8	x	.03333	x	339.90	=	90.64
2 x 12 x 8	1	x	.0160	x	420.00	=	6.72
2 x 12 x 10	12	x	.0200	x	420.00	=	100.80
2 x 12 x 12	44	x	.0240	x	420.00	=	443.52
2 x 12 x 14	2	x	.0280	x	420.00	=	23.52
2 x 12 x 16	88	x	.0320	x	420.00	=	1182.72
2 x 12 x 18	4	x	.0360	x	420.00	=	60.48
2 x 12 x 20	5	x	.0400	x	420.00	=	84.00

Figure 4-5
Factors for converting MBF price into total cost

When framing lumber is sold by the piece rather than by the MBF, it's easier to compute the price on small purchases. Here's an example. Let's say 2 x 4 x 8' studs are priced at $1.65 each. Joists measuring 2 x 6 x 14' cost $4.41 each, and 2 x 6 x 16' joists cost $5.04 each. Let's assume you need them in quantities of 400, 66 and 40. Here's how you calculate the total cost:

$$
\begin{aligned}
2 \text{ x } 4 \text{ x } 8\text{:} &\quad 400 \text{ @ } \$1.65 = \$660.00 \\
2 \text{ x } 6 \text{ x } 14\text{:} &\quad 66 \text{ @ } \$4.41 = \$291.06 \\
2 \text{ x } 6 \text{ x } 16\text{:} &\quad 40 \text{ @ } \$5.04 = \underline{\$201.60} \\
&\quad\quad\quad\quad\quad\quad\quad\ \$1,152.66
\end{aligned}
$$

If lumber is priced by the MBF and you want to buy it by the piece, the cost calculation is more difficult. Assuming again that you are buying lumber in quantities of 400, 66 and 40, the conventional math looks like this:

$$
\begin{aligned}
400 \text{ x } (2 \text{ x } 4 \text{ x } 8) \div (12 \text{ x } 1,000) \text{ x } \$309.38 &= \$660.01 \\
66 \text{ x } (2 \text{ x } 6 \text{ x } 14) \div (12 \text{ x } 1,000) \text{ x } \$315.00 &= \$291.06 \\
40 \text{ x } (2 \text{ x } 6 \text{ x } 16) \div (12 \text{ x } 1,000) \text{ x } \$315.00 &= \underline{\$201.60} \\
&\quad\ \$1,152.67
\end{aligned}
$$

Now look at Figure 4-5. Use these factors to simplify your calculations when lumber is priced by the MBF and you're buying it by the piece. Here's how:

Look down the first column until you find the lumber dimensions in our example.

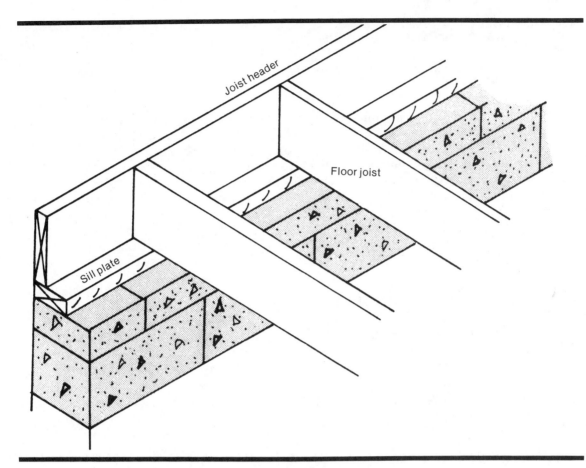

Figure 4-6
Sill plate and joist header

Let's look first at the 2 x 4 x 8' studs. In the next column enter the number of pieces (400). Multiply the number of pieces by the factor for 2 x 4 x 8' lumber (0.0053333) times the price per MBF ($309.38). This gives the total cost of $660.01.

Now calculate the 2 x 6 x 14' joists. Find the lumber dimensions in the first column. In the next column enter the number of pieces (66). Multiply the number of pieces by the factor for 2 x 6 x 14' lumber (0.014), times the price per MBF ($315.00). They'll cost $291.06.

Use the same procedure for the 2 x 6 x 16' joists. Find the dimensions and enter the number of pieces. Then multiply the number of pieces by the factor times the price per MBF. The total cost is $201.60.

Floor System Materials

We'll take the components of the floor system one at a time.

Posts and Pier Caps

The number of posts and pier caps, if any, will be clear on the plans. Multiply the number of items by the size of each.

Sill Plate

The sill plate, or mudsill, attaches the floor system to the foundation with anchor bolts (Figure 4-6). It must be at least 2'' thick (nominal measurement) and wide enough to provide not less than 1½'' bearing for the ends of the joists. Make sure the joints in the sill plate don't fall at window or door openings.

To estimate the material for the sill plate:

1)   Check the wall section of the blueprints for the size of the sill plate. In residential construction it's usually 2 x 6.

2)   Scale off the linear feet of foundation wall where the sill plate will be installed.

3)   Divide the total linear feet by the length you'll use for each piece of framing lumber. Example: If you use 12'0'' lengths, divide by 12; if you're using 14'0'' lengths, divide by 14. This gives you the number of pieces needed. To convert this to board feet, use the factors in the worksheet (Figure 4-2).

Let's try an example. Calculate how many pieces of framing lumber and how many board feet will be required for the foundation sill plate in Figure 4-7. Don't read any further to get my answer until you've done this. Then check your answer against mine.

• The plans show the sill plate to be 2 x 6.

• The linear feet of the foundation wall requiring a sill plate is 242'4''. There are several ways to get this figure. Some estimators start at the upper left corner and work clockwise, checking off each length of foundation and listing it until they get back to the upper left corner.

In a complex building, I'd work that way too. But for this plan, there's a simpler way with less chance for mistakes. Notice that the overall length is 64'. Twice 64' is 128'. Notice that the overall depth is 32'. Twice 32' is 64'. That brings our total to 192' with just two steps. Now pick up the little pieces: 26' for the short end wall and 24'4'' for the wall dividing the garage and utility area: 192' plus 26' plus 24'4'' is 242'4''.

Notice that there's no foundation wall under the girder that spans the 26' floor so no sill plate is needed.

• The plate will be 2 x 6 x 12'. And 242'4'' divided by 12 equals 20.19, or 21 pieces. You'll need 21 pieces of 2 x 6 x 12' lumber.

Now convert this to board feet:

$$21 \text{ (pieces)} \times 12' = 252 \text{ LF}$$

The factor from Figure 4-2 for 2 x 6 lumber is 1.0, so there are 252 board feet of lumber in the sill plate. List this in a separate category on your take-off sheet. The sill plate will have to be either treated material or foundation grade lumber from a decay-resistant species such as redwood. That may be the only treated material in your estimate.

Girders

Girders must bear on the walls at least 4'', with a minimum of 6'' of solid masonry supporting the girder. A 1/4'' bearing plate may be required where the girder rests on masonry blocks. All joints in a wood girder must be made over the column supports. Girders can be either single-member wood, built-up from several pieces of lumber, or steel. For most residential applications, built-up girders will be cheapest to buy and install. Nail built-up girders of three or more members from both sides, as follows:

• Two 20d nails at the ends of each piece and each splice.

• Two rows of 20d nails in between the splices at the top and bottom of each girder, 32'' o.c., with staggered nails.

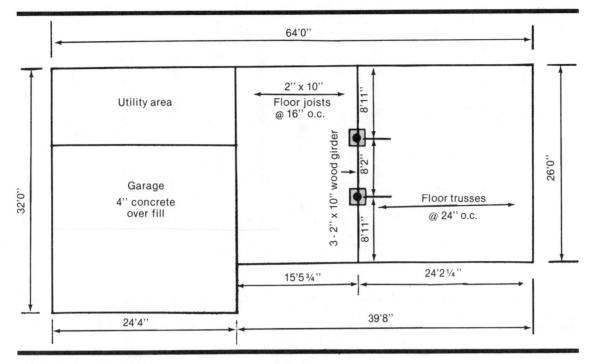

Figure 4-7
Foundation plan

The girder on the plans in Figure 4-7 was designed specifically for the intended span. Always use the species, grade and dimensions indicated on the plans when estimating girders and headers. This is probably the most expensive lumber on the job, but replacing it later (when the framing is complete) will cost a lot more.

To estimate the material for girders:

1) Check blueprints for the size of the girder and spans between column posts or piers.

2) Add the total length of the girder and calculate the most practical length of material. (Keep in mind that all joints must be made over the column supports.)

Look at Figure 4-7 again. It specifies a girder made of three 2 x 10's. The column posts are 8'11'' from each outside wall to the first column post, and 8'2'' between the two column posts.

Allow for adequate bearing on the walls and some overlap over the column posts. You may decide to order the girder material in 10'0'' lengths. You'll need nine of them. That's 150 board feet of lumber. If they're priced at $5.92 each, the cost of the girders will be $53.28.

As an alternative, you could order three pieces of 2 x 10 x 18' lumber and three 2 x 10 x 10' pieces. That's 140 board feet of lumber. If 18' lengths cost $10.75 each, the total cost is:

$$2 \text{ x } 10 \text{ x } 18': \; 3 \; @ \; \$10.75 \; = \; \$32.25$$
$$2 \text{ x } 10 \text{ x } 10': \; 3 \; @ \; \$ \; 5.92 \; = \; \underline{\$17.76}$$
$$\$50.01$$

There will be some waste in the lumber regardless of the length you choose, but using fewer pieces requires fewer splices. That cuts the labor cost.

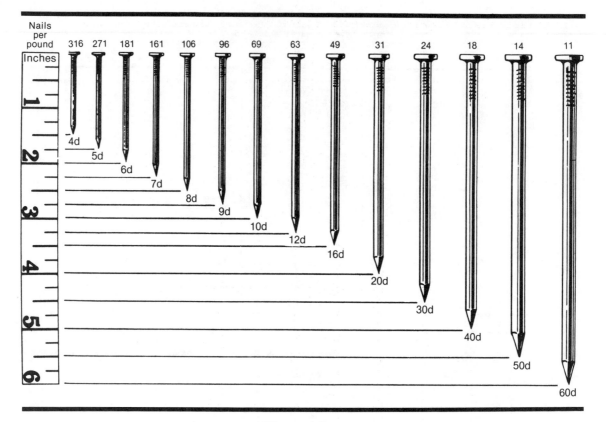

Figure 4-8
Sizes of common wire nails

Size of girder	BF per LF	Nails per MBF
4 x 6	2.15	26
4 x 8	2.85	20
4 x 10	3.58	16
4 x 12	4.28	13
6 x 6	3.21	21
6 x 8	4.28	16
6 x 10	5.35	13
6 x 12	6.42	11
8 x 8	5.71	15
8 x 10	7.13	12
8 x 12	8.56	10

Figure 4-9
Board feet per linear foot for girders, including normal waste

There are approximately 31 20d nails per pound. Following the recommended nailing schedule, it will require 1½ pounds of 20d nails for the girder. Figure 4-8 shows nail sizes and the approximate number per pound for "bright" (uncoated) nails. Nails are identified by their *penny* number. The smaller the number, the smaller the nail.

Figure 4-9 shows lumber and nails required for various sizes of built-up girders. Use it to check your girder calculations. In our example, the girder is 6 x 10 and 26' long. From the table, 6 x 10 girders will require 5.35 board feet per linear foot (including normal waste and overlap). That's 139.1 board feet and not too far from our estimate. From the

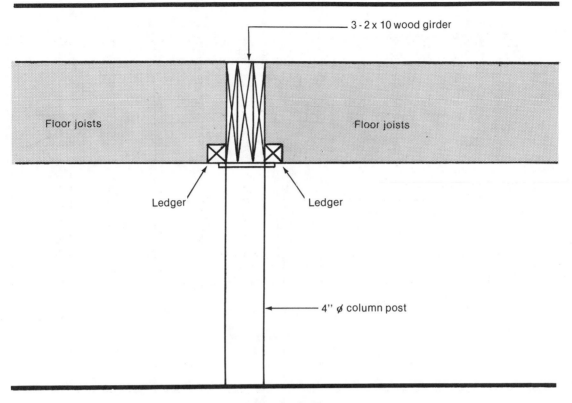

Figure 4-10
Floor joists framing into girder

table, 13 pounds of nails would be required for 1,000 BF. Our 139.1 BF would be 0.1391 times that, or 1.8 pounds. That's a little more than this nailing schedule calls for, but it might be a good estimate on another job.

Ledgers

When floor joists frame into the side of a wood girder, as shown in Figure 4-10, use either steel joist hangers or wood ledger strips to secure the joist. Wood ledger strips must be at least 2 x 2 and must be nailed to the girder with three 16d nails at each joist.

You can rip a 2 x 4 in half to make 2 x 2 ledger strips. If the length of the girder is 24'0", you could make the necessary 48' of ledger strips by ripping two 2 x 4 x 12' boards.

There are approximately 49 16d nails per pound. Allow two pounds of 16d nails for 24'0" of ledger strips.

You'll need this material for the sill plate, girder and ledger:

Sill plate	21-2 x 6 x 12' (252 BF)
Girder	3-2 x 10 x 18' (90 BF)
	3-2 x 10 x 10' (50 BF)
Ledger	2-2 x 4 x 12' (16 BF)
Nails	2 lbs. 16d common
	1½ lbs. 20d common

Floor Joists

The span of the joists is the distance between inner faces of the supports. Calculating maximum joist spans for various grades and species of lumber is a job for an engineer. That's beyond the scope of this book. But there are generally accepted span tables that most code authorities will accept. Tables for Southern Yellow Pine and Douglas Fir are

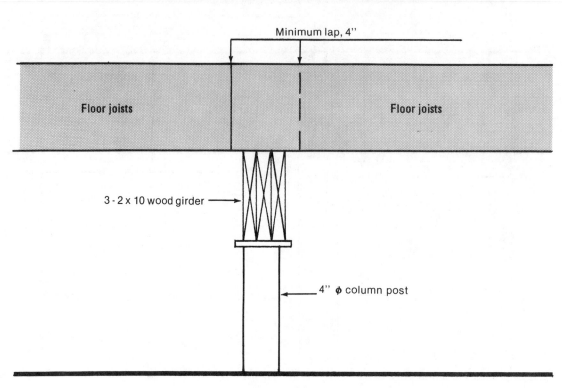

Figure 4-11
Floor joists framing on top of girder

at the end of this chapter (Figures 4-30 and 4-31). Use these as guidelines. In any case, the plans should show the size and spacing of the floor joists for each span. *Never use less lumber or a cheaper grade or species than is indicated on the plans and in the specs.*

Let's review how the floor joists, header joists and ledger strip will go together before we estimate the quantities required.

The joists must have a minimum bearing on the exterior wood sill plate of 1½''. We'll install a continuous 2'' header joist (band joist) to prevent lateral movement and to provide subfloor nailing. See Figure 4-6. You'll toenail floor joists to the sill plate with three 8d nails and then toenail the header to the sill plate with 8d nails spaced 16'' o.c. Nail the header to each floor joist with a minimum of two 16d nails.

We'll have to support floor joists framing into the side of a wood girder or beam with a ledger strip, as shown in Figure 4-10. We'll toenail the joists to the girder with three 10d or 16d nails.

Floor joists framing over girders and bearing partitions must have a minimum lap of 4'', as shown in Figure 4-11. We'll nail the joists together with three 16d nails and then toenail the joists to the girder or bearing partition with three 8d nails.

Plan for double floor joists under all parallel partitions. They'll be nailed together at the top and bottom, every 32'', with 10d or 16d nails.

Estimating the Floor Joists
Count the floor joists needed for each section separately. List the larger or "extra" joists first. These will be around stairways or under partitions. Then take off the regular joists. Begin at one side of the plan and work across the bay before going on to the next bay. Joists are nearly always laid across the shortest dimension of each floor. If the direction isn't clear, look at the wall section on the plan.

Remember that joists have to lap over one another enough so they can be spiked together. Allow about a foot of overlap. At 16'' spacing, 0.75 joists are needed for each

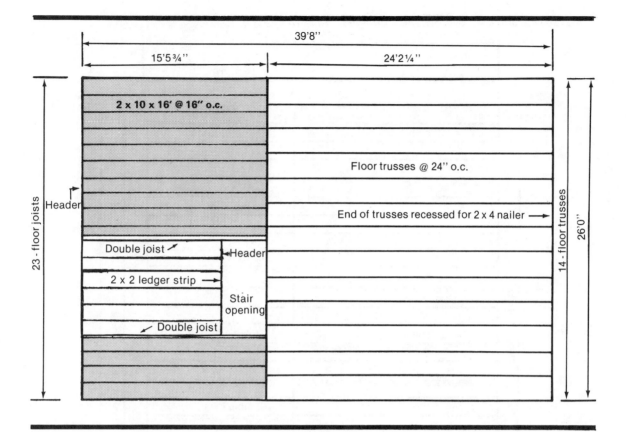

Figure 4-12
First floor plan

foot of width. If the span length is 20', 16 joists (0.75 times 20) will be required. This includes the "extra" joist required at the end of the span, but doesn't allow for doubling of any joist or header joist.

Multiply the number of joists by the board feet per joist to find the material needed. If joists are to be 16' long and of 2 x 12 lumber, each joist has 32 board feet and 16 joists would be 512 BF. Add for two headers (64 BF) and 32 BF more for one doubled joist. That's 608 board feet. Most estimators would add about 6% for waste (36 BF, or about one joist).

Don't deduct joists for small openings like stairways. You'll use the joists omitted to frame the opening.

Here's an example that's a little more complicated. Look at Figure 4-12. How many floor joists will be required for the section of the floor with the stair opening? What length will they be? Joist spacing is 16" o.c.

Here's the solution. The total linear feet perpendicular to the length of the joists is 26'0". The span between supports is 15'5¾", requiring 16' lengths. So how many 16' lengths of 2 x 10 are required for this section?

$$
\begin{array}{lrl}
\text{26.0' x .75} & = & 19.50 \\
\text{Starter} & & 1.00 \\
\text{Double joists (2)} & & \underline{2.00} \\
& & 22.50 \text{ or 23 joists (2 x 10 x 16')}
\end{array}
$$

If floor joists or floor trusses are spaced 24" o.c., multiply the linear feet perpendicular to the joists by 0.50 (50%) and add one joist for the starter and one for each double joist.

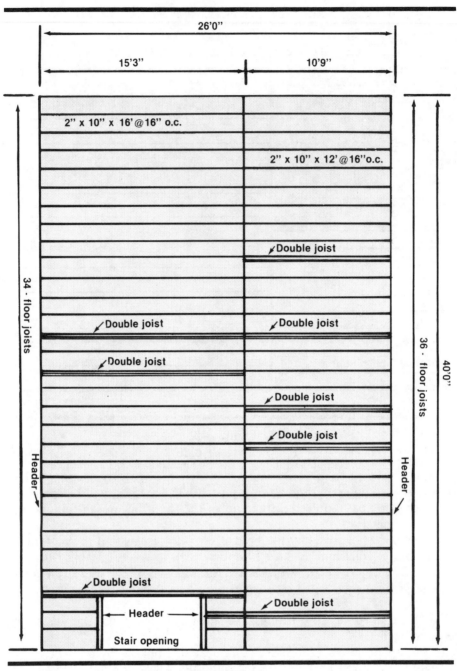

Figure 4-13
Second floor plan

The house shown in Figure 4-12 has two floor elevations on the first floor. The architect designed the floor trusses to provide the two elevations, and also to cover the 24'2¼'' span. The floor trusses are on 24'' centers. The total linear feet perpendicular to the trusses is 26'0''. How many trusses will you need?

$$26.0' \times .50 = 13$$

Starter $\underline{1}$

14 trusses

Figure 4-13 is the second floor plan. How many joists will it take?

Back section

40.0' x .75	=	30
Starter	=	1
Double joists (5)	=	5

36 joists (2 x 10 x 12')

Front section

40.0' x .75	=	30
Starter	=	1
Double joists (3)	=	3

34 joists (2 x 10 x 16')

The total number of floor joists required for the first and second floors:

First floor
23-2 x 10 x 16' joists (613 BF)
14- floor trusses

Second floor
34-2 x 10 x 16' joists (907 BF)
36-2 x 10 x 12' joists (720 BF)

Headers

Joist headers (or band joists) at the end of the joists prevent lateral movement of the floor joists and provide a nailing base for the subfloor.

To estimate the quantity of joist headers required, divide the total linear feet of headers by the length of the framing to be used.

How many pieces of 2 x 10 x 16' (the desired length for the headers) will be required for the house in Figures 4-12 and 4-13? First find the linear feet of headers:

First floor	26'0"
Second floor (40' + 40')	80'0"
Headers for stair openings	-0-

106'0"

106'0" ÷ 16' = 6.63 or 7 headers (2 x 10 x 16')

Note: We didn't allow anything for the headers for the stair openings because we'll make them from the cutouts from the joists.

Have Figure 4-14 handy when the floor joist estimate is complete. It shows board footage of joist per 100 square feet of floor, including header joists, doubled joists and

Size of joist	12" o.c.	16" o.c.	20" o.c.	24" o.c.	Nails per MBF
2 x 6	128	102	88	78	10
2 x 8	171	136	117	103	8
2 x 10	214	171	148	130	6
2 x 12	256	205	177	156	5

Includes header joists, doubled joists and typical waste but no trimmers or blocking.

Figure 4-14
Floor joists, board feet per 100 square feet of floor

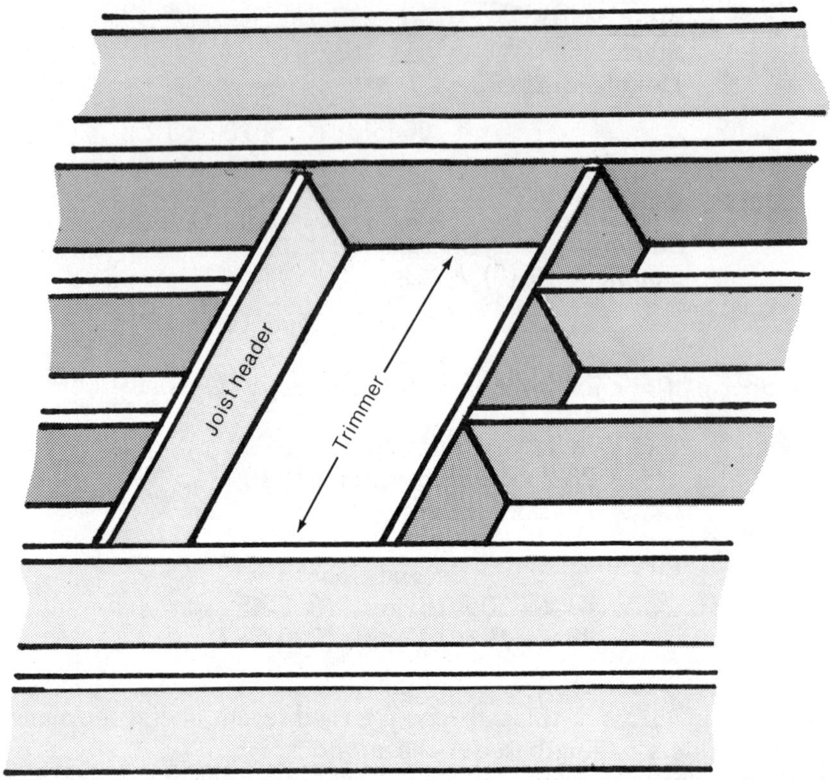

Figure 4-15
Joist header and trimmer

typical waste. To use the table, calculate the floor area in hundreds of square feet. Then multiply the appropriate figure in Figure 4-14 by the area. The answer is the board feet of lumber needed. If your estimate is 10% more or less than Figure 4-14, go back over your figures one more time.

Trimmers
The joist adjacent to an opening into which the header is framed is called a trimmer. Look at Figure 4-15. Most trimmers are estimated as floor joists.

Bridging
Floor joists with clear spans over 8' need bridging between the spans to stiffen them against twisting, and to transfer the floor load from one joist to the adjacent joists. Some of the different types of bridging are:

Wood cross-bridging— Look at Figure 4-16. Use 1 x 3 or 1 x 4 lumber for this type of bridging, with two 7d or 8d nails at each end. Estimate the quantity of bridging by adding the linear feet in each row. Multiply by 2 for 2 x 10 joists. For 2 x 12 joists, multiply by 2.5 for the total linear feet of bridging required. Allow 3.5 pounds of 8d nails per 100 linear feet of bridging.

Metal bridging— Order metal bridging by the joist size and spacing. Estimate two pieces of metal bridging for each space between joists. For joists 16'' o.c., multiply the linear feet of each run for the bridging by 0.75 (75%). For 24'' centers, multiply the linear feet of each run by 0.50 (50%).

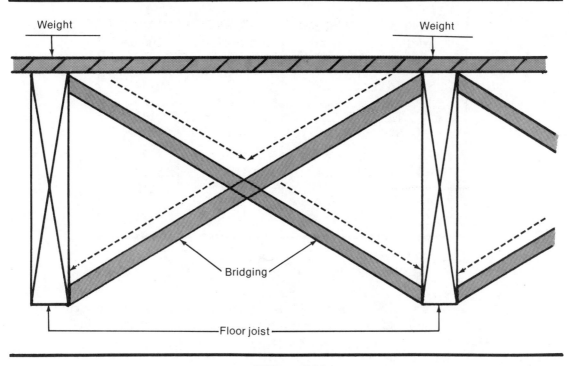

Figure 4-16
Bridging

Solid bridging— Use the same size members as the floor joists. Blocks have to fit tight between the joists.

For the house in Figures 4-12 and 4-13, let's estimate 1 x 3 wood cross-bridging. The linear feet required will be:

First floor:	24 LF	in row
Second floor:	40 LF	(back section)
	36 LF	(front section)
	102 LF	(for 3 rows)

The factor for 2 x 10 floor joists is 2.0. Multiply 102 LF by 2 to find 204 LF of bridging required. Order 210 LF of 1 x 3 lumber.

Note: On the first floor (Figure 4-12), no bridging is required between the floor trusses. In the front section of the second floor, the bridging stops at the stair opening.

Subfloor
The subfloor, sometimes called the floor deck or floor sheathing, is applied over the floor joists. It's the base for the finish floor. Subfloors in residential construction can be either wood boards or plywood, but plywood is more common.

Wood boards— The minimum thickness for wood board sheathing is 3/8'' and the maximum width is 8''. Install the boards diagonal to, or at right angles to, the floor joists. Take care that the end cuts are parallel to, and over, the center of joists. Maximum joist spacing is 16'' o.c. except when 25/32'' strip flooring is installed at right angles to joists and subfloor is installed diagonally. In this case, spacing may be 24'' o.c. Nail the wood boards to joists at each bearing with 8d common or 7d threaded (anchor-down) nails. Use two nails in 6'' boards and three in 8'' boards.

Nominal width		Finished width	BF per 100 SF	
			Laid perpendicular	Laid diagonal
1 x 3	S4S	2½	125	130
1 x 3	T&G	2½	138	144
1 x 4	S4S	3½	120	125
1 x 4	T&G	3¼	128	133
1 x 6	S4S	5½	114	119
1 x 6	T&G	5¼	120	125
1 x 8	S4S	7½	112	117
1 x 8	T&G	7¼	115	120
1 x 10	S4S	9½	110	115
1 x 12	S4S	11½	109½	114½

Figure 4-17
Waste factors for wood board subfloors

Figure 4-17 shows waste factors for wood board subfloors. These are only guidelines. There's no substitute for experience and accurate cost records when estimating material quantities. Here's how to find your own waste factors.

Your records show you installed 1,410 BF of 1 x 8 S4S as the subfloor for an area 42' x 28' (1,176 square feet). Your factor for that job is:

$$1{,}410 \text{ BF} \div 1{,}176 \text{ SF} = 1.20 \text{ (your factor)}$$

Use this factor for your next estimate for a 1 x 8 S4S subfloor.

Plywood— Use Structural-Interior type or Exterior type plywood. Use Exterior type when any surface or edge is exposed to weather. Install the plywood with the face grain at right angles to the joists and staggered so end joints break over different joists in adjacent panels.

The limiting factor in plywood subfloors is deflection under loads at the edges. Plywood must be continuous over two or more joists with the face grain across supports. Nail the plywood to joists at each bearing with 8d common or 6d threaded nails spaced 6'' o.c. along all panel edges, and 10'' o.c. along intermediate joists. Figure 4-18 shows the pattern. Figure 4-19 is a nail size chart for plywood subfloors.

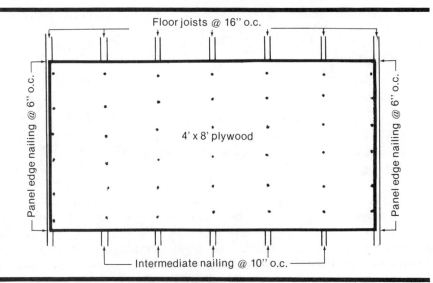

Figure 4-18
Nail detail for plywood subfloor

Plywood thickness (in inches)	Maximum span (in inches)	Nail size
1/2	16	6d threaded or 8d common
5/8	16	8d common
5/8, 3/4	20	8d common
3/4, 7/8	24	8d common

Note: 6d threaded nails (approximately 225 nails per pound)

Allow: 8 pounds per 1,000 SF
8d common nails (approximately 111 nails per pound)
Allow: 15   pounds per 1,000 SF (16" o.c.)
Allow: 11.5 pounds per 1,000 SF (24" o.c.)

Figure 4-19
Nails sizes for plywood subfloors

The next step is to estimate the number of sheets of plywood needed for the subfloor. Here's the formula:

To estimate plywood, divide the square feet of the floor area by the square feet in one piece of plywood.

Round your answer off to the next whole number. Assume you're estimating the plywood for 1,040 square feet of floor area. There are 32 square feet in a sheet of 4' x 8' plywood:

$$1,040 \text{ SF} \div 32 \text{ SF} = 32.5 \text{ or } 33 \text{ sheets}$$

Now let's do it the easy way. Look at Figure 4-20. Section A shows the factor for 4' x 8' plywood panels. Section B has the factor for 4' x 12' plywood. Look down the area column in Section A and find the floor area in our example (1,040 SF). Multiply the floor area by the factor (0.03125) to get the number of 4' x 8' plywood panels required. Order 33 panels.

Area (square feet) x	Factor =	Number of pieces	Area (square feet) x	Factor =	Number of pieces
1,040 x	.03125	= 32.50 (or 33)	1,040 x	.02083	= 21.66 (or 22)
1,280 x	.03125	= 40	1,280 x	.02083	= 26.66 (or 27)
1,450 x	.03125	= 45.31 (or 46)	1,450 x	.02083	= 30.20 (or 31)
1,676 x	.03125	= 52.38 (or 53)	1,676 x	.02083	= 34.91 (or 35)
1,814 x	.03125	= 56.69 (or 57)	1,814 x	.02083	= 37.79 (or 38)
A 4' x 8' plywood			**B 4' x 12' plywood**		

Figure 4-20
Factors for plywood panels

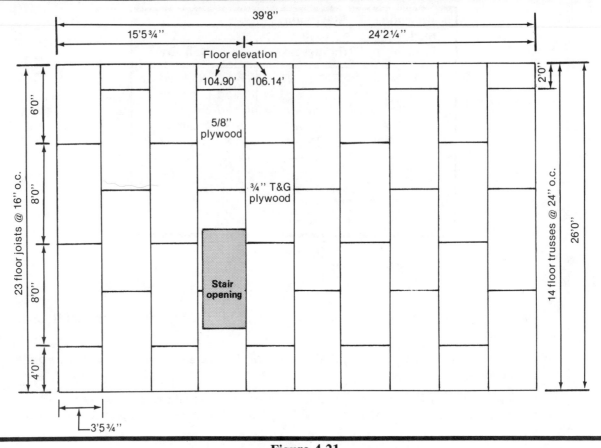

Figure 4-21
Plywood layout, first floor

Here's another example, look down the first column and find the floor area of 1,814 SF. Multiply the floor area by the factor (0.03125) to get the number of plywood panels required. The total comes to 56.69 panels. Round this up to 57 panels.

When you're using this table, keep in mind that the factor *does not include a waste allowance.* I'll explain how to figure waste in the next paragraph.

Our new formula for estimating plywood subfloors is:

Multiply square feet of floor area by the factor. Round fractions up to the next whole number. The factor does not include a waste allowance.

Deduct only large openings when estimating plywood. If the floor dimensions for the width and length are on a module of 4' (24', 48' or 64', for example), you don't need a waste factor. If the floor dimensions are on a module of 2' (26', 34', 50' or 66', for example) allow 3% to 5% for waste. If any of the dimensions vary from the module system, the waste factor will be higher. Uneven joist spacing can add even more to waste. Drawing a plywood layout to scale will help if a lot of cutting will be required.

Figures 4-21 and 4-22 show the plywood layout for the subfloor in the house we're estimating. Let's estimate the plywood required for the first and second floors. The subfloor will be 4' x 8' plywood nailed down with 8d common nails.

For the first floor (Figure 4-21), the right side with the floor elevation of 106.14' is 24'2¼'' x 26'0''. The floor trusses are 24'' o.c. and the plans call for 3/4'' T&G subfloor. Disregard the 2¼'' in the 24'2¼'' because the dimension is to the outside of the foundation and the floor trusses set back on the outside wall.

$$24'0'' \ \text{x} \ 26'0'' = 624 \ \text{SF}$$
$$624 \ \text{SF} \ \text{x} \ .03125 = 19.5 \ \text{or} \ 20 \ \text{sheets}$$

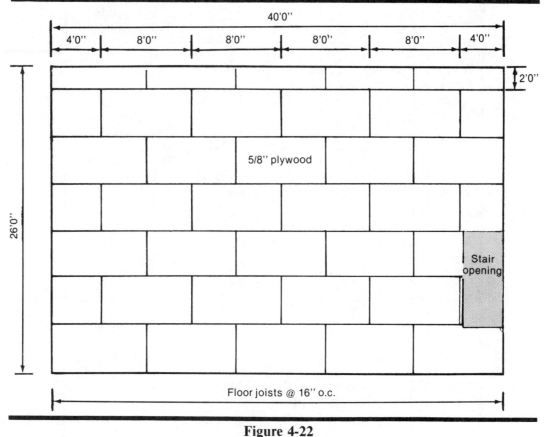

Figure 4-22
Plywood layout, second floor

To figure out how much waste you'll have, multiply the number of pieces ordered by the number of square feet per piece:

$$20 \ \times \ 32 \ SF \ = \ 640 \ SF \ (ordered)$$
$$19.5 \ \times \ 32 \ SF \ = \ \underline{624} \ SF \ (needed)$$
$$16 \ SF \ waste$$

You'll waste half of one sheet, or 16 SF. That's 3% waste for this floor. Order 20 sheets of 3/4'' x 4' x 8' T&G plywood for the right side of the first floor.

The left side of the first floor, with an elevation of 104.90', is 15'5¾'' x 26'0''. The floor joists are 16'' o.c. and the plans call for a 5/8'' plywood subfloor.

$$15.48' \ \times \ 26' \ = \ 402.48 \ or \ 403 \ SF$$
$$403 \ SF \ \times \ .03125 \ = \ 12.59 \ or \ 13 \ pieces$$

Order 13 sheets of 5/8'' x 4' x 8' plywood. How much waste will there be?

$$
\begin{array}{llr}
13 \ x \ 32 \ SF & = & 416 \ SF \\
\text{Area covered} & = & \underline{-403} \ SF \\
& & 13 \ SF \\
\text{Stair cutout} & = & \underline{+ \ 28} \ SF \\
\text{Waste} & & 41 \ SF \ (10\%)
\end{array}
$$

Total board feet	x	Factor	=	Pounds nails
3,708	x	.0100	=	37.08 (OR 37)

Allow 10 lbs. 16d common nails per 1,000 board feet
Floor joists and headers

Total board feet	x	Factor	=	Pounds nails
3,708	x	.00250	=	9.27 (OR 10)

Allow 2.5 lbs. 8d common nails per 1,000 board feet
Toenailing joist headers and floor joists

Total linear feet	x	Factor	=	Pounds nails
300	x	.03500	=	10.50 (OR 11)

Allow 3.5 lbs. 8d common nails per 100 linear feet
Wood cross-bridging

Total square feet	x	Factor	=	Pounds nails
1,814	x	.00800	=	14.51 (OR 15)

Allow 8 lbs. 6d threaded nails per 1,000 square feet
Plywood floor deck - 6d nails

Total square feet	x	Factor	=	Pounds nails
1,814	x	.01500	=	27.21 (OR 27)

Allow 15 lbs. 8d common nails per 1,000 square feet
Plywood floor deck - 8d nails

Total square feet	x	Factor	=	Pounds nails
1,040	x	.02700	=	28.08 (OR 28)

Allow 27 lbs. 7d threaded nails per 1,000 square feet
Board floor deck - 7d nails

Total square feet	x	Factor	=	Pounds nails
1,040	x	.0400	=	41.60 (OR 42)

Allow 40 lbs. 8d common nails per 1,000 square feet
Board floor deck - 8d nails

Figure 4-23
Factors for nails

The second floor dimensions are 40'0" x 26'0". The floor joists are 16" o.c. and the plans call for a 5/8" plywood subfloor. Figure 4-22 shows the plywood layout for the second floor. How many sheets do you need?

40' x 26' = 1,040 SF
1,040 SF x .03125 = 32.5 or 33 pieces

The waste calculations are:

$$
\begin{array}{lrl}
33 \times 32 \text{ SF} & = & 1,056 \text{ SF} \\
\text{Area covered} & = & -\,1,040 \text{ SF} \\
\hline
& & 16 \text{ SF} \\
\text{Stair cutout} & + & 28 \text{ SF} \\
\hline
\text{Waste:} & & 44 \text{ SF } (4\%)
\end{array}
$$

For all the subfloor in this house, order 46 sheets of 5/8'' x 4' x 8' C-D plywood and 20 sheets of 3/4'' x 4' x 8' T&G plywood.

Nails

Most builders buy nails for framing, sheathing, floor and roof decking in 50- or 100-pound quantities. You can buy nails by the pound, but the cost will be much higher than the 50-pound price. Save money by buying in 50-pound quantities whenever possible.

Allow extra nails for every job. Some nails will be needed for miscellaneous applications, such as forms, braces and scaffolding. Others will be discarded or wasted. Spacing of the floor joists (either 16'' o.c. or 24'' o.c.) will change the quantity of nails needed. For example, a plywood floor deck with joists 16'' o.c. will require 15 pounds of 8d common nails per 1,000 square feet. If the floor joists are spaced 24'' o.c. you'll need only 11.5 pounds of 8d common nails per 1,000 square feet. The factors shown in Figure 4-23 are for floor joists spaced 16'' o.c. and include 15% waste.

Floor System Labor

The manhours required to install a floor system will vary with the size and design of the building and the efficiency of your crew. The most accurate predictor of future costs is the cost of your job just completed. Be sure to keep good cost records on all work you do. Your weekly time sheets and daily logs are an invaluable guide.

Let's look at a typical job. Figures 4-24, 4-25 and 4-26 are weekly time sheets for the Baker job. The Baker house is a large two-story house with a crawl space but no basement. The floor joists rest on a steel beam. The first floor system is being installed before the factory-built house arrives at the job site.

What do the daily logs tell us? On Wednesday, June 30, carpenters spent 16 manhours installing the foundation sill plate. On Friday, July 2, they spent 32 manhours installing the steel beams and floor joists. Monday, July 5, was a holiday. On Tuesday, July 6, carpenters installed the bridging. They began installing the subfloor, but rain forced them to quit for the day. Only 14 manhours were recorded. On Wednesday, July 7, the crew spent 32 manhours finishing up the subfloor. A total of 94 manhours were required to install a first floor system of 1,956 square feet.

Let's use this information to find a manhour factor for estimating labor on future jobs. Figure 4-27 is a floor system labor worksheet. Look at Figure 4-24. Enter the total manhours from Figure 4-24 (94) in the first column. Enter the floor area (1,956) in the next column. Divide the manhours by the floor area to get the manhour factor (0.04806).

Use this manhour factor to estimate labor requirements for similar jobs. Here's the formula:

Multiply the manhour factor by the floor area (in square feet) to get the total number of manhours required to do the job. Then multiply the total manhours by the hourly pay rate to get the estimated labor cost.

Weekly Time Sheet

Page _/_ of _/_ pages

For period ending _7-3- 'xx_   _BAKER_ job

	Name	Exemptions	Days JUNE / JULY						Rate	Hours worked		Total earnings
			28 M	29 T	30 W	1 T	2 F	3 S		Reg.	Over-time	
1	D.L. WHITE		7½	5½	8	8	8	×		37		
2	W.C. MARTIN, MASONRY CONT.		✓	✓	×	×	×	×		—		
3	A.L. KING		×	×	8	8	8	×		24		
4	J.E. KING		×	×	8	8	8	×		24		
5	F.N. NEAL		×	×	8	8	8	×		24		
6												
7												
8												
9												
10												
11												
12												
13												
14												
15												
16												
17												
18												
19												
20												

Daily Log

Monday FOUNDATION BLOCKS — COORDINATING WORK W/ MASONS (7½ MANHOURS)
Tuesday FINISHED FOUNDATION BLOCKS — COORDINATING WORK (5½ MANHOURS)
Wednesday FOUNDATION SILL PLATE (16 MANHOURS) — FILL DIRT IN GARAGE AREA (16 MHRS.)
Thursday WATERPROOFING FOUNDATION (16 MANHOURS) — FILL DIRT IN PORCH (16 MANHOURS)
Friday SET STEEL BEAMS AND FLOOR JOISTS (32 MANHOURS)
Saturday × × × ×

Figure 4-24
Weekly time sheet

Weekly Time Sheet

Page _1_ of _1_ pages

For period ending _7-10-'xx_   _BAKER_ job

	Name	Exemptions	July 5 M	6 T	7 W	8 T	9 F	10 S	Rate	Reg.	Over-time	Total earnings
			Days							**Hours worked**		
1	D.L. WHITE		X	3½	8	8	X	X		19½		
2	A.L. KING		X	3½	8	8	X	X		19½		
3	J.E. KING		X	3½	8	8	X	X		19½		
4	F.N. NEAL		X	3½	8	8	X	X		19½		
5												
6												
7												
8												
9												
10												
11												
12												
13												
14												
15												
16												
17												
18												
19												
20												

Daily Log

Monday HOLIDAY (4TH OF JULY)
Tuesday BRIDGING – STARTED SUBFLOOR (14 MANHOURS) – RAIN
Wednesday FINISHED SUBFLOOR (32 MANHOURS) 1,956 SF ON FIRST FLOOR
Thursday FILL DIRT IN GARAGE AREA (32 MANHOURS)
Friday XXXX – WAITING ON DELIVERY OF FACTORY-BUILT HOUSE
Saturday XXXX

Figure 4-25
Weekly time sheet

Weekly Time Sheet

Page _1_ of _1_ pages

For period ending _7-17- 'XX_   _BAKER_ job

#	Name	Exemptions	Days July 12 M	13 T	14 W	15 T	16 F	17 S	Rate	Hours worked Reg.	Over-time	Total earnings
1	R. R. LEWIS		8	8	8	x	x	x		24		
2	C. A. LESTER		8	8	8	7½	8	x		39½		
3	D. L. WHITE		8	8	8	7½	8	x		39½		
4	A. L. KING		8	8	8	7½	8	x		39½		
5	J. E. KING		8	8	8	7½	8	x		39½		
6	F. H. NEAL		8	8	8	7½	8	x		39½		
7	W. R. FARLOW		8	8	8	7½	8	x		39½		
8	R. C. JONES		x	4½	8	7½	8	x		28		
9	A. A. NORMAN		x	8	8	7½	x	x		23½		
10												
11												
12												
13												
14												
15												
16												
17												
18												
19												
20												

Daily Log

FACTORY - BUILT HOUSE ARRIVED

Monday SET O/S PARTITIONS ON 1ST FLOOR (56 MANHOURS)

Tuesday SET I/S PARTITIONS ON 1ST FLOOR (68½ MANHOURS)

Wednesday SET FLOOR JOISTS ON 2ND FLOOR (72 MANHOURS)

Thursday SUBFLOOR ON 2ND FLOOR (60 MANHOURS) 1,696 SF ON 2ND FLOOR

Friday UNLOADED 2ND TRAILER (56 MANHOURS)

Saturday XXXXX

Figure 4-26
Weekly time sheet

Total manhours	÷	Floor area (square feet)	=	Manhour factor
94	÷	1,956	=	.04806

A First floor (over crawl space)

Total manhours	÷	Floor area (square feet)	=	Manhour factor
132	÷	1,696	=	.07783

B Second floor (over crawl space)

Total manhours	÷	Floor area (square feet)	=	Manhour factor
81	÷	1,230	=	.06585

C First floor (over basement)

Total manhours	÷	Floor area (square feet)	=	Manhours factor
108	÷	1,040	=	.10385

D Second floor (over basement)

Figure 4-27
Floor system labor worksheet

Use the same procedure to estimate the labor required for the second floor. The daily log on Figure 4-26 shows that on Wednesday, July 14, carpenters spent 72 manhours installing the floor joists on the second floor. On Thursday, July 15, they worked 60 manhours installing the subfloor. It took the carpenters 132 manhours to install a second floor system of 1,696 square feet.

Look at Figure 4-27 B. Enter the total manhours (132) in the first column. Enter the floor area (1,696 square feet) in the next column. Divide the manhours by the floor area. Our manhour factor for the second floor is 0.07783.

Figures 4-28 and 4-29 are weekly time sheets for the Brown job. This is a two-story house with a basement. It has a special floor system that requires floor trusses. The house is factory built, and the first floor system is included in the house package.

The daily log in Figure 4-28 tells us that the factory-built house was delivered on Tuesday, September 14, along with the first floor system. Carpenters spent 48 manhours unloading the truck and installing most of the first floor system. On Wednesday, September 15, they spent 33 manhours finishing the subfloor. A total of 81 manhours were required to install the first floor system. The total floor area was 1,230 square feet. This gives us a manhour factor of 0.06585 for the first floor. See Figure 4-27 C.

The daily log in Figure 4-29 shows that work on the second floor system for the Brown job began on Tuesday, September 21. It required 48 manhours. On Wednesday, September 22, carpenters spent 40 manhours installing the floor joists and bridging. The subfloor was finished on Thursday, September 23, in 20 manhours. A total of 108 manhours were required to install the second floor system. The total floor area was 1,040 square feet. Our manhour factor for this work is 0.10385. See Figure 4-27 D.

Keep daily logs for all of your jobs. Convert the manhours to manhour factors. Use these factors to estimate labor costs on future jobs.

Page 1 of 1 pages

Weekly Time Sheet

For period ending 9-18-'XX

BROWN job

	Name	Exemptions	Days SEPTEMBER 13 M	14 T	15 W	16 T	17 F	18 S	Rate	Hours worked Reg.	Over-time	Total earnings
1	C. A. LESTER		X	8	5½	3	8	X		24½		
2	D. L. WHITE		X	8	5½	3	8	X		24½		
3	A. L. KING		X	8	5½	2½	8	X		24		
4	J. E. KING		X	8	5½	2½	8	X		24		
5	W. R. FARLOW		X	8	5½	2½	X	X		16		
6	J. R. DAVIS		X	8	5½	2½	8	X		24		
7												
8												
9												
10												
11												
12												
13												
14												
15												
16												
17												
18												
19												
20												

Daily Log

Monday XXXX - FACTORY-BUILT HOUSE DUE TOMORROW

Tuesday FACTORY BUILT HOUSE ARRIVED W/ FLOOR SYSTEM FOR 1ST FLOOR FLOOR SYSTEM ON FIRST FLOOR (48 MANHOURS)

Wednesday FINISHED SUBFLOOR ON 1ST FLOOR (23 MANHOURS) 1,230 SF ON 1ST FLOOR

Thursday UNLOADED SECOND TRAILER - RAIN (16 MANHOURS)

Friday SET O/S AND I/S PARTITIONS ON 1ST FLOOR (40 MANHOURS)

Saturday XXXX

Figure 4-28
Weekly time sheet

Weekly Time Sheet

Page __/__ of __/__ pages

For period ending 9-25-'XX

__BROWN__ job

Name	Exemptions	Days SEPTEMBER 20 M	21 T	22 W	23 T	24 F	25 S	Rate	Hours worked Reg.	Over-time	Total earnings
1 C. A. LESTER		8	8	8	8	8	X		40		
2 D. A. WHITE		8	8	8	8	8	X		40		
3 A. L. KING		8	8	8	8	4	X		36		
4 W. R. FARLOW		8	8	4	4	8	X		32		
5 J. R. DAVIS		8	8	8	8	8	X		40		
6 R. R. LEWIS		X	8	4	4	8	X		24		
7											
8											
9											
10											
11											
12											
13											
14											
15											
16											
17											
18											
19											
20											

Daily Log

Monday TOP PLATES ON 1ST FLOOR PARTITIONS (40 MANHOURS)
Tuesday SET BEAMS AND STARTED FLOOR JOISTS ON 2ND FLOOR (48 MANHOURS)
Wednesday FINISHED FLOOR JOISTS AND BRIDGING ON 2ND FLOOR (40 MANHOURS)
Thursday FINISHED SUBFLOOR 1,040 SF (20 MANHOURS) – O/S PARTITIONS (20 MANHRS)
Friday FINISHED O/S AND I/S PARTITIONS ON 2ND FLOOR (36 MANHOURS); ROOF TRUSSES (8 MANHOURS)
Saturday XXXX

Figure 4-29
Weekly time sheet

Nominal size (inches)	Spacing (inches o.c.)	No. 1 Den. K.D. 2" dim. 2000 f	No. 2 Den. K.D. 2" dim. 1750 f	No. 3 Den. K.D. 2" dim. ---	No. 1 Den. 2" dim. 1700 f	No. 2 Den. 2" dim. 1400 f	No. 3 Den. 2" dim. ---	No. 1 Den. K.D. 2" dim. 2000 f	No. 2 Den. K.D. 2" dim. 1750 f	No. 3 Den. K.D. 2" dim. ---	No. 1 Den. 2" dim. 1700 f	No. 2 Den. 2" dim. 1400 f	No. 3 Den. 2" dim. ---
Pine, Southern Yellow (Dense Grain)													
							Floor Joists						
					30 lb. live load					40 lb. live load			
2 x 6¹	12	11' 4"	11' 4"	11' 4"	11' 4"	11' 4"	10' 4"	10' 6"	10' 6"	10' 4"	10' 6"	10' 6"	9' 2"
	16	10' 4"	10' 4"	10' 0"	10' 4"	10' 4"	9' 0"	9' 8"	9' 8"	9' 0"	9' 8"	9' 8"	8' 0"
	24	9' 0"	9' 0"	8' 2"	9' 0"	9' 0"	7' 4"	8' 4"	8' 4"	7' 4"	8' 4"	8' 4"	6' 6"
2 x 8	12	15' 6"	15' 4"	15' 4"	15' 4"	15' 4"	14' 0"	14' 4"	14' 4"	14' 2"	14' 4"	14' 4"	12' 8"
	16	14' 0"	14' 0"	13' 8"	14' 0"	14' 0"	12' 2"	13' 0"	13' 0"	12' 2"	13' 0"	13' 0"	10' 10"
	24	12' 4"	12' 4"	11' 2"	12' 4"	12' 4"	10' 0"	11' 6"	11' 6"	10' 0"	11' 6"	11' 6"	8' 10"
2 x 10	12	18' 4"	18' 4"	18' 4"	18' 4"	18' 4"	17' 10"	17' 4"	17' 4"	17' 4"	17' 4"	17' 4"	16' 0"
	16	17' 0"	17' 0"	17' 0"	17' 0"	17' 0"	15' 6"	16' 2"	16' 2"	15' 6"	16' 2"	16' 2"	13' 10"
	24	15' 6"	15' 6"	14' 2"	15' 6"	15' 6"	12' 8"	14' 6"	14' 6"	12' 8"	14' 6"	14' 6"	11' 4"
2 x 12	12	21' 2"	21' 2"	21' 2"	21' 2"	21' 2"	21' 2"	20' 0"	20' 0"	20' 0"	20' 0"	20' 0"	19' 4"
	16	19' 8"	19' 8"	19' 8"	19' 8"	19' 8"	18' 8"	18' 8"	18' 8"	18' 8"	18' 8"	18' 8"	16' 8"
	24	17' 10"	17' 10"	17' 2"	17' 10"	17' 10"	15' 4"	16' 10"	16' 10"	15' 4"	16' 10"	16' 10"	13' 8"

Figure 4-30
Floor joist span tables

Sample Floor System Estimate

Now that we've learned the easy way to estimate floor system materials and labor, let's apply it to a typical estimate. We'll estimate the materials and labor for a job that has a first floor of 1,814 square feet over a basement. A steel beam will be used. Here's how to estimate the material and labor costs for this job.

Materials
First we'll estimate the board lumber, plywood panels and nails for the job.

Board lumber: The lumber required for the sill plates, floor joists and band joists will be:

```
  5-2 x  6 x 12 (    60 BF) @ $315.00  MBF
 28-2 x  8 x 12 (   448 BF) @ $310.00  MBF
 16-2 x 10 x 12 (   320 BF) @ $330.00  MBF
108-2 x 10 x 16 (2,880 BF) @ $330.00  MBF
```

Use the factors in Figure 4-5 to compute the cost of the framing lumber.

```
2 x  6 x 12':   5 x 0.0120      x $315.00 = $ 18.90
2 x  8 x 12':  28 x 0.0160      x $310.00 = $138.88
2 x 10 x 12':  16 x 0.0200      x $330.00 = $105.60
2 x 10 x 16': 108 x 0.0266667   x $330.00 = $950.40
         Total                             $1,213.78
```

Use 1 x 4 for the cross bridging. It's priced at $12.80 per hundred linear feet (CLF). The multiplying factor is 0.01. We estimate that 300 linear feet are required. To find the cost, multiply the linear feet (300) by the factor (0.01) by $12.80. This comes to $38.40.

Figures 4-30 and 4-31 are the floor joist span tables I mentioned earlier in the chapter. Although the size of the joists will be indicated on the plans, use the tables to double-check the specifications if you have any questions.

Douglas Fir, Coast Region

Nominal size (inches)	Spacing (inches o.c.)	Select structural J & P 1950 f	Dense Construction J & P 1700 f	Construction J & P 1450 f	Standard J & P 1200 f	Utility J & P (1)	Select structural J & P 1950 f	Dense Construction J & P 1700 f	Construction J & P 1450 f	Standard J & P 1200 f	Utility J & P (1)
					Floor Joists						
				30 lb. live load					**40 lb. live load**		
2 x 6	12	11' 4''	11' 4''	11' 4''	11' 4''	8' 4''	10' 6''	10' 6''	10' 6''	10' 6''	7' 4''
	16	10' 4''	10' 4''	10' 4''	10' 4''	7' 2''	9' 8''	9' 8''	9' 8''	9' 8''	6' 4''
	24	9' 0''	9' 0''	9' 0''	9' 0''	5'10''	8' 4''	8' 4''	8' 4''	8' 2''	5' 2''
2 x 8	12	15' 4''	15' 4''	15' 4''	15' 4''	12' 4''	14' 4''	14' 4''	14' 4''	14' 4''	11' 0''
	16	14' 0''	14' 0''	14' 0''	14' 0''	10' 8''	13' 0''	13' 0''	13' 0''	13' 0''	9' 6''
	24	12' 4''	12' 4''	12' 4''	12' 4''	8' 8''	11' 6''	11' 6''	11' 6''	11' 0''	7'10''
2 x 10	12	18' 4''	18' 4''	18' 4''	18' 4''	16'10''	17' 4''	17' 4''	17' 4''	17' 4''	15' 2''
	16	17' 0''	17' 0''	17' 0''	17' 0''	14' 8''	16' 2''	16' 2''	16' 2''	16' 2''	13' 0''
	24	15' 6''	15' 6''	15' 6''	15' 6''	12' 0''	14' 6''	14' 6''	14' 6''	14' 0''	10' 8''
2 x 12	12	21' 2''	21' 2''	21' 2''	21' 2''	19' 8''	20' 0''	20' 0''	20' 0''	20' 0''	17' 8''
	16	19' 8''	19' 8''	19' 8''	19' 8''	17' 0''	18' 8''	18' 8''	18' 8''	18' 8''	15' 4''
	24	17'10''	17'10''	17'10''	17'10''	14' 0''	16'10''	16'10''	16'10''	16'10''	12' 6''

Figure 4-31
Floor joist span tables

Plywood panels: To find the number of pieces of 4' x 8' plywood, we'll use the factor in Figure 4-20 (0.03125). Remember that this factor doesn't include any allowance for waste.

Multiply the floor area (1,814 SF) by the factor (0.03125) to get the number of plywood panels. This comes to 56.69. Round up to 57 pieces.

Nails: Use the factor table in Figure 4-23 to estimate the pounds of nails required. *Note: The factors shown in Figure 4-23 are for floor joists spaced 16'' o.c.*

This job requires 3,708 BF of framing lumber. We'll use 16d common nails. The factor is 0.01. Multiply the board feet (3,708) by the factor (0.01) to get the pounds of nails required (37.08 or 37).

For toenailing headers and floor joists, we'll use 8d common nails. The factor is 0.0025. Multiply the total board feet (3,708) by the factor (0.0025) to get the pounds of nails required (9.27 or 10).

For cross bridging, we'll use 8d common nails. The factor is 0.035. Multiply the total linear feet (300) by the factor (0.035) to get the pounds of nails required (10.50 or 11).

For the plywood deck (with floor joists spaced 16'' o.c.), we'll use 6d threaded nails. The factor is 0.008. Multiply the total square feet (1,814) by the factor (0.008) to get the pounds of nails required (14.51, or 15).

Labor
Figure 4-27 C gives the manhour factor for a similar job with a first floor system over a basement. Use the manhour factor from this job (0.06585) to estimate the labor requirements for your new job. Multiply the floor area (1,814 SF) by the factor (0.06585) to get the number of manhours required (119.45, or 120). Multiply the number of manhours (120) by the hourly pay rate ($25.00) to get the estimated labor cost for the job ($3,000.00).

We've covered a lot of ground in this chapter. Unless you're already a seasoned estimator, a light reading won't be enough. Go back over the examples. Work them out yourself. Be sure you understand the way each number was developed. Try making several trial estimates yourself. Have someone check over your work to make sure nothing was omitted, and that all calculations are correct. When you're comfortable with everything in this chapter, when you could explain it to someone else, when there's nothing left to explore or understand here, then go on to Chapter 5.

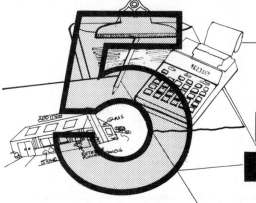

Estimating Exterior and Interior Walls

In this chapter we'll examine the cost variables for exterior and interior walls. But before we get into the details of estimating materials and labor, let's take a quick look at the wall components we're dealing with, and the construction standards we'll be following.

Studs

Studs are the vertical framing members in a wall. They're the backbone of every conventional wood-frame structure. The wall section of the plans will give the size and spacing of studs and the wall height. Finish materials are applied to the interior and exterior sides of the studs to complete wall construction.

You'll hear the term *partition* used to describe stud walls that don't carry more than their own weight. Exterior walls and some interior walls help support the roof or the floor above. In that case, the wall is called a *bearing wall* and has to be designed to carry the intended load. Interior walls that run parallel to ceiling joists usually don't have to support anything except their own weight and the weight of the wall finish applied to both sides. Their only purpose is to divide, or partition, the interior space. That's why non-bearing walls are called partition walls. Modern roof trusses make longer roof spans possible, reducing the number of interior walls that are bearing walls. In many homes, all interior walls are partitions.

Studs must be continuous lengths of lumber, without splices, and must be strong enough to support the design load. The minimum lumber dimension in a bearing wall is 2 x 4. Partition walls may be made from 2 x 2 or 2 x 3 material. Nail the studs to the sole plate with four 8d or two 16d common nails.

Figures 5-1 and 5-2 show two examples of wall framing, for a bearing and a non-bearing wall. Notice that the studs in the non-bearing wall are 1½'' longer, since there's a single instead of a double top plate.

Maximum stud spacing is 24'' o.c. when 2 x 4 studs support a ceiling and roof only. Studs should be 16'' o.c. when supporting one or two floors. If there are more than two floors, the studs should be at least 2 x 6, spaced not more than 16'' o.c.

Build corner posts with three 2 x 4's set to receive the interior finish. Note in Figure 5-3 that three short spacer blocks are used to complete corner framing.

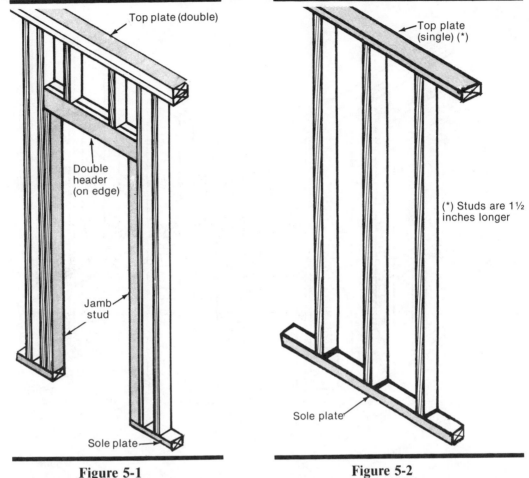

| **Figure 5-1** | **Figure 5-2** |
| Framing a bearing wall | Framing a non-bearing wall |

Wall Bracing

There are four common ways to brace stud walls against twisting and lateral loads:
1) Install wood board sheathing at approximately a 45-degree angle in the opposite direction from each corner. Note Figure 5-4.

2) Near each corner, cut 1 x 4 or wider boards into either the inner or outer face of the studs, sole plate and top plate at approximately a 45-degree angle. Figure 5-4 shows let-in bracing used with board sheathing installed horizontally. Figure 5-5 shows let-in bracing in balloon construction.

3) Install plywood sheathing in 4' x 8' sheets (Figure 5-6).

4) Install 25/32'' fiberboard in 4' x 8' sheets (Figure 5-6).

Framing Openings

Openings have to be framed to provide rigid support for windows and doors. Jamb studs support the header that spans the top of the opening. All jamb studs must extend in one piece from header to the sole plate. Figures 5-1 and 5-7 show properly framed openings. Note that there are two studs on each side of the opening, a full-length stud from bottom plate to top plate, and a jamb stud from bottom plate to header.

Plates

Sole plates— The sole, or bottom plate, rests on the subfloor. It's nailed to the floor

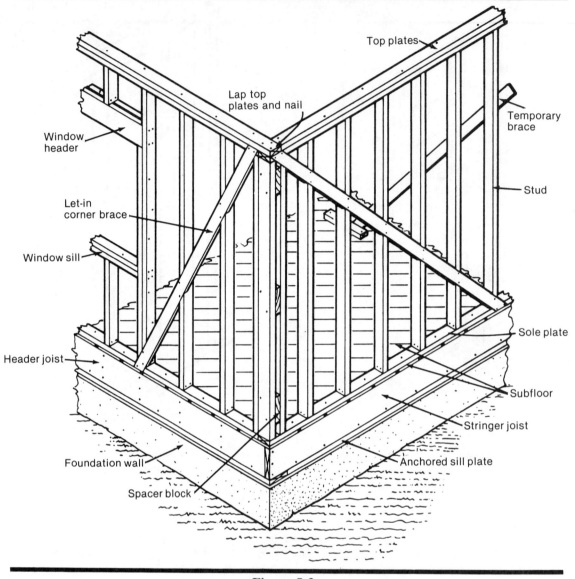

Figure 5-3
Wall framing with platform construction

joists, and studs are nailed to it (Figures 5-1 and 5-7). Plates in residential construction are usually 2 x 4's. The sole plate can be nailed to the floor joists with 16d common nails or 3½'' spiral thread nails spaced not more than 16'' o.c.

Top plates— There should be two 2 x 4 plates on all bearing walls. Lap the plate members at corners and intersecting partitions as in Figure 5-6. Make sure ends of the lower top plate meet over studs. Joints in the upper top plate should be spaced at least 24'' from joints in the lower top plate. Figure 5-8 shows sole plates and top plates at an end-wall in platform construction.

In non-bearing walls, only one top plate is needed. Refer back to Figure 5-2. When only one top plate is used, the studs for non-bearing walls have to be cut 1½'' longer than studs in bearing walls. You may find that it's cheaper and easier to use double top plates throughout the structure because nearly all studs can be cut the same length. That's why many builders use double top plates on all walls.

Nail the lower top plate at each stud with two 16d common nails. Nail the upper plate to the lower plate with 16d common or 3½'' spiral thread nails 16'' o.c.

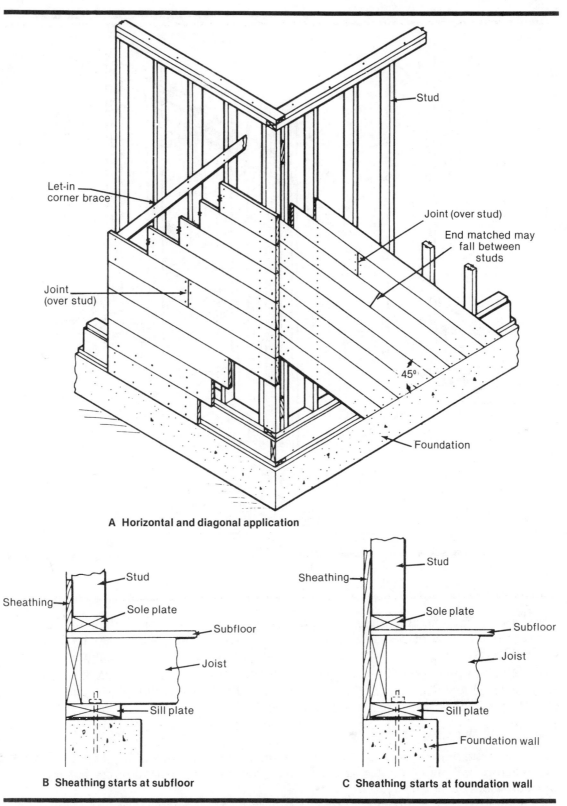

A Horizontal and diagonal application

B Sheathing starts at subfloor

C Sheathing starts at foundation wall

Figure 5-4
Application of wood sheathing

Wall Sheathing

Wall sheathing provides resistance to racking stresses caused by wind. It's also used to support the exterior finish material. Wood boards, plywood, fiberboard and gypsum

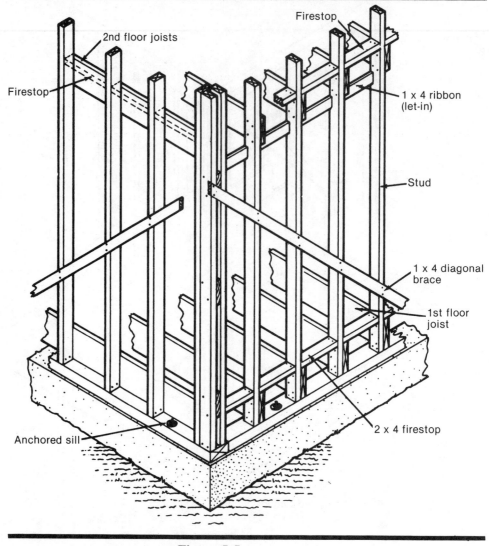

Figure 5-5
Wall framing with platform construction

board are the most common materials used for wall sheathing. Your building code may not require any exterior wall sheathing if certain types of wall cover are used and if corners are braced correctly. But the code varies from community to community. Be sure you know what the code requires before estimating the sheathing. Some types of sidewall cover require exterior wall sheathing. For example, Figure 5-9 shows insulating sheathing applied under shingles.

Comparing the Cost of Wall Systems

In many communities, preassembled wall systems are available from local vendors. The manufacturer will quote a price based on your plans and including delivery but probably without sales tax.

The labor cost for wall framing will be lower if preassembled wall sections arrive at the job site with sheathing already applied. But the material cost for prefab walls will be much higher. If the carpenters cut and assemble the wall on site, your labor costs will be higher but your material cost will be lower.

Which system should you use? The tables and worksheets in this chapter will help you decide which wall system is best for you. I'll suggest ways to use your cost records to produce accurate labor and material estimates for all wall framing.

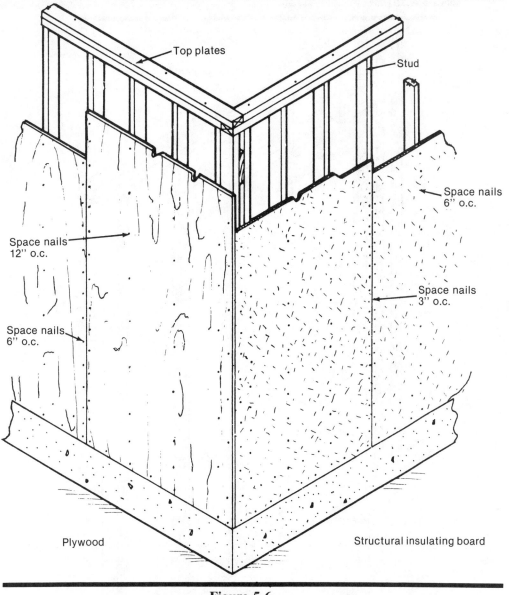

Top plates

Stud

Space nails
6" o.c.

Space nails
12" o.c.

Space nails
3" o.c.

Space nails
6" o.c.

Plywood

Structural insulating board

Figure 5-6
Vertical application of panels for wall bracing

Wall Systems Assembled on Site

If you're assembling the wall system on site, you'll need to make accurate estimates for framing lumber, sheathing and nails. I'll explain the easy way to make these calculations.

Figures 5-10 and 5-11 are the floor plans for the first and second floors of a house. I'll use them to explain in detail how to estimate the material for the exterior and interior walls.

Estimating Wall System Materials

Let's take the components of the wall system one at a time, keeping in mind the structural requirements we talked about at the beginning of this chapter.

Sole and Top Plates

When estimating plates, take off the linear feet of exterior and interior walls on each floor separately. But watch out for walls that are not made from 2 x 4 studs. For example, a wall may be 6" wide so a large plumbing drain line can be run through it.

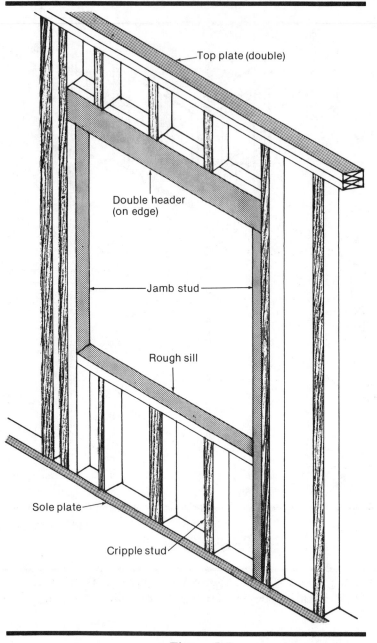

Figure 5-7
Window framing in a bearing wall

Some closet partition walls may be only 2'' wide to gain extra space. Be alert for unusual wall sizes.

A sole plate won't be needed across the bottom of doorways. But my advice is to ignore any opening less than 8 feet wide when taking off plates. Any lumber saved because a bottom plate isn't needed will be used elsewhere to replace defective lumber, or for blocking.

Multiply the linear feet of wall that will have double top plates by three. Multiply the linear of wall that will have a single top plate by two. Add the two lengths together to find the linear feet of plate needed. Divide this total by 12 if you're buying 12' lengths, and 14 if you're using 2 x 4 x 14's. The answer is the linear feet of plate required. If you're using 2 x 4 x 12's, divide the total by 12. If you're using 2 x 4 x 14's, divide by 14.

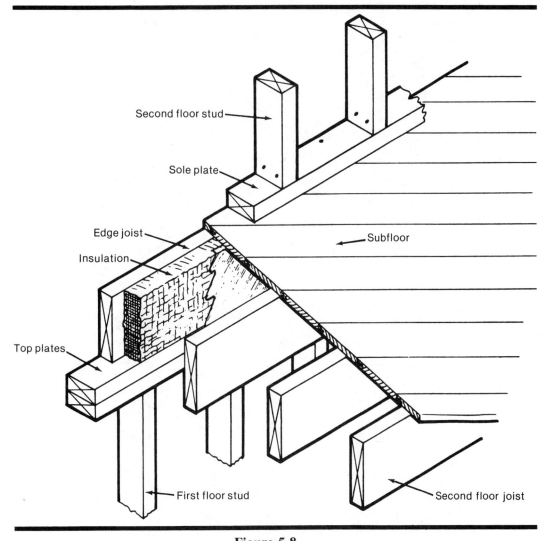

Figure 5-8
Sole plates and top plates

Estimate the number of 2 x 4 x 12's that will be required for the sole and top plates in Figures 5-10 and 5-11. Double top plates will be used on all walls, and all walls will use 2 x 4 studs.

Here's the solution:

```
            First Floor (Figure 5-10)
                Exterior walls........................192 LF
                Interior walls .......................213 LF
            Second Floor (Figure 5-11)
                Exterior walls........................132 LF
                Interior walls .......................185 LF
                                                      _____
                Total ............................722 LF


        722 x 3 =    2166 LF plates
             Less    -18 LF  (garage doors)
                     _____
                     2148 LF


        2148 LF divided by 12 = 179 (number of pieces)
```

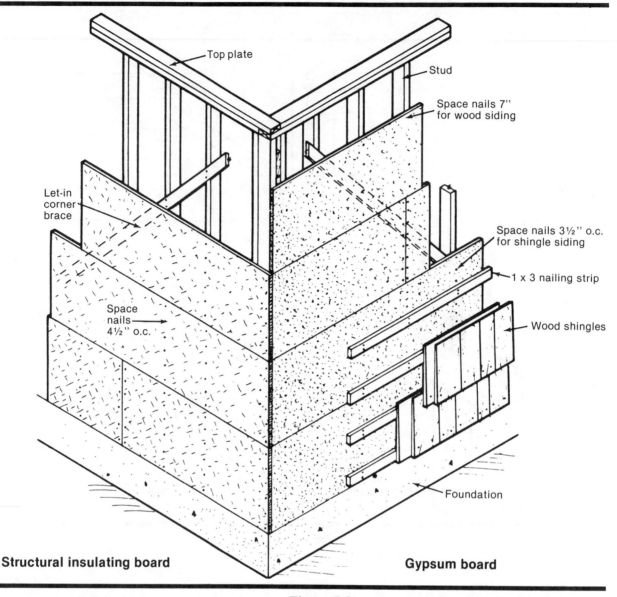

Labels in figure:
- Top plate
- Stud
- Space nails 7" for wood siding
- Let-in corner brace
- Space nails 3½" o.c. for shingle siding
- 1 x 3 nailing strip
- Space nails 4½" o.c.
- Wood shingles
- Foundation
- **Structural insulating board**
- **Gypsum board**

Figure 5-9
Horizontal application of panels

Now refer back to Figure 4-2, the worksheet for converting linear feet to board feet. It shows an easy way to calculate board feet. In our example, there are 2,148 LF of 2 x 4 x 12'. Multiply this by the factor for 2 x 4's (0.66667) to get 1,432 board feet.

Use the factors in Figure 4-2 in Chapter 4 to calculate the board feet for all the lumber in this chapter.

Studs

Estimating the number of studs in a straight wall without any window or door openings or intersecting walls is easy.

Multiply the linear feet of wall length by 0.75 for studs spaced 16" o.c., and by 0.50 for studs spaced 24" o.c.

For example, a wall 12'0" long with studs spaced 16" o.c. would take 10 studs:

12' x .75 = 9 + 1 starter = 10 studs

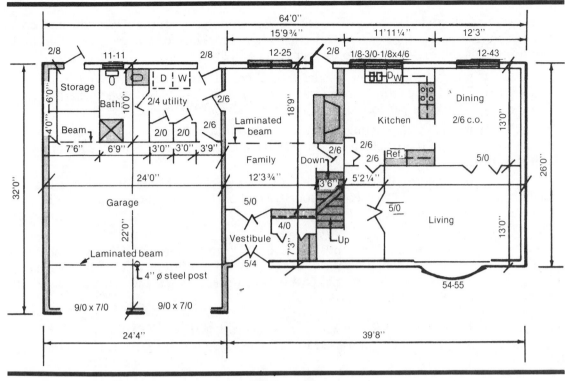

Figure 5-10
First floor plan

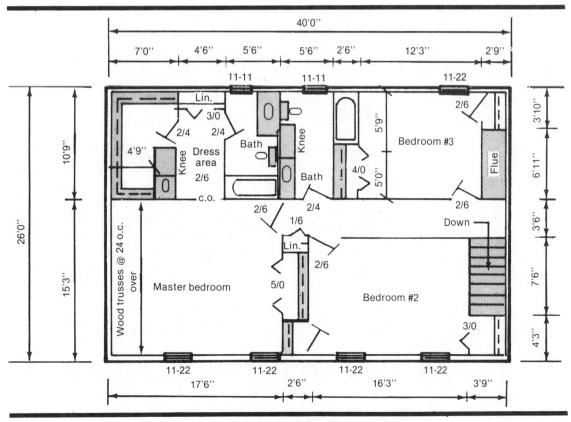

Figure 5-11
Second floor plan

Most walls with studs 16" o.c. will need far more lumber than that: Window and door openings, corner posts, T-posts at intersecting walls, blocking for partitions, double studs around plumbing lines — all add to lumber requirements.

A better estimate of the number of studs you'll need at 16" o.c. is one stud for each linear foot of wall. Some estimators add an additional two studs for each corner, or an arbitrary 50 to 100 studs per job, depending on the size of the house.

There's a common saying among builders: "Figure the number of 2 x 4's you'll need very carefully, then add a truckload. You may have enough!" This is an exaggeration, but it illustrates the point.

Let's figure the number of studs required for the exterior and interior walls for the first floor (Figure 5-10) and the second floor (Figure 5-11). From the estimate we did for the plates, we know there are 722 linear feet of wall. If we allow one stud for each linear foot, we'll need 722 studs.

Your yard probably sells precut studs that are 92⅝" long. Adding 4½" for the sole and two top plates will give a ceiling height of 8'1⅛" from the subfloor to the ceiling joists. There's very little difference in material cost between precut studs and other 2 x 4 x 8's, but there's a big savings in labor costs.

Estimating studs for gable ends— If you use rafters rather than roof trusses, and if it's a gable rather than a hip roof, you'll need to estimate studs for the gable ends. Here's how:

1)   Multiply the width of the gable by 0.75 for 16" o.c., or by 0.50 for 24" o.c. Add one stud for the starter to get the number of studs for each gable.

2)   Scale the length of the longest stud from the elevation on the plans. Divide the result by 2 to find the average stud length.

3)   Multiply the number of studs in each gable by the average stud length to find the linear feet of gable stud.

4)   Divide the linear feet of gable stud by 8 and round up to the next whole number. That's the number of 2 x 4 x 8' studs required for the gable.

5)   If all gables are the same size, as in Figure 5-12, multiply the quantity for one gable by the number of gables. That's the number of gable studs needed. If the gables vary in size, calculate each gable separately and add the totals.

Estimate the number of gable studs required for the three gables, plus the gable on the 6' offset for the garage area shown in Figure 5-12. The studs are spaced 16" o.c.
The width of each main gable is 26'0":

$$26' \times .75 = 19.5 \text{ or } 20 + 1 = 21 \text{ studs}$$

The longest gable stud is 1'6". Use this length for the average stud length because of the large gable vents.

$$21 \text{ studs} \times 1.5' = 31.5 \text{ LF}$$
$$31.5 \text{ LF} \times 3 \text{ gables} = 94.5 \text{ LF}$$

Add 11 LF for the two gables on the offset:

$$94.5 \text{ LF} + 11.0 \text{ LF} = 105.5 \text{ LF}$$

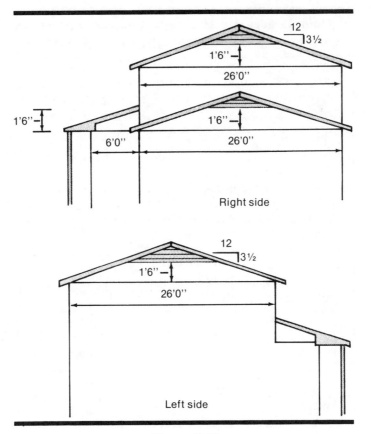

Figure 5-12
Figuring studs for gable ends

Divide by the length of each stud:

$$105.5 \text{ LF} \div 8 = 13.19 \text{ or } 14$$

Order 14 studs (2 x 4 x 8') for the gables.

The total studs required for the exterior, interior and gable walls in Figures 5-10, 5-11 and 5-12 are:

Exterior and interior walls	722 - 2 x 4 x 8
Gables	14 - 2 x 4 x 8
Allow for extras	64 - 2 x 4 x 8
Total	800 - 2 x 4 x 8

Order 800 studs (2 x 4 x 8'). That's 4,267 board feet.

Firestop Blocking

Some carpenters routinely install blocking between studs at the midpoint between top and bottom plates. These blocks increase wall stiffness and retard the spread of flame up the wall. But blocking also adds nearly one linear foot of 2 x 4 for each linear foot of wall. Consider omitting blocks. The code doesn't require it, in most cases, and the wall will support the roof or floor above perfectly well without it.

You'll have to install blocks at ceiling and floor levels in balloon framing so flame

Door width	Header size (on edge)	Header length	Estimate for each double header
2'0''	Two 2 x 4s	2' 5''	One 2 x 4 x 8'
2'4''	Two 2 x 4s	2' 9''	One 2 x 4 x 8'
2'6''	Two 2 x 4s	2'11''	One 2 x 4 x 8'
2'8''	Two 2 x 6s	3' 1''	One 2 x 6 x 8'
3'0''	Two 2 x 6s	3' 5''	One 2 x 6 x 8'
4'0''	Two 2 x 6s	4' 5''	One 2 x 6 x 10'
5'0''	Two 2 x 6s	5' 5''	One 2 x 6 x 12'
6'0''	Two 2 x 8s	6' 5''	One 2 x 8 x 14'

A   Headers for interior door openings

Header size (on edge)	Maximum width of rough stud opening	Header length
Two 2 x 4s	3'0''	Rough stud opening width plus bearing on two studs
Two 2 x 6s	6'0''	
Two 2 x 8s	8'0''	
Two 2 x 10s	10'0''*	Rough stud opening width plus bearing on four studs
Two 2 x 12s	12'0''*	

*Triple studs at jamb opening; headers to bear on two 2 x 4s on each end.

B   Headers for exterior openings

Figure 5-13
Header lengths

can't be sucked directly from the basement to the attic. Blocking may also be needed where a cavity wall opens up into a horizontal area such as a soffit or drop ceiling. Also plan to install blocks between studs along the run of stairs if the wall under the stairs isn't finished on both sides. But don't routinely estimate blocking between all studs. It's a waste of time and material.

Headers
Headers support the weight over openings such as doors and windows. See Figures 5-1 and 5-7. The size of the headers varies with the span of the opening and the weight it has to support. Calculating the material required for headers can be complex. But there are generally accepted standards that you can use on most jobs. Figure 5-13 is a table of header sizes for interior and exterior door openings. Longer headers and unusual situations will require help from an engineer qualified to make these calculations.

Interior doors— When estimating headers for interior doors, the length of each header is the door width plus 5''. Why add the 5''? Here's why:

Thickness of door jambs (2 @ ¾'') . . . . .1½''
Allowance for clearance . . . . ½''
Bearing on 2 studs (2 @ 1½'') . . . . .3''
                                                                              ___
      Total . . . . .5''

Location	Door width	Add for allow-ance	Header length	Header size (on edge)	Estimate for each double header
Bdr. 1	*2'6"*	*5"*	*2'11"*	*2 x 4*	*ONE 2 x 4 x 8'*

Figure 5-14
Headers for interior door openings

So the header length for a 2'6'' door would be 2'11''. Because the header is doubled, it will require 5'10'' (2 x 2'11'') for both headers. Estimate one 2 x 4 x 8' for this door opening. We've done this as an example on Figure 5-14, a worksheet for calculating headers for interior door openings.

Exterior doors and windows— Estimating the header lengths for door and window openings in exterior walls requires more time and caution. For example, when windows are twin or triple, allow additional material for the rough stud opening for each unit. To illustrate: a window with a sash opening 2'4'' wide may require a rough stud opening of 2'6½'' for a single unit, 5'0½'' for a twin unit, and 7'6½'' for a triple unit.

The thickness of outside door jambs is normally 1¼'' or 1⅜6''. Some doors are double (as in Figure 5-10) and some have side lites.

When you're estimating headers for exterior openings, add 3'' for the bearing to the rough stud opening for openings up to 8'. Add 6'' for the bearing to the rough stud opening for openings over 8' wide. For example; a 2/4 x 4/2 twin window with a rough stud opening width of 5'1'' will require two 2 x 6's for the header, as shown in Figure 5-15. The bearing on two studs is 3'' (2 x 1½'') plus the rough stud opening of 5'1'', which equals 5'4''. This will be the length of each header. Doubled, that's 10'8''. Estimate one 2 x 6 x 12' for the header for this window opening. Figure 5-15 is a worksheet for calculating headers for exterior openings.

Here's a consolidated list of material for the headers for the exterior and interior walls in Figures 5-10 and 5-11:

```
2 - 2 x 12 x 12 . . . . . . . . . . . . . . . . . . . . . . . . . 48  BF
4 - 2 x 10 x 10 . . . . . . . . . . . . . . . . . . . . . . . . . 67  BF
2 - 2 x  8 x  8 . . . . . . . . . . . . . . . . . . . . . . . . . 22  BF
7 - 2 x  6 x 12 . . . . . . . . . . . . . . . . . . . . . . . . . 84  BF
2 - 2 x  6 x 10 . . . . . . . . . . . . . . . . . . . . . . . . . 20  BF
2 - 2 x  6 x  8 . . . . . . . . . . . . . . . . . . . . . . . . . 16  BF
9 - 2 x  4 x 12 . . . . . . . . . . . . . . . . . . . . . . . . . 72  BF
3 - 2 x  4 x 10 . . . . . . . . . . . . . . . . . . . . . . . . . 20  BF
6 - 2 x  4 x  8 . . . . . . . . . . . . . . . . . . . . . . . . . 32  BF
                                                              ____
        Total . . . . . . . . . . . . . . . . . . . . . . . .381 BF
```

Unit	Rough stud opening	Add for Bearing	Header length	Header size (on edge)	Estimate for each double header
2/4 x 4/2	5'1"	3"	5'4"	2 x 6	ONE 2 x 6 x 12'

Figure 5-15
Headers for exterior openings

Use the multiplying factors from Figure 4-2, in Chapter 4, to calculate the board footage. Be sure your foreman has this material list. It'll save wasted time and material.

Temporary Wall Braces
After the exterior and interior walls are in place, you'll use temporary wall braces to keep them plumb and aligned until the upper top plate and ceiling joists or trusses are installed. These temporary wall braces are normally 2 x 4 x 12's. Estimating the number of 2 x 4 x 12's for temporary wall bracing is a guess, at best. My estimate would be 20 for this house. Remember that braces used on the first floor can also be used again on the second floor. If you guess wrong, don't worry. Most braces will become blocking, nailers, drop ceilings, or lookouts as construction continues.

For the first and second floors in Figures 5-10 and 5-11, order 20 pieces of 2 x 4 x 12'. That's 240 linear feet times 0.66667, or 160 board feet.

Corner Bracing
The corner bracing adds rigidity to the structure by protecting against lateral forces such as wind pushing against the walls. The most common way to brace corners is to use 1/2" x 4' x 8' plywood sheathing at the corners and 1/2" x 4' x 8' fiberboard sheathing vertically on the balance of the walls.

When estimating corner bracing, use one of the following methods:

1) If let-in bracing is used, estimate two 1 x 4 x 12's for each corner.

2) If sheet material is used, estimate two 4' x 8' pieces for each corner, and include these sheets with the wall sheathing estimate.

The corner bracing for the house in Figures 5-10 and 5-11 will be 1/2" x 4' x 8' plywood, and will be included with the wall sheathing estimate.

Wall Sheathing
Wall sheathing strengthens and adds rigidity to the exterior walls. It also adds additional insulation for the house. Many energy-conscious builders use polystyrene foam board sheathing with a reflective vapor barrier. We'll cover this later in the chapter on insulation.

You can use these materials for wall sheathing:

• *Wood board sheathing (Figure 5-4),* T&G, square edge or shiplapped. The minimum thickness is 3/4''. Maximum width is 12''. Corner bracing is required unless boards are installed diagonally.

• *Plywood sheathing (Figure 5-6).* The minimum thickness is 5/16'' with studs at 16'' o.c., and 3/8'' with studs at 24'' o.c. Plywood sheathing is acceptable for corner bracing if it's installed vertically. Nail plywood with 6d nails spaced 6'' o.c. along edges and 12'' o.c. along intermediate studs.

• *Fiberboard sheathing (Figure 5-6).* Minimum thickness is 1/2''. Corner bracing is required. Nail sheathing to studs at each bearing with 1½'' roofing nails (1¾'' roofing nails for 25/32'' sheathing) spaced 3'' o.c. along edges and 6'' o.c. along intermediate studs. Insulating board breaks easily at the edges, so the nails are spaced closer there.

• *Gypsum sheathing (Figure 5-9).* Minimum thickness is 1/2''. Corner bracing is required. Nail sheathing to studs at each bearing with 1½'' roofing nails with 3/8'' to 7/16'' heads, 4'' o.c. at edges and 8'' at intermediate supports.

• *Polystyrene foam board sheathing.* Follow manufacturer's recommendation for installing and nailing.

When estimating wall sheathing, first check the wall section of the plans for the type and thickness of the material to use. Some estimators deduct for large openings such as garage doors and picture windows. The cutouts from these openings can be used as fillers around band joists, and to help offset the material wasted in the gable sheathing. But note that any sheathing saved may be offset by the extra labor required to cut and fit small pieces around windows and doors.

The first step in estimating wall sheathing is to calculate the total linear feet of perimeter wall on each floor. Then multiply by the wall height to find the gross area in square feet.

Next, calculate the gross area in square feet of the gables: Multiply the rise from the plate to the ridge by the width of the gable. Scale the ridge height from the elevation on the plans if it isn't given. Then divide by 2. See Figure 5-16.

Calculate the area of each gable separately (if they are different sizes), then add all the

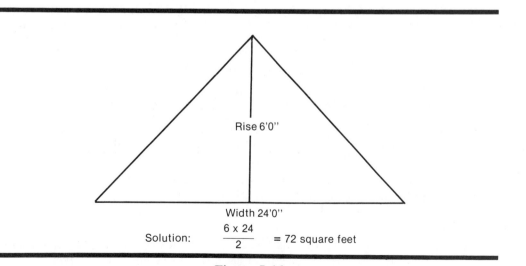

Figure 5-16
Calculating the area of gables

Nominal width		Finished width	BF per 100 SF	
			Laid perpendicular	Laid diagonal
1 x 3	S4S	2½	125	130
1 x 3	T&G	2½	138	144
1 x 4	S4S	3½	120	125
1 x 4	T&G	3¼	128	133
1 x 6	S4S	5½	114	119
1 x 6	T&G	5½	120	125
1 x 8	S4S	7½	112	117
1 x 8	T&G	7¼	115	120
1 x 10	S4S	9½	110	115
1 x 12	S4S	11½	109½	114½

Figure 5-17
Waste factors for wood board sheathing

totals to find the sheathing needed on gables. Finally, add the wall and gable areas to find the gross area for wall sheathing. If you decide to deduct for openings, subtract the opening area to get the net area to be sheathed.

Estimating wood board sheathing— Use the waste factors in Figure 5-17. These are the same as the factors for wood board subfloors in the last chapter. Multiply the appropriate factor by the net area to find the quantity of material to order.

Estimating panel sheathing— Panel sheathing has replaced wood boards for most applications. Applying panel sheathing takes less time than applying board sheathing.

For 4' x 8' sheets or panels, divide the net area in square feet by 32 and round up to the next whole number. That's the number of sheets to order. *Note:* You can also multiply the total square footage by the factor 0.03125 to find the number of sheets to order.

If plywood corners are used for bracing and the balance of the walls are fiberboard (or other types of panels), subtract the number of plywood sheets from the total number of sheets required.

Here's an example: Estimate the wall sheathing for the first and second floors in Figures 5-10 and 5-11, and the gables in Figure 5-12. We'll use 1/2" x 4' x 8' plywood on all corners for bracing, and 1/2" x 4' x 8' fiberboard sheathing on the balance of the house.

From Figure 5-10, the perimeter of the first floor is 192'0". From Figure 5-11, the perimeter of the second floor is 132'0". The height of each floor is 9'0" (8'0" ceiling height plus 1'0" for the floor joists).

First floor: . . . . 192' x 9' = 1728 SF
Second floor: . . . . 132' x 9' = 1188 SF

There are three main gables on the house (Figure 5-12). Each gable is 26'0" wide. But because of the large vents in each gable, the rise is only 1'6".

Rise (1.5') x width (26.0') ÷ 2 = 19.5 SF
19.5 SF x 3 gables = 58.5 SF

The 6" extension of the garage at the left front corner of the house has a shed-type roof with two gables. The total area for these two small shed-type gables is 9 SF. The total gable area is:

```
3 main gables . . . . . . . . . . . . . . . . . . . . . . . . . 58.5 SF
2 shed-type gables . . . . . . . . . . . . . . . . . . . . . . 9.0 SF
                                                            ─────
    Total . . . . . . . . . . . . . . . . . . . . . . . 67.5 or 68 SF
```

Gables require more waste, but the cutouts from the window and door openings will offset this waste. You don't need to make an additional allowance for waste here.
The total gross area for the wall sheathing is:

```
First floor . . . . . . . . . . . . . . . . . . . . . . . . . . . . 1728 SF
Second floor . . . . . . . . . . . . . . . . . . . . . . . . . . 1188 SF
Gables . . . . . . . . . . . . . . . . . . . . . . . . . . . . . .   68 SF
    Total gross area . . . . . . . . . . . . . . . . . . . . 2984 SF
Deduct for garage door openings . . . . . . . .  -126 SF
                                                            ─────
    Total net area . . . . . . . . . . . . . . . . . . . . . 2858 SF
```

2858 SF ÷ 32 SF = 89.31 or 90 panels

Note: You can also calculate the number of panels by multiplying the square feet by the factor for 4' x 8' panels (0.03125):

```
2858 SF x .03125 (factor) = 89.31 or 90 panels
    Total . . . . . . . . . . . . . . . . . . 90 panels
    Less . . . . . . . . . . . . . . . . . . -20 plywood corners
                                          ─────
                              70 fiberboard panels
```

Order 70 fiberboard panels (1/2" x 4' x 8') and 20 plywood sheathing corners (1/2" x 4' x 8').

Nails
The total board feet of lumber for the walls in Figures 5-10, 5-11 and 5-12 is:

```
Sole and top plates . . . . . . . . . . . . . . . . . . . . 1432
Studs . . . . . . . . . . . . . . . . . . . . . . . . . . . . . . 4267
Headers . . . . . . . . . . . . . . . . . . . . . . . . . . . .  381
Temporary braces . . . . . . . . . . . . . . . . . . . .  160
                                                      ─────
    Total . . . . . . . . . . . . . . . . . . . . . . . . . 6240 BF
```

Nails for studs, plates and headers— Using the nail allowance of 22 pounds of 16d common nails for 1,000 board feet, estimate the quantity of nails needed:

6240 BF x 22 ÷ 1000 = 137.28 or 138 pounds

Figure 5-18 is a table of multiplying factors for nails. If you prefer, use this table to shorten your calculations for nail quantities. The factor for nails for studs, plates and headers is 0.022. Here's how to use the multiplying factor:

6240 x .022 = 137.28 or 138 pounds

(A) Studs, Plates and Headers

Total board feet	x	Multiplying factor	=	Pounds nails
6,240	x	.022	=	*137.28* or *138*

Allow 22 lbs. 16d common nails per 1,000 board feet

(B) Fiberboard Sheathing

Total square feet	x	Multiplying factor	=	Pounds nails
2,240	x	.01	=	*22.40* or *23*

Allow 10 lbs. 1½'' roofing nails per 1,000 square feet

(C) Plywood Sheathing

Total square feet	x	Multiplying factor	=	Pounds nails
640	x	.008	=	*5.12* or *6*

Allow 8 lbs. 6d threaded nails per 1,000 square feet

Note: Includes an allowance for 15% waste.

Figure 5-18
Multiplying factors for nails

Order 138 pounds of 16d common nails.

Nails for sheathing— There are 70 pieces of 1/2'' x 4' x 8' fiberboard sheathing. The total square footage is 2,240 (70 times 32' equals 2,240 SF). Use 1½'' roofing nails to install the sheathing. The nail allowance is 10 pounds of 1½'' roofing nails per 1,000 square feet:

$$2240 \text{ SF x } 10 \div 1000 = 22.40 \text{ or } 23 \text{ pounds}$$

If you prefer to use the multiplying factor in Figure 5-18 B:

$$2240 \text{ SF x } .01 = 22.40 \text{ or } 23 \text{ pounds}$$

Order 23 pounds of 1½'' roofing nails.

We'll need 20 pieces of 1/2'' x 4' x 8' plywood sheathing for the corner. That's 640 square feet (20 x 32' equals 640 SF). Use 6d threaded nails for the plywood. According to Figure 5-18, allow eight pounds of nails per 1,000 square feet:

$$640 \text{ SF x } 8 \div 1000 = 5.12 \text{ or } 6 \text{ pounds}$$

Or you can use the multiplying factor from Figure 5-18 C (0.008). The calculation using this factor is:

$$640 \text{ SF} \times .008 = 5.12 \text{ or } 6 \text{ pounds}$$

Order six pounds of 6d threaded nails.

Summary of Wall System Materials
Here's a material list for the wall framing and sheathing for the house in Figures 5-10, 5-11 and 5-12:

Sole and Top Plates

179 - 2 x 4 x 12 . . . . .1432 BF

Studs

800 - 2 x 4 x 8 . . . . .4267 BF

Headers

2 - 2 x 12 x 12	48 BF
4 - 2 x 10 x 10	67 BF
2 - 2 x 8 x 8	22 BF
7 - 2 x 6 x 12	84 BF
2 - 2 x 6 x 10	20 BF
2 - 2 x 6 x 8	16 BF
9 - 2 x 4 x 12	72 BF
3 - 2 x 4 x 10	20 BF
6 - 2 x 4 x 8	32 BF
Total for headers	381 BF

Temporary Wall Braces

20 - 2 x 4 x 12 . . . . 160 BF

Wall Sheathing

70 - ½" x 4' x 8' fiberboard . . . . .2240 SF
20 - ½" x 4' x 8' C-D plywood . . . . 640 SF

Nails

138 lbs . . . . .16d common nails
23 lbs . . . . .1½" roofing nails
6 lbs . . . . .6d threaded nails

Now let me show you another way to figure the material needed for wall framing. Note from the calculation above that the plan in Figures 5-10 and 5-11 requires 6,240 board feet of lumber. Remember that number.

Now look at Figures 5-19 and 5-20. They show the board feet of lumber needed per square foot of wall. Let's apply these tables and see how close we come to our figure of 6,240 board feet.

You'll remember that we measured 324 linear feet of exterior wall for the home in Figures 5-10 and 5-11. To calculate the square feet of exterior wall, multiply 324 by 8: 324 times 8 is 2,592 square feet. Figure 5-19 says we need 1.05 board feet per square foot of exterior wall when using 2 x 4 studs at 16" o.c. Multiply 1.05 by 2,592 and you get 2,721.2. Call it 2,722 BF and remember that number also.

Now let's do the interior walls. There are 398 linear feet of interior wall, or 3,184 square feet (398 times 8 is 3,184). From Figure 5-20, note that 1.12 board feet of lumber are needed when interior walls are 2 x 4 at 16" o.c. Multiplying 1.12 by 3,184 we get

Size of studs	Spacing o.c.	BF per SF	Lbs. nails per 1000 BF
2" x 3"	12"	.83	30
2" x 3"	16"	.78	30
2" x 3"	20"	.74	30
2" x 3"	24"	.71	30
2" x 4"	12"	1.09	22
2" x 4"	16"	1.05	22
2" x 4"	20"	.98	22
2" x 4"	24"	.94	22
2" x 6"	12"	1.66	15
2" x 6"	16"	1.51	15
2" x 6"	20"	1.44	15
2" x 6"	24"	1.38	15

Board feet per square foot of wall including end stud, 3 plates, blocking, openings and waste.

Figure 5-19
BF of lumber per SF of exterior walls

Size of studs	Spacing o.c.	BF per SF	Lbs. nails per 1000 BF
2" x 3"	12"	.91	25
2" x 3"	16"	.83	25
2" x 3"	24"	.76	25
2" x 4"	12"	1.22	19
2" x 4"	16"	1.12	19
2" x 4"	24"	1.02	19
2" x 6"	16"	1.48	16
2" x 6"	24"	1.22	16

Board feet per square foot of wall including end stud, 3 plates, blocking, openings and waste.

Figure 5-20
BF of lumber per SF of interior walls

3,566.08 BF. Call it 3,566 and add it to the 2,722 we calculated for exterior walls in the table above. The total? It's 6,288 board feet, within 1% of the quantity we calculated the long way, figuring every stud, plate, brace and header! And note that Figures 5-19 and 5-20 include typical blocking, which wasn't included in our 6,240 BF figure. If we included some blocking, the figures would be nearly identical.

Figures 5-19 and 5-20 won't give the exact answer to every wall framing problem. But it's a quick way to check your calculations. Note that balloon framing requires slightly less material because the studs extend from the sill to the top plates of the second story. That saves plates at the second floor.

Compare Figures 5-19 and 5-20. Note that interior walls require slightly more material than exterior walls. That's because interior walls are usually shorter and have more ends and corners than exterior walls.

Should you use Figures 5-19 and 5-20 to figure wall framing or should you do it stick by stick? That's up to you, of course. But my recommendation is to use Figures 5-19 and 5-20 as a check at least. It takes only a minute or two to figure the board feet needed with these tables. That minute or two could prevent a costly mistake. If you find that these tables consistently come within 1% of the right answer, maybe they're all you need to figure materials for wall framing.

Figure 5-21 is a worksheet for computing the cost of the framing lumber. These are the same factors we used back in Figure 4-5, in Chapter 4. We'll use it to find the cost of the lumber from our final material list for the wall system.

Estimating Wall System Labor

The skill and productivity of your carpenters, the design of the house and the weather will all affect the labor cost. Allow for these variables when they can be identified. Use your cost records as a guide. They're your best guide to labor costs for your jobs.

Earlier in this chapter we talked about comparing the cost of preassembled wall systems and conventional site-fabricated walls. Before finishing this chapter, we'll look at some labor costs for each kind of wall system and see how much more or less on-site framing costs.

Lumber size	Number of pieces	x	Factor	x	Price per MBF	=	Cost of lumber
2 x 4 x 8	806	x	.00533	x	$310.00	=	1,331.75
2 x 4 x 10	3	x	.00667	x	310.00	=	6.20
2 x 4 x 12	208	x	.0080	x	310.00	=	515.84
2 x 4 x 14		x	.00933	x		=	
2 x 4 x 16		x	.01067	x		=	
2 x 4 x 18		x	.0120	x		=	
2 x 4 x 20		x	.01333	x		=	
2 x 6 x 8	2	x	.0080	x	315.00	=	5.04
2 x 6 x 10	2	x	.0100	x	315.00	=	6.30
2 x 6 x 12	7	x	.0120	x	3.15.00	=	26.46
2 x 6 x 14		x	.0140	x		=	
2 x 6 x 16		x	.0160	x		=	
2 x 6 x 18		x	.0180	x		=	
2 x 6 x 20		x	.0200	x		=	
2 x 8 x 8	2	x	.01067	x	310.00	=	6.62
2 x 8 x 10		x	.01333	x		=	
2 x 8 x 12		x	.0160	x		=	
2 x 8 x 14		x	.01867	x		=	
2 x 8 x 16		x	.02133	x		=	
2 x 8 x 18		x	.0240	x		=	
2 x 8 x 20		x	.02667	x		=	
2 x 10 x 8		x	.01333	x		=	
2 x 10 x 10	4	x	.01667	x	330.00	=	22.00

Figure 5-21
Worksheet for cost of lumber priced by MBF

Lumber size	Number of pieces	x	Factor	x	Price per MBF	=	Cost of lumber
2 x 10 x 12		x	.0200	x		=	
2 x 10 x 14		x	.02333	x		=	
2 x 10 x 16		x	.02667	x		=	
2 x 10 x 18		x	.0300	x		=	
2 x 10 x 20		x	.03333	x		=	
2 x 12 x 8		x	.0160	x		=	
2 x 12 x 10		x	.0200	x		=	
2 x 12 x 12	*2*	x	.0240	x	*420.00*	=	*2016*
2 x 12 x 14		x	.0280	x		=	
2 x 12 x 16		x	.0320	x		=	
2 x 12 x 18		x	.0360	x		=	
2 x 12 x 20		x	.0400	x		=	

Total $1,941.19

Figure 5-21 (continued)
Worksheet for cost of lumber priced by MBF

Figures 5-22 and 5-23 are weekly time sheets for the Brown job. These time sheets show the manhours required to erect a preassembled wall system. Figures 5-24 and 5-25 are weekly time sheets for the Lawson job. They show the manhours required to erect a wall system assembled on the job site. Let's compare the labor for the two jobs.

The Preassembled Wall System

The Brown job was a two-story factory-built house. The exterior walls were preassembled in panels not exceeding 16 feet in length for the first floor, and 14 feet for the second floor. The wall sheathing and windows (except the large picture window) were already in place. The door openings were framed in. The upper top plates were shipped loose.

The interior wall panels had all doors framed in. The first floor had 1,230 square feet of living area. The second floor had 1,040 square feet.

The daily log shows that on September 17 it took 40 manhours to erect the outside and inside wall sections on the first floor. On September 20 another 40 manhours were required to place the upper plates. That's a total of 80 manhours to erect the exterior wall panels and place the upper top plates for the first floor.

On September 23, the carpenters spent 20 manhours erecting the outside wall panels on the second floor. The next day, they spent 36 manhours putting up the remaining exterior and interior wall panels and upper top plates. The wall sections were then ready for the roof trusses. For the second floor, it took a total of 56 manhours to erect the exterior and interior wall panels and place the upper top plates.

Page____of____pages

Weekly Time Sheet

For period ending _9-18-XX_ _____BROWN_____job

	Name	Exemptions	13 M	14 T	15 W	16 T	17 F	18 S	Rate	Reg.	Over-time	Total earnings
			SEPTEMBER Days							Hours worked		
1	C. A. LESTER		×	8	5½	3	8	×		24½		
2	D. L. WHITE		×	8	5½	3	8	×		24½		
3	A. L. KING		×	8	5½	2½	8	×		24		
4	J. E. KING		×	8	5½	2½	8	×		24		
5	W. R. FARLOW		×	8	5½	2½	×	×		16		
6	J. R. DAVIS		×	8	5½	2½	8	×		24		
7												
8												
9												
10												
11												
12												
13												
14												
15												
16												
17												
18												
19												
20												

Daily Log

Monday XXXX FACTORY-BUILT HOUSE DUE TOMORROW

Tuesday FLOOR SYSTEM ON 1ST FLOOR (48 MANHOURS)

Wednesday FINISHED SUBFLOOR ON 1ST FLOOR (33 MANHOURS)...1230 SF

Thursday UNLOADED 2ND TRAILER ... RAIN (16 MANHOURS)

Friday SET O/S AND I/S PARTITIONS ON 1ST FLOOR (1230 SF... 40 MANHOURS)

Saturday XXXX

Figure 5-22
Weekly time sheet — Brown job

Weekly Time Sheet

Page____of____pages

For period ending **9-25-XX**   **BROWN**   job

	Name	Exemptions	Days SEPTEMBER						Rate	Hours worked		Total earnings
			20 M	21 T	22 W	23 T	24 F	25 S		Reg.	Over-time	
1	C.A. LESTER		8	8	8	8	8	x		40		
2	D.L. WHITE		8	8	8	8	8	x		40		
3	A.L. KING		8	8	8	8	4	x		36		
4	W.R. FARLOW		8	8	4	4	8	x		32		
5	J.R. DAVIS		8	8	8	8	8	x		40		
6	R.R. LEWIS		x	8	4	4	8	x		24		
7												
8												
9												
10												
11												
12												
13												
14												
15												
16												
17												
18												
19												
20												

Daily Log

Monday *TOP PLATES ON 1ST FLOOR PARTITIONS (40 MANHOURS)*
Tuesday *SET BEAMS AND STARTED FLOOR JOISTS ON 2ND FLOOR (48 MANHOURS)*
Wednesday *FINISHED FLOOR JOISTS AND BRIDGING ON 2ND FLOOR (40 MANHOURS)*
Thursday *FINISHED SUBFLOOR (20 MNHRS ON 2ND FLOOR)* 1040 SF *.. O/S PARTITIONS (20 MNHRS)*
Friday *FINISHED O/S AND I/S PARTITIONS ON 2ND FLOOR (36 MNHRS.)* 1040 SF *ROOF*
Saturday *XXXX*   *TRUSSES (8 MHRS)*

Figure 5-23
Weekly time sheet — Brown job

Weekly Time Sheet

Page____of____pages

For period ending **3-3-XX**   **LAWSON** job

	Name	Exemptions	FEB 26 M	27 T	28 W	MAR 1 T	2 F	3 S	Rate	Reg.	Over-time	Total earnings
			Days							**Hours worked**		
1	R·R· LEWIS		8	X	8	8	8	X		32		
2	C·A· LESTER		2	X	8	X	X	X		10		
3	O·L· WHITE		2	X	X	X	X	X		2		
4	R·C· JONES		8	X	8	8	8	X		32		
5	J·R· DAVIS		8	Y	X	X	8	X		16		
6												
7												
8												
9												
10												
11												
12												
13												
14												
15												
16												
17												
18												
19												
20												

Daily Log

Monday *FINISHED SUBFLOOR 1,682 SF (14 MANHOURS)... O/S PLATES (14 MANHOURS)*
Tuesday *RAIN*   *(16 MHRS)*
Wednesday *CHANGED BASEMENT STAIR OPENING (8 MANHOURS) LAID OUT ROOMS*
Thursday *LAID OUT WINDOWS AND DOORS, CUT STUDS FOR CORNER POSTS & TEES (16 MNHRS.)*
Friday *ASSEMBLED AND PLACED O/S AND I/S WALLS AND PARTITIONS (24 MANHOURS.)*
Saturday *XXXX*

Figure 5-24
Weekly time sheet — Lawson job

Weekly Time Sheet

For period ending *3-10-XX*   *LAWSON*   job

	Name	Exemptions	Days MARCH						Rate	Hours worked		Total earnings
			5 M	6 T	7 W	8 T	9 F	10 S		Reg.	Over-time	
1	R.R. LEWIS		6	8	7	8	8	X		37		
2	C.A. LESTER		7	4	5½	8	8	X		32½		
3	R.C. JONES		6	8	7	8	8	X		37		
4	J.R. DAVIS		X	4	5½	8	8	X		25½		
5	D.L. WHITE		X	4	5½	8	8	X		25½		
6												
7												
8												
9												
10												
11												
12												
13												
14												
15												
16												
17												
18												
19												
20												

Daily Log

Monday *RAIN UNTIL 10 A.M., FRAMED IN WINDOWS (19 MANHOURS)*
Tuesday *FINISHED FRAMING IN WINDOW AND DOORS ... TOP PLATES (28 MANHOURS)*
Wednesday *INSTALLED WALL SHEATHING (30½ MANHOURS) 1,682 SF FLOOR AREA.*
Thursday *ROOF TRUSSES (40 MANHOURS)*
Friday *FINISHED ROOF TRUSSES (10 MANHOURS)... STARTED ROOF SHEATHING (30 MNHRS.)*
Saturday *XXXX*

Figure 5-25
Weekly time sheet — Lawson job

Total manhours	÷	Floor area (square feet)	=	Manhour factor
1st floor 80	÷	1,230	=	.06504
2nd floor 56	÷	1,040	=	.05385

A Preassembled wall system

Total manhours	÷	Floor area (square feet)	=	Manhour factor
147.5	÷	1,682	=	.08769

B On-site wall system

Figure 5-26
Wall system labor worksheet

We've seen how many manhours were required to erect the preassembled wall system for the first and second floors on the Brown job. Now let's use this information to compute the manhour factors for a preassembled wall system. We'll use these manhour factors to estimate wall system labor for future jobs.

Manhour factors for a preassembled wall system— Figure 5-26 is a labor worksheet we'll use to find the manhour factors for both wall systems. First, the Brown job:

In the first column, enter the total manhours required to erect the preassembled wall system. The first floor took 80 manhours. The second floor required 56 manhours.

In the next column, enter the floor area (in square feet). The first floor had 1,230 SF of floor area. The second floor had 1,040 SF.

Now divide the total manhours (80 and 56) by the total floor areas (1,230 SF and 1,040 SF) to get the manhour factors. The manhour factor for the first floor is 0.06504. The factor for the second floor is 0.05385.

Notice that the manhour factor for the second floor is 17.2% less than the manhour factor for the first floor. Why? Because there are more partitions on the first floor, and the second floor layout is simpler.

Use these manhour factors as a guide to future estimates. To find the number of manhours required for your new job, just multiply the manhour factor (for each floor) by the number of square feet of floor area.

The On-Site Wall System
Look back to Figures 5-24 and 5-25. The weekly time sheets on the Lawson job show the manhours required to erect an on-site wall system. This job was a custom-built, one-story house. All of the framing lumber for the exterior and interior walls was cut and assembled on the job. The house had 1,682 SF of living area.

The daily log shows that on February 26 it took 14 manhours to place the sole plates for the outside walls. The next day it rained and no work was done. On the 28th, carpenters spent 16 manhours laying out the rooms and installing the sole plates. On March 1, they spent another 16 manhours to lay out the windows and doors, cut the studs and assemble the corner posts and ties. On Friday, March 2, carpenters assembled and placed the outside and inside wall panels. This required 24 manhours.

On March 5, it rained until 10:00 a.m. After that, the crew spent 19 manhours framing the windows. On March 6, 28 manhours were required to finish framing the windows and doors and install top plates. On Wednesday, the crew spent 30½ manhours installing wall sheathing.

This work on the Lawson job required a total of 147½ manhours. Now let's find the manhour factor for an on-site wall system.

Manhour factors for the on-site wall system— Look at Figure 5-26, section B. In the first column, enter the total manhours. In our example, this comes to 147.5. In the next column, enter the total SF of floor area. Then divide the total manhours (147.5) by the total SF of floor area (1,682). The manhour factor for the on-site wall system is 0.08769. You may recall that the manhour factor for erecting the preassembled wall system on the first floor of the Brown job was 0.06504. The factor for the Lawson job is 34.8% higher than that. The preassembled wall system required less labor.

Sample Comparison of Wall System Costs

We've seen how to use our cost records as a guide to easy, accurate wall system estimates. Now let's apply what we've learned.

We'll look at a one-story house with 2,270 SF of floor area. We'll compare the materials and labor for a preassembled wall system and the materials and labor for an on-site wall system.

Preassembled Wall System

First figure your material costs. Then compute your labor costs.

Materials— The materials for a preassembled wall system are the same as the materials for an on-site wall system, except that wall sheathing is usually fastened with staples instead of nails.

For our sample house with 2,270 SF of floor area, the wall system manufacturer looks at our plans and quotes a price of $4,175.00. This includes:

1) Openings for windows and doors already cut out (but no windows or doors are furnished).

2) Sheathing of 4' x 8' fiberboard, except corners. Corners are made of 1/2'' x 4' x 8' C-D plywood.

3) Delivery of the wall system to the job site.

Our total cost for materials for the preassembled wall system comes to $4,175.00 plus sales tax where required.

Labor— To estimate the labor required to erect the preassembled wall system, multiply the first floor manhour factor from Figure 5-26 A (0.06504) by the floor area (2,270 SF) to get 147.64 manhours. Round up to 148. Multiply the total manhours (148) by the hourly wage rate ($25.00) and you have $3,700.00. This is your labor estimate for the preassembled wall system.

The total cost for materials and labor for the preassembled wall system is:

Materials $4,175.00
Labor 3,700.00
Total. $7,875.00

On-Site Wall System

Materials— Now let's look at the cost for the materials for our sample on-site wall system.

> Framing lumber (see Figure 5-21) $1,940.37
> Wall sheathing
>   70 - ½" x 4' x 8' Fiberboard
>   20 - ½" x 4' x 8' C-D plywood
>   Total for wall sheathing 435.50
> Nails 74.80
>
>   Total $2,450.67

Labor— To estimate labor for the on-site wall system, multiply the on-site manhour factor (0.08769) by the floor area (2,270 SF) to get 199.06 manhours. Round this down to 199. Multiply 199 manhours by the wage rate per hour (in this example $25.00). The answer is $4,975.00. This is your labor estimate for the on-site wall system.

Our total cost for materials and labor for the on-site wall system is:

> Materials $2,450.67
> Labor 4,975.00
>
>   Total $7,425.67

Now let's compare the two wall systems.

> Cost for preassembled wall system $7,875.00
> Cost for on-site wall system $7,425.67

So for our sample one-story house with a total floor area of 2,270 SF, it will be cheaper to frame the walls on site.

But here's a factor you shouldn't overlook: Labor for wall framing can increase from 5% to 15% in cold weather. This could tip the balance in favor of preassembled walls.

Wall framing is only one part of the job. But combine a few hundred dollars saved here and a few hundred saved there and the total savings can be major. That can make the difference between success and just surviving in the construction industry. Take advantage of savings like this to build your profits and reputation as a progressive, cost-conscious builder.

In the next chapter, I'll suggest ways to accumulate savings on roof framing materials and labor.

Estimating Roof Systems

In this chapter we'll compare the two roof framing methods: roof trusses and conventional ceiling joists and rafters. Then we'll compare conventional roof framing with roof truss framing. Finally, we'll look at roof sheathing and roof covering. Along the way I've included some tables and worksheets that can help you make quick, accurate roof framing estimates.

Roof System Materials

Roof framing includes roof trusses or ceiling joists and rafters, sheathing, roof covering, and nails. We'll take a look at each part separately.

But first a word of advice: Use roof trusses whenever possible. They cut your costs because they go up much faster than ceiling joists and rafters built stick by stick. The labor savings can be considerable. Of course, it's not always possible to use roof trusses. Unusual roof design or an uncommon pitch may make conventional ceiling joists and rafters the only practical alternative. And in some communities roof trusses are not available at reasonable cost. That's why we'll cover both conventional framing and roof trusses in detail.

Roof Trusses

Roof trusses are a framework of individual structural members fabricated into one unit. They're designed to span the distance between walls without intermediate support.

All roof trusses must be designed by a qualified engineer or architect. The maximum spacing of roof trusses is determined by the anticipated load. That includes the sheathing material above the truss and the finish ceiling material underneath.

Trusses are available in a variety of sizes and shapes (Figure 6-1) and can be used for long or short spans, such as the roof over a porch, walk or breezeway. All trusses must be connected with metal plate connectors or nail-glued plywood gussets. Figure 6-2 shows the plywood gussets required on a 26' W truss.

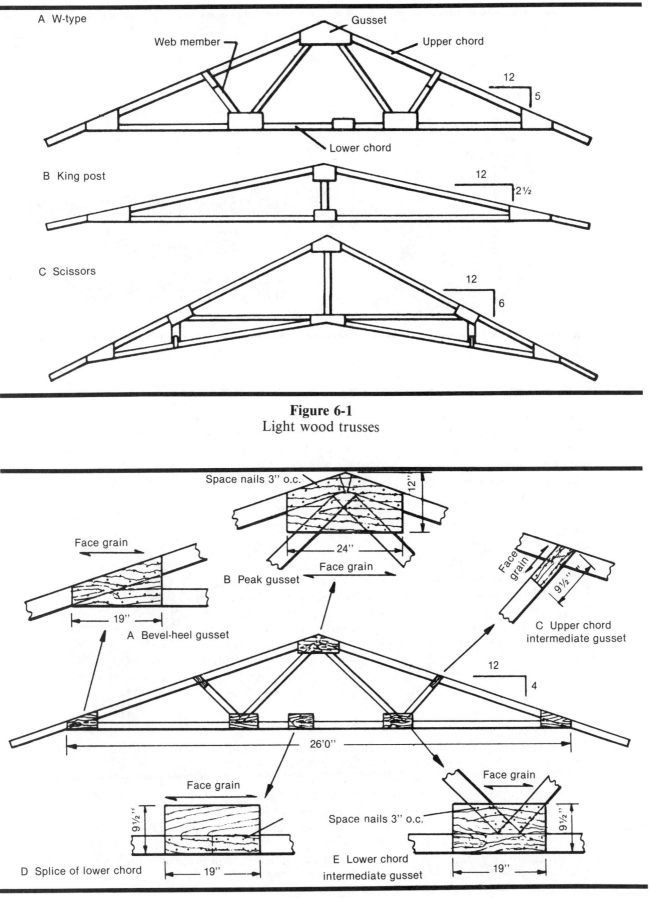

A W-type

Gusset

Web member

Upper chord

12

5

Lower chord

B King post

12

2½

C Scissors

12

6

Figure 6-1
Light wood trusses

Space nails 3" o.c.

12"

Face grain

24"

Face grain

B Peak gusset

Face grain

9½"

C Upper chord
intermediate gusset

19"

A Bevel-heel gusset

12

4

26'0"

Face grain

9½"

D Splice of lower chord

19"

Space nails 3" o.c.

9½"

E Lower chord
intermediate gusset

19"

Figure 6-2
Plywood gussets on a W truss

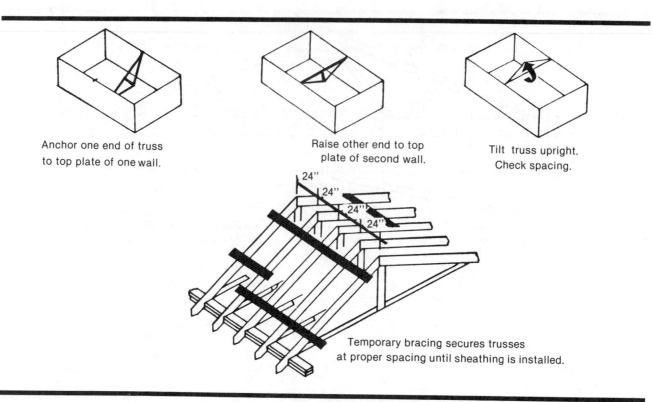

Anchor one end of truss to top plate of one wall.

Raise other end to top plate of second wall.

Tilt truss upright. Check spacing.

Temporary bracing secures trusses at proper spacing until sheathing is installed.

Figure 6-3
Installation of truss assemblies

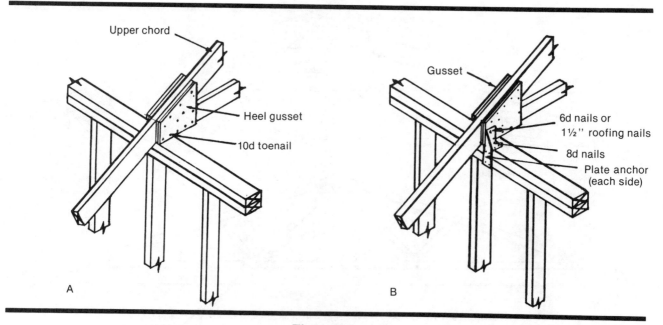

Upper chord

Heel gusset

10d toenail

A

Gusset

6d nails or 1½" roofing nails

8d nails

Plate anchor (each side)

B

Figure 6-4
Fastening trusses to wall plate

Figure 6-3 shows how to erect the truss assemblies. Toenail the heel joint of the truss to the wall plate with two 8d or 10d nails on each side. In areas subject to high winds (30 psf or over), provide additional anchorage by installing an 18 gauge galvanized metal strap (Figure 6-4).

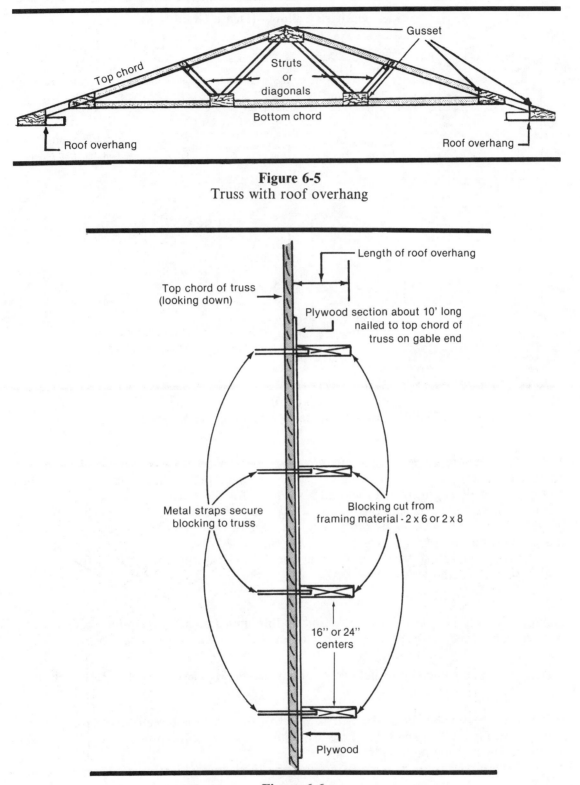

Figure 6-5
Truss with roof overhang

Figure 6-6
Fabricated gable roof overhang

The bottom chord of the truss acts as a ceiling joist; the top chord acts as a rafter. You can fabricate a roof overhang at the eave as shown in Figure 6-5. Cut blocking for the gable roof overhang from 2 x 6 or 2 x 8 framing and use it in the overhang at 16'' centers or 24'' centers. You can fabricate them in sections about 10' long and fasten them to the top chord of the truss with metal straps (Figure 6-6).

Pine, Southern Yellow - (Dense Grain)

Nominal size (inches)	Spacing (inches o.c.)	No. 1 Den. K.D. 2" Dim.		No. 2 Den. K.D. 2" Dim.		No. 3 Den. K.D. 2" Dim.		No. 1 Den. 2" Dim.		No. 2 Den. 2" Dim.		No. 3 Den. 2" Dim.		No. 1 Den. K.D. 2" Dim.		No. 2 Den. K.D. 2" Dim.		No. 3 Den. K.D. 2" Dim.		No. 1 Den. 2" Dim.		No. 2 Den. 2" Dim.		No. 3 Den. 2" Dim.	
		2000 f		1750 f		--		1700 f		1400 f		--		2000 f		1750 f		--		1700 f		1400 f		--	
		Ceiling Joists																							
		No Attic Storage												**Limited Attic Storage**											
		Ft.	In.	Ft.	In.	Ft.	In.	Ft.	In.	Ft.	In.	Ft.	In.	Ft.	In.	Ft.	In.	Ft.	In.	Ft.	In.	Ft.	In.	Ft.	In.
2 x 4	12	11	10	11	10	11	10	11	10	11	10	11	2	9	6	9	6	8	8	9	6	9	6	7	10
	16	10	10	10	10	10	10	10	10	10	10	9	6	8	6	8	6	7	6	8	6	8	6	6	10
	24	9	6	9	6	8	8	9	6	9	6	7	10	7	6	7	6	6	2	7	6	7	6	5	6
2 x 6 [1]	12	17	2	17	2	17	2	17	2	17	2	16	10	14	4	14	4	13	4	14	4	14	4	11	10
	16	16	0	16	0	16	0	16	0	16	0	14	8	13	0	13	0	11	6	13	0	13	0	10	4
	24	14	4	14	4	13	4	14	4	14	4	11	10	11	4	11	4	9	6	11	4	11	4	8	6
2 x 8	12	21	8	21	8	21	8	21	8	21	8	21	8	18	4	18	4	18	2	18	4	18	4	16	2
	16	20	2	20	2	20	2	20	2	20	2	19	10	17	0	17	0	15	8	17	0	17	0	14	0
	24	18	4	18	4	18	2	18	4	18	4	16	2	15	4	15	4	12	10	15	4	15	4	11	6
2 x 10	12	24	0	24	0	24	0	24	0	24	0	24	0	21	10	21	10	21	10	21	10	21	10	20	8
	16	24	0	24	0	24	0	24	0	24	0	24	0	20	4	20	4	20	0	20	4	20	4	17	10
	24	21	10	21	10	21	10	21	10	21	10	20	8	18	4	18	4	16	4	18	4	18	4	14	6

[1] Spans for 2" x 6" lumber having actual dressed size of 1⅝" x 5⅝" may be increased 2½%.

Note: (a) Spans may be increased 5% from those shown for rough lumber or lumber surfaced two edges (S2E).

(b) Spans shall be decreased 5% from those shown for lumber more than 2% but not more than 5% scant from American Lumber Standards size measured at a moisture content of 19% or less. Lumber scant more than 5% will not be acceptable.

Figure 6-7
Ceiling joist span table — Southern Yellow Pine

Estimating the number of trusses— Roof trusses are spaced 24" o.c. To calculate the number of trusses, first find the length of the wall that's perpendicular to the truss. Then multiply the wall length by 0.50, and add one truss for the starter.

For example, let's calculate the number of trusses required for a house with a 40' wall length. Multiply the wall length (40') by 0.50 to get 20 trusses. Add one truss for the starter. This house will require a total of 21 roof trusses.

If the roof line is broken into more than one section, calculate the trusses for each section separately and total them.

Ceiling Joists

Ceiling joists support the ceiling finish and and are not designed to support floor loads. If more than limited attic storage is expected over the ceiling joists, floor joists are required.

Here are some guidelines to help determine whether you need ceiling or floor joists:

1) Where the clear height of the attic is 5 feet or less, use the table titled "No Attic Storage" in Figures 6-7 and 6-8. These are span tables for ceiling joists made from Southern Yellow Pine or Douglas Fir.

2) Where the clear height of the attic is over 5 feet and a stair is not provided, use the table called "Limited Attic Storage" in Figure 6-7 or 6-8.

3) Where a permanent or folding stairway is provided, use the span tables for floor joists at the end of Chapter 4.

Douglas Fir - Coast Region

Nominal size (inches)	Spacing (inches o.c.)	Select Structural J & P 1950 f	Dense Construction J & P 1700 f	Construction J & P 1450 f	Standard J & P 1200 f	Utility J & P (¹)	Select Structural J & P 1950 f	Dense Construction J & P 1700 f	Construction J & P 1450 f	Standard J & P 1200 f	Utility J & P (¹)
		Ceiling Joists									
		No Attic Storage					**Limited Attic Storage**				
		Ft. In.	Ft. In.	Ft. In.	Ft. In.	Ft. In.	Ft. In.	Ft. In.	Ft. In.	Ft. In.	Ft. In.
2 x 4²	12	11 10	-- --	11 8	8 10	-- --	9 6	-- --	8 2	6 4	-- --
	16	10 10	-- --	10 0	7 8	-- --	8 6	-- --	7 2	5 6	-- --
	24	9 6	-- --	8 2	6 4	-- --	7 6	-- --	5 10	4 6	-- --
2 x 6	12	17 2	17 2	17 2	17 2	13 6	14 4	14 4	14 4	14 4	9 6
	16	16 0	16 0	16 0	16 0	11 8	13 0	13 0	13 0	12 10	8 4
	24	14 4	14 4	14 4	14 4	9 6	11 4	11 4	11 4	10 6	6 8
2 x 8	12	21 8	21 8	21 8	21 8	20 2	18 4	18 4	18 4	18 4	14 4
	16	20 2	20 2	20 2	20 2	17 6	17 0	17 0	17 0	17 0	12 4
	24	18 4	18 4	18 4	18 4	14 4	15 4	15 4	15 4	14 4	10 0
2 x 10	12	24 0	24 0	24 0	24 0	24 0	21 10	21 10	21 10	21 10	19 6
	16	24 0	24 0	24 0	24 0	22 6	20 4	20 4	20 4	20 4	16 10
	24	21 10	21 10	21 10	21 10	19 6	18 4	18 4	18 4	18 0	13 10

¹Denotes grade is not a stresss grade.
²Denotes light framing grade. (Not Industrial Light Framing).
Notes: (a) Spans may be increased 5% from those shown for rough lumber or lumber surfaced two edges (S2E).
(b) Spans shall be decreased 5% from those shown for lumber more than 2% but not more than 5% scant from American Lumber Standards size measured at a moisture content of 19% or less. Lumber scant more than 5% will not be acceptable.

Figure 6-8
Ceiling joist span table — Douglas Fir

To secure the joists, lap or butt the ends of ceiling joists over a bearing partition or beam, and toenail them to the bearing with four 10d nails in each pair of joists. See Figure 6-9 A.

When ceiling joists are used to provide resistance to rafter thrust, nail the joists together as in Figure 6-9 B.

The floor plan will show the size, spacing and direction the ceiling joists will run. Normally, the designer of the house will calculate the size and spacing shown on the plans. If the plans aren't clear, use Figures 6-7 and 6-8 as your guide. You can find the length of the joists and the direction they run by looking at the dimensions of the rooms on the floor plans. The joists usually run across the shorter span.

Ceiling joists seldom span the entire width of the building as trusses do. The direction they run will vary. Figure 6-10 shows a typical house plan with joists running in different directions. When estimating these joists, estimate each section separately.

Estimating ceiling joists is the same for hip or gable roofs, but the layout is different. In a hip roof, the run of the regular joists must stop short of the outside wall so the hip and jack rafters can clear them. Short ceiling joists are installed perpendicular to the regular joists as fillers to allow the rafters to reach the outside wall plate (Figure 6-11).

Estimate ceiling joists the same way you estimated floor joists:

Multiply the linear feet of the wall by 0.75 and add one joist for the starter if the spacing is 16" o.c. If the spacing is 24" o.c. multiply the linear feet of the wall by 0.50. Then add one joist for the starter.

Rafters
Size and spacing of the rafters must provide enough strength to support the roof covering and anyone walking on the roof. The building plans should show the intended size and spacing of rafters.

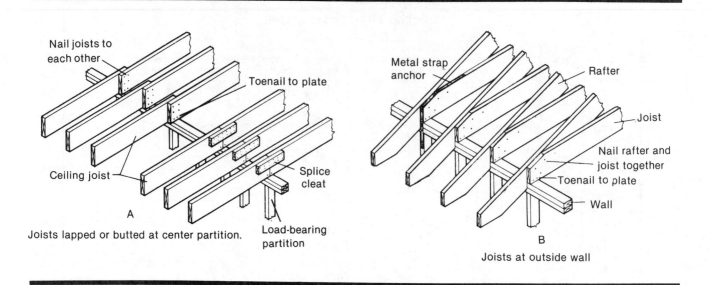

Figure 6-9
Ceiling joist connections

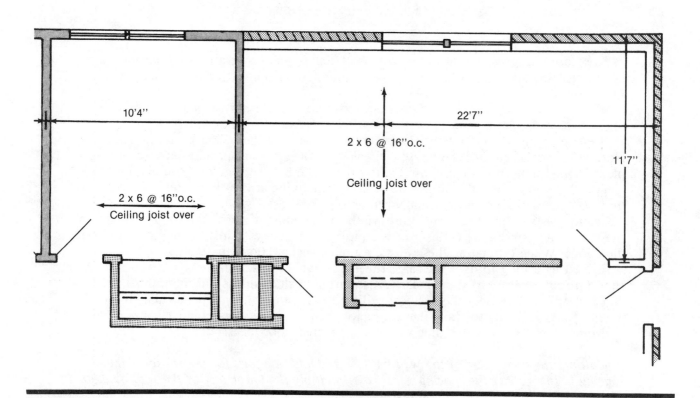

Figure 6-10
Ceiling joists running two directions

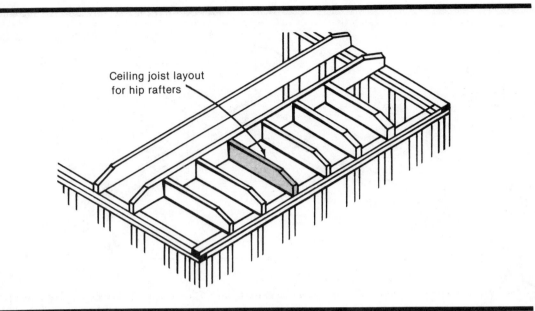

Figure 6-11
Ceiling joists for hip roof

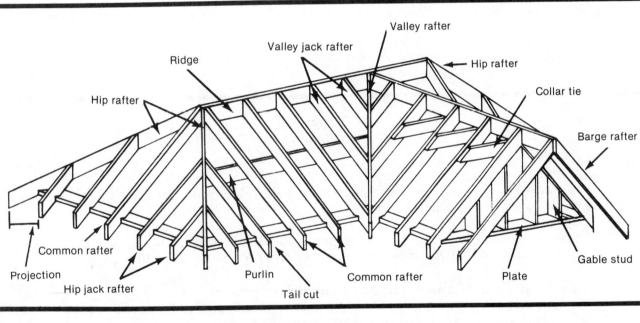

Figure 6-12
Types of rafters

Names for roof framing members are shown in Figure 6-12.

Estimating the material for rafters is more complicated than estimating the ceiling joists. On a sloped roof, rafters will always be longer than the ceiling joists that span the same distance. The steeper the slope, the longer the rafters must be.

Some builders scale rafter lengths off the elevation view of the blueprints. But blueprints sometimes shrink, making the scaled distance inaccurate. And on some jobs, you won't have a good elevation view for the entire roof.

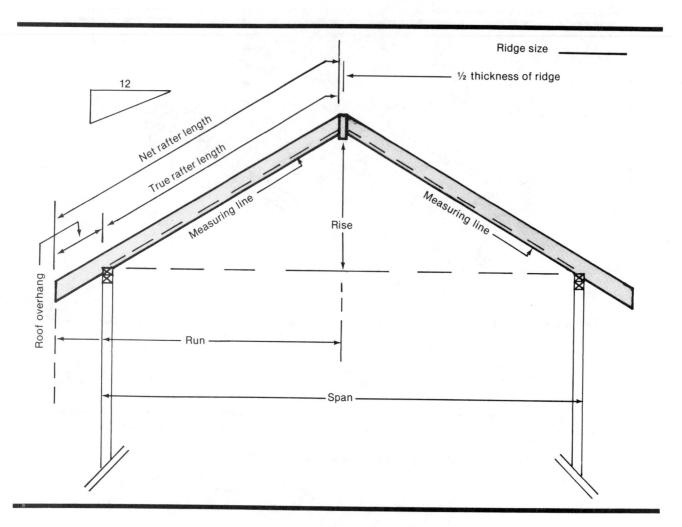

Figure 6-13
Common rafter terms

Let's look at the easy way to compute rafter lengths. We'll consider common rafters, hip and valley rafters, and shed roof rafters.

Common rafters— Figure 6-13 shows the terms you'll need to know to calculate the lengths of common rafters: *span, run, rise, true rafter length* and *net rafter length*.

Span: The distance between supporting members of the roof.

Run: One-half the span. For rafters with an overhang, the run includes the distance from the wall to the tail cut of the rafter.

Rise: The vertical distance from the plate line to the top of the measuring line (sloping dotted line).

True rafter length: The distance between the face of the ridge and the tail cut.

Net rafter length: The true rafter length plus the overhang, or the total length of the rafter.

Roof pitch	Run	x	Run factor	— (minus)	Factor for ½ thickness of ridge *	=	True rafter length **
1/12		x	1.00347	-	.06250	=	
1½/12		x	1.00778	-	.06250	=	
2/12		x	1.01379	-	.06250	=	
2½/12		x	1.02147	-	.06250	=	
3/12		x	1.03078	-	.06250	=	
3½/12	13.0'	x	1.04167	-	.06250	=	13.479' (13' 5¾")
4/12		x	1.05409	-	.06250	=	
5/12	12.573'	x	1.08333	-	.06250	=	13.558' (13' 6¹¹⁄₁₆")
6/12		x	1.11803	-	.06250	=	
7/12		x	1.15770	-	.06250	=	
8/12		x	1.20185	-	.06250	=	
9/12		x	1.25000	-	.06250	=	

*When ridge is 2" nominal framing (2 x 6's, 2 x 8's, etc.)
**True rafter length plus roof overhang equals net rafter length

Figure 6-14
Factors for common rafters

Now look at Figure 6-14. This is a factor table for cutting common rafters. You'll like the way it simplifies calculations. Here's how it works:

Suppose the roof pitch is 3½" of rise per 12" of run, and the span of the building is 26'0". The run will be one-half the span, or 13'0" (13.0').

Look down the first column to find the correct pitch (3½/12). In the next column, enter the run (13.0"). Multiply the run by the run factor (1.04167). Then subtract the ridge thickness factor (0.06250). This leaves 13.479' for the true rafter length.

To find the equivalent measurement in feet and inches, refer to Figure 6-15, a table of decimal equivalents of fractional parts of a foot. It's easy to use.

The first three columns show fractions of an inch. The first column shows 1/4", 1/2" and 3/4". The second column shows eighths of an inch: 1/8", 2/8", 3/8", up through 7/8". The third column shows sixteenths of an inch: 1/16", 2/16", 3/16", up through 15/16". The remaining columns show whole inches, from 0" through 11". Let's try a sample calculation.

In our example above, the true rafter length comes to 13.479'. Now look at Figure 6-15. Find 0.479, and read up the column to the whole-inch number at the top (5"). Look again at 0.479 in the table. Now read across the column to the fractional inch number at the far left (3 in the 4th column, indicating 3/4"). This table shows us that 0.479' is the same as 5¾". And our true rafter length is the equivalent of 13'5¾".

The plans probably show the roof overhang in inches measured horizontally from the exterior wall. The extra rafter length needed to produce this overhang will always be more than the horizontal distance. Compute the net rafter length by adding the run of the roof overhang to the run of the house. Then multiply the total run factor and subtract the ridge thickness factor. This gives you the net rafter length, including overhang.

4th	8th	16th	0"	1"	2"	3"	4"	5"	6"	7"	8"	9"	10"	11"
		0	.000	.083	.167	.250	.333	.417	.500	.583	.667	.750	.833	.917
		1	.005	.089	.172	.255	.339	.422	.505	.589	.672	.755	.839	.922
	1	2	.010	.094	.177	.260	.344	.427	.510	.594	.677	.760	.844	.927
		3	.016	.099	.182	.266	.349	.432	.516	.599	.682	.766	.849	.932
1	2	4	.021	.104	.188	.271	.354	.438	.521	.604	.688	.771	.854	.938
		5	.026	.109	.193	.276	.359	.443	.526	.609	.693	.776	.859	.943
	3	6	.031	.115	.198	.281	.365	.448	.531	.615	.698	.781	.865	.948
		7	.036	.118	.203	.286	.370	.453	.536	.620	.703	.786	.870	.953
2	4	8	.042	.125	.208	.292	.375	.458	.542	.625	.708	.792	.875	.958
		9	.047	.130	.213	.297	.380	.464	.547	.630	.714	.797	.880	.964
	5	10	.052	.135	.219	.302	.386	.469	.552	.635	.719	.802	.885	.969
		11	.057	.141	.224	.307	.391	.474	.557	.641	.724	.807	.891	.974
3	6	12	.063	.146	.229	.313	.396	.479	.563	.646	.729	.813	.896	.979
		13	.068	.151	.234	.318	.401	.484	.568	.651	.734	.818	.901	.984
	7	14	.073	.156	.240	.323	.406	.490	.573	.656	.740	.823	.906	.989
		15	.078	.161	.245	.328	.411	.495	.578	.661	.745	.828	.911	.995

Example: 8¼" = .688'

Figure 6-15
Decimal equivalents of fractional parts of a foot

For example, say the roof pitch is 3½'' for each 12'' run. The house run (to the exterior face of the wall) is 13'0'', and the horizontal roof overhang is 1'0''. The total run is 14'0'' (14.0'). Multiply 14.0' by the run factor (1.04167) to get 14.583'. Subtract the ridge factor (0.06250) to get a net rafter length of 14.521'. To convert this to feet and inches, refer to Figure 6-15. The net rafter length is 14'6¼''.

Of course, not all spans are given in even feet. Usually the span will be given in feet, inches and fractional parts of an inch. For example, let's say a building has a roof pitch of 5 in 12 and a span of 25'1¾'' (25.146'). The run of this span will be 12'6⅞'' (12.573'). Use the table of equivalents shown in Figure 6-15 to make your decimal conversions.

To calculate the true rafter length for this example, multiply the run (12.573') by the run factor (1.08333) to get 13.621'. Subtract the ridge thickness factor (0.06250) to get a true rafter length of 13.558' (13'6¹¹⁄₁₆'').

If the plans show the run of the roof overhang to be 2'5'' (2.417'), compute the net rafter length by adding the run of the roof overhang (2'5'') to the run of the house (12'6⅞''). This gives a total run of 14'11⅞'' (14.990'). Multiply the total run (14.990') by the run factor (1.08333) to get 16.239'. Then subtract the ridge thickness factor (0.06250) to get a net rafter length of 16.177' (16'2⅛'').

Hip and valley rafters— Hip and valley rafters run from the ridge to the plate at a 45-degree angle, ending at an outside corner. Valley rafters also run from the ridge to the plate at a 45-degree angle, but end at an inside corner. See Figure 6-12.

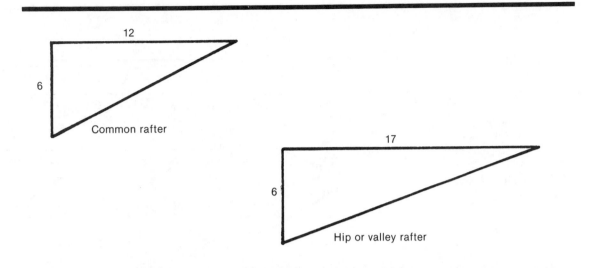

Figure 6-16
Rise in common and hip rafters

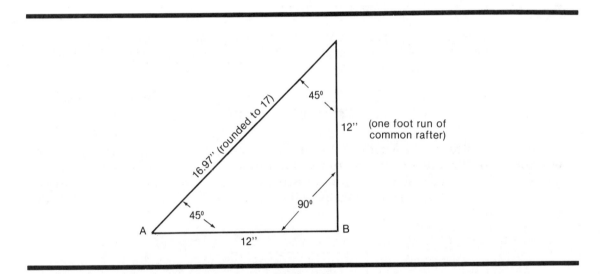

Figure 6-17
The hypotenuse of a right triangle

You remember that the roof pitch of common rafters is designated as the inches of rise per foot of run. Hip and valley rafters are designated as inches of rise per 17" of run. The number 17 is to the hip and valley rafter as 12 is to the common rafter.

Figure 6-16 shows the symbols used on most plans to indicate the rise of common and hip rafters. It's easy to understand why common rafter rise is indicated in inches per foot of run. But where did the 17" come from? Easy, if you remember any of your high school trigonometry. It's the hypotenuse of a right triangle with equal sides 12" long. Because the two sides of the triangle are equal, the angles are 45 degrees.

Hip and valley rafters run at 45-degree angles to the common rafters, so they in effect form the hypotenuse of a right triangle. Figure 6-17 shows the triangle with 12" sides.

Maybe you remember the Pythagorean theorem from high school math: The square of the hypotenuse of a right triangle equals the sum of the squares of the other two sides.

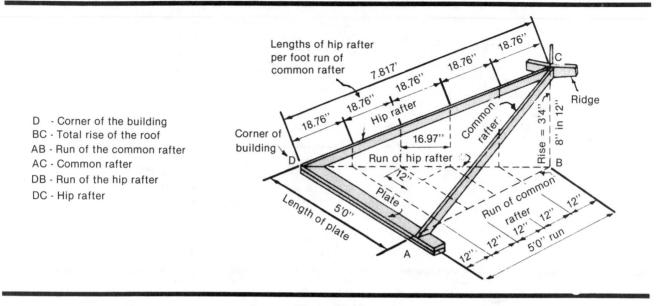

D - Corner of the building
BC - Total rise of the roof
AB - Run of the common rafter
AC - Common rafter
DB - Run of the hip rafter
DC - Hip rafter

Figure 6-18
Finding hip rafter length

Don't worry if you don't remember that, or even if you didn't take math in high school. You can still cut rafters to the right length, Pythagoras or not. But just in case you want to remember, here's the formula:

$$\sqrt{12^2 + 12^2} = 16.97$$

Because you calculate the length of the hip rafter per foot run of the common rafter, you'll use 17" instead of 12" for the run on hip rafters.

Look at Figure 6-18. It shows a hip rafter with an 8 in 12 rise, and a common rafter run of 5'0". We'll use the theorem again to find the hip rafter length per foot of run of the common rafter:

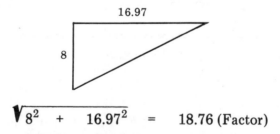

$$\sqrt{8^2 + 16.97^2} = 18.76 \text{ (Factor)}$$

So 18.76 is the factor you use to find the length of a hip or valley rafter with an 8" rise.

The length of a hip or valley rafter equals the run of the common rafter times the factor.

You'll find the per-foot factors for other rises in Figure 6-19. It also has factors per foot of run for common rafters and the length of jack rafters.

For the hip rafter shown in Figure 6-18, here's the calculation:

$$5.0' \times 18.76 = 93.8"$$
$$93.8" \div 12" = 7.817'$$

Pitch of Roof	Common Rafters: Length for each foot of run in inches	Jack Rafters: Length of shortest jack on 16 inch centers	Jack Rafters: Length of shortest jack on 24 inch centers	Hip and Valley Rafters: Length for each foot of run of common rafters in inches
12 ⌐				
1/12	12.042			
1½/12	12.093			
2/12	12.166			
2½/12	12.258			
3/12	12.369	16.485	24.740	17.234
3½/12	12.500	16.659	25.001	17.328
4/12	12.649	16.858	25.299	17.436
5/12	13.000	17.326	26.001	17.692
6/12	13.416	17.880	26.833	18.000
7/12	13.892	18.516	27.786	18.358
8/12	14.422	19.222	28.845	18.762
9/12	15.000	19.991	29.999	19.209
10/12	15.620	20.820	31.242	19.698
11/12	16.279	21.697	32.558	20.224
12/12	16.971	22.620	33.942	20.785

Figure 6-19
Rafter factors per foot run

Roof pitch	Run of common rafter	x	Factor	=	Length of hip or valley rafter (*)
3/12		x	1.43614	=	
3½/12		x	1.44398	=	
4/12		x	1.45297	=	
5/12		x	1.47432	=	
6/12		x	1.50000	=	
7/12		x	1.52980	=	
8/12	14.0'	x	1.56347	=	21.889' (21' 10 ¹¹/₁₆")
9/12		x	1.60078	=	
10/12		x	1.64148	=	
11/12		x	1.68531	=	
12/12		x	1.73205	=	

*Add the rafter overhang to this length.

Figure 6-20
Factors for hip and valley rafters

Now add the rafter overhang to find the net hip rafter length. Figure 6-20 is a factor table for computing the length of hip and valley rafters. It'll help simplify your calculations.

Let's say the roof has a pitch of 8 in 12 and a common rafter run of 14.0'. Look

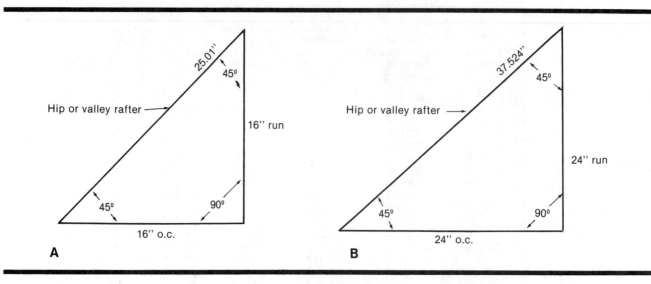

Figure 6-21
Hip or valley rafters spaced 16'' and 24'' o.c.

down the first column to find the correct pitch (8/12). In the next column, enter the run of the common rafter (14.0'). Multiply the run of the common rafter (14.0'') by the factor (1.56347) to get a hip or valley rafter length of 21.889' (21'10$\frac{1}{16}$''). This is the length of the hip or valley rafter to the plate.

If there's an overhang, be sure to include it in your calculation. If the run of the common rafter overhang is 2'0'', the total common rafter will be 16'0'' (14'0'' plus the 2'0'' overhang). Multiply the total run (16.0') by the factor for an 8/12 pitch (1.56347). This gives a net hip or valley rafter length of 25.016', or 25'0$\frac{3}{16}$''. Use Figure 6-15 for the decimal conversions.

Jack rafters— Any rafter that doesn't extend from the plate to the ridge is called a jack rafter. Look back at Figure 6-12. There are three kinds of jack rafters:

- Hip jacks, which run from the hip rafter to the plate

- Valley jacks, which run from the valley rafter to the ridge

- Cripple jacks, which run from a hip rafter to a valley rafter

Figure 6-19 shows the length of the shortest jack rafter on both 16'' and 24'' centers for different roof pitches. Let's look at a couple more triangles to see where these numbers come from. Diagram A in Figure 6-21 shows a hip or valley rafter spaced 16'' o.c., with a roof pitch of 8/12. The factor for this rafter from Figure 6-19 is 18.762.

The length of a hip or valley rafter is the factor times the run (in feet).

So multiply the factor (18.762) by the length in feet (1.333') to find the length of the hip or valley rafter — in this case 25.01'' per 16'' run of the common rafter.

To translate this into the length of the jack rafter:

$$\sqrt{25.010^2 \text{ less } 16^2} = 19.222''$$

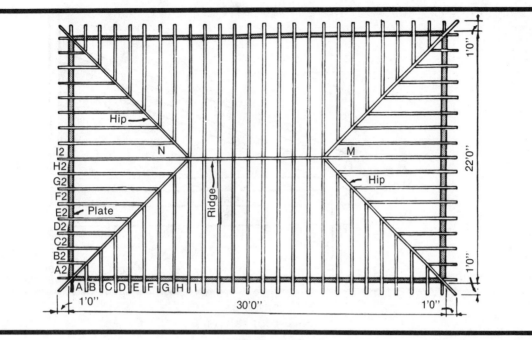

Figure 6-22
Framing detail for a hip roof

The length of the shortest jack rafter spaced 16'' o.c. for a roof pitch of 8/12 is 19.222''. Of course, you don't have to do these calculations yourself. Just look up the length in Figure 6-19. But I think it'll help you work with these lengths if you understand the reasoning behind the figures. So let's find the length of jack rafters for hip and valley rafters spaced 24'' o.c. Begin by looking at diagram B in Figure 6-21. It shows a hip or valley rafter at the same 8/12 rise, but this time spaced at 24'' o.c. The factor is the same — 18.762.

$$18.762 \text{ (factor)} \times 2.0' \text{ (24'' run)} = 37.524''$$

So the length of the jack rafter will be:

$$\sqrt{37.524^2 \text{ less } 24^2} = 28.845''$$

The length of the shortest jack rafter spaced 24'' o.c. for a roof pitch of 8/12 is 28.845''.

The length of the second jack rafter will be twice that of the shortest jack, the third jack rafter will be three times the length, and so on. This is true for both 16'' o.c. and 24'' o.c. spacing.

When estimating jack rafters, you don't need to calculate each length separately. Figure 6-22 shows a framing detail for a hip roof. Look at the lower left-hand corner, where the jack rafters are labeled from A through I and from A2 through I2. You can cut jack rafters A and H from the length of one common rafter. The same is true for A2 and H2. Also B and G, C and F and D and E. You can always cut two jack rafters from the length of one common rafter.

Estimate the number of jack rafters with the common rafters, and add two extra rafters per hip for waste.

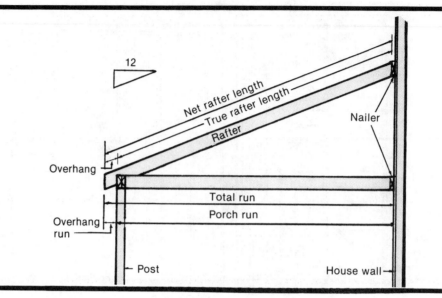

Figure 6-23
Shed roof rafters

Roof pitch	Run	x	Factor	— (minus)	Factor for full thickness of nailer *	=	True rafter length **
1/12		x	1.00347	-	.12500	=	
1½/12		x	1.00778	-	.12500	=	
2/12		x	1.01379	-	.12500	=	
2½/12		x	1.02147	-	.12500	=	
3/12		x	1.03078	-	.12500	=	
3½/12	12.0'	x	1.04167	-	.12500	=	12.375' (12'4½")
4/12		x	1.05409	-	.12500	=	
5/12		x	1.08333	-	.12500	=	
6/12		x	1.11803	-	.12500	=	
7/12		x	1.15770	-	.12500	=	
8/12		x	1.20185	-	.12500	=	
9/12		x	1.25000	-	.12500	=	

*When nailer is 2'' nominal framing (2 x 6's, 2 x 8's, etc.)
**True rafter length plus overhang equals net rafter length

Figure 6-24
Factors for shed roof rafters

Shed roof rafters— Figure 6-23 shows rafter layout for a shed roof. Figure 6-24 is the factor table for estimating shed roof rafters. Here's how to use the table.

Let's say we have a porch with a roof pitch of 3½ in 12 and a porch run of 12'0'' (12.0'). Look down the first column to find the correct pitch (3½/12). In the next

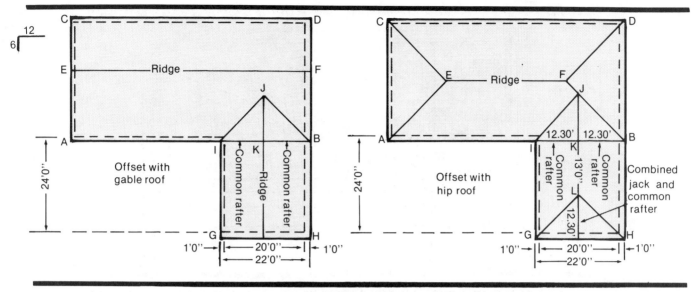

Figure 6-25
Gable and hip roof offset

column, enter the length of the porch run (12.0'). Multiply the run (12.0') by the factor (1.04167) to get 12.500'. Then subtract the nailer thickness factor (0.125) to get a true rafter length of 12.375' (12'4½'').

If the porch roof has an overhang of 6'' (0.5') measured horizontally, the total run of the roof would be 12'6'' (12.5'). Use this figure to compute the net rafter length.

Look down the first column to find the correct pitch (3½/12). In the next column, enter the length of the total run (12.5'). Multiply the length of the total run (12.5') by the factor (1.04167) to get 13.021'. Then subtract the nailer thickness factor (0.125) to get a net rafter length of 12.896' (12'10¾'').

Ridge

The ridge board is the highest horizontal member in the roof system. It should be one size larger than the rafters. For example, if the rafters are 2 x 6, make the ridge a 2 x 8.

The length of the ridge on a straight gable roof is the length of the building plus the overhangs. On intersection gable roofs, the ridge length is the length of the intersection plus the extension of the ridge to the adjacent roof. You can see this in Figure 6-25. Normally this ridge extension is equal to the total length of the common rafter on the building extension. For example, if the building extension, or offset, is 16'0'' and the length of the common rafter on the extension is 10'0'', the length of the ridge for the extension should be 26'0''.

The length of the ridge on a full hip roof is the length of the building less its width (Figure 6-26). On intersecting hip roofs, the length of the ridge will be the length of the intersection plus the overhang.

Estimators usually scale off the ridge length. If the plans are drawn to a true scale, this will be accurate enough when ordering materials. More accurate calculations will be needed when actually cutting the ridge.

Collar Beams

Collar beams are horizontal framing members which tie rafters together to overcome roof thrust — the tendency of the rafters to push outward against opposite walls. Collar beams are shown in Figure 6-27. They're located in the upper third of the attic space below the ridge. The maximum spacing of collar beams is 4' o.c.

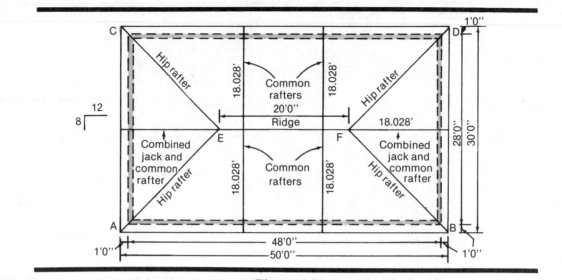

Figure 6-26
Hip roof area

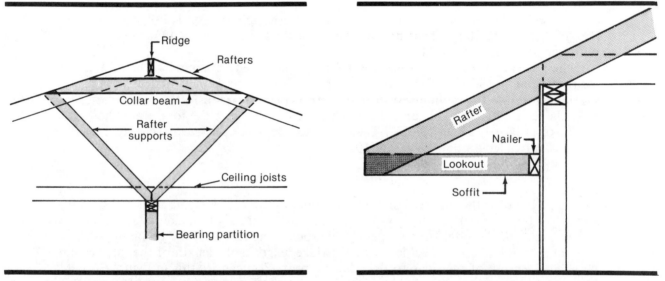

Figure 6-27
Collar beam and rafter supports

Figure 6-28
Framing for roof overhang soffit

If collar beams are spaced 4' o.c., divide the length of the house by 4 to determine the number required. Don't include the overhang in the length of the house. Normally, material 8'0" long will make one collar beam.

Rafter Supports
Rafter supports, or rafter braces, are sometimes used to keep the roof from sagging under the weight of roof loads. For maximum support, make them from 2 x 4's with the same spacing as the rafters. They should always run from the rafter to a bearing partition, as shown in Figure 6-27. The length of the rafter supports varies with the different roof pitches.
    To estimate rafter supports:

1)   Determine the location of the bearing walls from the floor plan of the blueprints.

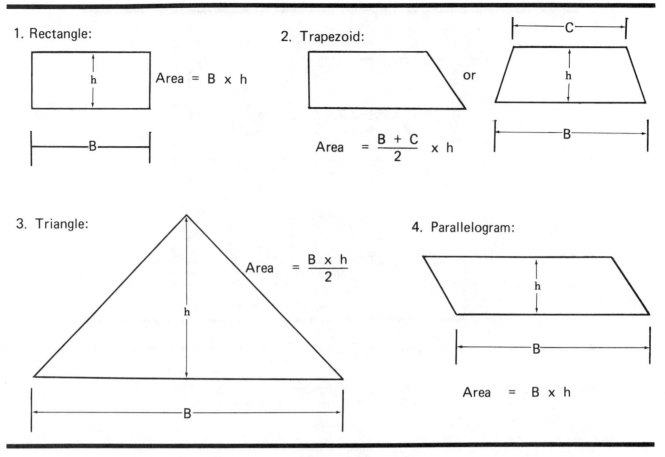

Figure 6-29
Finding the area of common roof shapes

2) From the side elevations, scale the length of the rafter supports from the rafters to the bearing partitions.

3) Allow one rafter support for each rafter.

Lookouts
Lookouts are short framing members nailed to the sides of rafters and extending to the wall of the house. They provide support for the soffit under the roof overhang. See Figure 6-28. There should be one lookout per rafter, including the gable overhang. The length of the lookouts is shown on the wall section of the blueprints. Most lookouts are made from 2 x 4 material. Don't forget to include the nailer shown in Figure 6-28. Allow one foot of nailer for every foot of eave.

Roof Sheathing
Plywood sheathing has replaced wood board sheathing in nearly all residential construction. One-half inch plywood is acceptable for rafter spacing of 16" o.c. or 24" o.c. In regions where heavy snow loads are common, you'll probably need 5/8" plywood. Use 6d threaded or 8d common nails and nail the plywood at each bearing 6" o.c. along all edges and 12" o.c. along intermediate members.

Roof area will always be more than floor area if the roof is anything but horizontal. You'll have to compute the roof area before ordering sheathing. That isn't easy if the roof shape is irregular. But nearly every roof you estimate can be broken down into simple shapes that are easy to figure. Figure 6-29 shows all the common shapes and the formula for computing the area of each.

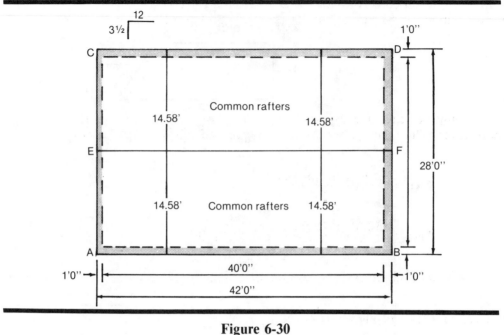

Figure 6-30
Gable roof area

Finding the area of a gable roof— The plain gable roof shown in Figure 6-30 is a rectangle. The formula for computing the area of a rectangle is:

Area equals base times height.

B, or base, in our example is the length of the eave A-B; and h, or height, is the length of the rafter to the center of the ridge. The roof area in Figure 6-30 is computed as follows:

Area equals eave length times rafter length.

So multiply 42.0' by 14.58' to find the area of section A-B-E-F, or half the roof. It's 612.36 square feet. Roof section C-D-E-F is the same size as A-B-E-F, so the total roof area in Figure 6-29 is double that, or 1,224.72 square feet.

Note that we're showing the length of the rafters in feet and decimal equivalents to make calculations easier. To convert feet and decimal equivalents to feet and inches, use the conversion chart, Figure 6-15.

Finding the area of a hip roof— The plain hip roof in Figure 6-26 has both trapezoids (sections A-B-E-F and C-D-E-F), and triangles (sections B-F-D and C-E-A). The formula for finding the area of a trapezoid is:

$$\text{Area} = \frac{B + C}{2} \times h$$

B is the length of the eave A-B or C-D, C is the length of the ridge E-F, and h is the length of the rafter to the center of the ridge. The roof area of the trapezoid sections of the roof in Figure 6-26 is:

$$\text{Area} = \frac{A\text{-}B + E\text{-}F}{2} \times \text{rafter length}$$

$$\text{Area} = \frac{50.0' + 20.0'}{2} \times 18.028"$$

Area = 630.98 SF (for section A-B-E-F)

630.98 x 2 = 1,261.96 SF

So far, the calculated area of the roof is 1,261.96 square feet. Now let's figure the area of the two remaining triangles. The formula for finding the area of a triangle is:

$$\text{Area} = \frac{B \times h}{2}$$

B is the length of the eave B-D or C-A, and h is the length of the combined jack and common rafter. The formula for the triangle parts of the roof in Figure 6-26 is:

$$\text{Area} = \frac{\text{D-B} \times \text{rafter length}}{2}$$

$$\text{Area} = \frac{30.0' \times 18.028'}{2} = 270.42 \text{ SF}$$

270.42 SF x 2 = 540.84 SF (sections B-F-D and C-E-A)

The total roof area in Figure 6-26 is:

Two trapezoid sections	1,261.96 SF
Two triangle sections	540.84 SF
Total	1,802.80 SF

Now you know how to find the area of odd-shaped roofs. But there's an easier way to find the area of a hip roof. You can figure it as a rectangle, just like we did earlier for the gable roof:

Area = A-B x length of rafter
Area = 50.0' x 18.028'
Area = 901.40 SF
901.40 SF x 2 = 1,802.80 SF (both sections)

You come up with the same answer either way. So take the easier route — use the formula for finding the area of a rectangle.

Finding the area of an offset— To estimate the roof area of an offset or intersection with a gable roof (Figure 6-25):

1) Compute the main roof of section A-B-E-F as solid; this will include the area of the triangle I-J-B in the offset.

2) Multiply the eave length I-G by the common rafter length in the offset for the area of one section. Multiply the area of one section by 2 for the total area. Example:

Area = I-G x rafter length
Area = 24.0' x 12.3' = 295.2 SF
295.2 SF x 2 = 590.4 SF

The roof area for the offset with a gable roof in Figure 6-25 is 590.40 square feet. Add this to the area of the main roof to find the total roof area.

To estimate the roof area of an offset or intersection with a hip roof (Figure 6-25):

1) Compute the main roof area of section A-B-E-F as if it were solid; this will include the area of the triangle I-J-B in the offset.

2) The remaining section I-G-K-L is a trapezoid. Remember the formula for finding the area of a trapezoid:

$$\text{Area} = \frac{\text{I-G} + \text{K-L}}{2} \times \text{rafter length}$$

$$\text{Area} = \frac{24.0' + 13.0'}{2} \times 12.30'$$

$$\text{Area} = \frac{37}{2} \times 12.30' = 227.55 \text{ SF}$$

$$277.55 \text{ SF} \times 2 = 455.10 \text{ SF}$$

The area of the triangle G-L-H is:

$$\frac{22' \times 12.30'}{2} = 135.3 \text{ SF}$$

The roof area for the offset with a hip roof in Figure 6-25 is:

Two trapezoids	455.10 SF
One triangle	135.30 SF
Total	590.40 SF

Note: The roof area of the offset with a gable roof (590.40 square feet) is the same as the offset with the hip roof. So you don't have to calculate the trapezoid and triangle sections separately. Calculate the offset with the hip roof as a rectangle.

A plain hip roof running to a point consists of four triangles. To get the roof area of the four sections, calculate the area of one section and multiply by four.

Roof Pitch	Factor	Divided By	Ratio
1/12	12.042	12	1.004
1½/12	12.093	12	1.008
2/12	12.166	12	1.014
2½/12	12.258	12	1.022
3/12	12.369	12	1.031
3½/12	12.500	12	1.042
4/12	12.649	12	1.054
5/12	13.000	12	1.083
6/12	13.416	12	1.118
7/12	13.892	12	1.158
8/12	14.422	12	1.202
9/12	15.000	12	1.250
10/12	15.620	12	1.302
11/12	16.279	12	1.357
12/12	16.971	12	1.414

Figure 6-31
Ratio of common rafter length to factors per foot run

Finding roof area using ratios— Here's the fastest way of all to compute roof area. Look at Figure 6-31. It has factors and ratios for roofs varying from 1/12 to 12/12 pitch. Just multiply the ratio in Figure 6-31 by the square feet of the floor area plus the roof extension. For example, in Figure 6-30, the roof pitch is 3½/12, and the area, including the roof overhang, is 1,176 square feet (42.0' x 28.0'). The ratio for a 3½/12 roof pitch from Figure 6-31 is 1.042.

$$1,176 \text{ SF} \times 1.042 = 1,225.39 \text{ SF}$$

Previously, we calculated the area of the gable roof at 1,224.72 square feet. As you can see, the answer is very close. And the method is much easier.

Estimating plywood panels for roof decking— For a fast and accurate method of estimating the plywood panels required for the roof deck, use the factors in Figure 4-20 in Chapter 4. Let's assume you're using 4' x 8' plywood panels for decking the gable roof we just used as an example. Rounded off, it has 1,255 square feet:

$$1,225 \text{ SF} \times .03125 \text{ (factor)} = 38.28 \text{ or 39 panels}$$

Figure 6-26 is a plain hip roof with a pitch of 8/12. The area, including the roof overhang, is 1,500 square feet (50.0' x 30.0'). The ratio for a 8/12 roof pitch from Figure 6-31 is 1.202.

$$1,500 \text{ SF} \times 1.202 \text{ (factor)} = 1,803 \text{ SF}$$

When we calculated the area before, it came out to 1,802.80 square feet.

Using the factor from Figure 4-20, the number of 4' x 8' plywood panels required for this roof will be:

$$1,803 \text{ SF} \times .03125 = 56.34 \text{ or 57 panels}$$

Note: If you use the ratios shown here to compute roof areas, be especially careful in the offsets or intersections. Any break in the roof line can cause an error in your figures.

A Quick Check to Spot Errors

Here's a quick way to check your roof framing material calculations for roof framing. It's based on the roof area, which you had to calculate when figuring the sheathing.

Figure 6-32 shows the framing lumber required for a hip roof when the roof surface is known. For example, if you're using 2" x 10" rafters at 24" o.c., you'll need about 121 board feet of lumber for each 100 square feet of roof surface. Slightly more or less lumber will be needed on most jobs. But if your estimate is very much below or above the number shown in Figure 6-32, better recheck those numbers!

Size of rafter	12" o.c.	16" o.c.	24" o.c.	Lbs. nails per 1000 BF
2 x 4	89	71	53	17
2 x 6	129	102	75	12
2 x 8	171	134	112	9
2 x 10	212	197	121	7
2 x 12	252	197	143	6

Note: Includes rafters, ridge, and collar beams but no ceiling joists, blocking, lookouts, rafter supports or nailers.

Figure 6-32
Board feet per 100 square feet of roof surface

Note that Figure 6-32 covers only rafters, the ridge board and collar beams. No ceiling joists, blocking, lookouts, rafter supports or nailers are included. These have to be added separately.

Sample Roof System Estimate

Look back to the house shown in Figures 5-10, 5-11 and 5-12 in Chapter 5. We'll go through the lumber estimate for the roof system step-by-step. We'll use ceiling joists and rafters instead of trusses.

Ceiling Joists

First floor: living room	19 - 2 x 6 x 14	(266 BF)
Kitchen and dining room:	19 - 2 x 6 x 14	(266 BF)
Second floor: front	31 - 2 x 8 x 16	(661 BF)
Second floor: back	31 - 2 x 6 x 12	(372 BF)
	Total	(1,565 BF)

Use the multiplying factors in Figure 6-33 to convert linear feet to board feet.

Ceiling backing, or nailers: (See Figure 6-34).
16 - 2 x 6 x 12 (192 BF)

Lumber size (thickness and width)	Factors
1" x 4"	.33333
1" x 6"	.50000
1" x 8"	.66667
1" x 10"	.83333
1" x 12"	1.00000
2" x 4"	.66667
2" x 6"	1.00000
2" x 8"	1.33333
2" x 10"	1.66667
2" x 12"	2.00000

Figure 6-33
Factors for converting linear feet to board feet

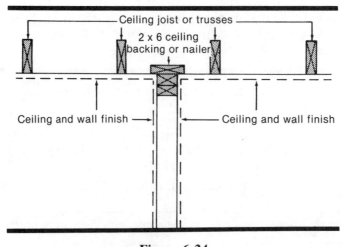

Figure 6-34
Wall parallel to ceiling joists

Rafters

First floor	40 - 2 x 6 x 16	
Second floor	66 - 2 x 6 x 16	
Total	106 - 2 x 6 x 16 (1,696 BF)	

Ridge

5 - 2 x 8 x 14 (93 BF)

Collar Beams

16 - 2 x 4 x 8 (85 BF)

Rafter Supports

50 - 2 x 4 x 12 (400 BF)

Lookouts

20 - 2 x 4 x 12 (160 BF)

Nails

From Figure 4-23 in Chapter 4, the nail allowance and multiplying factors are:

Framing allowance for floor joists and headers: Allow 10 pounds of 16d common nails per 1000 board feet. The multiplying factor is 0.01.

Framing allowance for toenailing: Allow 2.5 pounds 8d common nails per 1000 board feet. The multiplying factor is 0.0025.

Plywood allowance: Allow 8 pounds 6d threaded nails per 1000 square feet. The multiplying factor is 0.008.

There are 4,191 board feet of framing lumber in the roof system, so you'll need these nail quantities:

16d common nails—

4,191 BF x .01 = 41.91 or 42 lbs.

8d common nails—

4,191 BF x .0025 = 10.48 or 11 lbs.

There are 1,984 square feet of plywood for the roof sheathing. The nail requirement will be:

6d threaded nails—

1,984 SF x .008 = 15.87 or 16 lbs.

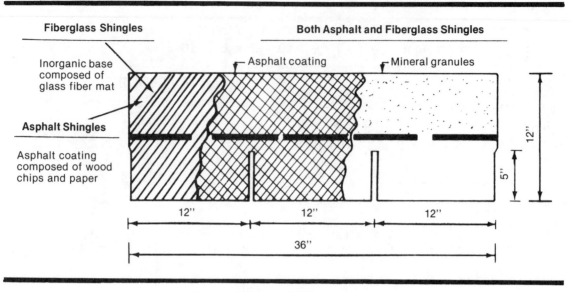

Figure 6-35
Asphalt and fiberglass shingles

Estimating Roof Coverings

Asphalt and Fiberglass Shingles

About 85% of the houses built in recent years have asphalt or fiberglass shingles. Asphalt shingles are made of organic material, usually wood chips and paper, impregnated with asphalt and mineral granules. Fiberglass shingles look very much like the asphalt, but they're made of an inorganic base composed of glass fiber mat.

Figure 6-35 shows the most popular asphalt and fiberglass shingle, a strip shingle 12'' wide and 36'' long, weighing 235-240 pounds per square. Most of these shingles have a self-sealing strip that's activated by the heat of the sun after it's installed. This bonds it to the next shingle.

The shingles are packed three bundles per square. A square is always the number of shingles required to cover 100 square feet of roof area. For example, it will take 80 12'' x 36'' shingles to cover one square, using a 5'' weather exposure. Here's how we figured it: Multiply 5'' (exposure) times 36'' (length) times 80 (number of shingles). The total is 14,400 square inches. Divide that by 144 (the number of square inches in a square foot). The answer? A square — 100 square feet.

To estimate asphalt or fiberglass shingles, calculate the roof area the same way you calculated roof sheathing. Divide the total roof area by 100 for the number of roofing squares required. Add an additional allowance to the roofing estimate for the starter strip, and the ridge and hip caps. Figure 6-36 shows that each strip shingle makes three caps.

Starter Course Shingles

Figure 6-37 has factor tables for starter courses, ridge and hip caps, and nails. Use table A in Figure 6-37 to compute the number of shingles required for the starter course. If you prefer to compute the number of squares required, use the bottom half of the table. Both tables assume the use of 12'' x 36'' asphalt or fiberglass shingles. Here's how to use each table:

Suppose you're building a house with a total eave length of 128 linear feet. In the top half of Figure 6-37 A, enter the eave length. Multiply the eave length (128) by the factor (0.33333) to get the number of shingles required for the starter course. It's 42.67, or 43 shingles.

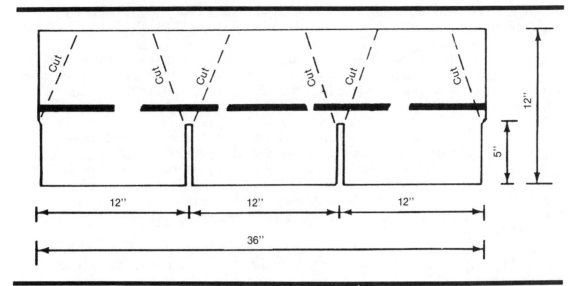

Figure 6-36
Ridge and hip caps

Eave length (linear feet)	x	Factor	=	Number		Length of ridge and hips (linear feet)	x	Factor	=	Number
Shingles: 128	x	.33333	=	42.67 OR 42		Shingles: 52	x	.80000	=	41.6 OR 42
Squares: 128	x	.00417	=	.53		Squares: 52	x	.01000	=	.52
A	**Factors for starter courses**					**B**	**Factors for ridge and hip caps**			

Number of squares	x	Factor	=	Number of pounds		Length of ridge and hips (linear feet)	x	Factor	=	Number of pounds
1" roofing nails: 29	x	1.5	=	43.5 OR 44		1½" roofing nails: 67	x	.02667	=	1.79 OR 2
1¾" roofing nails: 29	x	1.75	=	50.75 OR 51		1¾" roofing nails: 67	x	.03077	=	2.06 OR 2
C	**Factors for main roof nails**					**D**	**Factors for ridge and hip cap nails**			

Figure 6-37
Factors for shingles and roofing nails

Now look at the bottom half of table A. In the first column, enter the eave length (128). Multiply the eave length by the factor (0.00417) to get the number of squares of roofing you'll need for the starter course. In this example, it's 0.53 squares.

Hip and Ridge Cap Shingles
Table B in Figure 6-37 is a factor table for hip and ridge cap shingles. Use the top half to compute the number of shingles required for the hip and ridge caps. If you prefer to compute the number of squares required, use the bottom half. Both tables assume the use of 12" x 36" shingles with a 5" exposure.

Here's how to find the number of shingles needed for a roof with 52 linear feet of ridge and hips: In the top half of Figure 6-37 B, enter the total length (52 LF). Multiply the factor (0.8) to get 41.6, or 42 shingles.

Now let's find the number of squares needed. In the first column in the bottom half, enter the hip and ridge length (52 LF). Multiply the length by the factor (0.01) to get the number of squares of roofing required for the ridge and hip caps. In this example it's 0.52 squares.

Nails

Main roof— Use table C in Figure 6-37 to calculate the quantity of roofing nails required to shingle the main roof. Use the upper table for 1" nails and the lower table for 1¾" nails. Both tables assume you're using 12" x 36" shingles. Here's how to use the tables:

For 1" nails, enter the number of roofing squares in the first column of Figure 6-37 C. Let's say there are 29 squares. Multiply the number of squares (29) by the factor (1.5) to get 43.5, or 44 pounds of nails.

For 1¾" nails, enter the number of roofing squares in the bottom section of Figure 6-37 C. Multiply the number of squares (29) by the factor (1.75) to get 50.75, or 51 pounds of nails.

Hip and ridge caps— Use Figure 6-37 D to calculate the quantity of roofing nails required for the ridge and hip caps. Use the top for 1½" nails and the bottom section for 1¾" nails.

For 1½" nails, enter the total ridge and hip length in the first column of the top section. Multiply the length (67 LF) by the factor (0.02667) to get 1.79, or 2 pounds of nails.

For 1¾" nails, enter the total ridge and hip length in the bottom section. Multiply the length (67 LF) by the factor (0.03077) to get 2.06, or 2 pounds of nails.

Wood Shingles

Before 1940, most houses were roofed with wood shingles. In some parts of the country, they're still popular. Wood shingles are sawn from many species of wood, commonly cedar. Basic grades of red cedar are: Number 1, Blue Label (premium grade); Number 2, Red Label (good grade); and Number 3, Black Label (utility or economy grade.)

Each grade comes in lengths of 16", 18" and 24", and in random widths. They're packed four bundles per square. The approximate weight per square for the 16" shingles is 144 pounds; for the 18" shingles, 158 pounds; and for the 24" shingles, 192 pounds.

Figure 6-38 is a wood shingle exposure chart showing the approximate coverage of one square of wood shingles, based on weather exposures from 4" to 7½". The maximum recommended weather exposure for a 16" shingle is 5"; for an 18" shingle, 5½"; and for a 24" shingle, 7½". When estimating wood shingles, divide the roof area by the coverage for the weather exposure to be used. For gable roofs, add 10% for the starter strip and ridge. For hip roofs, add 15% for the starter strip, ridge and hips.

Shingle length	Minimum thickness	4"	4½"	5"	5½"	6"	6½"	7"	7½"
16"	5 in 2"	80	90	100	110	120	130	140	150
18"	5 in 2¼"	72½	81½	90½	100	109	118	127	136
24"	4 in 2"	--	--	--	--	80	86½	93	100

Figure 6-38
Wood shingle exposure chart

Handsplit and resawn	Approximate square foot coverage of one square of handsplit shakes based on these weather exposures:						
	5½"	6½"	7"	7½"	8"	8½"	10"
18" x ½" to ¾"	55*	65	70	75**	80	--	
18" x ¾" to 1¼"	55*	65	70	75**	80	85	--
24" x ½" to ¾"	--	65	70	75*	80	85	100**
24" x ¾" to 1¼"	--	65	70	75*	80	85	100**
32" x ¾" to 1¼"	--	--	--	--	--	--	100*

Note: *Recommended maximum weather exposure for 3-ply roof construction
**Recommended maximum weather exposure for 2-ply roof construction.

Figure 6-39
Handsplit shakes

For example, assume a gable roof with a roof area of 1,684 square feet will be covered with 16" red cedar shingles with a weather exposure of 4½". From Figure 6-38, we find that the coverage for that shingle is 90 square feet. To find the number of squares, divide the roof area by 90: 1,684 SF divided by 90 equals 18.71 squares. Add 10% (1.87) to that for the starter strip and ridge. Adding 18.71 and 1.87, we get 20.58 squares. Since there are four bundles per square, that's 4 times 20.58, or 82.32 bundles. Round up to 83.

Let's try another example. You're covering a 1,802 square foot hip roof with 24" red cedar shingles with a weather exposure of 7½". The coverage for a 24" shingle with a 7½" exposure is 100 square feet. Divide 1,802 by 100 to find 18.02 squares, plus 15% (2.70), equals 20.72 squares. Multiply by 4: 4 times 20.72 equals 82.33, or 83 bundles.

Wood Shakes

Handsplit and resawn shakes are split wood shingles with a rough texture. Cedar shakes are available only in Number 1 grade. They're sawn in lengths of 18", 24" and 32", and come in random widths, packed five bundles per square.

Shakes are much heavier than regular wood shingles. They vary in weight from approximately 225 pounds per square for the 18" x 1/2" x 3/4" shake, to double that for the 32" x 3/4" x 1¼". Figure 6-39 shows the approximate coverage of one square of handsplit shakes for weather exposures from 5½" to 10".

Estimate handsplit shakes just like we did wood shingles, using Figure 6-39 for the coverage. Here's an example: A gable roof with a roof area of 1,684 square feet will be covered with 24" red cedar handsplit shakes with a weather exposure of 10". The coverage for these shakes is 100 square feet. Divide 1,684 SF by 100 to find that you need 16.84 squares. Add 10% (1.68) to that to find a total of 18.52 squares. Since shakes are packed five bundles per square, multiply that by 5: 5 times 18.52 equals 92.60, or 93 bundles.

Nails for wood shakes— Use rust-resistant 1½" (4d) or 2" (6d) nails. Allow 2 pounds of 4d nails per square, or 3 pounds of 6d nails per square.

Computing the Roof Rise

Occasionally you'll want to know how much headroom there is in the attic. This may be important if heating or cooling equipment is to be installed in the attic, or if you have other work to do above the ceiling joists and below the rafters. How do we calculate the headroom available under the ridge?

Roof pitch	Run of common rafter	x	Factor	=	Rise
1/12		x	.08333	=	
1½/12		x	.12500	=	
2/12		x	.16667	=	
2½/12		x	.20833	=	
3/12		x	.25000	=	
3½/12		x	.29167	=	
4/12		x	.33333	=	
5/12		x	.41667	=	
6/12	*14.5'*	x	.50000	=	*7.250' (7'3")*
7/12		x	.58333	=	
8/12		x	.66667	=	
9/12		x	.75000	=	

Figure 6-40
Factors for roof rise

First, you'll need to know the rise of the roof. Figure 6-40 is a factor table for computing the roof rise. Here's how to use it:

Let's say we have a house with a roof pitch of 6 in 12 and a common rafter run of 14'6'' (14.5'). What's the rise of the roof?

Look down the first column to find the correct pitch (6/12). In the next column, enter the common rafter run (14.5'). Multiply the run (14.5') by the factor (0.5) to get a roof rise of 7.25' (7'3'').

This means that the vertical distance from the plate line to the top of the measuring line is 7'3''. How much head room do we have in this attic? Plenty. The attic could be floored and used for storage space.

Roof System Labor

That completes your material calculations for the roof. Now let's take a look at labor. As with every estimate, your cost records from previous jobs will be the most accurate guide to future labor requirements.

By now you know that there are many ways to compile manhour estimates. Whether you keep your records in units of square feet or square yards isn't important. But keep a record of the manhours required to handle every roof framing job.

Roof system labor includes the manhours required for framing (roof trusses or ceiling joists and rafters), sheathing, and roof covering. Let's look at the labor required for both the truss roof system and the ceiling joist and rafter system.

Truss Roof System
Figures 6-41, 6-42 and 6-43 are weekly time sheets for the Brown job. This is the same two-story house we've estimated in preceding chapters. The roof covers a floor area of 2,317 square feet over the living quarters and porches. Roof trusses were used throughout, except for a small area over a kitchen nook, where ceiling joists and rafters were used. Our daily log for Friday, September 24, shows that eight manhours were required to place the roof trusses over the kitchen and living room area.

Now look at Figure 6-42. On Monday, September 27, carpenters spent 18 manhours installing a supporting beam, ceiling joists and rafters over the kitchen nook. On Tuesday it rained. No work was done. On Wednesday the crew placed the roof trusses over the second floor and started installing the plywood sheathing. A total of 56 manhours were recorded. On Thursday it took 14 manhours to set the roof trusses on the porches. On Friday it rained again, and no work was done.

According to Figure 6-43, on Monday, October 4, carpenters spent 52 manhours installing the roof trusses on the back porch and starting the trusses for the front porch. On Tuesday they finished the front porch and began on the sheathing. A total of 56 manhours were recorded. On Wednesday they spent 32 manhours finishing the sheathing and applying felt.

It took the crew a total of 236 manhours to frame the roof as described here. The floor area covered was 2,317 square feet. Now let's use this information to compute a manhour factor for installing trusses.

Manhour factor for truss roof system— Figure 6-44 is a roof system labor worksheet. Use section A to compute the manhour factor for roof trusses. Section B is for computing the manhour factor for conventional ceiling joists and rafters.

Let's compute the manhour factor for the roof trusses on the Brown job. Enter the total manhours (236) in the first column of Figure 6-44 A. In the next column, enter the total square feet of floor area and porch area (2,317). Now divide the total manhours (236) by the total floor and porch area (2,317) to get a manhour factor of 0.10186.

To estimate the manhours required for a truss roofing system similar to the Brown job, just multiply the manhour factor (0.10186) by the total floor area. This gives you the total manhours required to do the job.

To find the cost of labor for the job, multiply the total manhours by the hourly rate of pay. This will be your labor estimate for the roof system using truss framing.

Ceiling Joist and Rafter System
Figures 6-45 through 6-49 are weekly time sheets showing the manhours required for the roof system on the Green job. This house was a large two-story dwelling with an attached double garage. Because the roof was designed with many offsets, it was impractical to use roof trusses. Ceiling joists and rafters had to be individually cut and placed.

According to the daily log for Friday, July 1 (Figure 6-45), it took 32 manhours to place the ceiling joists on the second floor. Another 32 manhours were needed to place the floor joists over the garage.

Monday, July 4, was a holiday. On Tuesday, carpenters spent 32 manhours placing floor joists and bridging over the garage. On Wednesday, they took 28 manhours to set the gables and prepare to place the rafters. On Thursday and Friday, a total of 92 manhours were required to place the rafters.

Now go to Figure 6-47. On Monday and Tuesday, July 11 and 12, the crew spent another 72 manhours placing rafters. On Wednesday, they spent 32 manhours finishing placing the rafters. Carpenters spent 80 manhours applying plywood roof sheathing on Thursday and Friday of that week.

The time sheet for the week of July 18 shows another 96 manhours to complete the application of the roof sheathing. On Thursday and Friday, workers spent 56 manhours installing roofing felt.

Weekly Time Sheet

Page____of____pages

For period ending 9-25-XX   BROWN   job

	Name	Exemptions	Days SEPTEMBER 20 M	21 T	22 W	23 T	24 F	25 S	Rate	Hours worked Reg.	Over-time	Total earnings
1	C. A. LESTER		8	8	8	8	8	X		40		
2	D. L. WHITE		8	8	8	8	8	X		40		
3	A. L. KING		8	8	8	8	4	X		36		
4	W. R. FARLOW		8	8	4	4	8	X		32		
5	J. R. DAVIS		8	8	8	8	8	X		40		
6	R. R. LEWIS		X	8	4	4	8	X		24		
7												
8												
9												
10												
11												
12												
13												
14												
15												
16												
17												
18												
19												
20												

Daily Log

Monday TOP PLATES ON 1ST FLOOR PARTITIONS (40 MANHOURS)

Tuesday SET BEAMS AND STARTED FLOOR JOISTS ON 2ND FLOOR (48 MANHOURS)

Wednesday FINISHED FLOOR JOISTS AND BRIDGING ON 2ND FLOOR (40 MANHOURS)

Thursday FINISHED SUBFLOOR, 1040 SF (20 MANHOURS ON 2ND FLOOR), O/S PARTITIONS

Friday FINISHED O/S + I/S PARTITIONS ON 2ND FLOOR (36 MNHRS) ROOF TROSSES 20 MANHOURS

Saturday XXXX   (624 SF) OVER KIT & LR (8 MNHRS)

Figure 6-41
Weekly time sheet

Weekly Time Sheet

Page____of____pages

For period ending 10-2-XX

BROWN job

	Name	Exemptions	Days SEPT 27 M	28 T	29 W	30 T	OCT 1 F	2 S	Rate	Hours worked Reg.	Over-time	Total earnings
1	R.R. LEWIS		X	X	8	2	X	X		10		
2	C.A. LESTER		3	X	8	2	X	X		13		
3	D.L. WHITE		3	X	8	2	X	X		13		
4	A.L. KING		3	X	8	2	X	X		13		
5	J.E. KING		3	X	8	2	X	X		13		
6	W.R. FARLOW		3	X	8	2	X	X		13		
7	J.R. DAVIS		3	X	8	2	X	X		13		
8												
9												
10												
11												
12												
13												
14												
15												
16												
17												
18												
19												
20												

Daily Log

Monday BEAM, CEILING JOISTS + RAFTERS OVER KITCHEN NOOK 53 SF (18 MANHOURS)
Tuesday RAIN
Wednesday ROOF TRUSSES ON 2ND FLOOR ... STARTED ROOF SHEATHING 1040SF (56 MNHRS)
Thursday STARTED PORCH TRUSSES ... RAIN (14 MANHOURS)
Friday RAIN
Saturday XXXX

Figure 6-42
Weekly time sheet

Weekly Time Sheet

Page____of____pages

For period ending 10-9-xx   BROWN ____job

	Name	Exemptions	Days OCTOBER						Rate	Hours worked		Total earnings
			4 M	5 T	6 W	7 T	8 F	9 S		Reg.	Over-time	
1	R.R. LEWIS		8	8	×	×	×	×		16		
2	C.A. LESTER		4	8	8	8	8	×		36		
3	D.L. WHITE		8	8	8	8	8	×		40		
4	A.L. KING		8	8	×	8	×	×		24		
5	J.E. KING		8	8	×	8	×	×		24		
6	W.R. FARLOW		8	8	8	8	4	×		36		
7	J.R. DAVIS		8	8	8	8	8	×		40		
8												
9												
10												
11												
12												
13												
14												
15												
16												
17												
18												
19												
20												

Daily Log

Monday PORCH TRUSSES IN BACK ·· STARTED FRONT PORCH TRUSSES (52 MANHOURS) (600 SF FRONT & BACK ROUTES)
Tuesday FINISHED FRONT PORCH TRUSSES ··· ROOF SHEATHING (56 MANHOURS)
Wednesday FINISHED ROOF SHEATHING & FELT ON HOUSE (32 MANHOURS)
Thursday SET WINDOWS AND FRONT DOOR ··· RAIN (48 MANHOURS)
Friday SET 3 DOORS IN BACK ··· STAIRS TO 2ND FLOOR (28 MANHOURS)
Saturday XXXX

Figure 6-43
Weekly time sheet

Total Manhours	÷	Floor area (square feet)	=	Manhour Factor
236	÷	2,317	=	.10186

A Trusses

Total Manhours	÷	Floor area (square feet)	=	Manhour Factor
592	÷	3,008	=	.19681

B Ceiling joists and rafters

Figure 6-44
Roof system labor worksheet

On Monday, July 25, 16 manhours were spent installing roofing felt. On Tuesday, workers finished installing the roofing felt and built a decorative roof overhang. This work required 24 manhours.

The total floor area covered on the Green job was 3,008 square feet. A total of 592 manhours were required to construct this roof system using ceiling joists and rafters. Let's use this information to compute a manhour factor for roof systems using ceiling joists and rafters.

Manhour factor for ceiling joist and rafter system— Look at Figure 6-44 B. In the first column, enter the total manhours (592). In the next column, enter the total square feet of floor area (3,008). Then divide the total manhours (592) by the total floor area (3,008 SF) to get a manhour factor of 0.19681.

To estimate the manhours required for a ceiling joist and rafter system similar to the Green job, just multiply the manhour factor (0.19681) by the total floor area. This gives you the total manhours required to do the job.

To estimate the cost of labor for the job, multiply the total manhours by the hourly rate of pay.

Now let's compare the manhour factors for the two different roof systems. The manhour factor for the Green job, using ceiling joists and rafters, is 0.19681. The manhour factor for the Brown job, using roof trusses, is 0.10186. *The manhour factor for the Green job is 93.2% higher than the manhour factor for the Brown job — almost double!* Those numbers show the value of keeping good cost records. If your own crew is installing the roof system, use trusses whenever the savings on labor exceed the extra cost of the trusses.

A roofing subcontractor can usually install the roofing more cheaply than your crew can. An experienced roofer can install over a square of asphalt or fiberglass shingles per hour on a gable roof if the roof pitch isn't over 6 in 12. If your own carpenters aren't experienced roofers, it may take them up to six manhours per square to do the same job.

If you don't have a skilled roofer on the payroll, get bids from several roofing subs. Using roofing subcontractors also releases your carpenters to do the work they do best.

One final note on the roofing estimate: Don't overlook the added expense for winter building. It can add from 5% to 15% to your roof framing costs.

If you build in a climate where cold weather is an important consideration, you'll be especially interested in the next chapter: estimating insulation.

Weekly Time Sheet

Page____of____pages

For period ending **7-2-xx**

____**GREEN**____ job

	Name	Exemptions	Days						Rate	Hours worked		Total earnings
			M	T	W	T	F	S		Reg.	Over-time	
1	D.L. WHITE		8	8	8	8	8	X		40		
2	C.A. LESTER		8	8	8	8	8	X		40		
3	A.L. KING		8	8	8	8	8	X		40		
4	J.E. KING		8	8	8	8	8	X		40		
5	D.L. WEST		8	8	8	8	8	X		40		
6	L.H. KIDD		8	8	8	8	8	X		40		
7	A.E. KIDD		8	8	8	8	8	X		40		
8	R.C. JONES		8	8	8	8	8	X		40		
9												
10												
11												
12												
13												
14												
15												
16												
17												
18												
19												
20												

Daily Log

Monday SET BALANCES OF PARTITIONS ON 1ST FLOOR ... STRAIGHTENED WALLS (40 MANHOURS) TOP PLATES ... STARTED FLOOR JOISTS ON 2ND FLOOR (24 MANHOURS)

Tuesday FLOOR JOISTS ON 2ND FLOOR ... BRIDGING (64 MANHOURS)

Wednesday CIRCLE STAIRS (32 MANHOURS) ... SUBFLOOR ON 2ND FLOOR (32 MANHOURS)

Thursday SET PARTITIONS ON 2ND FLOOR (64 MANHOURS)

Friday CEILING JOISTS ON 2ND FLOOR (32 MANHOURS) STARTED FLOOR JOISTS OVER GARAGE (32 MANHOURS)

Saturday XXXX

Figure 6-45
Weekly time sheet

	Weekly Time Sheet									Page___of___pages			

For period ending 7-9-X   GREEN   job

	Name	Exemptions	Days JULY						Rate	Hours worked		Total earnings
			4 M	5 T	6 W	7 T	8 F	9 S		Reg.	Over-time	
1	C. A. LESTER		X	8	4	8	4	X		24		
2	A. L. KING		X	8	8	8	8	X		32		
3	J. E. KING		X	8	8	8	8	X		32		
4	D. L. WEST		X	8	8	8	8	X		32		
5	L. H. KIDD		X	X	X	8	8	X		16		
6	R. C. JONES		X	X	X	8	8	X		16		
7												
8												
9												
10												
11												
12												
13												
14												
15												
16												
17												
18												
19												
20												

Daily Log

Monday HOLIDAY

Tuesday FINISHED FLOOR JOISTS AND BRIDGING OVER GARAGE (32 MANHOURS)

Wednesday SET GABLES... PREPARATION WORK FOR RAFTERS (28 MANHOURS)

Thursday RAFTERS (48 MANHOURS)

Friday RAFTERS (44 MANHOURS)

Saturday XXXX

Figure 6-46
Weekly time sheet

Weekly Time Sheet

Page____of____pages

For period ending __7-16-XX_____

__GREEN_____ job

	Name	Exemptions	Days JULY						Rate	Hours worked Reg.	Over-time	Total earnings
			11 M	12 T	13 W	14 T	15 F	16 S				
1	A. L. KING		8	8	8	8	8	x		40		
2	J. E. KING		8	8	8	8	8	x		40		
3	D. L. WEST		8	8	x	8	8	x		32		
4	L. H. KIDD		8	8	8	8	8	x		40		
5	R. R. LEWIS		x	8	8	8	8	x		32		
6												
7												
8												
9												
10												
11												
12												
13												
14												
15												
16												
17												
18												
19												
20												

Daily Log

Monday __RAFTERS (32 MANHOURS)__
Tuesday __RAFTERS (40 MANHOURS)__
Wednesday __FINISHED RAFTERS (32 MANHOURS)__
Thursday __STARTED PLYWOOD ROOF SHEATHING (40 MANHOURS)__
Friday __PLYWOOD ROOF SHEATHING ... FINISHED FRONT (40 MANHOURS)__
Saturday __XXXX__

Figure 6-47
Weekly time sheet

Weekly Time Sheet

Page____of____pages

For period ending 7-23-XX

GREEN job

	Name	Exemptions	Days JULY						Rate	Hours worked		Total earnings
			18 M	19 T	20 W	21 T	22 F	23 S		Reg.	Over-time	
1	R.R. LEWIS		8	8	8	8	X	X		32		
2	C.A. LESTER		8	8	8	8	8	X		40		
3	D.L. WEST		8	8	8	8	8	X		40		
4	L.H. KIDD		8	8	8	8	8	X		40		
5												
6												
7												
8												
9												
10												
11												
12												
13												
14												
15												
16												
17												
18												
19												
20												

Daily Log

Monday PLYWOOD ROOF SHEATHING (32 MANHOURS)
Tuesday PLYWOOD ROOF SHEATHING (32 MANHOURS)
Wednesday FINISHED PLYWOOD ROOF SHEATHING (32 MANHOURS)
Thursday STARTED 15 LB FELT ON ROOF (32 MANHOURS)
Friday ROOF FELT (24 MANHOURS)
Saturday XXXX

Figure 6-48
Weekly time sheet

Weekly Time Sheet

Page____of____pages

For period ending 7-30-XX

GREEN job

	Name	Exemptions	Days JULY 25 M	26 T	27 W	28 T	29 F	30 S	Rate	Hours worked Reg.	Over-time	Total earnings
1	C. A. LESTER		8	8	8	8	8	x		40		
2	D. L. WEST		8	8	x	x	8	x		24		
3	L.H. KIDD		x	8	8	8	8	x		32		
4												
5												
6												
7												
8												
9												
10												
11												
12												
13												
14												
15												
16												
17												
18												
19												
20												

Daily Log

Monday ROOF FELT (16 MANHOURS) TOTAL FLOOR AREA 2ND FLOOR & GARAGE 3008 SF
Tuesday CONSTRUCTED DECORATIVE ROOF OVERHANG...FINISHED ROOF FELT (24 MHR)
Wednesday O/S TRIM (16 MANHOURS)
Thursday O/S TRIM (16 MANHOURS)
Friday O/S TRIM (24 MANHOURS)
Saturday XXXX

Figure 6-49
Weekly time sheet

Estimating Moisture Protection and Insulation Costs

Every carpenter worthy of the name can tell the difference between quality framing and the slipshod work of a wood butcher. Unfortunately, many carpenters don't understand that the quality of their work is also reflected in the insulation and vapor barrier they install. There are good ways and bad ways to install insulation and vapor barrier, just as there are good ways and bad ways to install molding and trim. Everyone concerned with carpentry needs a good understanding of what insulation and vapor barrier can do for a home and how they should — and should not — be installed. Make a mistake when cutting baseboard and it just looks bad for the next 50 years. Make a mistake when installing vapor barrier and the building may not last 50 years.

This chapter is intended to do two things for you. As you might expect, it explains how to estimate the cost of thermal and moisture protection. That information is toward the end of the chapter. But before getting to that, I'm going to help you understand how important insulation and vapor barrier are in modern dwellings. Lumber and framing haven't changed much in the last 50 years. But insulation and vapor barrier are high-tech products that have evolved very quickly since the early 1970's. If you aren't as well informed on perm ratings and R-values as you are on lumber grades and span tables, this chapter will help bring you up to date.

How Moisture Affects the Home

Excess moisture accumulation is seldom a problem in homes built before the mid-1970's. Back when gasoline sold for 30 cents a gallon, no one worried about conserving energy. Poorly-insulated homes built before 1975 leaked plenty of air through walls and around doors and windows. Any moisture in the air quickly found a way out.

That isn't likely to happen in a home built under modern codes. In cold months, an airtight home traps and holds far more moisture than it needs. Trapped moisture promotes decay in wood, leading to joists and rafters that begin to rot and sag. Eventually they'll have to be replaced, at a cost much higher than the original installation cost.

Moisture can be present in three different forms: as a vapor (gas), liquid, or solid (ice). For our purposes, water in vapor form is most important. Water vapor travels in two principal ways; air movement and diffusion. Liquid water travels by capillary action.

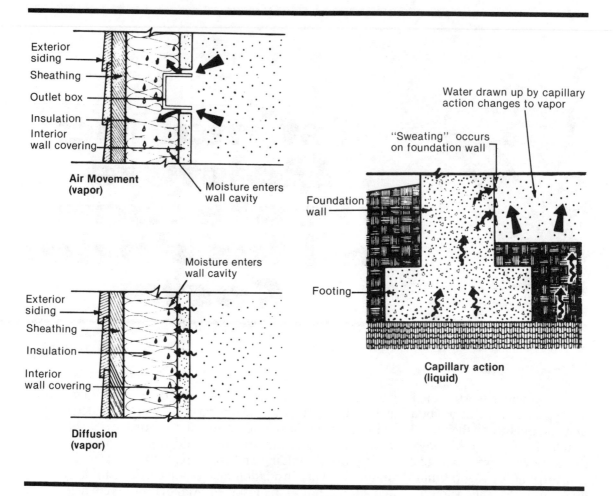

Figure 7-1
Moisture transfer methods

Figure 7-1 illustrates all three moisture transfer methods.

Air Movement

More moisture is moved by air movement than by either of the other methods. Air movement is determined by several factors, including vapor pressure, wind, convection, and temperature differences that set a *stack effect* in motion. Figure 7-2 shows how it works.

When moist air is heated in a home, high water-vapor pressure is created. (Water-vapor pressure is the increase made by water to the total atmospheric pressure). Moisture always tries to move toward areas of lower vapor pressure. So the warm moist air in the house tends to travel to the outside, where the pressure is lower. When outside temperatures are cooler than the warm, moist air, moisture condenses as it passes through building material in the wall, ceiling, roof and floor. Constant moisture discolors the surface at first and promotes rotting wood eventually.

This process works in reverse in warm, humid climates where the interior is cooled in summer. The higher vapor pressure is outdoors, pushing warm moist air *into* the house.

As wind strikes a building, it creates additional air pressure effects. The upwind side of the building (the side hit by the wind) has higher pressure than the opposite side where the pressure is lower. Walls on the low-pressure, or downwind, side of the house usually show more signs of moisture because warm, moist air is drawn to the outdoors through that section.

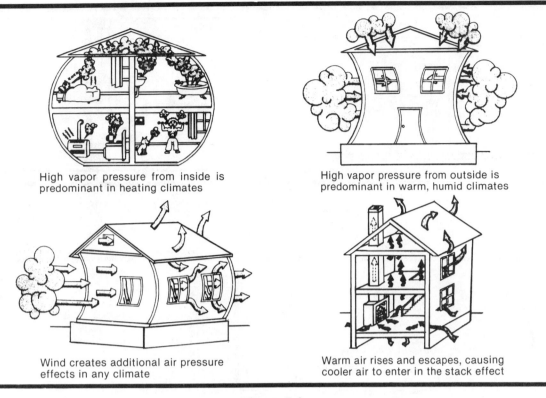

High vapor pressure from inside is predominant in heating climates

High vapor pressure from outside is predominant in warm, humid climates

Wind creates additional air pressure effects in any climate

Warm air rises and escapes, causing cooler air to enter in the stack effect

Figure 7-2
Moisture carried by air movement

Warm air always rises because of the stack effect. The higher the temperature of the air, the greater the upward thrust of that air. As warm air rises and escapes through the upper part of the house, it creates lower pressure at ground level. Cooler outdoor air is then pulled into the low pressure areas, and the cycle continues as this air is warmed and rises.

Convection describes the action of warm air moving upward until it cools or strikes cooler surfaces, such as windows. As the air is cooled, the amount of water vapor it can hold decreases, and condensation occurs. The cooler air then falls until it is reheated, and the process begins over again. Convection currents occur throughout the interior space of the home, powered by temperature differences. When convection currents move in wall cavities and other enclosed areas of the building, it reduces the thermal effectiveness of the insulation. Moisture problems are the result. Figure 7-3 shows how.

When a house in a cold climate has been weatherized by sealing, caulking and weatherstripping, air movement is reduced. Less heat and moisture escape. Tighter homes are more comfortable and have lower fuel bills. But they also trap more moisture, making exhaust fans and air management more important.

From your standpoint, the important point to remember is that there will usually be caulking and sealing to do on most jobs. Don't skimp on this important item. Your tradesmen should set doors and windows that fit snug and don't offer easy passage for moisture. Then be sure even the smallest cracks are caulked properly. Today, good craftsmen are energy-conscious craftsmen.

Diffusion
After a house has been thoroughly sealed, moisture transfer through diffusion becomes more important. Because the amount of water vapor that escapes through air movement has been cut to a minimum, water vapor will try to find another way out. As the vapor

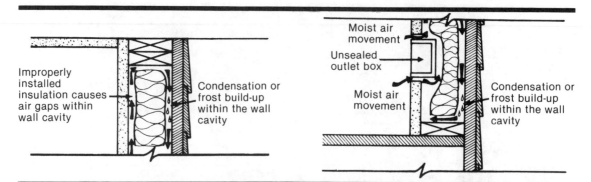

Figure 7-3
Moisture carried by convection currents

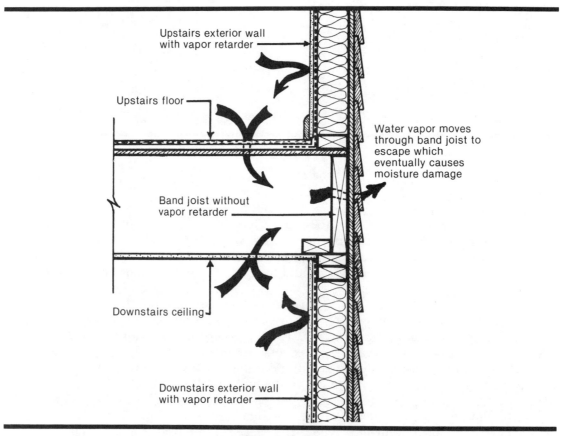

Figure 7-4
Water vapor diffusing through building materials

attempts to move from high pressure areas to low pressure areas, it will "diffuse," or pass directly through building materials. Look at Figure 7-4. Water vapor that penetrates a building surface may cool to the point where it turns to liquid or ice, causing severe damage.

Vapor retarders (also known as vapor barriers) slow diffusion through building materials. Good vapor retarders allow very little water to pass through them. With some of the new cold-climate building technologies, vapor barriers are used to slow both air movement and water vapor diffusion.

The air's temperature determines how much water vapor it will hold. Warmer air can hold much more moisture than cooler air. The *dew point* is the temperature at which water vapor condenses to liquid.

One goal with vapor barriers is to keep the warm, moist air in the house from coming in contact with temperatures below the dew point. That's why vapor barriers (such as plastic film) must be installed on the warm side of the wall. The cold side of the wall gets a layer of material that can breath (such as asphalt felt), to allow an escape path for any moisture in the wall.

Symptoms of Excess Moisture

Occasionally you'll have a job that involves correcting an existing moisture problem. Recognizing and diagnosing moisture problems is the first step in solving them. Once you've identified the symptoms and the source of the moisture, there will usually be several options. Some moisture problems can be handled best by educating the occupants. Others will require repairs.

Finding the source of excess moisture can be difficult. A little detective work and informed guessing will usually identify the most likely cause. Remember that some moisture sources are seasonal and won't be apparent during your inspection. For example, the soil in a crawl space may appear dry in midwinter. But in summer the soil may be saturated by irrigation water, drainage, or ground water.

One of the major challenges in solving excess moisture problems is that one symptom can have several causes. And it works the other way around also. One moisture source could be causing damage in many ways to many parts of the house.

Here's a list of the major symptoms you'll find in homes with moisture problems:

1) *Odors:* Odors are worse with high relative humidity. Musty odors may signal mold, mildew or rot. Also, odors from everyday household activities that seem to linger too long may be a signal of less-than-adequate ventilation.

2) *Damp feeling:* The sensation of dampness is common in areas with high relative humidity.

3) *Mold or mildew:* Growths of mold or mildew can often be seen in the form of a discoloration, ranging in color from white to orange, from green to brown to black. Even if you can't see them, you may know they're present by their musty odor. Mold and mildew are surface conditions but indicate that there's decay somewhere.

4) *Discoloration, staining and texture changes:* These usually indicate some degree of moisture damage. They may be black or dark streaks, or lines which border a discoloration. The area may not be wet at the time of inspection, but you can tell it has had moisture damage.

5) *Rot or decay:* Rot and wood decay show advanced moisture damage. Unlike surface mold and mildew, wood decay fungi penetrate the wood and make it soft and weak. Look for any type of rot or fruited bodies (mushroom-like growths). Decay fungi grow in a temperature range from just above freezing to 100 degrees. Wood decay usually happens fastest in the middle temperature ranges, from 50 to 75 degrees, if wood is more than 30% saturated with moisture. Fungi growth is slow below 50 degrees and above 90 degrees. At below-freezing temperatures, fungi go dormant. At 150 degrees most spores are killed.

6) *Water-carrying fungus:* This fungus is special. It carries water across surfaces, sometimes to distant locations. It looks like a fan, with vine-like strands coming out of it. These growths are papery, and usually have a dirty, white color with a tinge of

yellow. This fungus fan can spread over moist or dry wood, and can be found under carpet, behind cupboards, on framing between subfloors or on damp concrete foundations.

7)   *Fogging windows:* Condensation on windows and other smooth surfaces can have several causes. It may be a sign of excess moisture. You may need to insulate or warm the surface in question. Another possible cause is a faulty heating plant or some other flame-fired appliance which is leaking combustion gases into the living space. Combustion gases cause headaches, drowsiness, or other unexplained illnesses. Always check this possibility.

8)   *Sweating pipes, water leaks and dripping:* Water vapor may be condensing on cold pipes, or the pipes may be leaking.

9)   *Frost and ice:* Ice dams can occur in roof valleys and along the eaves. They frequently occur when there's insufficient ceiling or attic insulation and poor ventilation in the roof — problems that are aggravated by the freeze-thaw cycle. Snow or ice melts as the sun strikes the roof and as the interior roof surface is warmed from within. This moisture freezes again when temperatures drop, forming dams that impede drainage. Ice can build up under shingles, then melt and penetrate into the attic when temperatures rise. Frost or ice on any surface is an indication of possible trouble.

10)   *Paint peeling, blistering or cracking:* Moisture may be working from outside or inside the home to damage paint. Moisture is causing paint damage when you can see the raw surface between cracks or under blisters.

11)   *Corrosion:* Rusted metal is a sure sign that moisture is at work.

12)   *Deformed wooden surfaces:* Wood swells when it gets wet, and it warps, cups, and cracks when it dries. Shrinking, warping wood can cause new air leaks in a home.

13)   *Concrete and masonry efflorescence and chipping:* When water is passing through concrete or masonry, it may leave *efflorescence,* a white powder, on the surface. Freezing and thawing speed the process of deterioration, causing chipping and crumbling.

You may find sources of moisture both inside and outside the home. The three main sources of outdoor moisture are: poor drainage, blocked air circulation, and high outdoor relative humidity. Indoors, the situation is more complex: cooking, bathing, watering plants, etc.

Make yourself familiar with the more common moisture sources and possible solutions to each problem. That way you can avoid the problems in houses you build, and correct them in others.

Sources of Excess Moisture

Here are some of the causes of indoor moisture:

1)   *Continually high relative humidity indoors:* Too many occupants in a small building can cause problems. People, pets and plants give off moisture. Recommend more circulation and ventilation.

2)   *Too many internal sources from domestic activities:* Unvented bathrooms and kitchens are a common problem; cooking without lids, open-flame heating and cooking appliances, bathing, and drying clothes and towels indoors can produce excessive moisture. The residents should be using kitchen and bathroom exhaust fans. Install

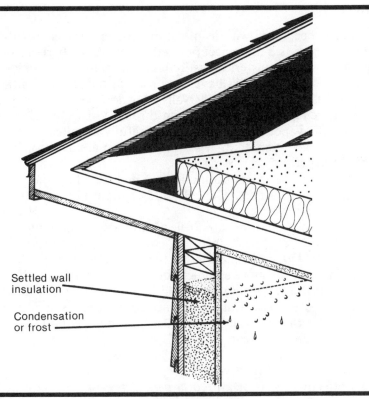

Settled wall
insulation

Condensation
or frost

Figure 7-5
Settled wall insulation causes condensation on cold surfaces

exhaust fan vents in the kitchen and bath if they aren't already there. Be sure the clothes dryer is vented to the outdoors.

3) *Lack of insulation:* Condensation is common in uninsulated walls and areas where insulation has settled or shifted, as shown in Figure 7-5. The solution: Seal any infiltration leaks, then insulate, using a vapor barrier. Check the existing insulation. Caulk the windows, and consider an insulated window.

4) *Vapor barrier deteriorated or missing:* Tightly-built and well-insulated homes need a durable vapor retarder, carefully installed on the warm side of the surface. If the vapor barrier is installed haphazardly, every point subject to air leakage is a target for condensation. Improper placement of vapor barriers is too common. For example, if a vapor barrier has been installed on the cold side of the wall surface, moisture may be condensing in the walls. If a low-perm vapor retarder is used on two sides of a wall surface, moisture may build up without an avenue of escape. In areas of high ground water, the lack of a ground-cover vapor barrier in the crawl space will allow water vapor to collect in the home.

5) *New construction or remodeling:* New foundations, concrete floors, brick fireplaces, sheetrock taping compound, paints, green lumber, wet wood or uncured masonry materials contain an enormous amount of moisture until they've had time to dry out thoroughly. New, tightly-constructed homes are likely to trap this moisture for much longer. Speed drying by increasing the ventilation and circulation, both during construction and during the first winter of occupancy.

Once you've found the source of moisture, the next decision is how to solve the problem. Sometimes it's enough just to explain the importance of using the bath and kitchen exhaust fans. But more complex problems will require more work on your part.

Vapor Barriers

Vapor barriers have been used with insulation in colder climates for the last several decades. Vapor *retarder* is a more accurate term than vapor barrier, since it doesn't actually stop all moisture transfer, it just reduces the rate of transmission.

In cold climates, vapor retarders have been used to reduce condensation by stopping water vapor from diffusing through the walls. But now we know that much more moisture is transferred by air movement than through diffusion. So to truly block most moisture transfer, the vapor retarder must be carefully installed to stop air leakage as well as diffusion. Vapor retarders that stop air leakage are a major improvement in modern home construction.

Remember that vapor retarders should always be located on the warm, or high-vapor pressure, side of the wall surface. The cold side of the wall has to breathe so that any moisture in the wall can escape.

Wall and ceiling vapor retarders aren't needed in areas where the average January temperature is above 35 degrees (California, coastal Oregon and Washington, southern Arizona and New Mexico, and the states of the old Confederacy). If the climate requires little winter heating but lots more summer cooling, (and especially if the building is unoccupied at night) the vapor barrier should be on the interior side of the wall.

In warm climates, the temperature difference across the insulation tends to be less, so less moisture migrates through the surface. Because the dew point is higher, it's less likely that condensation will occur.

Measuring Vapor Retarder Effectiveness

Vapor retarder effectiveness is measured in *perms,* a gauge of permeability. One perm equals one grain (or drop) of water per square foot per hour per unit vapor pressure difference. The lower the perm rating of a material, the better the material is at slowing moisture transfer.

Know the perm rating of the vapor barrier you plan to use in the walls. Any moisture that passes through the vapor barrier needs to escape through the outer wall surface. That's why any building paper on the wall exterior should be at least five times more permeable than the vapor barrier. Use this 1:5 ratio when choosing a vapor retarder and also when choosing sheathing materials for the outer skin of the house. Check with your building supply dealer for the perm ratings.

In the past, materials with a perm value of 1 or less were considered to be vapor barriers. Now, however, vapor barriers are available with a rating of 0.1 perm or less. Polyethylene films have extremely low perm ratings (usually 0.02 to 0.08 range) and are the best choice.

Asphalt-coated laminated papers and kraft-backed aluminum foil were once common. But these have installation problems, are not air tight, and tend to break down in high humidity. Stick with polyethylene film.

You install vapor barriers to avoid condensation problems. Unfortunately, poor placement, installation errors and omissions can aggravate problems rather than solve them. Here are some common errors:

• Installation on the wrong side of the wall surface: If low-perm products are used on the outer skin of a wall, and indoor humidity is high, moisture migrates to the wall and stays there. Low-perm sidings include vinyl and metal sidings, insulating sheathing with foil coverings, and low-perm plastics. Follow the manufacturer's instructions when installing any of these siding products.

• Double vapor retarders, or vapor retarders on both sides of a wall: Using a low-perm product on both sides of a wall or foundation can cause moisture buildup. The cold side of a wall or foundation must be able to breathe. Vapor retarders are not meant for use in party walls.

• Incomplete installation of vapor retarders: If you miss some areas of the house when you're installing the vapor retarder, the missed areas become escape routes for water vapor. If the home has constantly high indoor humidity, the missed areas will deteriorate eventually. Figure 7-4 shows a typical example. The vapor barrier is installed over walls and ceilings, but not band joists.

• Haphazard installation of vapor retarders: Vapor retarders aren't effective if they're not tightly installed. If you're using them to stop air infiltration as well as moisture transfer, the carpenter has to be very conscientious.

Millions of older houses have had insulation installed in wall cavities in the last decade, usually with the insulation blown in and no vapor retarder added. Utilities and other agencies sponsoring insulation work raised the question of the need for vapor barriers. A number of studies have found that while some condensation does occur, usually next to the cold inner surface of the exterior sheathing, wood rot and decay problems aren't common problems in most areas.

Researchers note that if moisture buildup within an insulated wall isn't extreme, it tends to correct itself. As the insulation gets wet, the insulation loses effectiveness, increasing heat loss. The temperature inside the wall then increases. This slows further condensation and steps up evaporation.

Wet insulation can pose problems in severe cases, however. First, the insulation becomes an excellent conductor of heat when really wet. Also, wet insulation touching electrical wiring or fixtures is a fire hazard. And there's some evidence that wet cellulose burns better than dry cellulose.

Remember that water vapor moves into wall cavities both by air movement and diffusion. But air movement is the more powerful force. That's why sealing air leakage points from the inside of the house is the first step in a conventional wall insulation job. Figure 7-6 shows the major penetration points. Seal around windows and doors, where the wall meets the ceiling and floor, and seal any cracks or holes in wall surfaces. Once air leakage points are closed off, you can apply vapor retarder paint to give wall surfaces some resistance to water vapor diffusion.

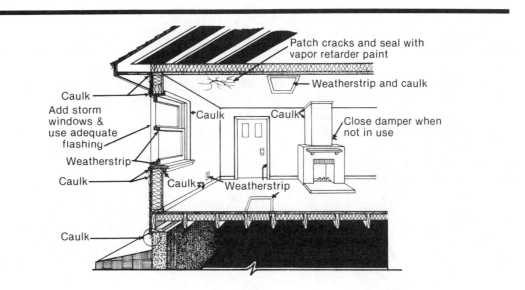

Figure 7-6
Seal air penetration points inside, then outside

When insulating rafters, allow 1″ minimum air space for ventilation

For thick ceiling insulation, install vent troughs for ventilation

Figure 7-7
Provide for ventilation at eaves

Vapor Retarders in the Attic

Installing attic ventilation is the best way to prevent moisture problems in attics. Until recently, most builders didn't use tightly installed vapor barriers except in the coldest climates. They believed that if a good vapor retarder was used in the walls and ceiling, too much moisture might accumulate in the house. Any water vapor that passes through the ceiling insulation can be vented away through attic vents.

However, when vapor barriers are used to stop both air and moisture transfer, a tight vapor barrier makes more sense for both new and newly remodeled homes in the condensation zone. A tight vapor barrier is the only way to avoid moisture damage if attic ventilation is poor, especially in homes with flat roofs or cathedral ceilings.

When using thicker attic insulation, be sure there is enough ventilation at the eaves. Install rigid vent troughs on the underside of the roof sheathing so insulation doesn't block the air flow. See Figure 7-7.

Vapor Retarders in Crawl Spaces and Floors

In all climate regions, lay vapor barrier on the soil under a crawl space to keep moisture from migrating up through the soil. Puncture-resistant 6-mil polyethylene works best. Hold it in place with bricks or concrete block. If you expect damage from people crawling in the crawl space, put a layer of sand over the plastic. Note that less crawl space venting is needed when soil cover vapor barrier is used.

Floor vapor barriers can be used with floor insulation in both cold and hot climates to stop condensation. But don't substitute them for ground cover vapor retarders. They're an addition, not a substitute. In cold climates, install the vapor retarder on the warm side, facing upward. In warm climates where air conditioning is needed all summer, install the vapor retarder face down. See Figure 7-8.

In new construction or remodeling in colder climates, install a continuous vapor barrier to stop air infiltration as well as moisture transfer. Make sure you provide an unbroken vapor barrier between floors, ceilings and interior walls. If these locations are left open to moisture, deterioration is inevitable.

Polyethylene vapor barrier used over friction fit insulation batts placed between framing members provides excellent insulation and vapor retardation. Your carpenter should work carefully to avoid punching holes in the polyethylene. Some holes are inevitable, of course. But they should be repaired with tape before the job is finished.

Energy-Saving Materials

The resistance of materials to the passage of heat is measured in R-value. Industry standard R-values are numbered; the higher the number, the more effective the insulation. The best favor you can do for any homeowner is to provide insulation with an R-value appropriate for the climate. The extra cost of doing it right will be repaid in energy savings every year for the entire life of the building.

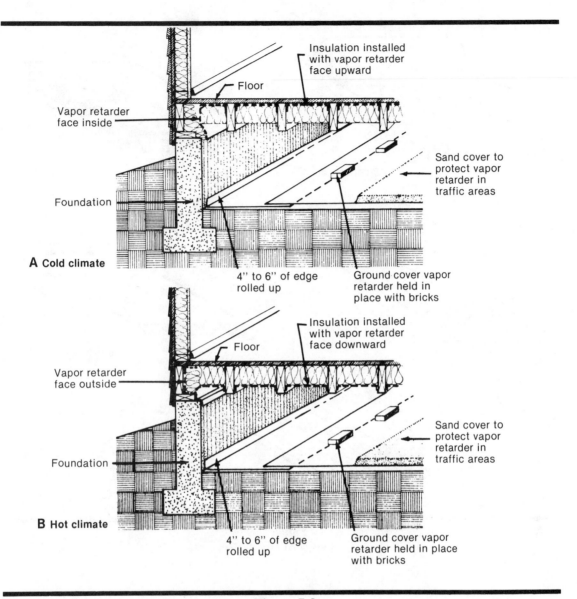

Figure 7-8
Vapor retarder locations for crawl spaces and floors

Here's one example of how much energy can be saved with a properly insulated house:
A house built before the energy crisis was fully insulated in the ceiling only. The builder
had installed no insulation in the walls or floors, and no storm doors. The windows were
single pane.

After two years, four additional inches of insulation were blown into the attic, the
walls were insulated with blown insulation and the floors (over an unheated basement)
were insulated with batts. Storm sash and storm doors were installed on all windows and
doors. The same family lived in the house during the entire period. In the 11 years after
the additional insulation was installed, the fuel consumption was reduced by an average
of 46% per year. Savings like this will continue for the life of the house — and the
family has the bonus of being more comfortable.

Types of Insulation
There are many types of insulation. Figure 7-9 shows the common types. Figure 7-10
gives the R-value of some kinds of insulation at different thicknesses.

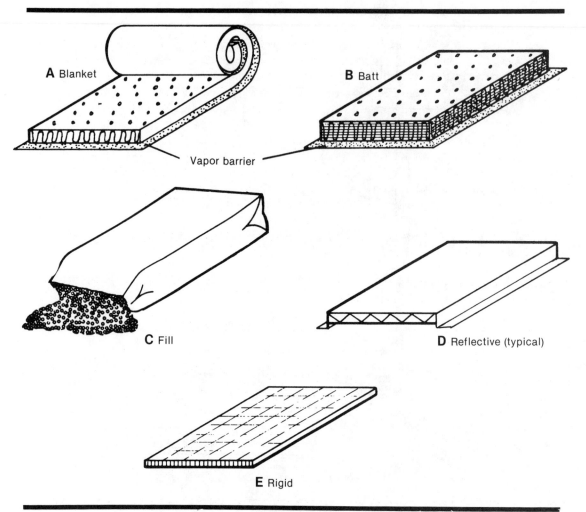

Figure 7-9
Types of insulation

R-value	Batts or blankets		Loose fill (poured-in)		
	Glass fiber	Rock wool	Glass fiber	Rock wool	Cellulosic fiber
R-11	3½" - 4"	3"	5"	4"	3"
R-19	6" - 6½"	5¼"	8" - 9"	6" - 7"	5"
R-22	6½"	6"	10"	7" - 8"	6"
R-30	9½" - 10½"*	9"*	13" - 14"	10" - 11"	8"
R-38	12" - 13"*	10½"*	17" - 18"	13" - 14"	10" - 11"
* Two batts or blankets required					

Figure 7-10
R-value and insulation thickness

Glass fiber and rock wool are available in batts, blankets and loose fill (poured-in). The batts and blankets are cut in sections 15'' or 23'' wide for stud or joist spacing of 16'' or 24'' o.c. They're available with or without a vapor barrier and are fire and moisture resistant. The loose fill (poured-in) insulation doesn't have a vapor barrier, so you need to buy and apply the barrier separately if one is required.

Cellulosic fiber, vermiculite and perlite are loose fill and don't have a vapor barrier. They're best suited for non-standard or irregular joist spacing or when space between joists has many obstructions. Check the bags to see if they meet federal specifications for fire resistance. They'll be clearly labeled if they do.

Rigid insulation boards are made from organic fiber, polystyrene foam and urethane. Rigid insulation boards made from organic fiber are used for wall sheathing, so they serve a dual purpose. Polystyrene and urethane rigid insulation boards have a higher R-value, but should be installed strictly according to the manufacturer's recommendations. Some manufacturers use aluminum foil facers for a vapor protection. The standard size is 4' x 8', with nominal thicknesses of 3/8'' through 1⅞''. You can special order thicknesses through 2¼''.

Weatherstripping and Caulk
Any room with windows or exterior doors will have some air leakage through cracks, especially when the wind blows. The cold air that leaks into the room adds an additional load on the heating system. Weatherstripping windows and doors, and sealing around cracks helps prevent infiltration.

Where to Insulate
Children in an elementary school were asked to share their ideas on how to ease the energy shortage. One child said, ''When the beds are empty, take the blankets and put them around the room to help hold in the heat.'' That child had the right idea. Figure 7-11 shows how to install a ''blanket of insulation'' around a house for efficient energy conservation.

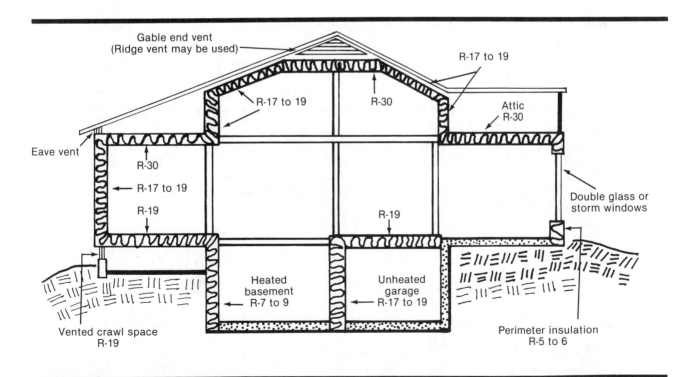

Figure 7-11
Installing a blanket of insulation

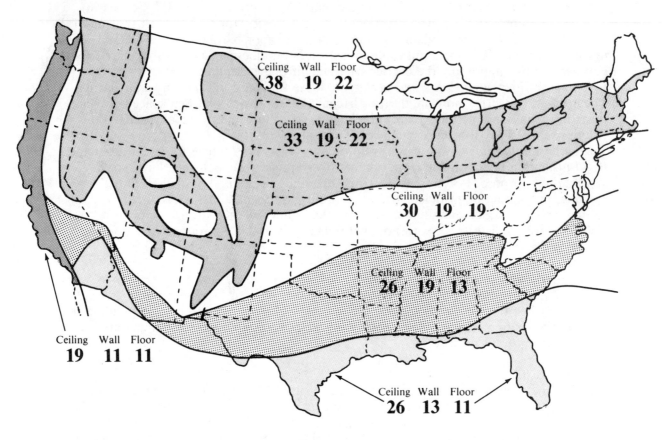

Ceiling Wall Floor
38 19 22

Ceiling Wall Floor
33 19 22

Ceiling Wall Floor
30 19 19

Ceiling Wall Floor
26 19 13

Ceiling Wall Floor
19 11 11

Ceiling Wall Floor
26 13 11

Figure 7-12
Recommended R-values

The R-value needed varies with climate. Generally, in warmer climates use R-19 for ceilings, R-11 for walls and R-11 for floors. In colder regions, use R-38 for ceilings, R-19 for walls and R-22 for floors. Figure 7-12 shows recommended R-values for different parts of the country.

Ceilings— Insulation for the ceiling can be either batts, blankets, loose fill (poured-in) or a combination of any two for the desired R-value (Figure 7-13). If insulation will be installed after the ceiling is finished, it saves time to carry the insulation to the attic and stockpile it there before the wallboard is installed. If the insulation can't be installed after the ceiling is finished, you'll have to staple it in place between joists before the drywall is installed. Be careful that the insulation doesn't block air flow at the soffit vents, gable end vents or roof vents.

Here are some interesting heat loss comparison figures:

1) 8" insulation (R-25.3) has 21% less heat loss than 6" insulation (R-19.0)

2) 10" insulation (R-31.7) has 35% less heat loss than 6" insulation.

3) 12" insulation (R-38) has 46% less heat loss than 6" insulation.

Walls— Exterior walls (excluding windows and doors) account for 13.2% of the total heat loss in a house. All building materials have some insulating value. When R-11 or R-13 batt or blanket insulation is added to the other building material, as in Figure 7-14, you can reach an R-value of 17 to 19, or more. Brick veneer with a dead air space can

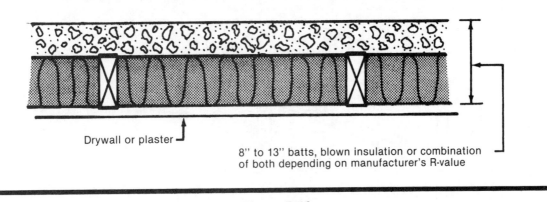

Figure 7-13
Ceiling insulation

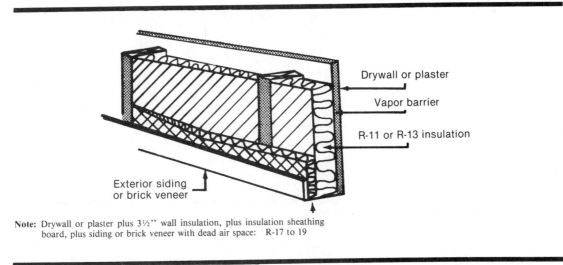

Note: Drywall or plaster plus 3½'' wall insulation, plus insulation sheathing
board, plus siding or brick veneer with dead air space: R-17 to 19

Figure 7-14
Wall insulation

add an extra R-3, or higher. A brick veneer wall with R-11 insulation between studs and a dead air space has 69% less heat loss than a brick veneer wall with no insulation between the studs.

Masonry walls with no insulation have a very high heat loss. But the addition of furring strips and R-7 to R-9 insulation (Figure 7-15) can reduce heat loss by as much as 83%.

Floors— Floors over heated rooms or basements need no insulation. Floors over unheated garages or vented crawl spaces should have insulation with about an R-19 value, depending on the climate (Figure 7-16). Install R-11 or R-19 insulation in floors over an unheated basement. For slabs on grade, as shown in Figure 7-17, install perimeter insulation of 1'' styrofoam or urethane (R-5 or R-6) at the edge of the slab, and 18'' to 24'' down the foundation or under the slab.

Windows— Windows and sliding glass doors account for about 40% of the total heat loss in a house. All cracks around windows should be filled with insulation and covered with a vapor retarder as shown in Figure 7-18.

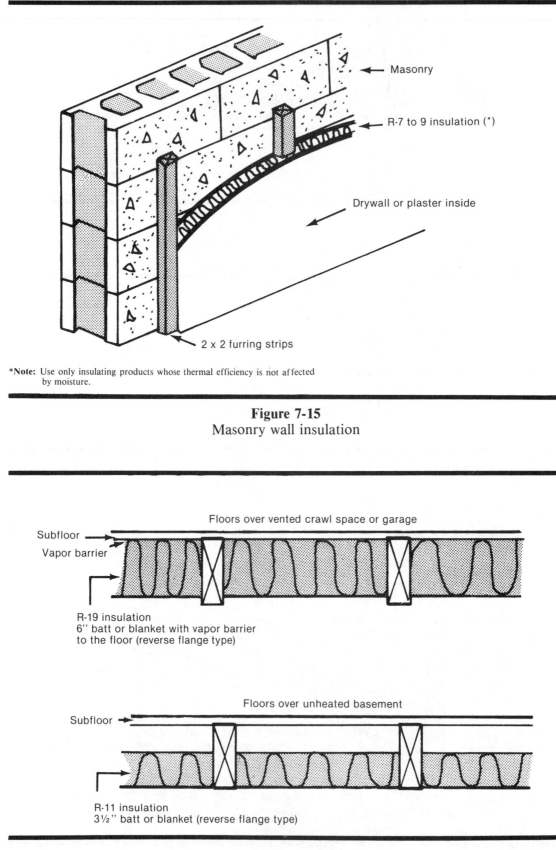

← Masonry

← R-7 to 9 insulation (*)

Drywall or plaster inside

2 x 2 furring strips

*Note: Use only insulating products whose thermal efficiency is not affected by moisture.

Figure 7-15
Masonry wall insulation

Floors over vented crawl space or garage

Subfloor
Vapor barrier

R-19 insulation
6'' batt or blanket with vapor barrier
to the floor (reverse flange type)

Floors over unheated basement

Subfloor

R-11 insulation
3½'' batt or blanket (reverse flange type)

Figure 7-16
Floor insulation

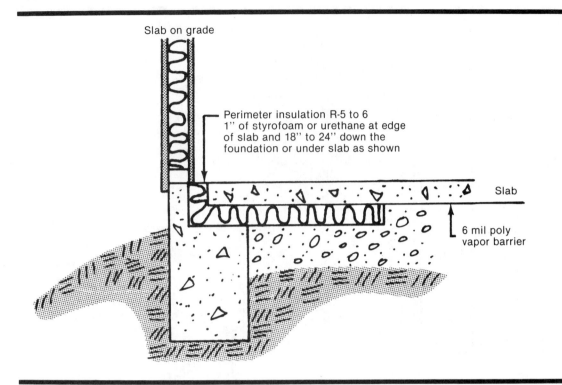

Slab on grade

Perimeter insulation R-5 to 6
1" of styrofoam or urethane at edge
of slab and 18" to 24" down the
foundation or under slab as shown

Slab

6 mil poly
vapor barrier

Figure 7-17
Perimeter insulation under slabs

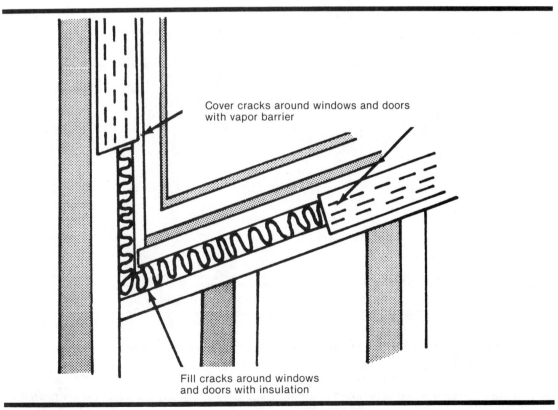

Cover cracks around windows and doors
with vapor barrier

Fill cracks around windows
and doors with insulation

Figure 7-18
Insulating around doors and windows

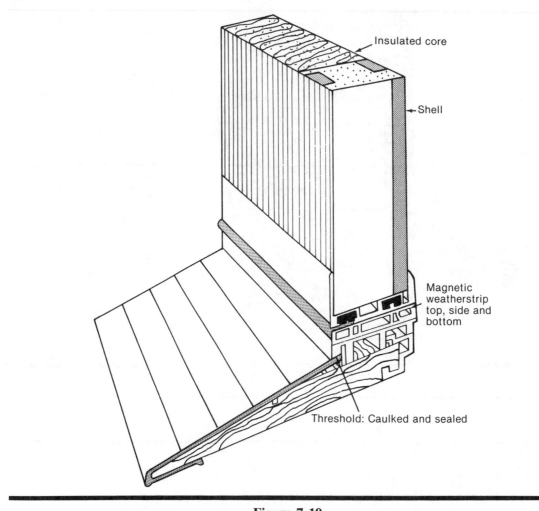

Insulated core

Shell

Magnetic
weatherstrip
top, side and
bottom

Threshold: Caulked and sealed

Figure 7-19
Insulated door

Look at these figures comparing window heat loss, when the windows are weatherstripped:

1)   Single pane and storm sash have approximately 50% less heat loss than single pane windows with no storm sash.

2)   Insulating glass has approximately 46% less heat loss than single pane windows with no storm sash.

Doors— Outside doors (excluding sliding glass doors) account for 2.4% of the total heat loss in a house. Fill all cracks around doors with insulation and cover with a vapor barrier. Here are the comparative figures:

1)   Solid core doors (1¾'') with storm doors have approximately 35% less heat loss than with no storm door.

2)   An insulated urethane and steel door with an R-13.8 value (Figure 7-19) with no storm door has approximately 85% less heat loss than a solid core door (1¾'') with no storm door. This same urethane and steel door with no storm door has approximately 76% less heat loss than a solid core door with a storm door.

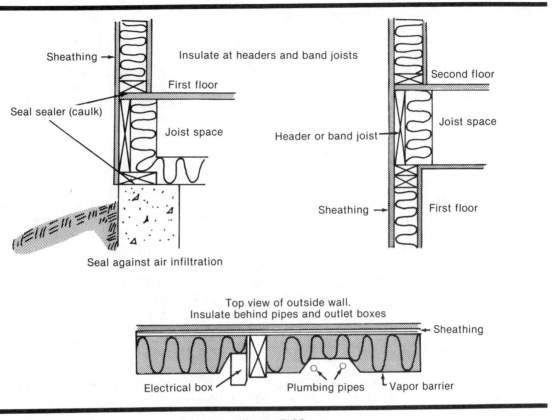

Figure 7-20
Remember to insulate little spaces

Install the Insulation Carefully

If you don't maintain the right insulation thickness, your insulation won't have enough R-value. The effectiveness of insulation depends on the workmanship of the carpenter who installs it. Compressing batts or blankets changes the density and reduces the insulation value. Blown insulation with too much air in the mixture results in a fluffy application that's less dense than required. In time it settles and isn't thick enough to provide the desired R-value.

Some of the more common installation problems are:

• Failure to fill small spaces around window and door frames with insulation, and to install a vapor retarder.

• Leaving void spaces between the framing members when batts or blankets aren't fitted correctly.

• Stapling batt or blanket flanges improperly, resulting in a poor vapor retarder. Staple with enough staples so there are no gaps and the insulation is held securely in place.

• Installing the batt or blanket under floors over crawl spaces with the vapor retarder facing the wrong way.

• Improper placement and fitting of batts or blankets where there's cross bracing between joists and purlins, or knee bracing between studs.

Figure 7-20 shows little spaces that are easy to forget. Don't let your installer make these mistakes.

Estimating Insulation Materials

To estimate insulation quantities for the walls, take the perimeter of the outside walls (plus any interior walls where insulation is required) and multiply by the wall heights. The result is the gross area. Deduct from the gross area any window and door openings 50 square feet or larger. This gives us the net area. Then divide the net area by the amount of insulation in each bag or roll. Let's say you need 1,968 square feet of R-11 insulation (3½'' x 15'') that's packed 88 square feet to the roll:

$$1,968 \text{ SF} \div 88 = 22.36 \text{ or } 23 \text{ rolls}$$

For ceiling and floor insulation, divide the area of the floor plan by the amount of insulation in each bag or roll. Round off to the next higher number for the total number of bags or rolls to order. For ceiling insulation where you'll need two layers of insulation for the correct R-value, estimate each layer and type separately. Here's an example: There are 1,040 square feet for R-30 insulation with trusses spaced 24'' o.c. You'll combine one layer of 6'' insulation (R-19) plus one layer of 3½'' insulation (R-11) for the R-30 value. The R-19 insulation is 6'' x 23'' and comes 75 square feet to the roll. The R-11 insulation is 3½'' x 23'', and a roll has 135.12 square feet:

$$1,040 \text{ SF} \div 75 = 13.87 \text{ or } 14 \text{ rolls of R-19}$$
$$1,040 \text{ SF} \div 135.12 = 7.70 \text{ or } 8 \text{ rolls of R-11}$$

If you're using polyethylene film as a vapor retarder, choose film that's as wide as the walls are high. Then divide the net area by the number of square feet per roll and round off to the next higher number for the number of rolls required. For example, say you're building a house with 1,968 square feet of wall area with an 8'0'' ceiling. Use 8'0'' wide polyethylene film. (It comes packed in 100' length, so there are 800 square feet per roll.)

$$1,968 \text{ SF} \div 800 = 2.46 \text{ or } 3 \text{ rolls}$$

Estimating Insulation Labor

Insulation labor will vary with the type installed, either batt, blanket or loose fill. Figure 7-21 shows some common manhour figures for installing insulation.

Your insulation labor estimates will be more accurate, of course, when they're based on your own cost records. Look at Figures 7-22 and 7-23. These are weekly time sheets showing the insulation and wallboard installation on the Brown job.

Our daily logs show that it took a total of 68 manhours to install 7,199 square feet of batt and blanket insulation in the ceilings, walls and floors on this job. Let's use this information to find the manhour factor for insulation labor.

Batt or blanket		Loose fill	
R-value	Square feet per manhour	Type	Cubic feet per manhour
11	180	Machine-blown	250
19	140	Hand-poured	20
30	120		

Figure 7-21
Manhour tables for installing insulation

	Name	Exemptions	Days OCTOBER 18 M	19 T	20 W	21 T	22 F	23 S	Rate	Hours worked Reg.	Over-time	Total earnings
1	D.L. WHITE		8	8	8	8	8	X		40		
2	J.R. DAVIS		8	8	8	8	8	X		40		
3												
4												
5												
6												
7												
8												
9												
10												
11												
12												
13												
14												
15												
16												
17												
18												
19												
20												

Weekly Time Sheet

Page____of____pages

For period ending 10-23-XX

BROWN ____job

Daily Log

Monday PREPARATION FOR WALLBOARD INSTALLATION (16 MANHOURS)
Tuesday PREPARATION FOR WALLBOARD INSTALLATION (16 MANHOURS)
Wednesday PREPARATION FOR WALLBOARD INSTALLATION (16 MANHOURS)
Thursday PREPARATION FOR 10,016 SF OF WALLBOARD INSTALLATION (16 MANHOURS)
Friday STARTED INSTALLING INSULATION (16 MANHOURS)
Saturday XXXX

Figure 7-22
Weekly time sheet

Weekly Time Sheet

Page____of____pages

For period ending 10-30-XX   BROWN   job

	Name	Exemptions	Days OCTOBER						Rate	Hours worked		Total earnings
			25 M	26 T	27 W	28 T	29 F	30 S		Reg.	Over-time	
1	D.L. WHITE		8	8	8	8	8	X		40		
2	J.R. DAVIS		8	8	8	8	8	X		40		
3	W.R. FARLOW		4	X	X	X	X	X		4		
4	D&A PLUMBING CO.		✓	✓	✓	X	✓	X		—.—		
5												
6												
7												
8												
9												
10												
11												
12												
13												
14												
15												
16												
17												
18												
19												
20												

Daily Log

Monday INSULATION (20 MANHOURS) - PLUMBING

Tuesday INSULATION (16 MANHOURS) - PLUMBING

Wednesday FINISHED 7,199 SF OF INSULATION (16 MANHOURS) - PLUMBING

Thursday O/S FRAMING (16 MANHOURS)

Friday O/S FRAMING (16 MANHOURS)

Saturday XXXX

Figure 7-23
Weekly time sheet

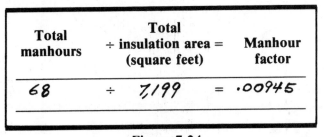

Figure 7-24
Insulation labor worksheet

Manhour factor for insulation— Look at Figure 7-24. In the first column, enter the total manhours required to install the insulation. In our example, 68 manhours were required to complete the insulation work. Now divide the total manhours (68) by the total square feet of insulation (7,199) to get a manhour factor (0.00945).

Use this factor for labor estimates on similar jobs. If you're estimating a job with 10,240 square feet of insulation in the ceilings, walls and floors, here's how to estimate the labor required:

Multiply the factor (0.00945) by the total insulation area (10,240 square feet) to get a total of 96.77 (rounded up to 97) manhours. This is the total labor to do the job. Multiply the estimated manhours (97) by the rate per hour for the labor cost.

Remember, energy conservation is a "must" in building homes today. But the investment in insulation, vapor retarders and caulk is largely wasted if your installers don't do a conscientious job. The care necessary to do a good job takes extra time. Make sure your craftsmen understand the level of quality that is expected of them, and allow for the extra time in your bid.

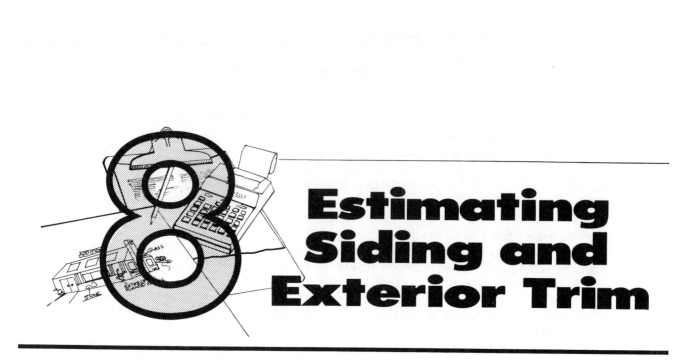

Estimating Siding and Exterior Trim

The siding and trim are the face your building presents to the world. Even the best-built, best-designed home can look no better than the siding that covers it. If your jobs include siding, be sure the materials are well-chosen and applied with care.

Siding and trim, properly installed, serve two purposes: First, they improve the appearance of the house. Second, they protect the framework from the weather. In this chapter I'll explain how to estimate siding and exterior trim.

Wood Siding

Wood siding comes in many styles, shapes, patterns and materials. A house may have a combination of siding and brick veneer, a combination of two or more types of siding, or simply one type of siding throughout.

Select a good quality siding that will hold paint. Any money you save by buying cheap siding will be lost when the house's appearance deteriorates soon after it's installed. Some of the different types of siding are:

- Bevel or lapped
- Board and batten
- Shiplap
- Tongue and groove
- Panel
- Wood shingles

Plywood siding comes in several popular designs that cost little more than textured plywood. Plywood offers excellent protection from air infiltration, an important consideration for energy conservation.

Wood siding, shingles and shakes should carry a grade stamp indicating that the product is intended for use as siding. There are too many grading organizations and grades for wood siding, shingles and shakes to make generalizations about what grades are required for what applications. Rely on your dealer for sound advice on how the products he sells should be used. If your dealer can't explain how some lumber product should be used, ask to use his copy of the lumber grading rules published by the association that graded the lumber.

Wood siding is usually made from redwood or cedar because these species are very durable, hold paint well and look good for years. Bevel, board and batten, shiplap, and tongue and groove sidings manufactured from these two wood species are popular in many parts of the U.S.

Cedar sidewall shingles are manufactured from select logs. No two shingles are exactly alike. They come in lengths of 16, 18 and 24 inches. One square of 16-inch shingles will cover 100 square feet if you use a 5-inch exposure. For the 18-inch length, use a 5½-inch exposure to cover 100 square feet, and for the 24-inch length, use a 7½-inch exposure. Cedar shingles are extremely durable and require no painting or staining.

Hardboard siding is manufactured both in siding strips and panels. It's made of wood chips and fiber pressed together to form a hard material. The thickness of lap siding is 3/8'' or 7/16''. It's available in widths up to 12 inches and lengths from 8 to 16 feet, in multiples of 2 feet. Hardboard panel siding is 1/4'', 3/8'' or 7/16'' thick, and 4 feet wide. It comes in lengths up to 16 feet.

Here are some guidelines to follow when installing wood siding, hardboard and plywood panel siding:

1)   Apply wood siding with corrosion-resistant nails which penetrate 1-inch into the studs or wood sheathing.

2)   Make sure the headlap is adequate to keep moisture out of the walls.

3)   Butt joints of horizontal sidings over studs, unless wood sheathing is used. Over sheathing, stagger the joints in adjacent pieces.

4)   Maximum spacing of the studs or blocking is 24'' o.c. for 3/8'' square edge ungrooved hardboard panels with or without sheathing. For all other hardboard, maximum spacing of studs or blocking is 16'' o.c.

Aluminum and Vinyl Siding

Aluminum siding is available in vertical V-groove, board and batten, and bevel siding. The bevel siding is the most popular. The paint on this siding is baked on and is very durable.

Vinyl siding is a product of modern chemistry. It never needs painting and is easily cleaned with soap and water. It's molded into various textures and shapes, the most popular being bevel siding.

Estimating Siding

To estimate any type of siding, first compute the wall area. Then add the gable area if you're installing gable siding. Disregard any openings less than 50 square feet.

Here's how to estimate the quantity of siding and nails to install different types of siding.

Board and Panel Siding

Figure 8-1 A is a factor table for different widths of wood bevel siding (lapped and rabbeted). Figure 8-1 B shows the factors for different widths of tongue and groove siding. Factors for vertical board siding are shown in Figure 8-1 C. For all three types of siding, factors are given for 8-inch, 10-inch and 12-inch nominal widths. These factor tables allow for lapping and waste.

Nominal width of siding	Net wall area (square feet)	x Factor	= Square feet of siding
8"		x 1.34	=
10"	1,184	x 1.26	= 1,491.84
12"		x 1.21	=

A Wood bevel siding (lapped or rabbeted)

Nominal width of siding	Net wall area (square feet)	x Factor	= Square feet of siding
8"	1,184	x 1.37	= 1,622.08
10"		x 1.33	=
12"		x 1.31	=

B Tongue and groove siding

Nominal width of siding	Net wall area (square feet)	x Factor	= Square feet of siding
8"		x 1.10	=
10"		x 1.08	=
12"	1,184	x 1.07	= 1,266.88

C Vertical board siding

Panel size	Net wall area (square feet)	x Factor	= Number of panels
4' x 8'	1,184	x .03125	= 37

D Panel siding

Figure 8-1
Factors for siding

Now let's try using these tables. Look down the first column and find the nominal width. In the next column, enter the net wall area (including the gable area, when appropriate). Multiply the net wall area by the factor to get the total square feet of siding required to do the job. Sample calculations are shown in Figure 8-1.

Use Figure 8-1 D when you're installing 4' x 8' siding panels. Again, multiply the net wall area by the factor to get the total number of panels required.

Cedar Sidewall Shingles

If you use the exposures I recommended earlier, just divide the net wall area by 100 and round off to the next even number of bundles for the number of squares. For example, 1,265 square feet of wall area is to be covered with 24" cedar shingles with an exposure of 7½". The shingles are packed four bundles per square:

$$1,265 \text{ SF} \div 100 = 12.65 \text{ squares}$$

The 12.65 squares rounds up to 12 squares plus three whole bundles.

If you're using other than the recommended exposures, consult the manufacturer's specification sheet for the coverage of one square for the exposure you're using.

The accessories for all siding, such as outside and inside corners, will vary with the type and size of siding used. Consult the manufacturer's specifications for the accessories you'll need.

Siding Nails

Figure 8-2 is a factor table for siding nails, covering nails for horizontal siding, panel siding, cedar shake siding, soffits and porch ceilings, and cornices. Here's how to use the table:

Look down the first column and find the nail size. In the next column, enter the wall area (for horizontal siding, panel siding and cedar shake siding), the ceiling area (for soffits and porch ceilings), or the total linear feet of cornice. Multiply this number by the factor to get the number of pounds of nails required to do the job.

Exterior Trim

The exterior trim of a house is installed at the same time the electrical, plumbing, heating and air conditioning are roughed-in and the interior walls are being finished. Use good grade exterior trim materials that are weather-resistant and able to hold paint. They'll look good as long as the house stands. And keep the number of joints to a minimum.

Although windows and exterior doors should be in place before the interior walls are finished, estimate them with the exterior trim. The materials for the exterior trim listed in this chapter are:

1) Windows, complete with weatherstripping, window locks and window pulls

2) Exterior doors, including garage doors, complete with door frames, weatherstripping, trim and hardware

3) Fascia, frieze and rake boards

4) Soffit and porch ceilings

5) Porch column posts

6) Gable louvers

7) Shutters

8) Flashing

9) Molding

Nail size	Wall area (square feet)	x Factor	=	Pounds of nails
6d		x .00600	=	
8d	1,184	x .00700	=	8.29 or 9
10d		x .01000	=	

A Horizontal siding

Nail size	Wall area (square feet)	x Factor	=	Pounds of nails
6d	1,184	x .01700	=	2 0,13 or 21
8d		x .02100	=	
10d		x .03000	=	

B Panel siding

Nail size	Wall area (square feet)	x Factor	=	Pounds of nails
6d		x .01000	=	
8d	1,184	x .01500	=	17.76 or 18

C Cedar shake siding

Nail size	Ceiling area (square feet)	x Factor	=	Pounds of nails
4d		x .01000	=	
6d	832	x .01250	=	10.40 or 11

D Soffit and porch ceiling

Nail size	Cornice length (linear feet)	x Factor	=	Pounds of nails
6d or 8d	550	x .01000	=	5.50 or 6

E Cornice

Figure 8-2
Factors for siding nails

Windows

Refer to the blueprints for the number, type and size of the windows. They may be wood or metal, or a combination of both, double-hung, casement, awning, sliding, fixed or combined. Are they single pane with storm windows and screens, or insulated glass with screens that must be bought separately? The plans and specifications will give this information.

Exterior Doors and Garage Doors

The plans and specifications will show the number, type and size of the exterior doors. The door frame for the main entrance door may have a special design. Look for it on the plans and specifications. The doors may be hollow or solid-core wood, or insulated with metal cladding. Sliding doors are made of metal or wood, with single pane or insulated glass. Screens are normally included with doors.

Find the number, size, type and design of the garage doors in the elevation section of the plans. Check the specifications to see if garage door openers are to be installed.

Fascia, Frieze and Rake Boards

The fascia is a vertical board nailed on the ends of rafters and trusses. It's part of the cornice (the part of the roof that projects from the wall). The frieze is a vertical board directly under the cornice, or porch ceiling, and adjacent to the wall or beam. Look at Figures 8-3, 8-4, 8-5 and 8-6. The rake is the sloping edge of a gable roof and the rake board is part of the gable trim. You can see them in Figure 8-5.

When estimating fascia, frieze and rake boards, find the size and grade of material in the plans and specs. From the elevations and cornice detail of the plans, compute the linear footage (including porches) of each different member listed. Add 5% to the total linear footage of each member for waste, and round off to the next multiple of 10. For example, assume the linear footage of 1 x 6 fascia from the prints is 136. Allowing 5% for waste, the linear footage is 142.80 (136 plus 5%). You would estimate 150 linear feet of 1 x 6 fascia boards.

Now suppose the specifications call for fascia, frieze and rake boards that are all 1 x 6. These blueprints show there are 193 linear feet of fascia board required. Add 5% for waste (9.65 linear feet) to get 202.65 linear feet. Now

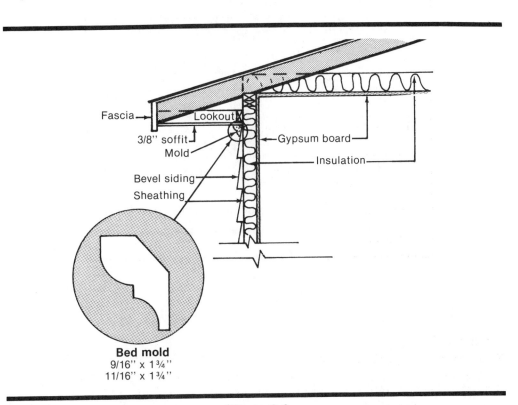

Figure 8-3
Siding and trim

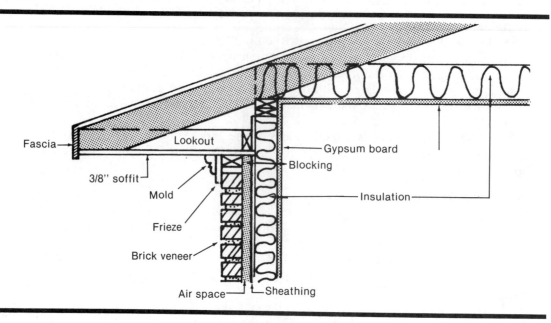

Figure 8-4
Brick veneer and trim

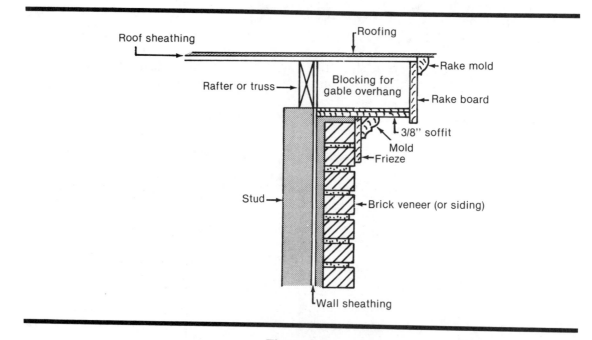

Figure 8-5
Gable overhang and trim

round up to the next multiple of 10. You'll need a total of 210 linear feet of 1 x 6 fascia board.

Once you know the total linear feet of fascia required, finding the cost is easy. Look at Figure 8-7. In the first column, enter the type and size of trim (or molding) you plan to use. In the next column, enter the total linear feet you'll need to do the job. In our example, this comes to 210 linear feet. Multiply the total linear feet (210) by the factor (0.01000) to get 2.10. Then multiply 2.10 by the price per hundred linear feet (CLF). That's $54.85 for this job. This gives you

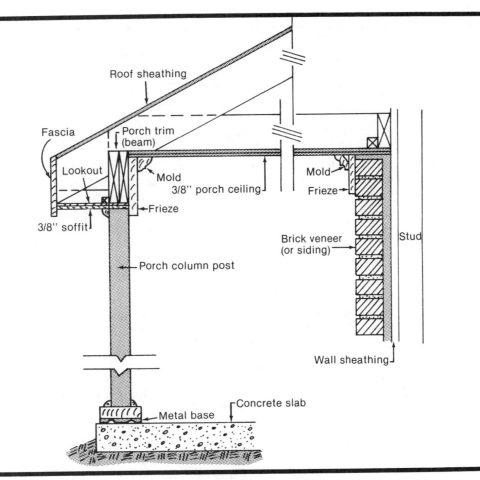

Figure 8-6
Porch trim

Type and size	Trim or molding length (linear feet)	x Factor	x	Price per CLF	= Cost of lumber
1"x 6" "B & Btr."	210	x .01000	x	$54.85	= $115.19
1"x 8" "B & Btr."	120	x .01000	x	69.50	= 83.40
2 1/4" Ranch Type Trim	400	x .01000	x	49.75	= 199.00
3 1/4" Base	340	x .01000	x	71.50	= 243.10
1/2" x 3/4" Oak Shoe	340	x .01000	x	31.00	= 105.40
11/16" x 3 5/8" Crown Mold	88	x .01000	x	88.25	= 77.66

Figure 8-7
Calculating trim and molding costs

a total cost of $115.19 for the fascia board. Use the same table to compute the cost of each of the other trim and molding pieces.

Note: The prices shown in this table are quoted per hundred linear feet (CLF). Use this table only when you need prices quoted per CLF.

Soffit and Porch Ceilings

The material most commonly used for the soffit and porch ceilings is A-C exterior plywood. Only one side of the plywood will show, so the reverse can be the lower C grade. The most common thicknesses are 1/4", 3/8", 1/2", 5/8" and 3/4". The 3/8" x 4' x 8' A-C exterior grade plywood is commonly used for soffits and porch ceilings because it's easy to handle and resists warping. Figures 8-3, 8-4, 8-5 and 8-6 show soffits and porch ceilings.

When estimating plywood for soffits and porch ceilings, compute the square footage of the area to be covered, then divide the total by the number of square feet in each piece of plywood used. Round off to the next higher number for the number of pieces. Let's say the plans show 296 square feet of area to be covered with 3/8" x 4' x 8' A-C plywood for the soffits and porch ceilings. Divide 296 square feet by 32 (the area of a 4' x 8' sheet). You need 9.25 (or 10) pieces of 3/8" x 4' x 8' plywood.

The factor for 4' x 8' sheets is 0.03125. You can get the same answer by multiplying the area by the factor:

$$296 \text{ SF } \times 0.03125 = 9.25 \text{ or } 10 \text{ pieces}$$

Porch Column Posts

These porch column posts may be wood, wrought iron or other metal. The type and design will be shown on the elevation section of the plans. The spacing of the column posts is designed by the architect for the load they will carry. Never increase the span between columns to more than is shown on the plans. Wood posts should always rest on a metal base, as shown in Figure 8-6, to prevent rot. A wood base exposed to dampness will rot very quickly.

When estimating porch column posts, get the number, type and size from the elevation section of the plans and the specifications.

Gable Louvers

These louvers, or vents, are designed by the architect for proper ventilation and appearance. The number, type and size of gable louvers are shown on the elevation section of the plans.

Shutters

Check the elevation sections of the plans for the number, size, type and design of shutters, if any.

Flashing

Provide flashing over all wall openings and intersections as shown in Figure 8-8. Use corrosion-resistant sheet metal.

When estimating metal flashing in rolls, allow 7 inches for the width of all wall openings and intersections. From the elevation sections of the plans, find the linear feet of all areas where flashing is required. If you're using 14" aluminum flashing, divide the total linear feet by 2. Here's an example: The plans show 100 linear feet of flashing will be required for the wall openings and intersections. You plan to use 14" aluminum flashing, so you divide the 100 linear feet by 2. You need 50 linear feet of 14" aluminum flashing.

Molding

Figure 8-9 shows the shape and size of common molds used for exterior trim. They're estimated by the linear feet. Allow 5% for waste.

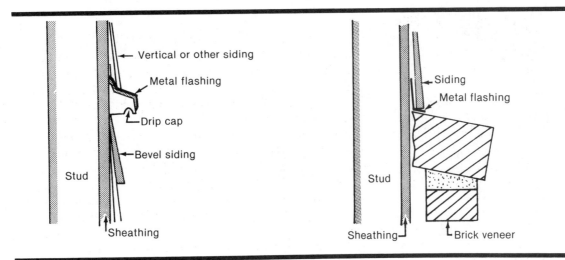

Figure 8-8
Flashing at intersections of different materials

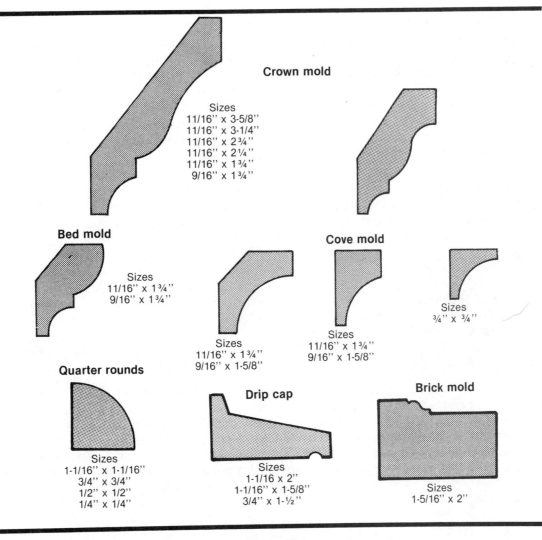

Crown mold

Sizes
11/16'' x 3-5/8''
11/16'' x 3-1/4''
11/16'' x 2¾''
11/16'' x 2¼''
11/16'' x 1¾''
9/16'' x 1¾''

Bed mold

Sizes
11/16'' x 1¾''
9/16'' x 1¾''

Cove mold

Sizes
11/16'' x 1¾''
9/16'' x 1-5/8''

Sizes
¾'' x ¾''

Sizes
11/16'' x 1¾''
9/16'' x 1-5/8''

Quarter rounds

Sizes
1-1/16'' x 1-1/16''
¾'' x ¾''
1/2'' x 1/2''
1/4'' x 1/4''

Drip cap

Sizes
1-1/16 x 2''
1-1/16'' x 1-5/8''
¾'' x 1-½''

Brick mold

Sizes
1-5/16'' x 2''

Figure 8-9
Molding

Exterior Trim Nails

Use rust-resistant nails for all exterior trim and molding. Most trim and molding can be fastened with 6d or 8d nails. Here's how to compute the quantity of nails required:

Look again at Figure 8-2 E. Use this table to compute the quantity of nails required for exterior trim and molding. Just multiply the factor by the total linear feet of exterior trim or molding to get the number of pounds of nails required.

Let's compute the nails required for our 210 linear feet of fascia board. Multiply the total linear feet (210) by the factor (0.01000). We'll need 2.1 (or 3) pounds of nails for this portion of the exterior trim and molding work. Use this same table to calculate the nails required for all the exterior trim and molding components.

Siding and Exterior Trim Labor

Labor estimates for siding and exterior trim can be based either on manhours per unit of material installed, or on manhours per square foot of floor space.

We'll figure it both ways in this chapter. Here are some figures to use if you base your estimate on units of material installed:

Siding: 4 to 8 manhours per 100 square feet

Cornice: 6 to 8 manhours per 100 linear feet

Gable (rake): 10 to 14 manhours per 100 linear feet

Other molding: 4 to 6 manhours per 100 linear feet

These estimates may or may not be accurate for work done by your own crew. Your best labor estimate for any task will always come from the figures you keep in your own cost records.

Installing siding and trim on the second floor will require more time than installing them on the first floor. Why? Because second-floor work requires scaffolding that must be erected and dismantled.

Scaffolding labor is charged to exterior trim and siding. The labor to install siding and trim on the second floor will generally be 25% to 35% higher than labor for the first floor.

Figures 8-10A through 8-10E are weekly time sheets for the Brown job. The daily logs show the labor required for siding and exterior trim. The siding and most of the exterior trim were on the second floor. This means that scaffolding was needed and extra labor was required to put it up. The house was brick veneer with 4' x 8' panel siding on the second floor.

The daily logs show that a total of 263 manhours were required to install the second-floor siding and exterior trim on a house (and attached garage) with a total floor area of 2,850 square feet. Let's use this information to find the manhour factor for siding and exterior trim.

Manhour Factor for Siding and Exterior Trim

Figure 8-11 is a labor worksheet for siding and exterior trim. In the first column, enter the total manhours. In our example, this comes to 263 manhours. Divide the total manhours by the total house and garage area (2,850 SF) to get a manhour factor of 0.09228. Now let's use the manhour factor to estimate a future job.

Let's say the new job we're bidding has a total house area of 1,875 square feet. Multiply the house area (1,875 SF) by the manhour factor (0.09228) to get 173.03 (or 173) manhours.

Weekly Time Sheet

Page____of____pages

For period ending __3-12-XX__   __Brown_____job

#	Name	Exemptions	March Days 7 M	8 T	9 W	10 T	11 F	12 S	Rate	Hours worked Reg.	Over-time	Total earnings
1	D.L. White		8	8	6½	8	8	X		38½		
2	A.L. King		X	8	8	8	8	X		32		
3	J.E. King		X	X	8	8	8	X		24		
4	Holston Drywall, Inc.		X	X	X	✓	X	X		—		
5												
6												
7												
8												
9												
10												
11												
12												
13												
14												
15												
16												
17												
18												
19												
20												

Daily Log

Monday __Started waterproofing foundation__
Tuesday __Finished parging -- started bituminous coating__
Wednesday __Finished bituminous coating -- Drain tile around basement__
Thursday __Drywall -- o/s trim (24 manhours)__
Friday __o/s trim (24 manhours)__
Saturday __XXXXX__

Figure 8-10A
Weekly time sheet

Weekly Time Sheet

Page____of____pages

For period ending 3-19-XX

Brown   job

	Name	Exemptions	Days March						Rate	Hours worked		Total earnings
			14 M	15 T	16 W	17 T	18 F	19 S		Reg.	Over-time	
1	D.L. White		8	8	4	6	8	X		34		
2	A.L. King		8	8	8	8	8	X		40		
3	J.E. King		8	8	4	6	8	X		34		
4	Holston Drywall, Inc.		X	✓	X	✓	✓	X		—		
5												
6												
7												
8												
9												
10												
11												
12												
13												
14												
15												
16												
17												
18												
19												
20												

Daily Log

Monday Siding (24 manhours)
Tuesday Siding (24 manhours)--Drywall finish
Wednesday Siding (16 manhours)
Thursday Siding--trim on back porch (20 manhours)--Drywall finish
Friday o/s trim (24 manhours)--Drywall finish
Saturday XXXXX

Figure 8-10B
Weekly time sheet

Weekly Time Sheet

Page____of____pages

For period ending **3-26-XX**

Brown job

#	Name	Exemptions	Days March 21 M	22 T	23 W	24 T	25 F	26 S	Rate	Hours worked Reg.	Over-time	Total earnings
1	D.L. White		8	8	8	8	8	X		40		
2	A.L. King		8	8	8	8	8	X		40		
3	J.E. King		8	8	8	8	8	X		40		
4												
5												
6												
7												
8												
9												
10												
11												
12												
13												
14												
15												
16												
17												
18												
19												
20												

Daily Log

Monday Trim on front porch (18 manhours)--started floor underlayment (6 manhours)
Tuesday Floor underlayment (24 manhours)
Wednesday Floor underlayment (24 manhours)
Thursday Finished floor underlayment (12 manhours)--o/s trim (12 man hours)
Friday o/s trim (24 manhours)
Saturday XXXXX

Figure 8-10C
Weekly time sheet

Weekly Time Sheet

Page____of____pages

For period ending 4-2-XX

Brown____job

	Name	Exemptions	Days March / April						Rate	Hours worked		Total earnings
			28 M	29 T	30 W	31 T	1 F	2 S		Reg.	Over-time	
1	D.L. White		8	8	8	8	8	X		40		
2	A.L. King		8	8	8	8	6½	X		38½		
3	J.E. King		8	8	8	8	6½	X		38½		
4												
5												
6												
7												
8												
9												
10												
11												
12												
13												
14												
15												
16												
17												
18												
19												
20												

Daily Log

Monday o/s trim (24 manhours)
Tuesday i/s trim (24 manhours)
Wednesday i/s trim (24 manhours)
Thursday i/s trim (24 manhours)
Friday i/s trim (21 manhours)
Saturday XXXXX

Figure 8-10D
Weekly time sheet

Weekly Time Sheet

Page____of____pages

For period ending 4-16-XX   Brown ____job

Name	Exemptions	Days April						Rate	Hours worked		Total earnings
		11 M	12 T	13 W	14 T	15 F	16 S		Reg.	Over-time	
1 J.E. King		5	8	8	8	8	X		37		
2 W.W. Peery, Paint Cont		✓	X	✓	✓	X	X		—		
3 D&A Plumbing Co.		X	X	X	X	✓	X		—		
4											
5											
6											
7											
8											
9											
10											
11											
12											
13											
14											
15											
16											
17											
18											
19											
20											

Daily Log

Monday o/s trim (5 manhours)--o/s & i/s painting

Tuesday o/s trim (8 manhours)

Wednesday o/s trim (8 manhours)--i/s painting

Thursday o/s trim (8 manhours)--o/s painting

Friday Formed in for concrete (8 manhours)-- plumbing

Saturday XXXXX

Figure 8-10E
Weekly time sheet

Total manhours	÷	House and garage area (square feet)	=	Manhour factor
263	÷	2,850	=	.09228

Figure 8-11
Labor worksheet for siding and exterior trim

Keep in mind that the manhour factor (0.09228) was developed on a job where most of the work was on the second floor. If all of the siding and exterior trim were on the first floor, the manhour factor would be reduced by about 25%. The manhour factor for first-floor siding and exterior trim is 0.06921.

If the new job we're bidding has siding and exterior trim work only on the first floor, estimate the labor by multiplying the house area (1,875 SF) by the first floor factor (0.06921), to get a total of 129.77 (or 130) manhours required to do the job.

Remember that in cold weather, the labor costs for exterior trim and siding will be approximately 10% more than in good weather.

And remember that your own manhour figures will always be more accurate for your crews. Keep accurate manhour figures on a form like the weekly time sheet, and use them to compute your own manhour factors.

In the next chapter we'll move inside for the interior wall and ceiling finish.

Estimating Finish Carpentry

After you've finished the rough-in work for the electrical, plumbing and HVAC subs and installed the insulation, it's time to finish the interior walls and ceilings. But first check to see if the plans show a drop ceiling over the kitchen cabinets and bathroom vanities, or any other carpentry work that has to be done before the wall finish is applied. You only want to finish those walls once!

Gypsum wallboard (sometimes called gypboard or sheetrock, and usually abbreviated G.W.B.) is the most common material for walls and ceilings, so we'll cover it first. Gypsum wallboard is popular because it has a high fire-rating, is inexpensive, goes up much faster than lath and plaster, and doesn't require highly skilled installers.

Gypsum Board

Gypsum board is a sheet material composed of a gypsum core faced with paper on both sides. It comes in standard sheets 4 feet wide and from 8 to 16 feet long. The standard thicknesses are 1/2'', 5/8'' and 3/4'', but you can order thicknesses of 1/4'' and 3/8'' for special applications, such as where you have to bend it.

Most wallboard has tapered edges along the length, although some types are tapered on all edges. This tapering permits a level surface after the joints are filled and taped. Wallboard is available with a foil back, which serves as a vapor retarder on exterior walls. You can also get it with vinyl or other prefinished surfaces, which are especially appropriate in commercial buildings.

In new construction, use 1/2'' wallboard for single-layer application. In laminated two-ply applications, use two 3/8'' sheets. The 3/8'' thickness is considered the minimum for 16'' stud spacing in single-layer applications, but it's usually only specified where there is a bend in the surface or in remodeling work.

Figure 9-1 lists maximum member spacing for the various thicknesses of gypsum board.

When you're applying wallboard in a single layer, you can lay the sheets either vertically or horizontally on the walls after the ceiling has been covered. Vertical application covers three stud spaces when studs are spaced 16'' o.c., and two when spacing is 24'' o.c. Center the edges on the studs, allowing only moderate contact between the edges of the sheets.

Installed long direction of sheet	Minimum thickness, gypsum board	Maximum spacing of supports (on center)	
		Walls	Ceilings
	In.	In.	In.
Parallel to framing members	⅜	16	--
	½	24	16
	⅝	24	16
Right angles to framing members	⅜	16	16
	½	24	24
	⅝	24	24

Figure 9-1
Maximum support spacing for gypsum board,
single-layer application

Apply sheets so the long edges are horizontal when you can use full-length sheets between opposite walls. This minimizes the number of vertical joints. Where joints are necessary, make them at windows or doors. Nail spacing is the same for horizontal or vertical application. When studs are spaced 16'' o.c., horizontal nailing blocks between studs are normally not required. But when spacing is greater, or an impact-resistant joint is required, use nailing blocks.

If you're using a laminated two-ply method of wallboard application, you'll start with an undercourse of 3/8'' material applied vertically and nailed in place. Then apply the finish 3/8'' sheet horizontally, usually in room size lengths, with an adhesive. Apply the adhesive in ribbons or spread it with a notched trowel. Follow the manufacturer's recommendations in any case.

Drive nails in the finish gypsum wallboard so the heads are slightly below the surface. A crowned head hammer will form a small dimple in the wallboard. Don't use a nail set. And be careful not to break the paper face.

Plywood

Prefinished plywood paneling is a another popular wall cover material. It's available in many species, finishes and textures. Sheet size is 4' x 8' or longer. They're applied vertically or horizontally, but must have solid backing at all edges. For 16'' o.c. studs, use at least 1/4'' thick plywood. For studs 20'' or 24'' o.c., 3/8'' plywood is the minimum acceptable thickness. Use casing or finish nails and adhesives to fasten prefinished plywood and other sheet materials to wall studs.

Hardboard and Fiberboard

Hardboard and fiberboard sheets are applied the same way as plywood. Hardboard must be at least 1/4'' thick when applied over open framing spaced 16'' o.c. Rigid backing of some type is required for 1/8'' hardboard.

Fiberboard in tongue-and-groove plank or sheet form must be 1/2'' thick when framing members are spaced 16'' o.c., and 3/4'' when 24'' spacing is used.

Fiberboard is also used to cover the ceiling and may be nailed or stapled to strips (furring) fastened to ceiling joists. See Figure 9-2. Acoustic tile is also suspended from wood or metal hangers attached to ceiling joists.

When ceiling tile (or floor tile) is installed, tile seldom fit exactly without some cutting. When tile have to be cut to fit, it's considered good practice to cut an equal amount

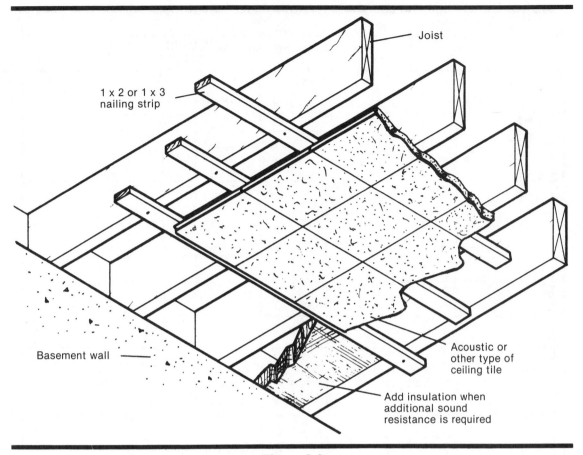

Figure 9-2
Installation of ceiling tile

from both sides of the room. On most jobs, all tile around the edge of the room will have to be cut. These cut tile are usually called the *border tile*. Figures 9-3 and 9-4 show two different ways to lay out 12" x 12" ceiling or floor tiles for a typical 12'6" x 16'8" room. One way to estimate the size of the border pieces is as follows:

1) *Room width:* Divide the width of the tile into the width of the room to get the number of whole pieces. In our example, the width of the room is 12'6" and we're using 12" x 12" acoustic tile. Divide 12'6" (150") by 12" (width of the tile). The answer is 12.50. There will be 12 whole pieces of tile plus 6" for the two borders. Divide the 6" by 2 to get the size of each of the two border pieces. A piece of tile will have to be cut to 3" for each row of tile for the width of the room. This shows clearly in Figure 9-3. Measure carefully when you cut the border tile. You'll find that many walls on opposite sides of a room are not quite parallel.

2) *Room length:* Divide the length of the tile into the length of the room to get the number of whole pieces. If the length of the room is 16'8", divide 16'8" (200") by 12" (length of tile). The answer is 16.67. This will be 16 whole pieces plus 8" for the two borders. Divide the 8" by 2 to find the width of each border. The border tiles for the length of the room will be cut to 4".

Now look at Figure 9-3 again. Don't you think it would look better if the border tiles were nearer in size to the whole tiles? If you agree, Here's the way to figure the borders so they're as large as possible:

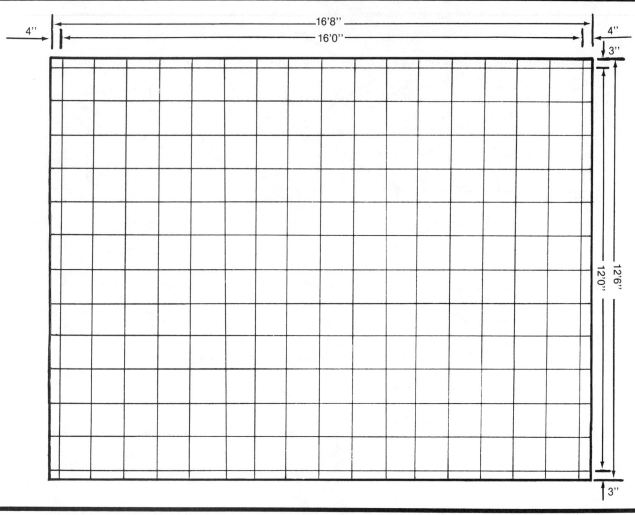

Figure 9-3
Laying out ceiling and floor tile (method 1)

Room width and length: Divide the width of the room by the width of the tile, as we did in the example above. *Now subtract one whole piece of tile from this number.* So we have 11 whole pieces plus 18" (12" plus 6") for the border. Finally, divide the 18" by 2 to get the size of each of the two borders. The answer is 9". So for the room width, each row of tile will end with a tile cut to 9"! Look at Figure 9-4.

The border tile for the length of the room in our example will be 16'8" (200") divided by 12" (length of tile). The answer is 16.67. *Again, subtract one whole piece of tile from this number.* That leaves 15 whole pieces plus 20" (12" plus 8") for the border. Divide this 20" by 2. The size of the cut tile for each border will be 10", as shown in Figure 9-4.

You'll always have a more attractive ceiling or floor if the border tile is more than 6" wide — and you'll use about the same amount of tile either way.

Wood Paneling
Real wood paneling is still popular in better quality homes. For informal treatment, natural or stained Knotty Pine, Douglas Fir, Chestnut, or Cypress are good choices. Wood paneling should be thoroughly seasoned to a moisture content near the average it reaches in service, in most areas about 8 percent. Let the material dry to the right moisture content by placing it around the wall of the heated room for as long as possible before installation.

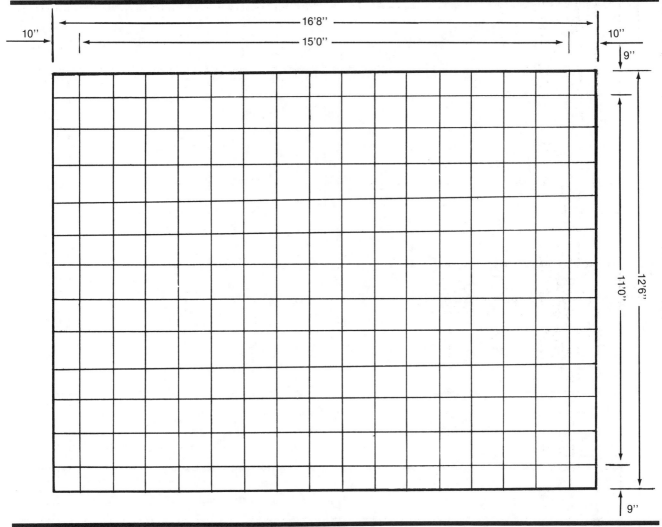

Figure 9-4
Laying out ceiling and floor tile (method 2)

Boards can be applied horizontally or vertically. Here's a guide to use when applying matched wood paneling:

• Apply the paneling over a vapor barrier and insulation if you're covering exterior wall framing or blocking (Figure 9-5).

• Don't use boards wider than 8'' unless there's a long tongue or matched edges. Wider boards swell and shrink too much.

• Thickness should be at least 3/8'' for 16'' o.c. framing, 1/2'' for 20'' o.c. spacing, and 5/8'' for 24'' o.c. spacing.

• Maximum spacing of supports for nailing should be 24'' o.c. with blocking for vertical applications. See Figure 9-5.

• Use 5d (1¾'') or 6d (2'') nails. Figure 9-6 shows the sizes of common wire nails.

Estimating Wallboard Material

Begin your wallboard estimate by calculating the area of the walls and ceiling in each room, closet, hall and stairway.

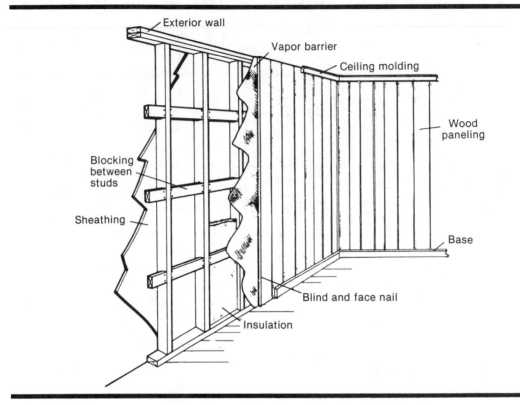

Figure 9-5
Blocking between studs for vertical wood paneling

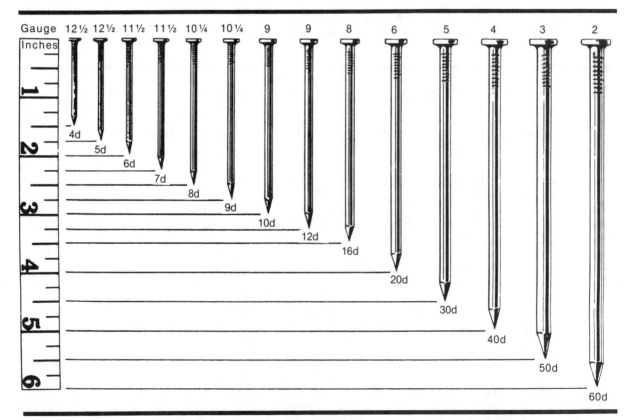

Figure 9-6
Sizes of common wire nails

	Length of room																		
	2'	3'	4'	5'	6'	7'	8'	9'	10'	11'	12'	13'	14'	15'	16'	17'	18'	19'	20'
2'	68	86	104	122	140	158	176	194	212	230	248	266	284	302	320	338	356	374	392
3'	86	105	124	143	162	181	200	219	238	257	276	295	314	333	352	371	390	409	428
4'	104	124	144	164	184	204	224	244	264	284	304	324	344	364	384	404	424	444	464
5'	122	143	164	185	206	227	248	269	290	311	332	353	374	395	416	437	458	479	500
6'	140	162	184	206	228	250	272	294	316	338	360	382	404	426	448	470	492	514	536
7'	158	181	204	227	250	273	296	319	342	365	388	411	434	457	480	503	526	549	572
8'	176	200	224	248	272	296	320	344	368	392	416	440	464	488	512	536	560	584	608
9'	194	219	244	269	294	319	344	369	394	419	444	469	494	519	544	569	594	619	644
10'	212	238	264	290	316	342	368	394	420	446	472	498	524	550	576	602	628	654	680
11'	230	257	284	311	338	365	392	419	446	473	500	527	554	581	608	635	662	689	716
12'	248	276	304	332	360	388	416	444	472	500	528	556	585	614	643	672	701	730	759	788
13'	266	295	324	353	382	411	440	469	498	527	556	585	614	644	674	704	734	764	794	824
14'	284	314	344	374	404	434	464	494	524	554	584	614	644	674	705	736	767	798	829	860
15'	302	333	364	395	426	457	488	519	550	581	612	643	674	705	736	768	800	832	864	896
16'	320	352	384	416	448	480	512	544	576	608	640	672	704	736	768	800	832	864	896
17'	338	371	404	437	470	503	536	569	602	635	668	701	734	767	800	833	866	899	936
18'	356	390	424	458	492	526	560	594	628	662	696	730	764	798	832	866	900	934	968
19'	374	409	444	479	514	549	584	619	654	689	724	759	794	829	864	899	934	969	1004
20'	392	428	464	500	536	572	608	644	680	716	752	788	824	860	896	932	968	1004	1040

(Width of room is labeled along the left side.)

Figure 9-7
Wall and ceiling area (in SF) for rooms with 8'0" ceilings

Room	Size	Ceiling height
GARAGE	24'0" WIDTH x 22'0" LENGTH	10'0"

Perimeter of walls: __24'__ width + __22'__ length x 2 = __92__ linear feet

Walls: __92__ LF (perimeter) x __10'__ (ceiling height) = __920__ SF

Ceiling: __24'__ width x __22'__ length = __528__ SF

Total square feet of walls and ceiling __1,448__ SF*

__1,448__ square feet divided by 9 = __160.89__ square yards

*If openings are to be deducted, deduct them from this total.

Figure 9-8
Wall and ceiling area (in SF) for rooms with other than 8'0" ceiling heights

Use Figure 9-7 as a shortcut. It shows the total square feet of walls and ceiling for rooms of different sizes, assuming a ceiling height of 8'0". If a room is 14'0" x 16'0", for example, it will have 704 square feet of wall and ceiling area. A hall 3'0" x 18'0" has 390 square feet of wall and ceiling area.

Here's a tip. Estimate all walls as if they had no door or window openings, unless an opening is more than 25 square feet. The pieces cut out probably can't be used anywhere else. Also, this overestimate gives you a small allowance for waste.

When a room is larger than the dimensions given in Figure 9-7, or when the ceiling isn't 8'0" high, use the worksheet in Figure 9-8 to calculate the wall and ceiling area.

Total surface area (square feet)	x	Factor	=	Number of panels	Total surface area (square feet)	x	Factor	=	Number of panels
10,016	x	.03125	=	*313*	*10,016*	x	.02083	=	*208.63 or 209*
A 4' x 8' wallboard					**B 4' x 12' wallboard**				

Figure 9-9
Factors for wallboard panels

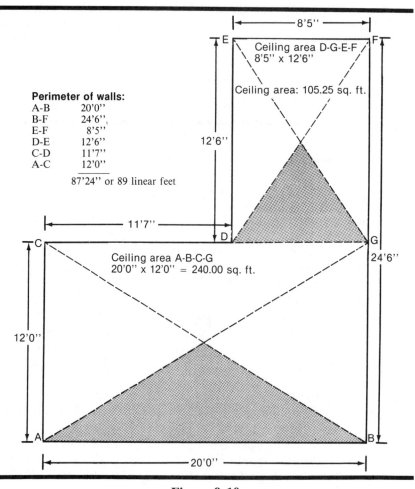

Perimeter of walls:
A-B   20'0''
B-F   24'6''
E-F   8'5''
D-E   12'6''
C-D   11'7''
A-C   12'0''
87'24'' or 89 linear feet

Ceiling area D-G-E-F
8'5'' x 12'6''

Ceiling area: 105.25 sq. ft.

Ceiling area A-B-C-G
20'0'' x 12'0'' = 240.00 sq. ft.

Figure 9-10
Estimating drywall for irregularly shaped rooms

We've used this one to do our example, but there's a blank one in the back of the book that you can photocopy or have printed.

If a garage that's 22'0'' x 24'0'' has a ceiling 10'0'' high, what's the total wall and ceiling area? Figure 9-8 shows that there are 1,448 square feet of walls and ceiling in this garage.

If you want to convert that into square yards, simply divide by 9. In our example, 1,448 square feet divided by 9 equals 160.89, or 161 square yards.

Once you know the total wall and ceiling area, you can figure the number of sheets of wallboard to order. Use Figure 9-9 A to find the number of 4' x 8' panels you'll need. Section B is for 4' x 12' panels. You'll find blank copies of the tables in the back of the

Wallboard size	Approximate weight (each panel)	Bending Radii Length	Width
¼" x 4' x 8'	35 lbs.	5'	15'
⅜" x 4' x 8'	50 lbs.	7½'	25'
⅜" x 4' x 12'	75 lbs.	7'	25'
½" x 4' x 8'	67 lbs.	10'*	---
½" x 4' x 12'	100 lbs.	10'*	---
⅝" x 4' x 8'	90 lbs.	---	---
⅝" x 4' x 12'	135 lbs.	---	---

*Bending two ¼" pieces successively permits radii shown for ½".

Figure 9-11
Gypsum board weight and bending radii

book. Here's how to use these two factor tables.

In the first column, enter the total square feet of wall and ceiling area. We're assuming that there are 10,016 square feet of surface area to be covered. Multiply the total surface area by the factor to get the number of panels required. Figure 9-9 A shows that if you use 4' x 8' panels, you'll need 313 panels to complete the job. If you're using 4' x 12' panels, section B shows that you'll need only 209 panels.

Figure 9-10 shows how to estimate the drywall required for odd-shaped rooms. You'll add each wall length to find the total wall perimeter, then multiply that by the wall height. Next, break the room down into regular-shaped sections. Calculate the ceiling area separately for each section. Add the ceiling area figures to the wall area to get the total area for the entire room. Then use the factor table to find the number of sheets of drywall.

Figure each type and each thickness of wallboard separately. For example, estimate all 1/2" wallboard first. Then calculate quantities for water-resistant wallboard (greenboard), foil-backed wallboard, etc.

When wallboard is delivered to the job site, be conscious of how much weight you're storing in each room. Too much weight in one place can deflect joists. Figure 9-11 shows gypsum board weight (and the minimum bending radii). Use this table to determine how much wallboard weight you're bringing onto the job site. Here's how this table works:

Using our example in Figure 9-9 B, we'll need to store 209 pieces of 1/2" x 4' x 12" gypsum wallboard. According to the chart in Figure 9-11, each piece of 1/2" x 4' x 12'

Total surface area (square feet) x	Factor =	Pounds of nails	Total surface area (square feet) x	Factor =	Number of tubes
10,016 x	.00500 =	50.08 or 50	10,016 x	.00200 =	20.03 or 20
A 1⅜" annular ring nails			B Adhesive		

Figure 9-12
Factors for wallboard fasteners

gypsum wallboard weighs approximately 100 pounds. This makes a total weight of 20,900 pounds of wallboard to be delivered and stored at the job site. Divide 20,900 pounds by 2,000 to get 10.45 tons of wallboard. That's a little more than two full-grown African elephants.

So when the wallboard arrives, divide it up and store it throughout the house. Don't put that 10½ tons across two or three joists in a single room! And be sure to stack it so that the length of the wallboard is perpendicular to the floor joists. This distributes the weight over a greater number of joists.

Fasteners

Gypsum wallboard is hung with nails and adhesives. Use both nails and adhesive on each sheet. Figure 9-12 A is a factor table for 1⅜'' annular ring nails. Figure 9-12 B is a factor table for adhesive. Use these tables for single-layer application. Here's how:

In the first column, enter the total square feet of wallboard surface area. In our example, this is 10,016 square feet. Then multiply the total area by the factor to get the number of pounds of nails and the number of tubes of adhesive required. We'll order 50 pounds of annular nails and 20 tubes of adhesive.

Finishing Materials

Use Figure 9-13 to compute the quantity of finishing materials needed. Section A is a factor table for rolls of tape (based on 250 feet per roll). Section B has factors for five-gallon cans of joint compound for smooth finishes. Use section C for figuring joint compound for ceilings treated with textured finish. Here's how to use these three tables.

In the first column, enter the total square feet of wallboard surface area. We'll use 10,016 square feet again. Then multiply the total area by the factor to get the number of rolls of tape or cans of joint compound required.

Look at Figure 9-13. We'll need 17 rolls of tape and 10 five-gallon cans of joint compound. If the ceilings have a textured finish, we'll need 25 cans of joint compound.

We've seen the easy way to calculate the materials required for wallboard. Now let's take a look at wallboard labor.

Total surface area (square feet)	x	Factor	=	Number of rolls
10,016	x	.00167	=	16.73 OR 17

A Rolls of tape

Total surface area (square feet)	x	Factor	=	Number of cans
10,016	x	.00100	=	10.02 OR 10

B Cans of joint compound

Total surface area (square feet)	x	Factor	=	Number of cans
10.016	x	.00250	=	25.04 OR 25

C Cans of joint compound (for ceilings with textured finish)

Figure 9-13
Factors for wallboard finishing materials

Weekly Time Sheet			Page____of____pages

For period ending _10-23-XX_   _BROWN_ ___job

	Name	Exemptions	Days OCTOBER						Rate	Hours worked		Total earnings
			18 M	19 T	20 W	21 T	22 F	23 S		Reg.	Over-time	
1	D.L. WHITE		8	8	8	8	8	X		40		
2	J.R. DAVIS		8	8	8	8	8	X		40		
3												
4												
5												
6												
7												
8												
9												
10												
11												
12												
13												
14												
15												
16												
17												
18												
19												
20												

Daily Log

Monday *PREPARATION FOR WALLBOARD INSTALLATION (16 MANHOURS)*
Tuesday *PREPARATION FOR WALLBOARD INSTALLATION (16 MANHOURS)*
Wednesday *PREPARATION FOR WALLBOARD INSTALLATION (16 MANHOURS)*
Thursday *PREPARATION FOR 10,016 SF OF WALLBOARD INSTALLATION (16 MANHOURS)*
Friday *STARTED INSTALLING INSULATION (16 MANHOURS)*
Saturday *XXXX*

Figure 9-14
Weekly time sheet

Estimating Wallboard Labor

Most carpenters are able to hang drywall. But on larger jobs the general contractor will probably subcontract the drywall work to a drywall specialist. Drywall subs usually bid by the square foot and will include in their price both labor and materials, or the labor only.

Drywall subs want to have all the framing and furring done before wallboard application begins. Make sure all the drop ceilings for cabinets are framed in. Nailers should be installed on inside corners on partitions running parallel to the ceiling joists. These are needed to anchor the ends of wallboard sheets at the corners. Your carpenters will have to cut all openings in the walls and ceilings for bathroom accessories and access doors. This preparation and coordination is essential on every drywall job.

Look at Figure 9-14. It's a weekly time sheet showing carpenter labor for preparation for wallboard installation. It shows a total of 64 manhours needed to complete the preparation work for wallboard installation. Let's use this information to find the manhour factor for coordination work for installing wallboard.

Manhour Factor for Wallboard Preparation: Figure 9-15 is the worksheet for computing the factor for wallboard preparation labor. In the first column, enter the total manhours required for wallboard installation (64). In the next column, enter the total square feet of wallboard installed (10,016). Then divide the total manhours (64) by the total area (10,016 square feet) to get the manhour factor (0.00639). Of course, your factor will be at least slightly different.

Use your manhour factor to estimate future jobs. Here's an example. If a job has an estimated 12,000 square feet of gypsum wallboard, multiply the total area (12,000 SF) by the factor (0.00639) to get a total of 76.68 (or 77) manhours. If the hourly labor cost is $25.00, the cost of the coordination work for wallboard installation labor will be $1,925.00.

Some drywall subs charge by the number of pieces installed. In this example, it would be 250 pieces (48 square feet in each 4' x 12' panel).

Thin-Coat Plaster

Thin-coat plaster has almost replaced lath and plaster for plastered walls. Because it doesn't contain as much water, there's less time lost waiting for the plaster to dry. It dries in about 24 hours to a hard and durable finish. Thin-coat plaster is applied over a plaster base of gypsum core with a special face paper. These plaster base sheets are 4 feet wide, and for residential construction, 12 feet long. They're available in 1/2" and 5/8" thickness. The plaster is specially formulated and applied over the plaster base 1/16" to 3/32" thick.

Estimate the quantity of plaster base by the square feet just as we estimated the quantity of drywall. Application of thin-coat plaster is done by plasterers who specialize in this trade. They'll submit a bid for either the labor and material or the labor only. The bid will probably be based on the square yards of wall and ceiling to be covered, rather than on the total job.

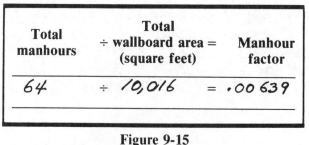

Total manhours	Total ÷ wallboard area = (square feet)	Manhour factor
64	÷ 10,016 =	.00639

Figure 9-15
Wallboard labor sheet

Estimating Interior Trim and Stairs

The final stairway is installed after the finish carpentry is done. But rough stairs have to be laid out and framed earlier so tradesmen can move from level to level. That's why stair carriages are usually cut and installed at the framing stage. Use rough lumber for temporary treads until you're ready to finish the interior trim.

Every stairway is unique, with its own design and construction problems. That makes estimating the cost of stair work more difficult — but not impossible. All stairways have some things in common. They have to be safe, meet code requirements, have adequate headroom for people and be strong enough and wide enough for moving furniture.

Main stairs leading to the second floor or split-level floors are usually enclosed and may be carpeted. They should be both easy to use and attractive because they're a main focus of the interior design. Service stairs leading to a basement or garage are more utilitarian. Appearance is less important. They can be somewhat steeper and made of less expensive materials. But even here safety and convenience are more important than economy.

Most finish and service stairs are constructed in place. Main stairs can be assembled with prefabricated parts, which include housed stringers, treads, and risers. Basement stairs are usually made of 2 x 12 carriages and plank treads.

Oak, birch, maple and similar hardwoods are appropriate for exposed surfaces on main stairways. Use less expensive softwoods, like Douglas fir or southern pine, for treads and risers for the basement or service stairways. Combine a hardwood tread with a softwood or lower grade hardwood riser for an economical stairway with greater resistance to wear. Stairs that will be covered with carpet can have plywood treads and risers.

Three types of stairway runs are used in house construction: the straight run (Figure 10-1 A), the long "L" (Figure 10-1 B), and the narrow "U" (Figure 10-2 A).

Another type is similar to the long "L" except that *winders* substitute for the landing. It's shown in Figure 10-2 B. Your building code may prohibit or restrict stairs like this. Even if your code permits them, don't use stairs with winders if you can avoid it. It's less safe and convenient than the long "L". If you *have* to use it because there's not enough space for a long "L," follow the rules for tread width in the section on tread width and riser height.

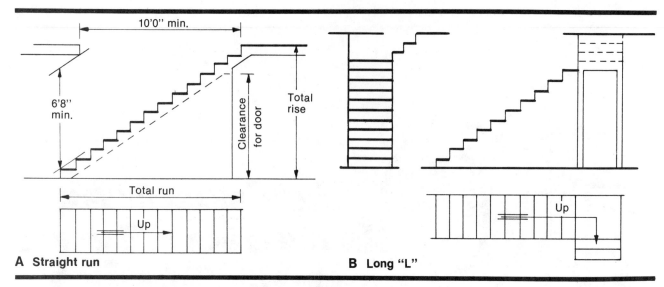

Figure 10-1
Common types of stair runs

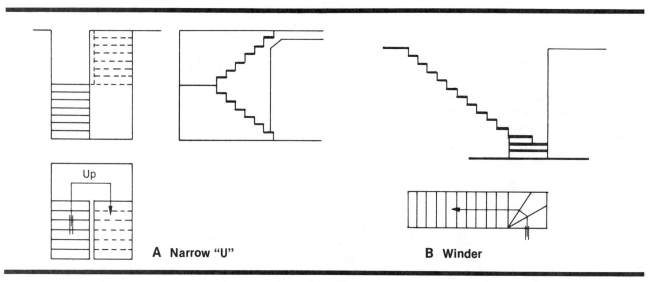

Figure 10-2
Space-saving stairs

Even though there are several different kinds of stairs, the same layout rules apply to all kinds. Let's review these rules so you can see how to calculate the quantity of materials needed.

Planning the Stair Layout

Let's begin with the guidelines for stair carriages.

The Carriages or Stringers

Carriages need a minimum effective depth of at least 3½" (see Figure 10-3 A), with solid bearing at the top and bottom. Figure 10-3 B shows the carriage bearing on a ledger nailed to the header. The bottom of the stair carriages may rest on, and be anchored to,

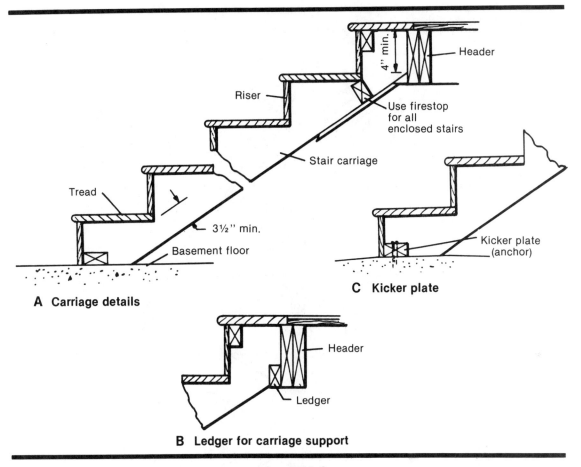

Figure 10-3
Carriage details for basement stairs

the basement floor. But it's better to use an anchored 2 x 4 or 2 x 6 treated kicker plate (Figure 10-3 C).

The maximum distance between carriages is 30'' for nominal 1¼'' treads, and 36'' for nominal 2'' treads. Factory-built stairs with wedged and glued treads and risers may be supported by two carriages if the stairs aren't wider than 42''.

A more finished staircase for an enclosed stairway might lead from the main floor to the attic. It combines the rough notched carriage with a finished stringer along each side (Figure 10-4 A). The finished stringer is fastened to the wall before the carriages. Treads and risers are cut to fit snugly between the stringers and fastened to the rough carriage with finishing nails. An alternative is to nail the rough carriage directly to the wall and notch the finished stringer to fit (Figure 10-4 B).

Use firestops at the top and bottom of all stairs, as shown in Figure 10-3 A.

Tread Width and Riser Height
Poorly designed stairs cause falls. Take the time to understand stair design principles and follow these principles on every stair job. That will help prevent painful and potentially serious accidents for the life of the home.

Anyone climbing or descending stairs shouldn't have to guess where the next step will be. It should be predictable. There shouldn't be any surprises. When going down stairs carrying bulky packages or when going up stairs in the dark, you should know where the next step will be even if you can't see it. That's what makes a stairway safe. You know where to put your foot and climb or descend without stumbling, putting a foot squarely on the next step without watching each foot.

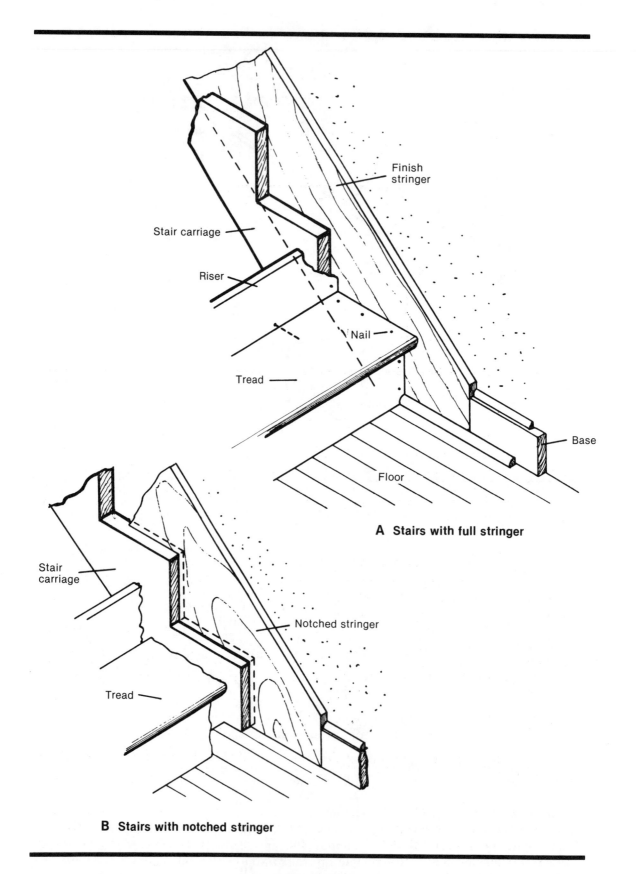

Finish stringer

Stair carriage

Riser

Nail

Tread

Base

Floor

A Stairs with full stringer

Stair carriage

Notched stringer

Tread

B Stairs with notched stringer

Figure 10-4
Enclosed stairway details

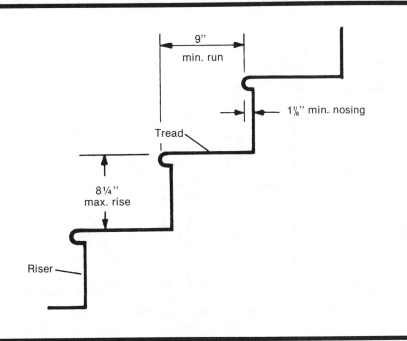

Figure 10-5
Tread and riser dimensions

A safe, predictable stairway follows some rules about the height of each riser and the width of each tread (step). Stair layout professionals don't violate these rules.

First, every tread must be (within about 1/4") the same width as every other tread in that stairway. Second, every riser must be (within about 1/4") the same height as every other tread in that stairway. These two rules help the person climbing predict where the next step will be without looking.

If the combination of run and rise is too great, it strains your leg muscles and takes too much effort. If the combination is too small, your foot will tend to kick the riser at each step. There's no single rule about how high risers should be or how wide treads should be. That would be impossible. The height between floors varies too much and the overall length of the stairway may be restricted in some cases.

But there are several popular rules for calculating the proper relationship between the width of each tread and the height of each riser. You'll hear about the "Rule of 17½." The width of each tread and the height of each riser, when added together must equal 17½". I think that's more restrictive than necessary. A stairway can violate the Rule of 17½ and still be safe. Here's the rule I prefer to follow:

1) Each riser in the main stairs should be no more than 8¼" high.

2) The height of one riser plus the width of one tread should never be less than 17" or more than 19".

For closed stairs, consider a 9" tread width the minimum, and an 8¼" riser height the maximum, even for basement stairways. Look at the dimensions in Figure 10-5. Try to design your risers shorter than 8¼", if possible. The nosing projection should be at least 1⅛". Don't make it much greater than that, however, or the stairs will be awkward and difficult to climb.

If you must use stairs with winders instead of a long "L," make sure the winders are at least as wide as the tread width on the straight run when measured 18" from the

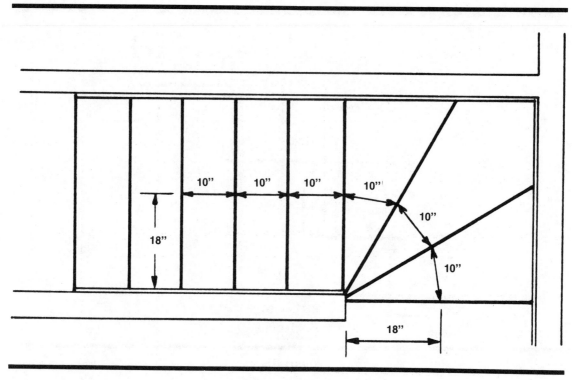

Figure 10-6
Minimum width for winders

narrow end. Figure 10-6 shows typical winders. If the standard tread is 10'' wide, the winder should be at least 10'' wide at the 18'' line.

I won't go into any more detail on riser height and tread length here other than to say that figuring and cutting these dimensions requires care and precision. If you want more information, the best book of stair tables I know of is *Stair Builders Handbook*, published by Craftsman Book Company. An order form for this manual is bound into the last few pages of this book.

You can use simple 1½''-thick treads without risers for basement stairs. Appearance will be better and maintenance easier, however, if you use finished tread material and nominal 1'' boards or plywood for risers. Fasten them to the carriages with finishing nails.

The Landing
There are also design rules for landings. When the landing at the top of a flight of stairs has a door opening onto it, the landing should be at least 2'6'' long. You'll commonly find this situation on the stairs leading up from the basement. Make middle landings at least 2'6'' long, as well. Look at Figure 10-7.

Headroom
Every stairway needs enough headroom so you don't hit your head on the header above when climbing or descending. For main stairways, the clear vertical distance should be at least 6'8''. Basement or service stairs should provide at least a 6'4'' clearance. These dimensions are shown in Figure 10-8.

Stairway Width
Make the main stairs a minimum of 2'8'' wide, clear of the handrail. If space is available, allow 3'6'' between the centerline of the enclosing side walls, creating a stairway about 3 feet wide. Split-level entrance stairs should be even wider. For basement

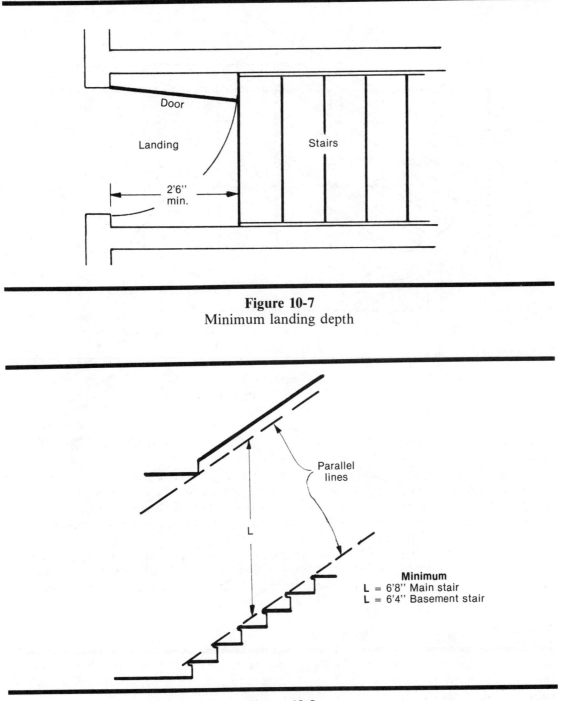

Figure 10-7
Minimum landing depth

Figure 10-8
Minimum headroom

stairs, the minimum clear width is 2'6''.

The Handrails

Provide a handrail on a least one side of any stairway with three or more risers. When stairs are open on two sides, there should be protective railings on each side. The handrails should have a minimum height of 30'' and a maximum height of 34'', measured vertically from the nosing of the treads below.

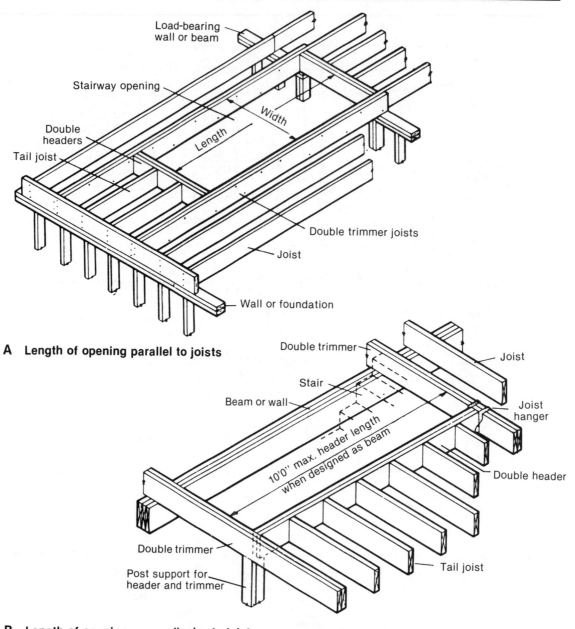

A Length of opening parallel to joists

B Length of opening perpendicular to joists

Figure 10-9
Framing for stair openings

Openings for Stairways

Openings in the floor for stairways, fireplaces, and chimneys are framed out during construction of the floor system. The long dimension of stairway openings may be either parallel or at right angles to the joists. It's much easier to frame a stairway opening when its length is parallel to the joists. For basement stairways, the rough opening may be about 9'6'' long by 32'' wide (two joist spaces). Openings in the second floor for the main stair are usually a minimum of 10 feet long (see Figure 10-1 A). Widths may be 3 feet or more. Depending on the short header required for one or both ends, the opening is usually framed as shown in Figure 10-9 A, when joists run parallel to the length of the opening.

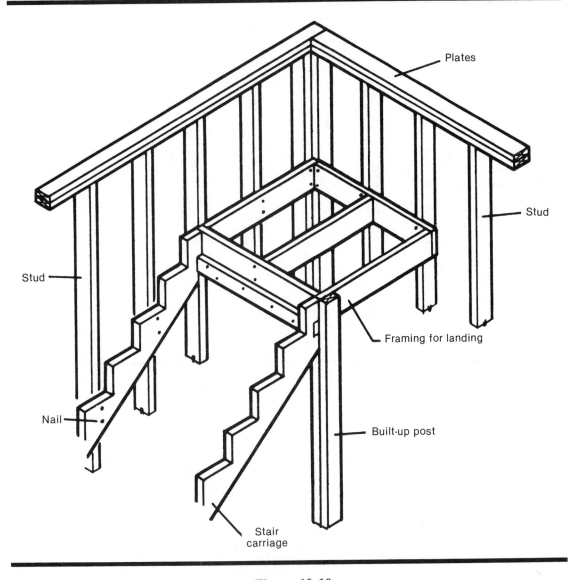

Figure 10-10
Framing for stair landing

When the length of the stair opening is perpendicular to the length of the joists, a long double header is required (Figure 10-9 B). A header under these conditions without a supporting wall beneath is usually limited to a 10-foot length. A load-bearing wall under all or part of this opening simplifies the framing because joists bear on the top plate of the wall rather than the header above.

The framing for an L-shaped basement stairway is usually supported by a post at the corner of the opening or by a load-bearing wall beneath. When an L-shaped stair leads from the first to the second floor, frame the landing as shown in Figure 10-10. The platform frame is nailed into the enclosing stud walls and provides a nailing area for the subfloor as well as a support for the stair carriages.

Finished or Main Stairs

Many better homes have an open main stairway with railing and balusters ending in a newel post. A decorative main stairway like this takes more time to build than the stairways we've talked about so far in this chapter. Here's a summary of the differences:

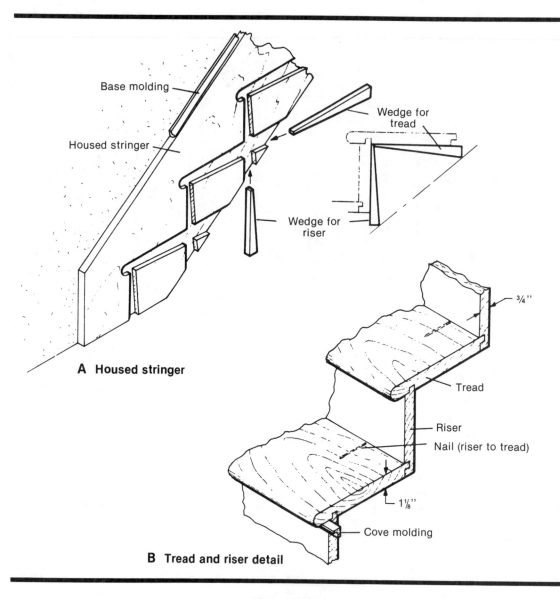

Figure 10-11
Main stair detail

- Housed carriages replace the rough carriages.

- Treads and risers are routed and grooved.

- Open stairways have a decorative railing and balusters.

- Wood species are used which will take a natural finish.

The supporting member of the finished main stairway is the housed stringer, shown in Figure 10-11 A. One is used on each side of the stairway, fastened to the finished walls. They are routed to fit both the tread and riser. The stair is assembled with hardwood wedges which are spread with glue and driven under the ends of the treads and in back of the risers. Then nails are used to fasten the riser to the tread between the ends of the step (Figure 10-11 B). When treads and risers are wedged and glued into housed stringers, the maximum allowable width is usually 3'6''.

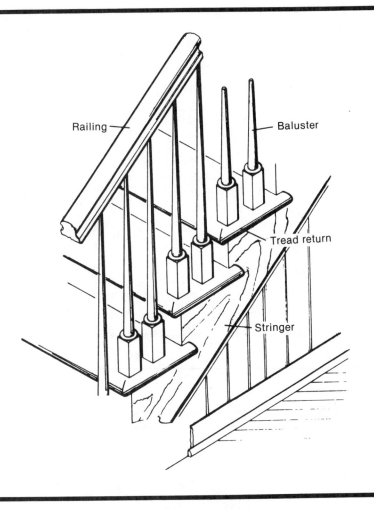

Figure 10-12
Details of open main stairway

When stairs are open on one side, the design usually calls for a railing and balusters. Balusters are fastened to the end of the treads which have a finished return (Figure 10-12) and to a railing which ends at the newel post. The balusters may be turned to form doweled ends, which fit into drilled holes in the treads and the railing. Complete the stairway trim with a stringer and appropriate moldings.

Estimating Stairs

Start your estimate by searching for the floor-to-floor rise on the plans. If the plans don't show the number of risers, calculate it by doing a stair layout like the one shown in Figure 10-13. Convert the floor-to-floor rise into inches, divide by 8 and round off the answer. For example, in Figure 10-13, the floor-to-floor rise is 8'10⅜'', or 106⅜'' (106.38''). Divided by 8, that's 13.3 risers. You'll use either 13 or 14 risers.

If you use 13 risers, each riser will be 8³⁄₁₆'', which is near the maximum permissible riser height of 8¼'' for main stairs. If you use 14 risers, each riser will be 7⅝'', which is more acceptable. There is always one less tread than riser. For 14 risers, you'll have 13 treads.

Once you know the number of risers and treads, you can begin estimating the material for the stairs and landings. We'll start with the carriages.

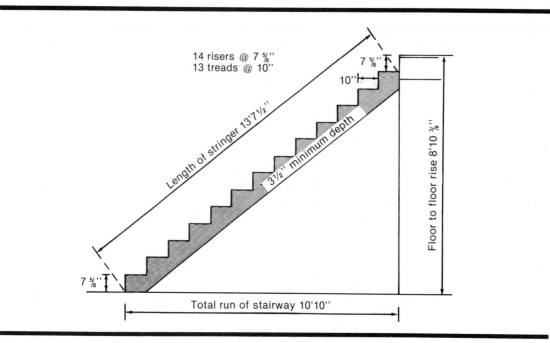

Figure 10-13
Stair layout

Floor to floor rise		Approximate length of stringers (*)
3'0''	. . . .	6'0''
4'0''	. . . .	7'0''
4'6''	. . . .	7'6''
5'0''	. . . .	9'0''
5'6''	. . . .	9'6''
6'0''	. . . .	10'0''
6'6''	. . . .	11'0''
7'0''	. . . .	12'0''
7'6''	. . . .	12'6''
8'0''	. . . .	13'0''
8'6''	. . . .	14'0''
9'0''	. . . .	15'0''
9'6''	. . . .	15'6''
10'0''	. . . .	16'0''

(*) The stair stringer length depends on the number and dimensions of the risers and treads. The length of the stringer increases as the number of risers increases.

Figure 10-14
Approximate carriage lengths

Estimating Stair Carriages

Remember, there must be at least 3½'' of solid wood between the cutout and the bottom of the carriage, unless it's supported by other construction. For most stairs, you'll use 2 x 12's for the carriages. If the stairs are wider than 2'6'', you'll need a center carriage, also.

Figure 10-14 is a table of approximate carriage lengths for different floor levels. Use it as a guideline for estimating stair carriages. Remember that these lengths are only

Width of room	Length of room																		
	2'	**3'**	**4'**	**5'**	**6'**	**7'**	**8'**	**9'**	**10'**	**11'**	**12'**	**13'**	**14'**	**15'**	**16'**	**17'**	**18'**	**19'**	**20'**
2'	4	6	8	10	12	14	16	18	20	22	24	26	28	30	32	34	36	38	40
3'	6	9	12	15	18	21	24	27	30	33	36	39	42	45	48	51	54	57	60
4'	8	12	16	20	24	28	32	36	40	44	48	52	56	60	64	68	72	76	80
5'	10	15	20	25	30	35	40	45	50	55	60	65	70	75	80	85	90	95	100
6'	12	18	24	30	36	42	48	54	60	66	72	78	84	90	96	102	108	114	120
7'	14	21	28	35	42	49	56	63	70	77	84	91	98	105	112	119	126	133	140
8'	16	24	32	40	48	56	64	72	80	88	96	104	112	120	128	136	144	152	160
9'	18	27	36	45	54	63	72	81	90	99	108	117	126	135	144	153	162	171	180
10'	20	30	40	50	60	70	80	90	100	110	120	130	140	150	160	170	180	190	200
11'	22	33	44	55	66	77	88	99	110	121	132	143	154	165	176	187	198	209	220
12'	24	36	48	60	72	84	96	108	120	132	144	156	168	180	192	204	216	228	240
13'	26	39	52	65	78	91	104	117	130	143	156	169	182	195	208	221	234	247	260
14'	28	42	56	70	84	98	112	126	140	154	168	182	196	210	224	238	252	266	280
15'	30	45	60	75	90	105	120	135	150	165	180	195	210	225	240	255	270	285	300
16'	32	48	64	80	96	112	128	144	160	176	192	208	224	240	256	272	288	304	320
17'	34	51	68	85	102	119	136	153	170	187	204	221	238	255	272	289	306	323	340
18'	36	54	72	90	108	126	144	162	180	198	216	234	252	270	288	306	324	342	360
19'	38	57	76	95	114	133	152	171	190	209	228	247	266	285	304	323	342	361	380
20'	40	60	80	100	120	140	160	180	200	220	240	260	280	300	320	340	360	380	400

Figure 10-15
Total area of floor or ceiling in square feet

approximate. The actual length depends on the number and dimensions of the risers and treads.

Here's an example. Assume you have a floor-to-floor rise of 8'10⅜'', as shown in the stair layout in Figure 10-13. You're using 14 risers at 7⅝'' and 13 treads at 10''. The carriage will be 13'7½'' long. Since these stairs are 3'6'' wide, you would order three 2 x 12 x 14' lengths. That's 84 BF of lumber for the three carriages.

During framing the carpentry crew will cut and install the carriage. If hardwood treads and risers will be installed after framing is finished, cut temporary treads from scrap plywood or lumber. There's normally enough waste material available on site to make temporary treads. I don't usually estimate any extra material for the rough treads.

Estimating Finish Stair Materials

The finish material for the stairs includes treads, risers, skirtboard or finish stringer, and molding. A balustrade consisting of the balusters, handrail, turnout, newel post, and rosettes may be used on the open side of main stairs. If the stair opening is enclosed by a wall on each side, only a handrail and handrail brackets are needed.

For basement stairs, risers are optional. The handrail is secured to the wall with handrail brackets at the top of the stairs and a post (normally a 4 x 4) at the bottom.

Estimating Stair Labor

The labor to frame and install the risers, treads and handrails will vary with the type of stairs and the efficiency of the craftsmen. The figures that follow assume that experienced stair builders are used for this work. The labor for basement stairs with open risers and two handrails may be as low as 10 manhours per set of stairs. Circular stairs and other ornate main stairs with an elaborate balustrade system may require 80 or more manhours. That's a pretty wide range of times, I know. But stair types range from plain vanilla to some fairly exotic variations. Keep good cost records on stair-building labor. Your own records will be the most accurate guide for your operation.

Panel size	Net floor area (square feet)	x Factor	= Number of panels
4' x 8'	1,184	x .03125	= 37

Figure 10-16
Factors for underlayment

Interior Trim and Molding

When the wallboard is up and the walls have dried, it's time to begin the interior trim, the last carpentry work done in a house. This includes flooring, floor underlayment, baseboard, baseshoe, wall molding and paneling, interior doors (including trim and hardware), window trim, kitchen cabinets and counter tops, vanities, bars, closet shelves, stair trim, mirrors and medicine cabinets, tub and shower doors, decorative beams, and room dividers. Let's start with flooring and floor underlayment.

Flooring and Floor Underlayment

Use Figure 10-15 to compute the floor area for a room. For example, a room 12'0'' x 16'0'' has 192 square feet of floor space. Once you know the area, you can calculate the material required for flooring and floor underlayment.

To find the total quantity of flooring or underlayment needed, add together the areas of each room, closet and hallway in the house. If you're installing 4' x 8' panel underlayment, use the factor shown in Figure 10-16 to compute the number of panels required. Here's an example:

A kitchen 12'0'' x 15'0'' has 180 square feet of floor space. Multiply the net floor area (180 SF) by the factor (0.03125) to get a total of 5.63 (or 6) underlayment panels.

Here's another example. To cover a floor area of 2,460 square feet with 4' x 8' particleboard, multiply the area (2,460 SF) by the factor (0.03125) to get 76.88 (or 77) particleboard panels.

Wood Flooring

Wood flooring is manufactured from both hardwood and softwood trees. But the terms *hard* and *soft* don't refer to the hardness or softness of the wood. Generally, wood from a broadleafed tree is called hardwood, and wood from trees with needles is called softwood. Oak and maple are the most popular hardwood flooring. Southern pine and Douglas fir are the most popular softwood flooring.

Flooring comes in three types: strip, plank and blocks. Strip flooring is available in widths of 1½'' and 2'', in thicknesses of 3/8'' and 1/2''. For 25/32'' thickness, the widths are 1½'', 2'', 2¼'' and 3¼''. The length of the flooring varies from 1'0'' to 16'0''. The most popular strip flooring is 25/32'' x 2¼'' tongue-and-grooved end matched. It weighs about 2,100 pounds per thousand square feet in oak or maple.

To estimate 25/32'' x 2¼'' T&G end-matched flooring, multiply the area to be covered in square feet by the factor of 1.38. This tells you the number of board feet of flooring needed. Note this: Square feet and board feet are the same for 1'' sheathing and flooring. This factor allows for side and end matching and 5% for waste.

Nail flooring from 10'' to 12'' o.c. with 7d (2¼'') flooring nails, or machine nail with 2'' power cleats. Allow 20 pounds 7d spiral flooring nails, or 1 box (5,000) 2'' power cleats per 1,000 square feet for 25/32'' x 2¼'' flooring.

Plank flooring is usually random width, with wooden plugs of a contrasting color.

	Length of room																		
Width of room	**2'**	**3'**	**4'**	**5'**	**6'**	**7'**	**8'**	**9'**	**10'**	**11'**	**12'**	**13'**	**14'**	**15'**	**16'**	**17'**	**18'**	**19'**	**20'**
2'	8	10	12	14	16	18	20	22	24	26	28	30	32	34	36	38	40	42	44
3'	10	12	14	16	18	20	22	24	26	28	30	32	34	36	38	40	42	44	46
4'	12	14	16	18	20	22	24	26	28	30	32	34	36	38	40	42	44	46	48
5'	14	16	18	20	22	24	26	28	30	32	34	36	38	40	42	44	46	48	50
6'	16	18	20	22	24	26	28	30	32	34	36	38	40	42	44	46	48	50	52
7'	18	20	22	24	26	28	30	32	34	36	38	40	42	44	46	48	50	52	54
8'	20	22	24	26	28	30	32	34	36	38	40	42	44	46	48	50	52	54	56
9'	22	24	26	28	30	32	34	36	38	40	42	44	46	48	50	52	54	56	58
10'	24	26	28	30	32	34	36	38	40	42	44	46	48	50	52	54	56	58	60
11'	26	28	30	32	34	36	38	40	42	44	46	48	50	52	54	56	58	60	62
12'	28	30	32	34	36	38	40	42	44	46	48	50	52	54	56	58	60	62	64
13'	30	32	34	36	38	40	42	44	46	48	50	52	54	56	58	60	62	64	66
14'	32	34	36	38	40	42	44	46	48	50	52	54	56	58	60	62	64	66	68
15'	34	36	38	40	42	44	46	48	50	52	54	56	58	60	62	64	66	68	70
16'	36	38	40	42	44	46	48	50	52	54	56	58	60	62	64	66	68	70	72
17'	38	40	42	44	46	48	50	52	54	56	58	60	62	64	66	68	70	72	74
18'	40	42	44	46	48	50	52	54	56	58	60	62	64	66	68	70	72	74	76
19'	42	44	46	48	50	52	54	56	58	60	62	64	66	68	70	72	74	76	78
20'	44	46	48	50	52	54	56	58	60	62	64	66	68	70	72	74	76	78	80

Figure 10-17
Perimeter of room in linear feet

This imitates the flooring used in colonial times. Block or parquet flooring is made of pieces of strip flooring bonded together edgewise to form a square unit, usually 9'' x 9''. They have tongue and groove edges and can be either nailed to the subfloor or laid in mastic over concrete or wood.

Wood flooring may come unfinished or with a factory finish. If the flooring is unfinished, it must be finished after installation by sanding and applying a filler, stain and finish. Floor finishing should be done by specialists in this work. They will contract for labor and material at a designated price per square foot, or by the job.

For manhour tables for installing different types of wood flooring, go to Figures 12-27 and 12-28, in Chapter 12.

Baseboard, Baseshoe, Molding and Paneling

Look at Figure 10-17. Use this chart to compute the perimeter of different size rooms. For example, a room 12'0'' x 18'0'' has a perimeter of 60 linear feet. A closet 3'0'' x 7'0'' has a perimeter of 20 linear feet. Once you know the perimeter of a room, you can order the material required for baseboard, baseshoe, and molding. No door openings have been deducted in this table.

To compute the number of 4'-wide hardboard or plywood panels required, use the factor from Figure 10-18. Just enter the room perimeter in the first column. Then multiply the perimeter by the factor to get the number of panels required.

Wall Molding

Wall molding, including chair rails and panel molding, is a relatively inexpensive way to give a room a luxurious look. Although they can by used in any room, they're commonly used in living rooms, dining rooms, family rooms and foyers. Figure 10-19 shows the common types of wall molding.

Room perimeter (linear feet)	x	Factor	=	Number of panels
54	x	.25000	=	13.50 or 14

Figure 10-18
Factor for interior paneling (4' wide)

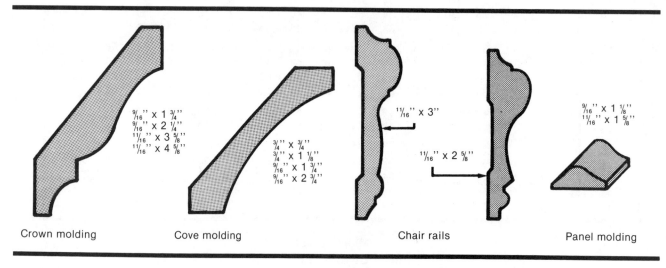

Crown molding   Cove molding   Chair rails   Panel molding

Figure 10-19
Wall molding

Chair rail comes in a variety of designs and sizes. The recommended height from the floor to the top of the chair rail is 32''. Use nails and a good grade of adhesive to keep the chair rail from separating from the wall between nails. Chair rail can be used on all walls in a room or on just one. A mural or other scenic wall fabric on the wall above the chair rail can be very effective.

Panel mold is applied to the wall between the chair rail and baseboard. It too should be applied both with a good grade of adhesive and nails. There are many ways to use panel mold. Here are some suggestions: As shown in Figure 10-20, the distance from the inside wall corner to the panel mold may vary from 4'' to 6'', but it should be equal on each side. If the chair rail butts into a window or door casing between the two opposite walls, the distance from this casing to the panel mold should also be equal on each side. For a perfectly balanced design, distances a, b, c and d in Figure 10-20 should all be equal. After the panel mold has been installed, the wall can be decorated with paint or wall fabric.

Chair rail and panel mold is estimated by the linear foot. Find the linear feet of design patterns for the panel mold and then add 10% for waste.

Use 8d (2½'') finish nails with adhesive for the chair rail. Allow 2 pounds of nails per 100 linear feet. Use 6d (2'') finish nails with adhesive for the panel mold and figure 1/2 pound of nails per 100 linear feet.

It will take your carpenter about six manhours to install each 100 linear feet of chair rail or panel mold.

Interior Trim Nails
You'll need to calculate nail quantities for floor underlayment, baseboard, baseshoe and paneling, as well as adhesive for paneling.

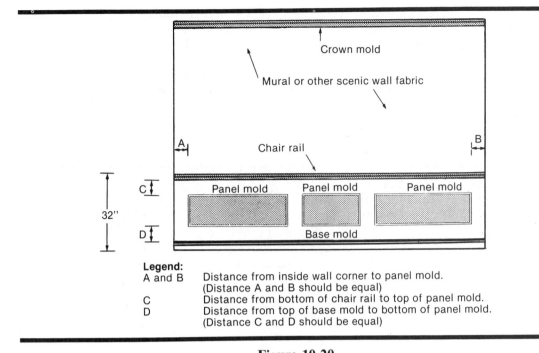

Legend:
A and B   Distance from inside wall corner to panel mold.
(Distance A and B should be equal)
C   Distance from bottom of chair rail to top of panel mold.
D   Distance from top of base mold to bottom of panel mold.
(Distance C and D should be equal)

Figure 10-20
Installing wall molding

Floor area (square feet)	x	Factor	=	Pounds of nails
2,640	x	.02000	=	52.80 or 53

A Floor underlayment

Baseboard length (linear feet)	x	Factor	=	Pounds of nails
850	x	.01000	=	8.50 or 9

B Baseboard

Baseshoe length (linear feet)	x	Factor	=	Pounds of nails
250	x	.00500	=	1.25 or 2

C Baseshoe

Figure 10-21
Factors for finish nails and adhesive

Paneling area (square feet)	x	Factor	=	Boxes of colored nails
448	x	.01000	=	4.48 or 5

A 1⅝" colored nails

Paneling area (square feet)	x	Factor	=	Pounds of finish nails
448	x	.01000	=	4.48 or 5

B 4d finish nails

Paneling area (square feet)	x	Factor	=	Number of tubes
448	x	.01000	=	4.48 or 5

C Adhesive

Figure 10-22
Factors for paneling nails and adhesive

Figure 10-21 is a factor table for finish nails and adhesive for underlayment, baseboard and baseshoe. Use section A to compute the quantity of 6d ring-grooved nails needed for floor underlayment. Just multiply the floor area by the factor to get the pounds of nails required. Use section B to compute the quantity of 8d finish nails required for baseboard. Section C gives you the factor for computing the quantity of 6d finish nails required for baseshoe.

To estimate the quantity of nails and adhesive you'll need for paneling, use Figure 10-22. Section A covers 1⅛" colored nails, section B includes 4d finish nails, and section C is for the adhesive.

Interior Doors and Trim

Interior doors are normally hollow-core flush or paneled, 1⅜" thick. The complete door unit consists of the door frame, door, door butts, door stops, casing on both sides and the door lock. Prehung doors are the most popular and are widely used because they reduce labor costs. They come prehung in the door frame with the door butts, door stops and casing installed. The unit probably will not include the door lock, but the cross hole and bolt hole will be drilled for the standard 2⅜" backset for a cylindrical lockset.

When estimating interior doors, find the number and size from the floor plan or the door schedule. The specifications will determine the type of doors to use.

Use 8d finish nails for installing door casing. Allow 1/2 pound of nails per opening.

Manhours for installing doors: The labor to set a door, install and sand the joints and install the door lock may be estimated at 3 manhours per door.

For other kinds of interior doors, such as sliding or bi-fold, estimate 4 to 5 manhours per door to assemble and set the door frame, install the casing on two sides, and install the hardware and door.

Window Trim

The side and head casing of windows are normally the same design and kind of wood as the door trim. The window trim consists of casing, stool, apron, stops, window lock and window lift. Some windows are designed so the stops can be used on four sides, eliminating the stool. The casing is placed on all four sides, giving the window a framed appearance. Metal windows don't normally require casing, only a window sill. On these windows the drywall or plaster makes a return to the metal window, eliminating the casing and apron.

Window trim can be purchased by the linear foot, or in sets for each window. If you buy it by the linear feet, add an allowance of 20% for cutting and waste. Many manufacturers of wood windows also manufacture window trim. The trim will probably be sold in sets for each window they make. The sets will include the casing, stops, mullions, stool and apron (if required). No allowance for waste is necessary when the window trim is purchased in sets. The number and type of windows, the trim, locks and window lifts are shown in the plans, the window schedule, and specifications.

Use 6d (2") or 8d (2½") finishing nails for the window trim. All joints should be glued, nailed and sanded before they're finished. Allow 1/4 pound of nails for each side.

Manhours to install window trim: The labor to install the window trim will vary, depending on the size and type of window. A 3' x 3' single window unit will require about 50% less labor to trim than a large triple window or picture window. Previous cost records are your best guide.

Kitchen Cabinets and Vanities

You never know the exact sizes of kitchen cabinets and bathroom vanities until the drywall or plastering is finished. There's always some variation between the scale dimensions on the blueprint and the actual finished dimensions. When it's done, you can measure for the exact cabinet space.

Mills have designed complete units and sections ready to install. The cabinets are made to standard dimensions, but they're available in enough different sizes to fit almost any space, using filler strips. Kitchen cabinets usually are in two parts: base cabinets, the

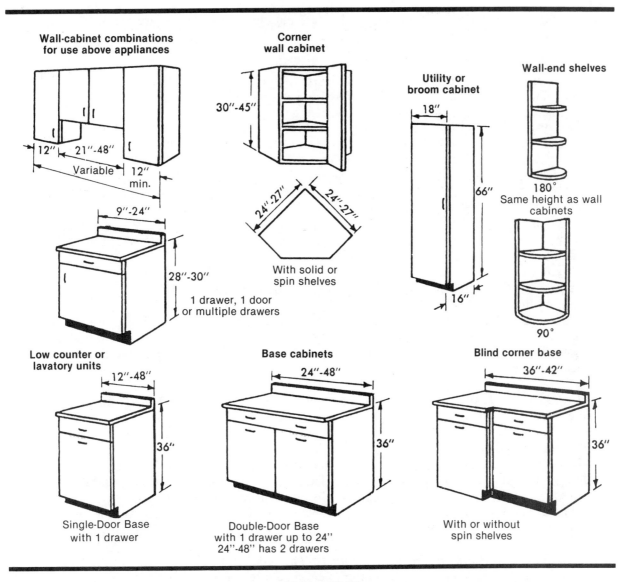

Figure 10-23
Types and sizes of cabinets

rather wide lower portion to be covered with a counter top, and wall cabinets, the shallow upper portion that hangs on the wall. Both are shown in Figure 10-23.

The counter tops are usually made from laminated plastic such as Formica, or they're covered with ceramic or plastic tile. If the counter top will be made in the mill, don't order it until the base cabinets are in place. This will enable you to get a more perfect fit.

Manhours for setting cabinets: Here are my manhour factors for installing cabinets. Use them until you have good labor figures for your own crews. For cabinets built on the job, allow 3.5 manhours per linear foot for the base cabinet (this includes installing cabinet tops), and 1 manhour per linear foot for the wall cabinets.

For installing factory-built cabinets, allow 2 manhours to install a 36''-wide base unit, and the same for a 36''-wide wall unit. This figure includes the time needed to install factory-made tops.

On larger jobs, where you're installing over 100 square feet of factory-built cabinets, including counter tops and molding, estimate 7 manhours per 100 square feet of face area.

Closet Shelves

The floor plan of the blueprints shows the size of the closets. For clothes closets, the floor plan will indicate the shelf and rod with a dotted line under the shelf for the rod. For linen closets the number of shelves will be given.

The material for clothes closets consists of 12'' shelving material, 1'' x 4'' cleats or ribbons, clothes rod and supports, and rosettes. The shelf is normally 66'' from the floor. If the material is purchased separately, scale the length of the closet from the floor plan and order the shelves and cleats in linear feet. Purchase the clothes rod for the length of the closet, and allow one pair of rosettes per rod. If the clothes rod is longer than 48'', you'll need one or more rod supports.

The material for linen closets consists of shelving material and cleats. When estimating the material in linear feet, order in lengths that require the least amount of waste. For example, a linen closet 3'0'' in length requires five shelves. If you order one 1'' x 12'' x 16', you can cut the five shelves from this one piece of material with only 1'0'' waste. If you ordered the shelving in 8' lengths, it would require three 1'' x 12'' x 8' pieces, resulting in 9'0'' of waste.

Prehung shelves are widely used today. They come complete with all hardware for any type of closets, and are adjustable for different closet lengths. When estimating prehung closet shelves, list each closet separately and order the prehung shelves as required for each closet length.

Manhours for closet shelves: Estimate the labor for closet shelves at 3 manhours per 100 linear feet of shelving.

Mirrors and Medicine Cabinets

Mirrors add glamor to a bathroom. They accent certain architectural features, and can double the apparent size of a small room. They can be used over vanities in bathrooms to replace medicine cabinets, or on side walls adjacent to the cabinet.

Mirrors and medicine cabinets will be shown on the floor plan. Detail sections or the specs will give you the number and size.

Manhours for mirrors and medicine cabinets: The labor to install mirrors and medicine cabinets may be estimated at 8 manhours per 55 square feet of mirror area. You can use the factor of 0.14545 manhours per square foot of mirror area. For example, the labor to install a 3' x 7' mirror (21 square feet) would be:

$$0.14545 \times 21 = 3.05 \text{ or } 3 \text{ manhours}$$

Tub and Shower Doors

The number, type and size of tub and shower doors are shown on the floor plans, detail sections and specifications. Allow 2 manhours per door for installation.

Bathroom Accessories

The bathroom accessories include paper holders, towel racks, soap dishes, grab bars, and shower curtain rods (if a shower door isn't used). The number, type and style will be selected by the owner. An allowance for the bathroom accessories is normally made. Allow 1/4 manhour per unit for the labor to install the accessories.

Miscellaneous

This will include any special items not shown on the prints which the owner wants. Valances, room dividers, and artificial beams would be included here. Additional materials such as nails, glue, adhesive, wood filler, sandpaper and tub and tile caulking not listed elsewhere may also be listed here.

Weekly Time Sheet

Page____of____pages

For period ending *3-26-XX* _____   _____*BROWN*_____job

	Name	Exemptions	Days MARCH 21 M	22 T	23 W	24 T	25 F	26 S	Rate	Hours worked Reg.	Over-time	Total earnings	
1	D.L. WHITE		8	8	8	8	8	×		40			
2	A.L. KING		8	8	8	8	8	×		40			
3	J.E. KING		8	8	8	8	8	×		40			
4													
5													
6													
7													
8													
9													
10													
11													
12													
13													
14													
15													
16													
17													
18													
19													
20													

Daily Log

(6 MANHOURS)

Monday *TRIM ON FRONT PORCH (18 MANHOURS) — STARTED FLOOR UNDERLAYMENT*

Tuesday *FLOOR UNDERLAYMENT (24 MANHOURS)*

Wednesday *FLOOR UNDERLAYMENT (24 MANHOURS)*

Thursday *FINISHED FLOOR UNDERLAYMENT (12 MANHOURS) — O/S TRIM (12 MANHOURS)*

Friday *O/S TRIM (24 MANHOURS)*

Saturday *XXXX*

Figure 10-24
Weekly time sheet

Weekly Time Sheet

Page____of____pages

For period ending 4-2-XX   BROWN   job

	Name	Exemptions	MARCH 28 M	29 T	30 W	31 T	APRIL 1 F	2 S	Rate	Hours worked Reg.	Over-time	Total earnings
1	D. L. WHITE		8	8	8	8	8	x		40		
2	A. L. KING		8	8	8	8	6½	x		38½		
3	J. E. KING		8	8	8	8	6½	x		38½		
4												
5												
6												
7												
8												
9												
10												
11												
12												
13												
14												
15												
16												
17												
18												
19												
20												

Daily Log

Monday   O/S TRIM (24 MANHOURS)
Tuesday I/S TRIM (24 MANHOURS)
Wednesday I/S TRIM (24 MANHOURS)
Thursday I/S TRIM (24 MANHOURS)
Friday   I/S TRIM (24 MANHOURS)
Saturday XXXX

Figure 10-25
Weekly time sheet

Weekly Time Sheet

Page____of____pages

For period ending __4-9-XX__   __BROWN__ job

#	Name	Exemptions	4 M	5 T	6 W	7 T	8 F	9 S	Rate	Reg.	Over-time	Total earnings
			Days APRIL							Hours worked		
1	D.L. WHITE		8	8	8	8	8	X		40		
2	A.L. KING		8	8	8	8	8	X		40		
3	J.E. KING		8	8	8	8	8	X		40		
4	W.W. PEERY, PAINT		✓	✓	✓	✓	X	X		—		
5	CONTRACTOR											
6												
7												
8												
9												
10												
11												
12												
13												
14												
15												
16												
17												
18												
19												
20												

Daily Log

Monday _I/S TRIM (24 MANHOURS) — I/S PAINTING_
Tuesday _I/S TRIM (24 MANHOURS) — I/S PAINTING_
Wednesday _I/S TRIM (24 MANHOURS) — I/S PAINTING_
Thursday _I/S TRIM (24 MANHOURS) — I/S PAINTING_
Friday _I/S TRIM (24 MANHOURS)_
Saturday _XXXX_

Figure 10-26
Weekly time sheet

Weekly Time Sheet

Page____of____pages

For period ending __4-30-xx__   __BROWN__ job

#	Name	Exemptions	Days APRIL 25 M	26 T	27 W	28 T	29 F	30 S	Rate	Hours worked Reg.	Over-time	Total earnings
1	D. L. WHITE		X	6	8	X	3½	X		17½		
2	A. L. KING		X	3½	8	8	8	X		27½		
3	J. E. KING		X	6	8	X	3½	X		17½		
4	D. L. WEST		X	X	8	X	3½	X		11½		
5												
6												
7												
8												
9												
10												
11												
12												
13												
14												
15												
16												
17												
18												
19												
20												

Daily Log

Monday XXXX
Tuesday PANELING IN FAMILY ROOM — I/S TRIM (15½ MANHOURS)
Wednesday PANELING IN FAMILY ROOM — I/S TRIM (32 MANHOURS)
Thursday VANITY CABINETS IN BATHROOMS (8 MANHOURS)
Friday FINISHED PANELING (18½ MANHOURS)
Saturday XXXX

Figure 10-27
Weekly time sheet

Page____of____pages

Weekly Time Sheet

For period ending __5-7-XX__   __BROWN__ job

	Name	Exemptions	2 M	3 T	4 W	5 T	6 F	7 S	Rate	Reg.	Over-time	Total earnings
			Days MAY							Hours worked		
1	D. L. WHITE		8	8	8	7	X	X		31		
2	A. L. KING		8	8	8	7	X	X		31		
3	J. E. KING		4	8	8	7	X	X		27		
4	D. L. WEST		4	8	8	7	X	X		27		
5	D & A PLUMBING		X	X	✓	✓	X	X		—		
6	W. W. PEERY, PAINT		X	X	✓	✓	✓	X		—		
7	CONTRACTOR											
8												
9												
10												
11												
12												
13												
14												
15												
16												
17												
18												
19												
20												

Daily Log

Monday *TRIM IN FAMILY ROOM (16 MANHOURS) — FORMS FOR CONCRETE (8 MANHOURS)*

Tuesday *KITCHEN CABINETS (32 MANHOURS)*   CLEANED BRICK (16 MANHOURS)

Wednesday *FINISHED KITCHEN CABINETS (16 MANHOURS) — PLUMBING - I/S PAINTING*

Thursday *FORMS FOR CONCRETE (18 MANHOURS) — PLUMBING - I/S PAINTING*
          CLEANED BRICK (10 MANHOURS)

Friday *I/S PAINTING*

Saturday *XXX*

Figure 10-28
Weekly time sheet

Interior Trim Labor

Use your weekly time sheets from previous jobs to estimate interior trim labor. Look at Figures 10-24 through 10-28. The daily logs show that a total of 420 manhours were required to install the interior trim for a house (and attached garage) with a total floor area of 2,850 square feet. Now let's compute the manhour factor for interior trim.

Manhours for interior trim: Look at Figure 10-29. In the first column, enter the total manhours (420). Divide the total manhours by the total house and garage area (2,850 SF) to get a manhour factor of 0.14737.

Now let's use the interior trim manhour factor to bid on a new job. Suppose you're bidding on a house with a total floor area of 3,290 square feet. Multiply the house area (3,290 SF) by the factor (0.14737) to get 484.85, or 485 manhours. Use this as your interior trim manhour estimate for the new job.

Close supervision of the finish work is essential. Remember, the finish work will always be seen. It's a gauge of the carpenter's skill and craftsmanship.

In this chapter we've learned how to make easy, accurate trim estimates. In the next chapter, I'll give you some tips on how to avoid trouble with your subcontractors.

Total manhours	÷	House and garage area (square feet)	=	Manhour factor
420	÷	2,850	=	.14737

Figure 10-29
Labor worksheet for interior trim

Staying Out of Trouble with Subcontractors

From time to time you're going to have the opportunity to subcontract some portion of the work to a specialty contractor. For example, suppose a job includes 25 squares of wood shingles. If you don't have an expert shingle installer on your payroll, a shingle specialist may be willing to take the job at a fixed cost which is substantially below your labor and material cost for the same work. The shingle sub probably has experienced tradesmen, specialized equipment and buys from low-cost suppliers that let him do the work at a price (including his markup) which is less than your cost. In a case like that, why not do it the easy way? Accept the sub's proposal.

There's one major advantage to subcontracting parts of a construction project: Subcontractors give you a set price. You know the actual cost before work begins. In theory, the subcontractor accepts the risk of loss if costs exceed his estimate. The work should be done for the price quoted and no more. But experienced builders know it isn't always that simple. Yes, the subcontractor's quote was firm, but it was based on a particular set of plans and specifications. Now he claims that you're asking him to do something that wasn't in the plans and wasn't included in his bid. You pay or he doesn't do the work!

You don't see it that way, of course, but you may have little choice. The work has to be done or you don't get paid. And you may not be able to pass this extra cost along to the owner or general contractor. The plans assume a complete building that complies with the building code and is ready for occupancy. The owner won't pay extra for what he thinks was included in your bid, even if the subcontractor insists it wasn't in *his* bid. The result: you're stuck in the middle with extra costs that reduce your profit.

In this chapter, I'll suggest ways to avoid getting stuck in the middle and how to escape most of the common subcontract problems. I'll set up some basic guidelines to reduce your risk of loss. Finally, I'll discuss the key subcontracts: electrical, plumbing, HVAC, excavation and fill, masonry, and roofing.

The Basics of Subcontracts

Experienced contractors are usually quick to spot potential problems with subcontracts. Once you've had a dispute on some point with a subcontractor, you're likely to anticipate similar problems in the future. But that's the expensive way to learn contracting and estimating.

How can you be sure that a subcontractor's bid will cover all the work you expect to have done? Easy! Keep a checklist of the common items that run up subcontract costs in residential construction. Review this checklist before you accept any bid.

Common subcontract problems include: who buys insurance and who has to pay the taxes, separate owner-subcontractor agreements, subcontractor payment dates, and qualified bids. Let's look at how problems come up in these areas and suggest ways to keep your subcontracts trouble free.

Proof of Insurance and Taxes

Subcontractors operate their own businesses, hire their own employees and are responsible for FICA and FUTA taxes, Workers' Compensation, and liability insurance for their employees. But you can still be held responsible for a sub's unpaid employee taxes or for an injury to or by a subcontractor's tradesman. That's why you should always have proof of insurance coverage and deal only with reputable subs who comply with the tax laws.

Owner-Subcontractor Agreements

Sometimes the owner will enter into a separate agreement with your subcontractor. That puts you in a difficult position. You have no authority over that sub's workers, but have to share space with them and coordinate the work they do. Have a written understanding with the owner stating who is liable for personal injury or personal property damage caused by that subcontractor or his employees.

Subcontractor Payments

Make sure every subcontract states clearly when the subcontractor will be paid. Will he receive a single payment when his work is finished? Or will he be paid as each phase is complete? Be clear on this, and get it in writing.

Bids "Per Plans and Specs"

Get subcontract bids "per the owner's plans and specs" and with no other qualifications, if possible. The chance of a dispute is greater when the sub doesn't bid "per plans and specs."

A subcontract based on plans drawn up by the sub or a subcontract that includes ambiguous terms is sure to cause trouble. The more descriptions, explanations and qualifications the subcontractor submits with his bid, the more likely you are to get stuck with additional costs.

If the sub doesn't bid per the owner's plans and specs, he's required to do only what he proposes and no more. If the sub omits something that's in the owner's plans, it will be your responsibility to correct it. That puts you in the middle again. And that can be a very expensive position.

Electrical and HVAC subs routinely draw up their own plans. That's fine as long as the subcontractor's plans become the owner's plans and are submitted as part of your bid. Make the sub's qualifications part of your contract. That should keep you out of many disputes and save more than a few dollars.

Unexpected Problems

Even the most complete, professional plans and specs may omit some important point, have inconsistent provisions or leave room for misunderstanding. It's not necessarily the architect's fault. Detailed planning of even a simple home is a complex and demanding task.

A few changes and some improvising are inevitable on nearly every project. And the bigger the job, the more changing and improvising will be needed. That's just the nature of construction. When subcontracted work costs more than you allowed for in your bid, make a detailed record of the problems, how they could have been avoided and how you resolved them. Document the claims of the subcontractor very carefully to prepare your case for extra compensation.

Keep a correspondence file and make handwritten summaries of phone calls or conversations that relate to the increased costs. These notes that you make to yourself will be admissible in court if the dispute becomes a legal matter. The more complete your records of the facts, the more likely you are to recover the full amount of the subcontractor's additional charges.

The Electrical Subcontract

The installation of the electrical, plumbing, and HVAC systems are done by specialized trades. Most places require a license and a permit to perform these specialties. The work must conform to the local building code, and one or more inspectors will inspect for compliance. The rough-in for these trades follows the installation of the roof and precedes the finish walls and ceilings.

We'll cover the electrical sub first. And here's one of the most important things to remember: *Never compromise on the quality or safety of the electric wiring.*

Here are some general recommendations for modern, safe, but economical electrical systems:

1) Install adequate outlets and switches. Wire for future needs as well as present needs.

2) Install switch-controlled outlets instead of ceiling fixtures.

3) Consider omitting lights in closets where hallway or room lights will provide enough light.

4) The location of wall outlets is measured from the finished floor to the center of the outlet or switch box. Here are the recommended heights for the common outlets:

   - Telephone outlets: 12 inches
   - Duplex receptacles: 12 inches
   - Light switches: 48 inches
   - Receptacles for wall fans: 78 inches

Your local power company may be willing to supply an electrical layout for the house at no cost. The layout in the plans may not be adequate for the appliances and equipment planned. This can save the owner the additional expense of adding more wiring later.

What to Include in the Electrical Subcontract
The electrical contractor will normally bid on the labor and material for the rough-in electrical work: wiring, boxes for outlets, switches and fixtures, the entrance panel and circuit breakers, and cover plates for the outlets and switches. His bid normally includes hanging the light fixtures (but not furnishing them) and the hook-up for the appliances, such as the water heater, oven, and dishwasher, shown on the plans and specifications. Any special equipment, including the hook-up for the heating, cooling and ventilating system, the installation of smoke detectors, intercom systems, central vacuum systems, sump pumps, door bells, telephone and television service lines and boxes, should be included in the bid.

There should be a clear understanding on where the electrical contractor's responsibility begins. It normally begins at the meter. If the electric service line to the house is underground, the electric power company may install this line but charge for the service. A long run from the street to the house will increase the cost.

Electrical Subcontract Checklist

1) What's the cost of service line to house? _____

2) What's the cost of hook-up for temporary electric service? _____

3) What's the cost of labor and material for rough-in? (This includes wiring, outlets, boxes and plates, boxes for the fixtures, switches, connectors, the entrance panel, and circuit breakers.) _____

4) Who covers the following items:

   Cost of light fixtures _____

   Installation of light fixtures _____

   Hook-up for appliances _____

   Hook-up for heating, cooling and ventilating equipment _____

   Hook-up and installation of special equipment _____

   Telephone boxes and service to house _____

   Television boxes and service to house (if required)

   _____

5) Is the subcontractor providing insurance for his employees?

   _____

Figure 11-1
Electrical Subcontract Checklist

Figure 11-1 is a list for checking a bid from an electrical subcontractor. Make sure every item on the list is included and fully covered.

The Plumbing Subcontract

The plumbing must provide adequate water, proper drainage, and venting for the dwelling. As with the electrical system, most communities require a license and permit to do plumbing work. All plumbing must comply with the local building code and will be inspected for compliance. If you're building in an area with no public water service or sewer system, the local health department will probably have the final authority over the private water supply and the private sewage discharge system.

Residential plumbing rough-in includes the plumbing work required preliminary to the setting of the fixtures. Your carpenters can help the plumbers by framing walls wide enough for the soil and vent stacks. They should also arrange the floor joists to carry the bathtub load without excessive deflection. Too great a deflection will sometimes cause an opening above the edge of the tub. Joists should be doubled at the outer edge of the tub, and the intermediate joist should be spaced to clear the tub drain. Metal hangers or wood blocking should also be used to support the tub at the wall.

Where You Can Save on the Plumbing
Good plumbing design can save money. Consider the following:

1) Concentrate plumbing fixtures as much as possible to reduce the amount of piping required. In a two-story house, stack the fixtures. Locate the bathroom directly above the kitchen or a downstairs bathroom, with all fixtures back to back and on the same wall. In a single-story house, locate the kitchen and bathroom, or kitchen and laundry room, with the fixtures back to back.

2) Install an electric water heater in an area not suitable for other use. For example, you might put it under a stairway, in the crawl space, or in a corner base cabinet in the kitchen.

3) Automatic washers, dishwashers, and garbage disposals increase the load on a septic tank. Too small a tank will need more frequent cleaning. It's much cheaper to install a large tank at the time of construction than to replace an inadequate system later.

4) Be sure the water and sewer lines are placed below the frost line — even after finish grading. Finish grading for the landscaping may remove so much soil that the water line is nearly exposed — causing frozen water pipes in cold weather.

What to Include in the Plumbing Subcontract
Taking off the plumbing rough-in material is work for experienced personnel. Let the plumbing contractor do it. The fixtures, such as the kitchen sink, garbage disposal, bathtubs, shower stalls, water closets, lavatories and faucets are normally selected by the owner and installed by the plumber.

The plumbing specifications should state the type and size of the water supply pipes and the drain pipes. If the plumber is furnishing any fixtures, including the water heater, the specifications should make clear the type and size fixture to be furnished. The fixtures furnished by the owner should be noted in the specifications. Responsibility for installing the fixtures should be made clear.

Make sure the specs clearly define the limits of responsibility for water supply lines and sewer lines outside the house. Some plumbing contractors will bid on the work to a specified distance outside of the foundation, such as 5 or 10 feet. The cost of extending the water supply and the sewer lines to the point of connection and discharge will be extra. The responsibility for digging the water and sewer lines and covering them should be defined in the specifications. The plumbing contractor usually won't extend his area of responsibility beyond the property line without a separate bid.

Figure 11-2 is a checklist that can help you spot potential problems with a plumbing subcontract.

The HVAC Subcontract

Every residential and commercial building needs heating, ventilating and air conditioning work. Let's start with heating.

Heating
Modern houses may heat with oil, gas, electric and bio-fueled furnaces, space heaters, electric radiant heat with heating cables in the ceiling, heat pumps that are also air conditioners, or even solar heaters.

Plumbing Subcontract Checklist

1) What's the cost of the water supply line from point of connection to the house, including the trench for the water pipe? _____

2) Does the subcontract include temporary water service hook-up? _____

3) Is the cost of the sewer line from house to point of discharge, including the trench for the sewer pipe, included in the bid? _____

4) What's the cost of the labor and material for the rough-in? (This includes type and size of water supply pipes, type and size of drain pipes, type and size of vent pipes, number and location of outside water faucets and all material required to make the necessary connections.) _____

5) If any plumbing fixtures are included in the subcontract, what will they cost? _____

6) Does it cover installation of plumbing fixtures? _____

7) Does it cover installation of special equipment such as water softeners, pressure relief valves, sump pumps, shower doors and so on? _____

Figure 11-2
Plumbing Subcontract Checklist

Regardless of which type of heating system is chosen, it has to be designed and installed correctly. If the heating unit is too small or not installed properly, it won't provide sufficient heating; if the heating unit is too large, it'll be unnecessarily expensive to purchase and operate.

Heating and cooling capacity depends on the size of the house and the calculated heat loss and gain. Installing adequate insulation in the house and reducing the window area will cut down heat transfer and reduce both operating costs and the initial cost of the heating unit.

For electric baseboard heat or radiant heat, the capacity of the heating unit will range from 6 to 10 watts per square foot of living area, depending on the heat loss. A room with 200 square feet and high heat loss will probably require 2,000 watts to heat. The same room with low heat loss (good insulation, insulated windows, little glass) would probably need only 1,200 to 1,500 watts of capacity.

Air Conditioning
The capacity of the air conditioning system also depends on the size of the house and the calculated heat loss.

Through-the-wall and window-type air conditioners, which cool only a limited area, are normally measured in Btu's per hour. Central air conditioning is designed to cool the entire building, or a major part of the building, such as one floor. It's measured in tons of refrigeration (one ton equals 12,000 Btu's per hour).

If air conditioning is required most of the year and if the heating season is relatively short, a heat pump is probably the best choice for heating and cooling. It supplies heat in the winter and air conditioning in the summer by reversing the compression cycle. Most heat pumps have a built-in auxiliary resistance heating unit that automatically switches on when the outside temperature is too cold for the heat pump to operate efficiently. Except in really cold weather, heat pumps are more efficient than resistant-type heaters.

Heating efficiency is measured by comparing the amount of heat delivered with the energy required to create that heat. This is known as the *Coefficient of Performance* or COP. Electric resistance heaters have a COP of 1; that means it takes 1 watt of electricity to deliver the heat equivalent of 1 watt. Air-source heat pumps generally have COP's of 2; they deliver two times more energy than they consume. Water-source heat pumps normally have a COP of at least 3. Cooling efficiency is usually measured in terms of the *Energy Efficiency Ratio* or EER. The EER is similar to COP, but it's calculated using different units of measure. With EER's, higher ratings are better. EER's of 8 or 9 are possible.

Here's a rule of thumb you can use when estimating heat pump capacity needed for a house: One ton of refrigeration (12,000 Btu's) will serve 600 square feet. A house with 1,800 square feet of living area on one floor will probably require a three-ton heat pump. A two-story house with 1,200 square feet of living area on the first floor and 800 square feet of living area on the second floor will probably require a two-ton heat pump for the first floor and a 1½-ton heat pump for the second floor.

What to Include in the HVAC Subcontract

Be sure to verify with your HVAC subcontractor whether the heat pump has an auxiliary resistance heating system that will automatically switch on in very cold weather. And leave no doubt about who is responsible for constructing the concrete pad for the compressor.

Specialty Subcontracts

Let's look at some points to remember before accepting bids from the other specialty subcontractors — excavation and fill, masonry, and roofing.

Excavation and Fill

Figure 11-3 is an excavation subcontract checklist. Be sure to ask the questions in it when setting up your excavation subcontract.

Masonry

Foundation block is priced either per block or by the job. Brick masons normally charge a fixed fee per thousand bricks, plus extra for fireplaces, hearths, special walls, and steps. Some masons bid by the job per the plans and specs. Either system works well as long as the subcontractor includes all the work in his bid, does a quality job, and leaves a clean site when the work is finished. But ask for a certificate of insurance showing that the sub carries liability and Workers' Compensation insurance.

Make sure that you and the masonry sub have a clear understanding of the points in the checklist in Figure 11-4. The time you spend going over these items with the masonry subcontractor is insignificant compared to the cost of correcting mistakes later. And here's something else to consider: Even though the sub will provide tools, equipment, masons and helpers, you'll still have some important preparation and cleanup costs to include in your estimate. For example, your carpenters will have to frame an opening for the chimney and frame around the prefab fireplace, if they're part of the plans. If the masonry sub doesn't include cleaning the brick in his contract, your carpenter helpers

---

Excavation Subcontract Checklist

1) Are the grade elevations specified for cuts and fills? _____

2) If fill dirt is necessary, is the method of compaction specified? _____

3) Will it cost extra to move excavation equipment onto the job site? _____

4) If so, how much will it cost? _____

5) If rock removal is required, or if there's disturbed earth (such as an underground spring), is the extra cost specified in the contract? _____

6) Will this extra work be charged by the contract or by the hour? _____

7) How much will it cost? _____

8) Does the contract require the removal of trees, stumps, debris, old buildings and fences? _____

9) If so, how much will it cost? _____

10) Will the excavated soil have to be hauled away during the construction period? _____

11) Does the contract include the cost of this hauling? _____

12) Does it specify the cost of hauling the soil *back* to the job site? _____

13) Will there be an extra charge for equipment during cold and wet weather? _____

Figure 11-3
Excavation Subcontract Checklist

---

will probably have to do it. Don't overlook these costs. Keep good records when they do occur, so you'll have an accurate basis for estimating the prep and cleanup on the next job. Divide the actual costs on a typical job by the number of brick used, to find a manhour factor to speed future estimates.

Roofing

Roofing subcontractors normally charge by the square (100 square feet). The cost per square depends on the roofing material, roof pitch, and the number of valleys, vents and metal drip caps. Make it clear whether flashing is to be installed by the carpenters or the roofers.

Masonry Subcontract Checklist

1) How many courses of blocks are required?   _____

2) Who is responsible for leveling the foundation walls?   _____

3) How will they be leveled?   _____

4) If brick is to be set on the block, on which course does it begin?   _____

5) What is the maximum spacing for anchor bolts?   _____

6) On which block course will they set lintels for the foundation windows and doors?   _____

7) Did you verify the following information?

    The location of all corners and their dimensions   _____

    The size of block in each section of the foundation   _____

    The size and location of windows, vents and doors in the foundation wall   _____

    The size and location of notches for beams, girders or floor joists   _____

    The location and size of all piers   _____

    How piers will be constructed   _____

    Where solid masonry blocks will be required   _____

    The location and spacing of wall ties   _____

    Where and how mortar joints will be tooled   _____

    The correct mix for mortar   _____

8) In cold weather, what precautions will the masons take to keep mortar from freezing?   _____

Figure 11-4
Masonry Subcontract Checklist

Verify insurance coverage before signing a contract with the roofer. Workers' Compensation insurance for roofers is one of the major costs for a roofing contractor.

Get the roofing sub to sign a complete specification sheet as part of the contract. The specs should include:

1) Felt paper: weight

2) Metal drip edging

3) Roof vents: type and size

4) Flashing: type and size, where used, how installed. Are valleys open, closed or woven? Who applies the roof cement?

5) Roof shingles: type and weight

6) Nails: size and number per shingle

7) Insurance: If the roofing contractor doesn't have Workers' Compensation and liability insurance for his employees, you must provide it. Ask for a certificate of insurance.

Miscellaneous Subcontracts

You may also use subcontractors for insulation, plaster or drywall, concrete finishing, painting, floor and wall covering, paving and landscaping. Here are some points to remember about agreements with each of these subs:

Insulation: The insulation sub's bid will be for labor and materials per plans and specs. Close supervision is important here. There are many "easy-to-overlook" areas that need insulation and vapor barriers. Make sure your sub doesn't overlook any of them.

Plaster or drywall: The plaster sub may bid on labor and materials for the entire job, or may quote a fixed fee (per square yard) for labor only. The drywall sub normally bids only on the cost of labor per square foot to hang and finish. Some drywall subs may bid on the labor and material for the entire job.

Concrete: These subs normally charge a fixed fee per square foot. They pour and finish the concrete after the forms and screeds are in place. In my part of the country, the carpenters place the forms and screeds. In other areas, the concrete people do it. If it's the carpentry sub's responsibility on your job, make sure the carpentry work is coordinated with the concrete work to avoid delays.

Paint: Paint subs may bid for labor only or for the labor and materials for the entire job per plans and specs. The bid should include both interior and exterior work.

Make sure the bid includes these items:

• All nail holes will be filled.

• All woodwork will be sanded before the first coat of paint is applied, and sanded between each coat thereafter.

• The woodwork is to have a perfectly smooth finish when the painting is finished.

Floor and wall covering: You may want to sub out the installation of wall-to-wall carpet, resilient floor tile, masonry floor covering, wall tile, and wall fabric. The owner normally selects the materials. The subcontract will probably be for the labor only.

12 Estimating Manhours for Carpentry

No book on carpentry would be complete without labor time estimates. Use the manhour figures in this chapter when compiling labor costs for all types of carpentry work. I've developed these figures from my own experience, the experience of other carpenters and carpentry contractors, and from cost studies done by others. I believe this is the most comprehensive list of labor times ever published for carpentry work.

But before you begin to use these figures, understand that there is no single manhour estimate that covers all jobs. Experienced construction estimators know that no two jobs are exactly alike. Labor productivity varies from job to job, even if the crew remains the same. That's why your judgment is an essential part of every estimate. It's also why judgment is needed when using the figures in this chapter.

The figures I give here are not based on "ideal" conditions. They assume conditions typical of what most carpentry contractors face on well-managed jobs. If your jobs don't fall in that category, your labor times will be different. Here's what I mean by "typical" conditions:

Size of the job is moderate, about what most contractors handling this type of work are accustomed to bidding.

The materials needed are readily available at a storage point relatively close to the point of installation. The materials are service grade and meet generally accepted standards for the type of use intended.

Layout and installation are relatively uncomplicated because the plans and specifications are adequate, access to the work is good, and work done by other trades was done according to the plans and is professional quality.

Labor productivity is fair to good. The carpentry crew is experienced in this type of work, motivated to complete the work as required, and is just large enough to get the job done using routine procedures.

Temperature and working conditions do not adversely affect progress of the job.

Tools and equipment appropriate for the job are available and used to best advantage during the course of construction.

Work is professional quality. Exceptional work involving great detail, decorative materials, custom treatments or unique skills is not considered. Any defects or omissions are remedied before the crew leaves the job site. *Only new construction* is involved.

Repair, replacement and remodeling-type work often involves problems of limited access, matching of materials, working with non-standard sizes, patching, and control of the construction environment. The estimates will be a useful guide only to the extent that repair or remodeling work is similar to new construction.

Scope of the Work Described

The manhour figures in this chapter will be a useful guide if you can visualize what work is included and what work is excluded from the tasks listed. No manhour estimate is useful if there is doubt about what the figures actually cover. But it would be nearly impossible to describe in detail every element of each manhour estimate in this chapter.

It is safe to assume, however, that every task essential to performing the work has been included in the estimate. If the scope of work covered still is not clear, understand that estimates are for the "complete" job and include all of the associated work usually performed along with the named task unless noted otherwise.

But be aware that estimates include work by carpenters only. This should help you define what is included and excluded from each table. For example, manhours for installing a cabinet (by a carpenter) would not include the time to stain and seal the cabinet (by a painter).

Two categories of work are specifically included and excluded from the manhour tables:

Non-productive labor is not included unless noted otherwise. On larger crews it is assumed that the supervisor works along with the crew when not actually directing the work.

Mobilization and demobilization on the site are included. Time usually spent unloading tools, materials and equipment, and preparing to do the work, is included in the manhour estimates. So is time spent reloading tools and equipment at job completion and cleanup of surplus material. Naturally, no travel time or delays off the site are included unless specifically noted.

How Accurate Are the Tables?

This chapter is the product of personal judgment. Crew productivity varies widely. Even the most well-informed, professional judgment cannot guarantee that the figures here will apply to the job you're estimating.

Overall, the manhour estimates here will be accurate to within about 20% on most jobs where conditions are similar to the conditions outlined. On most of the remaining jobs the figures will be too high by 20% or more — estimating more manhours than are actually required. This is intentional, as an estimate slightly too high is better than an estimate slightly too low. Most contractors would agree.

Let's look at an example. I list labor installing asphalt strip shingles at 1.5 manhours per 100 square feet. A skilled shingle specialist working under ideal conditions on a larger job will be able to handle considerably more work than this. You'll hear claims of 200 or more square feet per manhour. At that rate a two-man crew would finish two 1600 square foot roofing jobs in a day. That's an excellent rate. But it's not a rate most estimators should use until they saw their crews produce results like that on several jobs.

Now look at the other extreme. Estimators who have figured asphalt shingles on commercial, better industrial, or military jobs, claim that 2 to 2.5 manhours per 100 square feet is a reasonable figure. I don't doubt the validity of these estimates for that type of work.

Most jobs fall between these extremes. Many experienced roofing contractors would insist that their crews can average close to 100 square feet per manhour. Thus a two man crew would finish that 1600 square foot job in one 8 hour day.

Again, I don't doubt the validity of these figures. But I note that they are based on specialized crews working under experienced supervisors and with exactly the right equipment.

To summarize, reasonable estimates for installing asphalt strip shingles may vary from

0.5 to 2.5 manhours per square, with most experienced crews producing about 100 square feet per hour.

Why the difference? There are many reasons. The highest and lowest productivity rates vary from the conditions outlined above, and probably don't include and exclude the same tasks. Many shinglers can put down 200 square feet of shingles in an hour. But every shingle job involves checking and cleaning the deck, moving tools and materials into place, laying out the job, placing felt and starter strips, some flashing work, making minor repairs, and cleanup. All of this should be included in any realistic estimate and is included in my 1.5 manhours per square estimate.

Another difference is the type of work itself — even though the material applied fits the same description. Commercial jobs nearly always receive higher quality workmanship than the typical residential job. Every tradesman worthy of your payroll will give more care and attention to a highly visible roof on a commercial building covered with top quality shingles than a garage roof using strictly standard grade shingles.

Recognize also that an experienced crew working under the direct supervision of an owner-entrepreneur will out-produce less motivated tradesmen on nearly every job. And a crew working on a piecework basis will do its level best to get the job done by quitting time so a return trip isn't necessary the next day.

No single figure will cover all work, and a 500-word essay would be needed to describe most common situations. I have selected what I feel are reasonable first approximations for labor productivity. Use these figures when the productivity of the crew is unknown and the exact type of work isn't specified. In this case of asphalt strip shingles, 1.5 manhours was my choice. And that brings me to my final, and most important point.

Every manhour estimate in this chapter is a poor second choice when compared to the figures you develop yourself from the work your crews have handled. Your most reliable guide will always be your own cost records. Where you must supplement your experience with the reference data in this chapter, I hope my judgment proves worthy of your trust.

Adjusting for Adverse Weather

Bad weather increases your cost, both in wasted manhours and ruined materials. Your framing crew won't work nearly as fast on the hottest afternoon in September as they do on a clear, cool morning in May. Rain and wet weather also increase your costs. Mud slows the work and makes more clean-up necessary. Cold weather also reduces the efficiency of your carpentry crews.

Since the estimates in this chapter assume that temperature and weather conditions don't delay the work, what, you might ask, do I do when the weather is going to be bad? Before I get into the actual manhour estimate, let me answer that question. I'll make a few generalizations about labor productivity in bad weather. I'll also point out some ways that bad weather increases your material costs. Most important, I'll suggest what can be done to keep costs in line when you have to work in bad weather.

Working in Hot Weather

There are two additional costs for framing during hot, dry weather: stud loss due to increased warping, and a labor productivity decrease. The loss of studs can be as high as 5%, even if you're using kiln-dried lumber. To reduce the damage, don't break open the stud packages (wrapped in metal bands) until the studs are ready for use.

Framing productivity drops during hot weather. The drop may be as much as 20% compared to working in more moderate weather. Consider scheduling the framing crew to start work early in the morning, and stop work before the temperature gets too hot.

Roofing productivity drops even more dramatically in hot weather. After a few hours in 100 degree heat, no one can work at top productivity. Weather like that practically stops production. If you don't stop work, the roofers will damage the asphalt shingles with their shoes. Then you have a leaky roof.

Generally, any time the temperature is over 90 degrees for an hour or more, figure that productivity will drop by 10% to 20%. For roofing work, productivity may fall 20% to 40%.

Working in Wet Weather

In wet weather the first question is usually access to the site. If your crew has trouble getting materials to where they're needed, there's no sense scheduling work. Usually access can be improved by draining surface water away from access roads and away from the foundation. You can also improve productivity by dumping gravel to form walkways around the foundation and having the foresight to stack lumber on higher ground. The best time to cut drainage channels and stack lumber on high ground is before the rains begin, of course.

Framing speed is very important in wet weather. It's important to get the house *blacked-in*, or enclosed, so other work can go on even in the rain. A house is blacked-in when the asphalt or roofing felt is placed on the roof. In wet weather you may be asked to place asphalt felt on the roof as soon as the roof sheathing is down so the house is blacked-in before roofing is complete.

Framing lumber used in wet weather should be covered immediately after it's delivered to the building site. That prevents weathering. Wetting of the surface of the wood by rain, followed by rapid drying when the sun comes out, causes checking and deterioration of the wood surface. Wood will also discolor easily in wet weather. Lumber may turn dark in less than two weeks if it's exposed to rainy weather.

Leaving lumber and plywood in the rain results in delaminated plywood, lumber that warps or turns black, and warped siding.

Don't plan to lay asphalt shingles on a wet deck or underlayment. That will cause buckling and ruin the roof's appearance. Asphalt shingles have to go down on an absolutely dry surface.

Roofing materials should always be stored off the ground in wet weather. Store them on a platform or wood pallets. Roll roofing should be stored on end.

Gypsum board is easily damaged by wet or rainy weather. It should always be kept dry, preferably by storing it inside a building under the roof. If you have to store gypsum board outside, stack it off the ground on a level platform and cover it with a plastic tarp to protect it from moisture.

Finish lumber requires special attention in wet weather. The finish lumber like trim and molding is kiln-dried to reduce shrinkage and expansion after it's installed. Don't try to install molding or trim that's wet. Don't let your yard deliver finish lumber until the house is enclosed. Finish lumber can be stored outside temporarily if it's stacked off the ground and covered.

Doors, flooring and millwork should be stored in a clean, dry, well-ventilated space. If they get wet, warping, swelling and raised fine grain will result. Warping and cracks occur in wooden doors when they absorb moisture in humid weather, then dry out quickly, as happens when the air conditioning is turned on. Doors should be conditioned indoors for several days to the prevailing local humidity before hanging or finishing. Steel doors don't need conditioning, of course.

Light rain can make the site an unpleasant place to work. But I think the psychological effect of occasional and light rain is more important than the rain itself. Light rain will stop work only if your crew wants to stop work. Rain isn't like cold weather that numbs fingers and requires heavier clothing. Neither is it like very hot weather that saps a carpenter's energy. Your carpenters will work at near top productivity in light rain if they want to work. If they want to go fishing, any rain at all provides the excuse.

Always try to have some inside work for the carpentry crew in case of wet weather. Installing insulation or framing partitions are examples. These inside jobs can keep the men busy in wet weather so less production time will be lost.

Carpentry in Cold Weather

Figure that carpenter productivity will drop as much as 30% in the winter in cold climate areas. Low temperatures slow movement and require that your crews wear heavy clothes. Your carpenters wouldn't be human if they didn't spend a little extra time in their cars sipping coffee, and take a minute now and then to adjust their coats and boots when the temperature drops to freezing.

Why, then, should you work in cold weather? There may be a couple of reasons. Maybe you're finishing up work that was started in the summer or fall. Or maybe you're finishing up so you can get paid. Maybe your general contractor just demands it so he can sell the house.

In spite of the extra costs for working in cold weather, there are some advantages:

• You can keep your key employees.

• Your cash flow continues year-round.

• That steady cash flow helps pay overhead expenses, which are *always* year-round.

• Winter work beats seasonal labor and material cost increases.

Most materials are more available in winter because the demand isn't as great as it is in the spring, summer and fall. But materials stored in the winter must be protected, and this can be costly. Schedule delivery so the materials won't have to be stored longer than necessary. This is especially true with lumber. When wet lumber freezes, it causes excessive checking and breaks down the cell structure.

Framing

Wood is actually stronger when cold — as long as it doesn't get wet. Lumber is easy to work with in cold weather and the quality of the work may be better if there isn't any rain. But winter framing may take longer. Consider using wall panels and roof trusses that take less assembly on site.

But there are some problems with wood in winter. Repeated freezing and thawing will affect the strength of any wood that has too much moisture. Moisture left in the wood freezes and breaks down the wood cells, reducing the bending strength. That happens with all types of lumber.

Here are some hints for framing in the winter:

• Protect lumber from the effects of weather during delivery and until it's part of the building. Don't leave it exposed on the site. Store it off the ground and use polyethylene sheets to protect it from the snow and ice. Don't have it delivered until you're ready to use it. Reduce to an absolute minimum the time you have to store it on-site.

• On-site labor costs can be dramatically lowered by using preassembled wall panels and roof trusses.

• Finish carpentry should be done after the heat has been turned on in the house and the temperature is stable. Finish carpentry installed in a cold house causes expansion problems like sticking doors and windows once warm weather returns.

Roofing

All snow, ice and frost must be off the roof deck before any roofing materials are placed. Trapped moisture in any form can cause shingles to bubble or buckle, and in extreme cases can cause the roof deck to rot.

Store roofing materials indoors where they'll be dry. If this isn't possible, stack them on a dry platform covered with polyethylene for protection against snow, ice and frost.

Roofing nails are easier to work with than staples in the winter. Nails won't split or crack the shingles as easily as staples do. Many roofers use 1½'' roofing nails rather than 7/8'' nails because the longer nails are easier to grip in cold weather.

It takes longer to lay a roof in winter, mainly because numb fingers don't move as quickly as warm fingers. Also, extra time is needed to prepare the roof deck. Figure from 20% to 40% more time for roofing in cold weather.

Drywall goes up nearly as fast in cold weather, but don't do any taping or finishing until the heat is turned on. Finishing drywall when the temperature is below 50 degrees F usually results in poor quality work.

The cost of heating a house during construction, with either a temporary or permanent heater, may cost from $200 to $400 from the time it's enclosed until it's completed. Don't forget this cost in your estimate for winter building.

Loss of Productivity
The loss of productivity during cold weather is caused by several factors. Some of them are:

- Low temperatures
- Wind chill
- Ground frost
- Slow body movement
- Limited dexterity
- Heavy clothing
- Warm-up breaks
- Material protection
- Snow removal
- Restricted use of materials

Psychological as well as physical factors influence production. If the weather is very cold, the workers may spend half their time getting warm. The threat of injury from cold exposure seems to serve as a distraction for men working in cold weather. And there are a few workers who would rather collect unemployment checks than work in cold weather.

Production decreases from December through March for most carpentry contractors who build in cold weather. For most jobs, figure that work will take 10% to 30% longer from December through March, or any time the temperature drops below freezing.

The Manhour Tables

Follow the suggestions in preceding chapters in this manual and you should have little trouble estimating material quantities. Material estimates are relatively easy. It's the labor estimates that separate the men from the boys in the carpentry contracting business. That's where you'll make or lose money on most jobs. If your labor estimate is only a guess, chances are you'll lose either the job or your shirt.

It's hard to estimate labor accurately because productivity is much higher for some craftsmen and crews than it is for others. And it's higher on some days than others for the *same* crew. No labor estimate fits all jobs. But don't assume it's impossible to estimate labor accurately. There are some reasonable standards that will apply on most jobs. That's what I've tried to describe in the rest of this chapter.

Use the labor figures I recommend here only until you've got better figures based on your crews, your jobs, your supervisors and your work conditions. The cost of work done today by *your* crews, on *your* jobs, under *your* supervision and at *your* labor rates, is the best predictor of labor costs on your next job. This is true now and always will be,

Size	Material			Labor	
	C.F. concrete per L.F.	C.F. concrete per 100 L.F.	C.Y. concrete per 100 L.F.	Manhours per 100 L.F. for hand excavation	Manhours per C.Y. for concrete placement
6 x 12	0.50	50.00	1.9	3.8	1.1
8 x 12	0.67	66.67	2.5	5.0	1.1
8 x 16	0.89	88.89	3.3	6.4	1.1
8 x 18	1.00	100.00	3.7	7.2	1.1
10 x 12	0.83	83.33	3.1	6.1	1.0
10 x 16	1.11	111.11	4.1	8.1	1.0
10 x 18	1.25	125.00	4.6	9.1	1.0
12 x 12	1.00	100.00	3.7	7.2	1.0
12 x 16	1.33	133.33	4.9	9.8	1.0
12 x 20	1.67	166.67	6.1	12.1	0.9
12 x 24	2.00	200.00	7.4	15.8	0.9

Reduce excavation hours by ¼ for sand or loam. Increase excavation hours by ¼ for heavy clay soil.

Placement labor is based on ready-mix concrete direct from chute. Add 50% if concrete is pumped into place. Add 60% if concrete is placed with a crane and bucket. Add two hours per cubic yard if concrete is wheeled 40 feet into place and an additional 25% for each additional 40 feet.

Excavation includes loosening and one throw from trench only.

Figure 12-1
Labor and materials for excavating and pouring
footings, foundations and grade beams

no matter how estimates are compiled and no matter what type of job you're figuring. That's why making and saving good cost records is so important. No one can do it for you. You have to do it yourself. But until you have, try to get by with the figures that follow.

Footings
Here's the standard manhour factor for pouring concrete footings directly from the chute of a concrete truck:

1.0 manhour per cubic yard

If 18 cubic yards of concrete were required for a footing, the estimated manhours to pour this concrete would be 1.0 times 18, or 18.

But be careful. This manhour factor doesn't include excavation, forming, setting grade stakes, finishing, or stripping forms. Stepped footings will take longer. If the concrete truck can't discharge concrete directly into the form, more labor will be required. Figure 12-1 suggests manhour requirements for excavating and pouring footings, foundations and grade beams. Allow about 20 manhours per ton for handling, setting and tying steel in footings and foundations. Lighter bars will take more time per ton and heavier bars will take less time per ton. Add 50% to your estimate if the bars have to be welded in place. These figures assume that the bars arrive on site cut and bent to shape. If cutting and bending will be done on site, allow 20 manhours per ton if there are less than 40 bends per hundred linear feet. Lighter bars and more bending will require more time per ton, of course.

Work Element	Unit	Manhours Per Unit
Wall footings		
1 use	S.F.	.098
3 uses	S.F.	.074
5 uses	S.F.	.068
Column footings		
1 use	S.F.	.120
3 uses	S.F.	.087
5 uses	S.F.	.080
Grade beam or tie beam footings		
1 use	S.F.	.088
3 uses	S.F.	.065
5 uses	S.F.	.060

Labor is manhours for each use of plywood forms. Unit is one square foot of contact area. These figures include fabrication, erection, stripping, and repairing forms for multiple uses. For steel forms, use the labor hours for 5 uses less 10%.

Figure 12-2
Labor forming footings

Footing forms— To estimate the manhours required to build forms for footings:

Multiply the face area of concrete in square feet by 0.098

This includes any forms for stepped footings that may be required.

The estimated manhours to construct the forms for a 24''-wide footing for a foundation 65'0'' by 32'0'' (194'0'' linear feet) would be: 2.0' (24'' wide) times 194.0' equals 388 square feet. Multiply 388 SF by 0.098 to get 38.02, or 38 manhours. Figure 12-2 shows manhours required to form wall, column and grade beam footings.

Foundations

Figure 12-3 show manhours for forming and stripping concrete foundation walls. Concrete placement will average 1 hour per cubic yard when concrete can be poured

Work element	B.F. per S.F. of forms	Make and place forms			Removing forms	
		S.F. in 8 hours	Carpenter hours	Labor hours	S.F. in 8 hours	Labor hours
Foundation wall forms						
4' to 6'	2	190-210	4.0	2.0	640	1.3
7' to 8'	2	165-190	4.5	2.3	550	1.5
9' to 10'	2.5	150-160	5.3	2.5	450	1.8
11' to 12'	3	135-150	5.5	2.8	425	1.9

Figure 12-3
Labor and materials for 100 S.F. of foundation wall forms

Work Element	Unit	Manhours Per Unit
Concrete block, lightweight		
4" block	100 S.F.	10.50
6" block	100 S.F.	11.70
8" block	100 S.F.	12.80
10" block	100 S.F.	15.00
12" block	100 S.F.	17.90
Concrete block, hollow, standard weight		
4" block	100 S.F.	11.00
6" block	100 S.F.	12.00
8" block	100 S.F.	13.00
10" block	100 S.F.	15.00
12" block	100 S.F.	18.10

Time includes set-up, clean-up, joint striking one side only, cutting, pointing, steel alignment and mortar mixing.

Figure 12-4
Labor placing concrete block

directly from the chute. For other conditions, use the modifications suggested in Figure 12-1.

If the foundation wall is concrete block, Figure 12-4 has estimated manhours for placing the block. Whether the foundation is block or concrete, don't forget to include these costs:

1) Spreading crushed stone in the basement
2) Parging foundation walls
3) Brushing on bituminous coating
4) Installing drain tile

Parging foundation walls— To estimate the manhours needed for parging foundation walls, use:

2 manhours per 100 square feet

The labor to parge 902 square feet of foundation wall would be: 902 SF divided by 100 times 2, or 18.04 manhours. To shorten this calculation, use the multiplying factor 0.0200. Multiply 902 SF by 0.02 to get 18.04 manhours. Parging thinner coats and interior surfaces will take less time. See Figure 12-5 for other manhour estimates for parging.

The time required to brush on a bituminous coating will be about 1.1 manhours per 100 square feet on most foundation jobs. Figure 12-6 shows times for various types of coatings and multiple coats.

Installing drain tile— To estimate labor for installing drain pipe, use:

1.5 manhours per 10 linear feet

Here's how you would figure the labor to install 106 linear feet of drain tile: 106 LF divided by 10 times 1.5 equals 15.90, or 16 manhours. To shorten this calculation, use the multiplying factor 0.15000. Multiplying 106 LF by 0.15000 equals 15.90, or 16 manhours.

Work Element	Unit	Manhours Per Unit
Cement parging		
½" for interior faces	100 S.F.	1.2
¾" for interior faces	100 S.F.	1.2
1" for interior faces	100 S.F.	1.6
Cement parging to exposed wall		
½" for exposed faces	100 S.F.	1.6
¾" for exposed faces	100 S.F.	1.6
1" for exposed faces	100 S.F.	2.0

Time includes set-up, preparation, application, repair and clean-up. On larger jobs, reduce the estimated time from 10% to 20%.

Figure 12-5
Labor for cementitious dampproofing

Work Element	Unit	Manhours Per Unit
Asphalt dampproofing		
Primer plus one coat	100 S.F.	1.5
Primer plus two coats	100 S.F.	2.3
Primer plus three coats	100 S.F.	3.1
Troweled on cold asphalt		
One coat	100 S.F.	1.1
Troweled on hot fibrous asphalt		
Primer plus one coat	100 S.F.	1.7
Primer plus two coats	100 S.F.	2.8
Primer plus three coats	100 S.F.	4.0
Asphaltic paint dampproofing		
Per coat — brush on	100 S.F.	1.1
Per coat — spray on	100 S.F.	1.0

Time includes set-up, preparation and clean-up.

Figure 12-6
Labor for bituminous dampproofing

Cold weather can add from 5% to 15% in labor costs for footing and foundations. When your job will be in the winter, don't forget to allow for this extra labor cost.

Once the concrete work is finished, framing can begin. In the next section I'll cover each framing task in the order the work is usually done. Figure 12-7 summarizes the manhour estimates listed in this section and provides some additional estimates.

Floor System
The floor system includes the plate (sill), girder or beam, floor joists, ledgers (if needed), bridging and subfloor. Most standard estimate manhour factors are calculated for the number of manhours to install a given number of linear feet (for the sills), board feet (framing lumber) or square feet (plywood subfloor).

Sills— 3 manhours per 100 linear feet

Work Element	Unit	Manhours Per Unit
Mudsill, 2" x 6"		
Bolted	100 L.F.	3.0
Shot	100 L.F.	2.5
Basement beams (girders)		
2" x 8", built-up	1000 B.F.	26
2" x 10", built-up	1000 B.F.	18
Basement posts	1000 B.F.	18
Box sills	1000 B.F.	29
Floor joists		
2" x 6" to 2" x 8"	1000 B.F.	13
2" x 10" to 2" x 12"	1000 B.F.	10
Headers, tail joists and trimmers		
2" x 6" to 2" x 8"	1000 B.F.	16
2" x 10" to 2" x 12"	1000 B.F.	14
Bridging 2" x 3"	50 sets of 2	4
Subflooring, boards		
Straight	1000 B.F.	15
Diagonal	1000 B.F.	17
Subflooring, plywood, 4' x 8'	1000 B.F.	10
Stud walls, including plates, blocks and bracing		
2" x 4"	1000 B.F.	25
3" x 4", 2" x 6"	1000 B.F.	20
Ceiling joists		
2" x 6" to 2" x 8"	1000 B.F.	16
2" x 10" to 2" x 12"	1000 B.F.	14
Ceiling backing		
2" x 6" to 2" to 8"	1000 B.F.	15
2" x 10" to 2" to 12"	1000 B.F.	14
Attic floor	1000 B.F.	13
Headers for wall openings		
2" x 4"	1000 B.F.	41
2" x 6"	1000 B.F.	28
Gable-end studs	1000 B.F.	28
Fire stop wall blocks	1000 B.F.	30
Corner braces	1000 B.F.	35
Partition plates and shoe	1000 B.F.	23
Partition studs	1000 B.F.	25
Wall backing	1000 B.F.	20
Grounds	1000 L.F.	12
Knee wall plates and studs		
2" x 4"	1000 B.F.	35
2" x 6"	1000 B.F.	25
Wall sheathing, boards, diagonal		
1" x 6"	1000 B.F.	15
1" x 8"	1000 B.F.	14
1" x 10"	1000 B.F.	13

Figure 12-7
Labor for rough carpentry

Work Element	Unit	Manhours Per Unit
Wall sheathing, plywood		
4' x 8' sheets, includes paper	1000 S.F.	12
Wall sheathing, composition		
½"	1000 S.F.	10
¾"	1000 S.F.	11
1"	1000 S.F.	12
Siding, plywood, 4' x 8' sheets	1000 S.F.	13
Corner boards	1000 B.F.	40
Common rafters		
2" x 6"	1000 B.F.	25
2" x 8"	1000 B.F.	19
2" x 10"	1000 B.F.	15
2" x 12"	1000 B.F.	13
Hip, valley, jack rafters	1000 B.F.	30
Roof sheathing, boards		
1" x 6", S4S	1000 B.F.	15
1" x 6", center match	1000 B.F.	18
1" x 8", shiplap	1000 B.F.	17
1" x 10", shiplap	1000 B.F.	13
Roof sheathing, plywood, gable	1000 S.F.	12
Hip roof	1000 S.F.	16
Window and door headers	Each	.6
Make and install rough door buck	Each	1.2
Furring concrete or masonry walls	1000 L.F.	46
Wood plaster grounds on masonry	1000 L.F.	38

Time includes layout, all precutting, stacking, repairing and clean-up as required.

Figure 12-7 (continued)
Labor for rough carpentry

If your job has 350 linear feet of sill, 350 LF divided by 100 times 3 equals 10.5 or 11 manhours. The multiplying factor for sills is *.03000.*

Built-up girders— 18 manhours per 1,000 board feet

If the built-up girder requires 240 board feet of framing lumber, the manhours estimated to build and install it will be 240 BF divided by 1,000 times 18, which equals 4.32, or 5 manhours. The multiplying factor is *.01800.*

Floor joists— 1 manhour per 100 board feet

If there will be 2,860 BF of framing lumber for joists, the estimated manhours to install it will be 2,860 BF divided by 100 times 1, equaling 28.6, or 29 manhours. The multiplying factor is *0.01000.*

Subflooring, diagonal— 17 manhours per 1,000 board feet

Board feet and square feet are the same for 1-inch sheathing. If there are 2,800 BF of 1 x 6 T&G subfloor, the estimated manhours to install it will be 2,800 BF divided by 1,000 times 17, which equals 47.6, or 48 manhours. The multiplying factor is *0.01700.*

Plywood subfloor— 1 manhour per 100 square feet

If there are 2,800 square feet of plywood subfloor, the estimated manhours to install it will be 2,800 SF divided by 100 times 1, which equals 28 manhours. The multiplying factor is *0.01000*.

Here's a word of caution. When labor manhours are based on board feet, linear feet or square feet of lumber, any error in estimating the lumber will have a similar effect on the labor estimate. Double-check your figures before applying the manhour factors.

Increase the manhours from 5% to 15% if the floor system is to be installed in cold weather.

Exterior and Interior Walls
The labor manhour factors in this section include estimates for conventional site-fabricated walls. For details on estimating labor costs for pre-assembled wall systems, review Chapter 5.

Exterior and partition wall studding and plates— These manhour estimates include installing the studs and plates on the first and second floor, knee walls (where they are needed), dormers, gables and headers over openings:

25 manhours per 1,000 board feet

If your job requires 6,240 board feet of studding and plates, 6,240 divided by 1,000 times 25 equals 156 manhours. To shorten this calculation use the factor *0.02500*: 6,240 BF times 0.02500 equals 156 manhours.

Plywood or composition wall sheathing— 12 manhours per 1,000 square feet

If your job includes 2,858 square feet of wall sheathing, 2,858 SF divided by 1,000 times 12 equals 34.30, or 35 manhours. The multiplying factor is *0.01200*: 2,858 square feet times 0.01200 equals 34.30, or 35 manhours.

Roof System
The roof system includes roof trusses or ceiling joists and rafters and sheathing.

Plain gable rafters— 25 manhours per 1,000 board feet

If your job requires 4,191 board feet of common rafter, 4,191 BF divided by 1,000 times 25 equals 104.78, or 105 manhours. Use the multiplying factor *0.02500*: 4,191 BF times 0.02500 equals 104.78, or 105 manhours.

Hip rafters, no dormers— 30 manhours per 1,000 board feet.

If your job requires 4,191 board feet of hip, valley and jack rafters, 4,191 BF divided by 1,000 times 30 equals 125.73, or 126 manhours. The multiplying factor for this calculation is *0.03000*: 4,191 BF times 0.03000 equals 125.73, or 126 manhours.

Rafter supports and collar beams— 25 manhours per 1,000 board feet

If your job requires 485 board feet of rafter supports and collar beams, 485 BF divided by 1,000 times 25 equals 12.13, or 13 manhours. The multiplying factor is *0.02500*: 485 BF times 0.02500 equals 12.13, or 13 manhours.

If the rafter supports and collar beams are 2 x 4 and are estimated in linear feet, the multiplying factor is *0.01667*: 728 LF times 0.01667 equals 12.14, or 13 manhours.

Roof sheathing, plywood (plain gables)— 12 manhours per 1,000 square feet

If your job requires 1,984 square feet of plywood sheathing, 1,984 SF divided by 1,000 times 12 equals 23.81, or 24 manhours. The multiplying factor is *0.01200:* 1,984 SF times 0.01200 equals 23.81, or 24 manhours.

Roof sheathing, plywood (hips and valleys)— 16 manhours per 1,000 square feet

Item	Lumber per 1000 S.F. of floor	Manhours per 1000 S.F. of floor
Sills, pier blocks, floor beams	145 BF	16
Floor joists, blocking, bridging	1,480 BF	26
Subfloor, plywood	1,150 BF	10
Studs, plates, headers, blocks, bracing	2,250 BF	80
Wall sheathing, plywood	1,200 SF	13
Ceiling joists, beams, trimmers, blocks	1,060 BF	36
Rafters, collar beams, ridge boards	1,340 BF	26
Roof sheathing, plywood	1,250 SF	14
Total	**9,875**	**221**

Figure 12-8
Labor and materials for framing and sheathing

Work Element	Unit	Manhours Per Unit
Beams		
6" x 8" to 6" x 10"	1000 B.F.	25.0
8" x 12" to 8" x 16"	1000 B.F.	27.0
10" x 12" to 10" x 16"	1000 B.F.	28.0
Columns		
6" x 6"	1000 B.F.	24.0
8" x 8"	1000 B.F.	25.0
10" x 10"	1000 B.F.	26.0
12" x 12"	1000 B.F.	30.0
14" x 14"	1000 B.F.	32.0
Light canopy framing		
2" x 4"	1000 B.F.	21.0
2" x 8"	1000 B.F.	20.0
3" x 8"	1000 B.F.	19.0
Steel joist bridging		
Cross strapping	100	0.7
Compressible type bridging	100	0.9

Time includes layout, all precutting where necessary, repairing and clean-up.

Figure 12-9
Labor for commercial grade rough carpentry

Span in feet	Unit	Manhours assembly	Manhours placement
20, placed by hand	Each	2	3
30, placed by hand	Each	4	4
40, placed by crane	Each	10	3
50, placed by crane	Each	16	3
60, placed by crane	Each	19	3
80, placed by crane	Each	25	4

Suggested crew: Hand placement - 2 carpenters and 2 laborers.
Crane placement - 1 operator, 2 to 3 men on guylines.

Figure 12-10
Labor for roof trusses

Covering 1,984 square feet of hips and valleys would be 1,984 SF divided by 1,000 times 16 equals 31.74, or 32 manhours. The multiplying factor is *0.01600:* 1,984 SF times 0.01600 equals 31.74, or 32 manhours.

Here's a quick way to check the accuracy of your framing estimates. Figure 12-8 shows the lumber and time needed to frame one and two story residential buildings. Use this table for preliminary estimates and to check your final bid. The quantities shown are for each 1,000 square feet of floor area. If your estimate is for a 1,600 square foot home, multiply labor and material quantities in the table by 1.6 to find your estimated quantity.

Figure 12-8 is based on a wide variety of jobs and will be accurate to within about 10% on most residences. The framing time may be lower by as much as 50% on highly repetitive tract jobs where homes are built from the same plan and lumber is precut and stacked for quick assembly. Homes with small rooms, complex roof shapes, and homes designed by an architect will take longer.

Figure 12-9 shows labor estimates for carpentry on commercial projects.

If you use roof trusses instead of rafters and ceiling joists, manhour estimates are listed in Figure 12-10.

Work Element	Unit	Manhours Per Unit
Wood shingles		
16'' perfections, 5½'' exposure	SQ.	2.3
18'' perfections, 6'' exposure	SQ.	2.0
Split or sawn cedar shakes, 10'' exposure		
24'' long, ½'' to ¾'' thick	SQ.	2.9
White cedar shingles, 5'' exposure		
16'' long	SQ.	2.5
Fire retardant cedar shingles		
16'', 5'' exposed	SQ.	2.6
18'' perfections, 5½'' exposed	SQ.	2.2

Time assumes pitch less than 6 in 12 roof. Sidewalls will take 10 to 20% longer unless exposures are increased.

Figure 12-11
Labor for wood shingles and shakes

Shingle and Shake Roofing

Occasionally you'll be called on to estimate the cost of applying roofing shingles. If you have an experienced roofer on your payroll, you may be able to do this work as economically as a roofing subcontractor. Figure 12-11 shows labor estimates for wood shakes and shingles. Estimates for composition (asphalt or fiberglass) shingles are in Figure 12-12.

Type of roofing	Shingles per 100 S.F.	Nails per shingle	Length of Nail*	Nails per 100 S.F.	Pounds per 100 S.F. (approximate)		Manhours per 100 S.F.
					12 Ga. by ⁷⁄₁₆" head	11 Ga. by ⁷⁄₁₆" head	
Roll roofing on new deck	--	--	1"	252**	0.73	1.12	1.0
Roll roofing over old roofing	--	--	1¾"	252**	1.13	1.78	1.25
19" selvage over old shingles	--	--	1¾"	181	0.83	1.07	1.0
3 tab sq. butt on new deck	80	4	1¼"	336	1.22	1.44	1.5
3 tab sq. butt reroofing	80	4	1¾"	504	2.38	3.01	1.85
Hex strip on new deck	86	4	1¼"	361	1.28	1.68	1.5
Hex strip reroofing	86	4	1¾"	361	1.65	2.03	2.0
Great American	226	2	1¼"	479	1.79	2.27	2.5
Great Dutch lap	113	2	1¼"	236	1.07	1.39	1.5
Individual hex	82	2	1¾"	172	.79	1.03	1.5

*Length of nail should always be sufficient to penetrate at least ¾" into sound wood. Nails should show little, if any, below underside of deck.
**This is the number of nails required when spaced 2" apart.

Figure 12-12
Labor and materials for composition roofing

Insulation

Loose ceiling insulation can be either poured by hand over ceilings or blown in. On larger jobs it will usually be cheaper to rent a blowing machine to blow the insulation into place. If insulation is poured in place by hand, estimate productivity at 20 cubic feet per manhour. If it's blown into place, figure production at 250 cubic feet per manhour. Use Figure 12-13 to convert cubic feet to square feet at the depth required.

Figure 12-14 shows manhour estimates for placing batt and blanket insulation.

Siding and Exterior Trim

Labor manhour factors for siding and trim are figured by the square foot of siding and linear foot of trim. Figure 12-15 shows labor estimates for siding and siding trim.

Cornice— 6 to 8 manhours per 100 linear feet

For 550 linear feet of cornice using the factor 7 manhours per 100 linear feet, the calculation will be: 550 LF feet divided by 100 times 7 equals 38.50, or 39 manhours.

Gable (rake)— 10 to 14 manhours per 100 linear feet

Fill Thickness	Material Number of S.F. covered by C.F. @ density ratings				
	6 lbs.	7 lbs.	8 lbs.	9 lbs.	10 lbs.
1"	21.1	18.0	15.9	14.1	13.0
2"	10.6	9.1	8.0	7.1	6.4
3"	7.1	6.1	5.3	4.7	4.2
4"	5.3	4.6	4.0	3.5	3.2
5"	4.2	3.6	3.2	2.8	2.6
6"	3.6	3.0	2.7	2.4	2.2
7"	3.1	2.6	2.3	2.0	1.9
8"	2.6	2.3	2.0	1.8	1.6

Figure 12-13
Coverage for poured ceiling insulation

Item	Manhours per 1000 S.F.
Unfaced fiberglass in walls with studs 16" o.c.	
3½", R-13	5.5
6½", R-19	7.1
Paper faced fiberglass in walls with studs 16" o.c.	
3½", R-13	6.3
6½", R-19	8.2
Unfaced fiberglass between ceiling joists 16" o.c.	
3½", R-13	5.5
6½", R-19	7.1
9½", R-30	8.3
Unfaced fiberglass in walls with studs 24" o.c.	
3½", R-13	3.9
6½", R-19	5.0
Paper faced fiberglass in walls with studs 24" o.c.	
3½", R-13	4.4
6½", R-19	5.8
Unfaced fiberglass between ceiling joists 24" o.c.	
3½", R-13	3.9
6½", R-19	5.0
9½", R-30	5.9

Coverage includes space taken by studs and joists. Times listed include set-up and cleanup, unloading, stacking and installing. Paper-backed insulation is stapled with an automatic stapler. Suggested crew is one carpenter and one helper.

Figure 12-14
Labor installing batt and blanket insulation

Work Element	Unit	Manhours Per Unit
Bevel siding		
½'' x 6'', 3' to 7' long	1000 S.F.	19.0
½'' x 6'', 6' to 18' long	1000 S.F.	17.0
½'' x 8'', 3' to 7' long	1000 S.F.	17.0
¾'' x 8'', 3' to 7' long	1000 S.F.	18.0
¾'' x 10'', 6' to 18' long	1000 S.F.	18.5
Tongue and groove siding		
1'' x 4''	1000 S.F.	21.5
1'' x 6''	1000 S.F.	20.5
Board and batten siding, 1'' x 12''	1000 S.F.	29.0
Coved channel siding, 1'' x 8''	1000 S.F.	24.5
Plywood siding, 4' x 8' panels		
⅜''	1000 S.F.	14.0
⅝''	1000 S.F.	16.0
Trim pieces		
Edging, 1'' x 3''	10 L.F.	0.4
Corner, 1'' x 3'' x 3''	10 L.F.	0.5
Base trim, 1'' x 4''	10 L.F.	0.35

Figure 12-15
Labor installing siding

Other molding— 4 to 6 manhours per 100 linear feet

Installing siding and trim on the second floor will require more time than installing them on the first floor. Why? Because second-floor work requires scaffolding that must be erected and dismantled.

Scaffolding labor is charged to exterior trim and siding. It will take 25% to 35% more time to install siding and trim at the second floor level.

Interior Wall and Ceiling Finish

Drywall installation (or plastering) is normally done by a subcontractor. Before this work can begin, the carpenters have to install nailers and furring to support the finish wall material. Make sure all the drop ceilings for cabinets are framed in and nailers have been installed at inside corners on partitions running parallel to the ceiling joists. All openings in the walls and ceilings for bathroom accessories and access doors must be cut and framed in. This work by the carpenters is usually called *preparation and coordination work*.

Carpenter's preparation work— 6 to 8 manhours per 1,000 square feet of wallboard or plaster applied

For 10,016 square feet of wallboard and a manhour factor of 6 manhours per 1,000 of wall and ceiling, the calculation is: 10,016 square feet divided by 1,000 times 6, which equals 60.10, or 60 manhours. Using the multiplying factor of *0.00600* (for 6 manhours per 1,000 square feet) the calculation is: 10,016 square feet times 0.00600 equals 60.10, or 60 manhours.

Interior Trim and Stairs

The labor to install floor underlayment will vary with the amount of cutting and fitting that has to be done. For most jobs, these manhour factors will be:

Work Element	Unit	Manhours Per Unit
Solid core exterior doors		
3'0" x 7'0" x 1¾" thick	Each	3.4
3'0" x 7'0" x 2¼" thick	Each	3.5
Exterior fire doors		
3'0" x 7'0", 1 hour rating	Each	3.7
3'0" x 7'0", 1½ hour rating	Each	3.7
Hollow core 3'0" x 6'8" x 1¾" exterior doors with frames		
3'0" x 6'8"	Each	3.5
4'0" x 7'0"	Each	3.6
Interior doors		
3'0" x 7'0", hollow core	Each	3.5
3'0" x 7'0", solid core	Each	3.6
Architectural type doors with transom and panels		
3'0" x 7'0" x 1¾" thick	Each	5.2
Acoustical doors		
3'0" x 7'0" class 36 STC	Each	4.4
3'0" x 7'0" class 40 STC	Each	4.4
Exterior combination storm and screen doors, excluding frames		
3'0" x 6'8"	Each	2.2
French doors 1¾" fir, job hung		
3'0" x 6'8"	Each	4.0
Closet bi-passing, 1⅜" thick, complete with pulls and tracks		
4'0" x 6'8"	Each	2.2
6'0" x 6'8"	Each	2.6

Time includes move on and off site, unloading, stacking, setting frame and trim, hanging door, installing lockset, repair and cleanup as needed, but no finishing.

Figure 12-16
Labor for installing doors and frames

Underlayment— 1 to 2 manhours per 100 square feet

Using 65 pieces of 4' x 8' floor underlayment (2,080 square feet) and the multiplying factor of 2 manhours per 100 square feet: 2,080 square feet times 0.02000 equals 41.60, or 42 manhours.

Interior doors and trim— The labor to install a door, install and sand the casing on two sides, and install the lockset may be estimated at:

3 manhours per door

Figure 12-16 shows labor estimates for installing other types of doors. These figures include assembling the door, setting the door frame, installing the casing on two sides, sanding, and installing the hardware and door. Figure 12-17 shows labor estimates for installing door weatherstripping.

Work Element	Unit	Manhours Per Unit
Door weatherstripping, spring bronze or brass, 2 jambs and 1 head, wood door		
3' to 4' width	Each	1.0
Over 4' to 6' width	Each	1.2
Door weatherstripping, interlocking, metal, 2 jambs, head and sill seal, wood door		
3' to 4' width	Each	1.6
4' to 6' width	Each	2.0

Figure 12-17
Labor for installing door weatherstripping

Windows and trim— The labor to install windows and trim will vary with the size and type of window. A 36'' x 36'' single window will require about 50% less labor to trim than a large triple window or picture window. Figure 12-18 shows labor estimates for windows. On most jobs you'll have both large and small windows. The labor savings on the small windows will offset the extra labor needed on the large units. Many estimators just count the windows and multiply the total by an installation time for an average size window.

Work Element	Unit	Manhours Per Unit	Work Element	Unit	Manhours Per Unit
Casement windows and screens			8'4'' x 5'2''	Each	5.2
1 leaf, 1'10'' x 3'2''	Each	1.4	Bow bay windows and screens		
2 leaves, 3'10'' x 4'2''	Each	1.9	8' x 5'0''	Each	5.1
3 leaves, 5'11'' x 5'2''	Each	2.4	9'9'' x 6'8''	Each	7.6
Picture windows			7' x 5'0''	Each	7.1
4'6'' x 4'6''	Each	3.0	8'9'' x 5'0''	Each	7.7
5'8'' x 4'6''	Each	3.2	7'6'' x 6'0''	Each	7.6
9' x 5'	Each	3.7	8'9'' x 6'6''	Each	8.4
10' x 5'	Each	4.0			
11' x 5'	Each	4.4	One member casing on windows, ordinary work	Each	1
Double or single hung windows and screens			Hardwood, first class work	Each	1½ to 2
2'0'' x 3'2''	Each	1.1	Two member casing on windows, ordinary work	Each	1½ to 2
2'0'' x 4'6''	Each	1.6	Hardwood and first class work	Each	2 to 4
2'8'' x 3'2''	Each	2.0	Window trim on brick walls, ordinary work	Each	1½ to 2
2'8'' x 5'2''	Each	2.1	First class or difficult work	Each	2 to 4
3'4'' x 5'2''	Each	2.4			
5'6'' x 5'2''	Each	3.4			

Time is for setting factory-made assembled windows in a prepared opening and includes move on and off site, unloading, stacking, installing, repairing and cleanup as needed.

Figure 12-18
Labor installing windows and trim

Work Element	Unit	Manhours Per Unit
Base cabinets, 36" high		
24" wide	Each	1.2
36" wide	Each	1.4
Base corner cabinets, 36" wide	Each	3.2
Wall cabinets, 12" deep		
12" x 18"	Each	0.9
18" x 18"	Each	1.0
18" x 36"	Each	1.1
24" x 36"	Each	1.5
Factory formed tops, 4" backsplash		
24" wide	L.F.	0.20
32" wide	L.F.	0.21
Backsplash only, 4" high	L.F.	0.08
Cutting blocks, custom sizes	S.F.	0.42
Broom closets, 7' high	Each	1.8

Time includes layout, unloading and all necessary trim work, cleanup and repairs as needed. Time does not include any floor or wall preparation or demolition work.

Figure 12-19
Labor installing cabinets and tops

Kitchen cabinets and vanities— Manhour estimates for cabinet work are:

Base section, job built:
3.5 manhours per linear foot

Wall section, job built:
1.0 manhours per linear foot

Install factory-built base section, 36" wide unit:
2.0 manhours per unit

Install factory-built wall section, 36" wide unit:
1.5 manhours per unit

These manhour factors include installing the counter tops and molding.

Here's the manhour factor on a larger job for installing factory-built cabinets, including the counter tops and molding, based on the square feet of face area:

7 manhours per 100 square feet of face area

Figure 12-19 shows labor estimates for cabinets and counter tops. Larger tops can be much harder to set than smaller tops. Tops that are more than 8' long in any dimension may present special problems and require larger crews for setting. Be sure the top you order can be maneuvered into place without removing any doors or framing.

Baseboard and baseshoe— *4 to 6 manhours per 100 linear feet*

Closet shelves— *3 manhours per 100 linear feet*

Work Element	Unit	Manhours Per Unit
Exterior trim		
Corner boards, verge, fascia	100 L.F.	4
Cornice, 3 member	100 L.F.	12
Porch post, plain	Each	1
Porch post, built-up	Each	2
Clothes closets		
One shelf, hookstrip, hook and pole	Each	2
Open shelving and cleats	Each	0.5
Linen closet, shelving and cleats	Each	3
Baseboard		
Two member, ordinary work	100 L.F.	4 to 6
Two member, hardwood, first class or difficult work	100 L.F.	6 to 8
Three member, ordinary work	100 L.F.	5 to 7
Three member, hardwood, first class or difficult work	100 L.F.	7 to 9
Picture molding		
Ordinary work	100 L.F.	2.7 to 3
Hardwood, first class or difficult work	100 L.F.	4 to 5
Chair rail		
Ordinary work	100 L.F.	2.5 to 3
Hardwood, first class or difficult work	100 L.F.	3 to 4
Plate rail		
Two member, ordinary work	100 L.F.	10 to 12
Two member, first class work	100 L.F.	12 to 15
Interior cornice		
Ordinary work	100 L.F.	10 to 16
First class or difficult work	100 L.F.	18 to 22

Time includes layout, all pre-cutting, stacking, repair and clean-up.

Figure 12-20
Labor for finish carpentry

Figure 12-20 shows installation estimates for interior and exterior trim and molding.

Mirrors and medicine cabinets— 8 manhours per 55 square feet of mirror area

Here's the multiplying factor per square foot of mirror area: *0.14545.* The labor to install a mirror 3' x 7' (21 square feet) will be estimated like this: 21 SF times 0.14545 equals 3.05, or 3 manhours. Figures 12-21 and 12-22 show manhour estimates for installing surface-mounted and recessed bathroom accessories.

Tub and shower doors— 2 manhours per door

Several important finish items are covered in Figures 12-23 to 12-28. Figure 12-23 gives labor hours for interior paneling. Figure 12-24 shows labor times for gypsum drywall. Use Figures 12-25 and 12-26 when installing suspended systems and tile. Figures 12-27 and 12-28 cover wood strip and block flooring.

Work Element	Unit	Manhours Per Unit	Work Element	Unit	Manhours Per Unit
Soap dish	Each	.24	Towel pin	Each	.13
Clothes hook, single	Each	.12	Towel ladder & bar	Each	.39
Clothes hook, double	Each	.12	Mirror 18" x 24"	Each	.44
Crystal shelf, 6" deep	L.F.	.26	Mirror shelf, 18" x 24"	Each	.52
Stainless steel shelf, 6" deep	L.F.	.26	Government type mirror, 18" x 24"	Each	.53
Towel bar, 12" long	Each	.25	With shelf	Each	.60
Towel bar, 18" long	Each	.26	Shelf, 18" wide x 6" deep	Each	.40
Towel bar, 24" long	Each	.27	Pull down utility shelf	Each	.66
Soap & grab bar combined	Each	.20	Straight grab bars, 24"	Each	.39
Towel ring	Each	.13	Angular grab bars, 24" x 36"	Each	.80
Tumbler & toothbrush holder	Each	.24	Wall to floor grab bars	Each	.65
Toilet paper holder, single roll	Each	.26	Straddle grab bars	Each	1.00
Toilet paper holder, double roll	Each	.26	Special shaped grab bars (custom)	Each	1.30
Toilet paper dispenser, box type	Each	.39	Towel & waste receptacle, 10.5 gal.	Each	.90
Soap dispenser, globe type	Each	.20	Sanitary napkin dispenser & receptor	Each	1.45
Soap dispenser, box type	Each	.33	Sanitary napkin receptacle	Each	.92

These figures assume blocking has been installed where needed to carry each fixture if installation is on a frame wall.

Figure 12-21
Labor installing surface-mounted bathroom accessories

Work Element	Unit	Manhours Per Unit
Toilet paper holder, single	Each	.30
Soap holder	Each	.18
Soap & grab bar combined	Each	.24
Tumbler holder	Each	.24
Tumbler & toothbrush holder	Each	.24
Paper towel dispenser	Each	.36
Concealed lavatory service unit	Each	.57
Facial tissue dispenser	Each	.26
Towel & soap dispenser with mirror	Each	1.20
Towel dispenser & receptacle	Each	1.20
Towel dispenser	Each	1.80
Towel & waste receptacle, 10.5 gal. capacity	Each	1.10
Sanitary napkin dispenser	Each	1.80

These figures assume fixtures are installed in prepared openings.

Figure 12-22
Labor installing recessed bathroom accessories

Work Element	Unit	Manhours Per Unit
Plastic faced hardboard, including molding and trim		
⅛"	100 S.F.	2.8
¼"	100 S.F.	2.9
Plywood, 4' x 8' panels, including trim		
¼"	100 S.F.	3.5
½"	100 S.F.	4.4
Plank paneling		
¼"	100 S.F.	3.9
¾"	100 S.F.	5.0
¾", random width	100 S.F.	5.4
Cedar closet lining		
1" x 4" plank	100 S.F.	5.9
¼" plywood	100 S.F.	4.5

Allow about 25% more time for ceiling installation. Deduct 5 to 15% when 9' or 12' high plywood panels can be used. If installation is on metal studs, add 10% to the times listed.

Figure 12-23
Labor installing wall paneling

Work Element	Unit	Manhours Per Unit	Work Element	Unit	Manhours Per Unit
Drywall on one face of metal or wood studs or furring			Drywall for beams and soffits		
1 layer, ⅜"	100 S.F.	1.8	1 layer, ½"	100 S.F.	4.0
1 layer, ½"	100 S.F.	1.9	1 layer, ⅝"	100 S.F.	3.9
1 layer, ⅝"	100 S.F.	2.1	2 layers, ½"	100 S.F.	7.3
2 layers, ⅜" (mastic)	100 S.F.	2.7	2 layers, ⅝"	100 S.F.	8.0
2 layers, ½" (mastic)	100 S.F.	3.0	Drywall, glued		
2 layers, ⅝" (mastic)	100 S.F.	3.4	1 layer, ½"	100 S.F.	2.0
Drywall for columns, pipe chases or fire partitions			1 layer, ⅝"	100 S.F.	1.9
1 layer, ⅜", nailed	100 S.F.	4.4	Screwed drywall		
1 layer, ½", nailed	100 S.F.	4.5	1 layer, ½"	100 S.F.	1.9
1 layer, ⅝", nailed	100 S.F.	4.6	1 layer, ⅝"	100 S.F.	2.2
2 layers, ½", mastic	100 S.F.	8.5	Additional time requirements		
2 layers, ⅝", mastic	100 S.F.	8.9	Add for ceiling work	100 S.F.	.6
3 layers, ½", mastic	100 S.F.	12.5	Add for walls over 9' high	100 S.F.	.5
3 layers, ⅝", mastic	100 S.F.	13.0	Add for resilient clip application	100 S.F.	.4
1 layer, 1½", coreboard	100 S.F.	4.0	Add for vinyl covered drywall	100 S.F.	.4
			Add for thincoat plaster finish	100 S.F.	1.4
			Deduct for no taping, finish or sanding	100 S.F.	.9

Time includes move on and off site, unloading, stacking, installing drywall, repair and cleanup as needed. Taping, joint finishing and sanding are included.

Figure 12-24
Labor installing gypsum drywall

Work Element	Unit	Manhours Per Unit
Concealed zee splines, 1½" carrying channels 4' o.c. with 3/16" rod hangers		
Zee runners @12" o.c.	100 S.F.	3.3
Zee runners @24" o.c.	100 S.F.	3.0
Nailable channel system, 1½" carrying channels 4' o.c. with 3/16" rod hangers		
Nailing channels 12" o.c.	100 S.F.	3.3
Nailing channels 16" o.c.	100 S.F.	2.7
Metal pan snap system, 1½" carrying channels 4' o.c. with 3/16" rod hangers, snap type runners		
Runners 1' o.c.	100 S.F.	2.5
Runners 2' o.c.	100 S.F.	2.1
Runners 3' o.c.	100 S.F.	2.0
Runners 4' o.c.	100 S.F.	1.6
Runners 5' o.c. custom	100 S.F.	2.6
Exposed grid 1½" tee bar, with 3/16" rod hangers and cross tee runners		
2' x 2' grid	100 S.F.	2.3
2' x 3' grid	100 S.F.	2.2
2' x 4' grid	100 S.F.	2.1
3' x 3' grid	100 S.F.	1.9
4' x 4' grid	100 S.F.	1.8
5' x 5' grid	100 S.F.	1.4
1' x 4' grid	100 S.F.	2.5
Add for rods hung from:		
Explosive set studs	100 S.F.	1.0
Drilled & set expansion shield	100 S.F.	4.7
Concrete embedded insert	100 S.F.	2.7

Suspension system includes layout, handling, fitting and placing ceiling framework under a steel deck, cleanup and repairs as needed. Heights over 9' will add about 10% to manhours for each 2' of additional height. No tile or panel installation included in these figures.

Figure 12-25
Labor for suspended ceiling systems

Work Element	Unit	Manhours Per Unit
Fiber tiles laid in suspension grid		
24" x 24"	100 S.F.	.8
24" x 48"	100 S.F.	.5
Asbestos board laid in grid, with 1" insulation blanket		
24" x 24"	100 S.F.	.9
24" x 48"	100 S.F.	.6
Adhesive mounted tiles		
12" x 12"	100 S.F.	1.3
12" x 24"	100 S.F.	.7
24" x 24"	100 S.F.	.6
Aluminum panels laid in grid		
12" x 12"	100 S.F.	1.6
12" x 24"	100 S.F.	1.4
Perforated steel panel in grid		
12" x 48" snap in	100 S.F.	1.4
24" x 24" snap in or lay in	100 S.F.	1.3
24" x 48" lay in	100 S.F.	1.1
48" x 24"	100 S.F.	1.3

Time includes handling, cutting panels as needed, installation, scaffolding and cleanup. Heights over 9' will add about 10% to manhours for each 2' of additional height. No suspension system installation is included in these figures.

Figure 12-26
Labor for suspended ceiling panels

Work Element	Unit	Manhours Per Unit
Fir flooring (4' to 20' long 1'' x 4'')		
C and better vertical grain	100 S.F.	3.1
C and better flat grain	100 S.F.	3.0
Oak flooring ($^{25}/_{32}$'' x 2¼'')		
Clear quartered	100 S.F.	3.5
Clear plain	100 S.F.	3.6
Select plain	100 S.F.	3.9
Number one common	100 S.F.	3.9
Prefinished prime grade	100 S.F.	4.0
Maple flooring ($^{25}/_{32}$'' x 2¼'')		
First grade	100 S.F.	5.2
Second grade and better	100 S.F.	5.0
Maple flooring ($^{25}/_{32}$'' x 3¼'')		
First grade	100 S.F.	3.8
Second grade and better	100 S.F.	3.0
Pine flooring ($^{25}/_{32}$'' x 2¼'')		
First grade	100 S.F.	3.8
Second grade and better	100 S.F.	3.5

Time includes move on and off site, unloading, stacking, placing, repair and cleanup as needed, but no sanding or finishing. Figure sanding at 1 hour per 100 square feet and filling holes and 2 coats of lacquer at 1.5 hours per 100 square feet.

Figure 12-27
Labor for installing wood strip flooring

Work Element	Unit	Manhours Per Unit
Parquet, prefinished		
$^{5}/_{16}$'' thick	100 S.F.	6.0
½'' thick	100 S.F.	6.1
Parquet, prefinished, top quality		
$^{5}/_{16}$'' thick	100 S.F.	6.2
½'' thick	100 S.F.	6.4
Simulated parquet and tile flooring, 5 ply, ⅝'' thick plywood	100 S.F.	3.5
Wood block flooring (factory type)		
Creosoted 2'' thick	100 S.F.	3.7
Creosoted 2½'' thick	100 S.F.	4.0
Creosoted 3'' thick	100 S.F.	4.3
Natural finish end grain 1½'' thick	100 S.F.	3.8
Expansion strip 1'' thick	100 L.F.	2.7

Time includes move on and off site, unloading, stacking, cleanup and repair as needed, but no sanding or finishing.

Figure 12-28
Labor for installing wood block flooring

Work Element	Unit	Manhours Per Unit
Erecting stairwork, hours per 9' rise		
Building ordinary plain box stairs on the job	Each	8 to 16
Rails, balusters and newel post for above	Each	4 to 8
Erecting plain flight of stairs built-up in shop	Each	6 to 8
Erecting two short flights	Each	10 to 12
Erecting open stairs	Each	10 to 12
Erecting open stairs with two flights	Each	12 to 16
Newels, balusters and hand rail for the above	Each	6 to 8
Erecting prefabricated wood stairs, hours per 9' rise		
Circular, 6' diameter, oak	Each	23.0
Circular, 9' diameter, oak	Each	31.0
Straight, 3' wide, assembled	Each	3.0
Straight, 4' wide, assembled	Each	3.2

Figure 12-29
Labor erecting stairs

Stairs

The labor to frame and install the risers, treads and handrails will vary with the type of stairs and the efficiency of the craftsmen. The labor for an 8- to 10-foot rise of basement stairs with open risers and two handrails may be as low as 10 manhours. Circular stairs and other ornate main stairs with an elaborate balustrade may require 80 or more manhours. Figure 12-29 suggests manhour estimates for stair work.

Worksheets

- **Rough Carpentry**
- **Footings and Foundations**
- **Floor Systems**
- **Interior and Exterior Walls**
- **Roof Systems**
- **Siding and Exterior Trim**
- **Interior Wall and Ceiling Finish**
- **Interior Trim**
- **Weekly Timesheet**

Rough Carpentry Worksheets

Lumber Cost per Thousand Board Feet (MBF)

Lumber size	Price per piece	x	Factor	=	Price per MBF	Lumber size	Price per piece	x	Factor	=	Price per MBF
2 x 4 x 8		x	187.50	=		2 x 8 x 14		x	53.57142	=	
2 x 4 x 10		x	150.00	=		2 x 8 x 16		x	46.87501	=	
2 x 4 x 12		x	125.00	=		2 x 8 x 18		x	41.66667	=	
2 x 4 x 14		x	107.14290	=		2 x 8 x 20		x	37.50	=	
2 x 4 x 16		x	93.74997	=		2 x 10 x 8		x	75.00	=	
2 x 4 x 18		x	83.33333	=		2 x 10 x 10		x	60.00	=	
2 x 4 x 20		x	75.00	=		2 x 10 x 12		x	50.00	=	
2 x 6 x 8		x	125.00	=		2 x 10 x 14		x	42.85715	=	
2 x 6 x 10		x	100.00	=		2 x 10 x 16		x	37.50	=	
2 x 6 x 12		x	83.33333	=		2 x 10 x 18		x	33.33333	=	
2 x 6 x 14		x	71.42857	=		2 x 10 x 20		x	30.00	=	
2 x 6 x 16		x	62.50	=		2 x 12 x 8		x	62.50	=	
2 x 6 x 18		x	55.55556	=		2 x 12 x 10		x	50.00	=	
2 x 6 x 20		x	50.00	=		2 x 12 x 12		x	41.66667	=	
2 x 8 x 8		x	93.74997	=		2 x 12 x 14		x	35.71429	=	
2 x 8 x 10		x	75.00	=		2 x 12 x 16		x	31.25	=	
2 x 8 x 12		x	62.50	=		2 x 12 x 18		x	27.77778	=	
						2 x 12 x 20		x	25.00	=	

Total Lumber Cost

Lumber size	Number of pieces	x	Factor	x	Price per MBF	=	Cost of lumber
2 x 4 x 8		x	.00533	x		=	
2 x 4 x 10		x	.00667	x		=	
2 x 4 x 12		x	.0080	x		=	
2 x 4 x 14		x	.00933	x		=	
2 x 4 x 16		x	.01067	x		=	
2 x 4 x 18		x	.0120	x		=	
2 x 4 x 20		x	.01333	x		=	
2 x 6 x 8		x	.0080	x		=	
2 x 6 x 10		x	.0100	x		=	
2 x 6 x 12		x	.0120	x		=	
2 x 6 x 14		x	.0140	x		=	
2 x 6 x 16		x	.0160	x		=	
2 x 6 x 18		x	.0180	x		=	
2 x 6 x 20		x	.0200	x		=	
2 x 8 x 8		x	.01067	x		=	
2 x 8 x 10		x	.01333	x		=	
2 x 8 x 12		x	.0160	x		=	
2 x 8 x 14		x	.01867	x		=	
2 x 8 x 16		x	.02133	x		=	
2 x 8 x 18		x	.0240	x		=	
2 x 8 x 20		x	.02667	x		=	
2 x 10 x 8		x	.01333	x		=	
2 x 10 x 10		x	.01667	x		=	
2 x 10 x 12		x	.0200	x		=	
2 x 10 x 14		x	.02333	x		=	

Total Lumber Cost (continued)

Lumber size	Number of pieces	x	Factor	x	Price per MBF	=	Cost of lumber
2 x 10 x 16		x	.02667	x		=	
2 x 10 x 18		x	.0300	x		=	
2 x 10 x 20		x	.03333	x		=	
2 x 12 x 8		x	.0160	x		=	
2 x 12 x 10		x	.0200	x		=	
2 x 12 x 12		x	.0240	x		=	
2 x 12 x 14		x	.0280	x		=	
2 x 12 x 16		x	.0320	x		=	
2 x 12 x 18		x	.0360	x		=	
2 x 12 x 20		x	.0400	x		=	

Converting Linear Feet to Board Feet

Lumber size (thickness and width)	Linear feet	x	Factor	=	Board feet
1'' x 4''		x	.33333	=	
1'' x 6''		x	.50000	=	
1'' x 8''		x	.66667	=	
1'' x 10''		x	.83333	=	
1'' x 12''		x	1.00000	=	
2'' x 4''		x	.66667	=	
2'' x 6''		x	1.00000	=	
2'' x 8''		x	1.33333	=	
2'' x 10''		x	1.66667	=	
2'' x 12''		x	2.00000	=	

Converting Board Feet to Linear Feet

Lumber size (thickness and width)	Board feet	x	Factor	=	Linear feet
1'' x 4''		x	3.00	=	
1'' x 6''		x	2.00	=	
1'' x 8''		x	1.50	=	
1'' x 10''		x	1.20	=	
1'' x 12''		x	1.00	=	
2'' x 4''		x	1.50	=	
2'' x 6''		x	1.00	=	
2'' x 8''		x	.75	=	
2'' x 10''		x	.60	=	
2'' x 12''		x	.50	=	

Footings and Foundations Worksheets

Crushed Stone Quantities for Foundation

Thickness	Factor	Foundation area (square feet)	Cubic yards
3"	.00926	x	=
3½"	.01080	x	=
4"	.01235	x	=
4½"	.01389	x	=
5"	.01543	x	=
5½"	.01698	x	=
6"	.01852	x	=

Cubic yards crushed stone _____ x 1.35 = _____ tons crushed stone

Concrete Block Quantities

12" x 8" x 16" blocks

Factor	Foundation length (linear feet)	Number of courses	Number of blocks
.75 x		x	=

8" x 8" x 16" blocks

.75 x		x	=

4" x 8" x 16" blocks

.75 x		x	=

Concrete block quantities (by square foot method)

8" x 8" x 16" blocks

Factor	Foundation area (square feet)	Number of blocks
1.125 x		=

Masonry Cement and Sand Quantities

Factor	Number of blocks	Bags of masonry cement	Factor	Number of blocks	Tons of sand
.024	x	=			
.03 (25% waste)	x	=	.003	x	=

Parging Cement and Sand Quantities

Factor	Foundation area (square feet)	Bags of masonry cement	Factor	Foundation area (square feet)	Tons of sand
.01848	x	=	.00231	x	=

Bags of masonry cement	_____	Tons of sand	_____
Add for waste (_____%)	_____	Add for waste (_____%)	_____
Total	_____	Total	_____

Crushed Stone Quantities for Drain Tile

Factor	Drain tile (linear feet)	Cubic yards crushed stone
.05232	x	=

Cu. yds. crushed stone _____ x 1.35 = _____ tons crushed stone

Cost Estimate Worksheet for Footings

Layout $_____

Concrete Quantity
   Regular footings:
      Size: _____ width x _____ depth x _____ lin. ft. = _____ cu. ft.
      Size: _____ width x _____ depth x _____ lin. ft. = _____ cu. ft.

   Column footings: (*number* _____)
      Size: _____ w x _____ d x _____ lf x _____ no. = _____ cu. ft.

   Chimney footings: (*number* _____)
      Size: _____ w x _____ d x _____ lf x _____ no. = _____ cu. ft.

   Vertical rise for stepped footings:
      Size: _____ w x _____ thickness x _____ height = _____ cu. ft.

   Other (specify):
   _____ _____ cu. ft.

   Total cubic feet _____ divided by 27 = _____ cubic yards
   Cost per cubic yard $_____ x _____ cubic yards = $_____
   Total cost of concrete (test: _____ psi) $_____

Other Material
   Reinforcing rods:
      Linear feet of _____ (size) reinforcing rod _____
      Cost per foot $_____
      Total cost of reinforcing rods $_____

   Plywood forms:
      Quantity and size _____
      Total cost of forms $_____

   Framing lumber:
      Quantity and size _____
      Total cost of lumber $_____

   Cost of other material:
   _____ $_____
   Subtotal material cost: $_____
   Plus sales tax (% _____): $_____
   Total material cost: $_____

Labor Cost
   Estimated cost of excavation: $_____
   Estimated cost to form and pour: $_____
   Total labor cost: $_____

Total Cost of Footings: $_____

Cost Estimate Worksheet for Foundations

Crushed stone fill under concrete slab:
_____ tons stone @ _____ = $_____

Masonry blocks:
_____ 12" x 8" x 16" @ _____ =
_____ 8" x 8" x 16" @ _____ =   _____
_____ 4" x 8" x 16" @ _____ =   _____
_____ Total blocks $_____

Mortar and sand:
_____ bags masonry cement @ _____ $_____
_____ tons sand @ _____ =   _____

                                                            $_____

Basement windows, foundation vents and basement doors:
_____ basement windows (size _____) @ _____ = $_____
_____ foundation vents (size _____) @ _____ =   _____
_____ basement doors (size _____) @ _____ =   _____

                                                            $_____

Lintels, beams, column posts, anchor bolts, and reinforcing steel:
_____ lintels (size _____) @ _____ = $_____
_____ beams (size _____) @ _____ =   _____
(If necessary itemize on separate sheet and enter total cost here)
_____ column posts (size _____) @ _____ =   _____
_____ anchor bolts (size _____) @ _____ =   _____
_____ reinforcing steel (size _____) @ _____ =   _____

                                                            $_____

Waterproofing and drain tile:
_____ bags masonry cement @ _____ = $_____
_____ tons sand @ _____ =   _____
_____ (5-gal. cans) bituminous coating @ _____ =   _____
_____ lin. ft. drain tile @ _____ =   _____
_____ ells @ _____ =   _____
_____ tons stone @ _____ =   _____

                                                            $_____

Miscellaneous materials:
(Itemize on separate sheet and enter totals here)

                            Cost of material $_____
                         Sales tax (_____%)
                         Total cost of material   (1) $_____

Masonry labor:
_____ blocks @ _____ =   (2) $_____

Other labor:
(Itemize on separate sheet and enter totals here)   (3) $_____

(Add lines 1, 2 and 3 for total foundation cost) $_____

Floor Systems Worksheets

Plywood Paneling Quantities

4' x 8' sheets				4' x 12' sheets			
Area (square feet) x	Factor	=	Number of pieces	Area (square feet) x	Factor	=	Number of pieces
x	.03125	=		x	.02083	=	
x	.03125	=		x	.02083	=	
x	.03125	=		x	.02083	=	
x	.03125	=		x	.02083	=	
x	.03125	=		x	.02083	=	

Floor System Nail Quantities (for 16'' o.c. joists)

Total board feet	x	Factor	=	Pounds nails
Floor joists and headers - 16d common nails				
	x	.01000	=	
Toenailing joist headers and floor joists - 8d common nails				
	x	.00250	=	
Total linear feet Wood cross bridging - 8d common nails				
	x	.03500	=	
Total square feet Plywood floor deck - 6d threaded nails				
	x	.00800	=	
Total square feet Plywood floor deck - 8d common nails				
	x	.01500	=	
Total square feet Board floor deck - 7d threaded nails				
	x	.02700	=	
Total square feet Board floor deck - 8d common nails				
	x	.04000	=	

Interior and Exterior Walls Worksheets

Nail Quantities for Walls

Studs, Plates and Headers - 16d common nails

Total board feet	x	Multiplying Factor	=	Pounds nails
	x	.022	=	

Fiberboard Sheathing - 1½'' roofing nails

Total square feet	x	Multiplying Factor	=	Pounds nails
	x	.01	=	

Plywood Sheathing - 6d threaded nails

Total square feet	x	Multiplying Factor	=	Pounds nails
	x	.008	=	

Note: Includes an allowance for 15% waste.

Headers for Interior Openings

Page _____ of _____ pages

Location	Door width	Add for allow-ance	Header length	Header size (on edge)	Estimate for each double header

Headers for Exterior Openings

Unit	Rough stud opening	Add for Bearing	Header length	Header size (on edge)	Estimate for each double header

Roof Systems Worksheets

Shed Roof Rafter Lengths

Roof pitch	Run	x	Factor	— (minus)	Factor for full thickness of nailer *	=	True rafter length **
1/12		x	1.00347	-	.12500	=	
1½/12		x	1.00778	-	.12500	=	
2/12		x	1.01379	-	.12500	=	
2½/12		x	1.02147	-	.12500	=	
3/12		x	1.03078	-	.12500	=	
3½/12		x	1.04167	-	.12500	=	
4/12		x	1.05409	-	.12500	=	
5/12		x	1.08333	-	.12500	=	
6/12		x	1.11803	-	.12500	=	
7/12		x	1.15770	-	.12500	=	
8/12		x	1.20185	-	.12500	=	
9/12		x	1.25000	-	.12500	=	

*When nailer is 2'' nominal framing (2 x 6's, 2 x 8's, etc.)

**True rafter length plus overhang equals net rafter length

Shingle and Roofing Nail Quantities

Starter courses

Eave length (linear feet)	x	Factor	=	Number
Shingles:	x	.33333	=	
Squares:	x	.00417	=	

Ridge and hip caps

Length of ridge and hips (linear feet)	x	Factor	=	Number
Shingles:	x	.80000	=	
Squares:	x	.01000	=	

Main roof nails

Number of squares	x	Factor	=	Number of pounds
1'' roofing nails:	x	1.5	=	
1¾'' roofing nails:	x	1.75	=	

Ridge and hip cap nails

Length of ridge and hips (linear feet)	x	Factor	=	Number of pounds
1½'' roofing nails:	x	.02667	=	
1¾'' roofing nails:	x	.03077	=	

308

Common Rafter Lengths

Roof pitch	Run	x	Run factor	— (minus)	Factor for ½ thickness of ridge *	=	True rafter length **
1/12		x	1.00347	-	.06250	=	
1½/12		x	1.00778	-	.06250	=	
2/12		x	1.01379	-	.06250	=	
2½/12		x	1.02147	-	.06250	=	
3/12		x	1.03078	-	.06250	=	
3½/12		x	1.04167	-	.06250	=	
4/12		x	1.05409	-	.06250	=	
5/12		x	1.08333	-	.06250	=	
6/12		x	1.11803	-	.06250	=	
7/12		x	1.15770	-	.06250	=	
8/12		x	1.20185	-	.06250	=	
9/12		x	1.25000	-	.06250	=	

*When ridge is 2'' nominal framing (2 x 6's, 2 x 8's, etc.)

**True rafter length plus roof overhang equals net rafter length

Hip and Valley Rafter Lengths

Roof pitch	Run of common rafter	x	Factor	=	Length of hip or valley rafter*
3/12		x	1.43614	=	
3½/12		x	1.44398	=	
4/12		x	1.45297	=	
5/12		x	1.47432	=	
6/12		x	1.50000	=	
7/12		x	1.52980	=	
8/12		x	1.56347	=	
9/12		x	1.60078	=	
10/12		x	1.64148	=	
11/12		x	1.68531	=	
12/12		x	1.73205	=	

*Add the rafter overhang to this length

Roof Rise

Roof pitch	Run of common rafter	x	Factor	=	Rise
1/12		x	.08333	=	
1½/12		x	.12500	=	
2/12		x	.16667	=	
2½/12		x	.20833	=	
3/12		x	.25000	=	
3½/12		x	.29167	=	
4/12		x	.33333	=	
5/12		x	.41667	=	
6/12		x	.50000	=	
7/12		x	.58333	=	
8/12		x	.66667	=	
9/12		x	.75000	=	

Siding and Exterior Trim Worksheets

Siding Quantities

Wood bevel siding (lapped or rabbeted)

Nominal width of siding	Net wall area (square feet)	x Factor	= Square feet of siding
8"		x 1.34 =	
10"		x 1.26 =	
12"		x 1.21 =	

Vertical board siding

Nominal width of siding	Net wall area (square feet)	x Factor	= Square feet of siding
8"		x 1.10 =	
10"		x 1.08 =	
12"		x 1.07 =	

Tongue and groove siding

Nominal width of siding	Net wall area (square feet)	x Factor	= Square feet of siding
8"		x 1.37 =	
10"		x 1.33 =	
12"		x 1.31 =	

Panel siding

Panel size	Net wall area (square feet)	x Factor	= Number of panels
4' x 8'		x .03125 =	

Trim and Molding Lumber Cost

Type and size	Trim or molding length (linear feet)	x Factor	x	Price per CLF	=	Cost of lumber
		x .01000	x		=	
		x .01000	x		=	
		x .01000	x		=	
		x .01000	x		=	
		x .01000	x		=	
		x .01000	x		=	
		x .01000	x		=	
		x .01000	x		=	
		x .01000	x		=	
		x .01000	x		=	

Nail Quantities for Siding and Trim

Horizontal siding

Nail size	Wall area (square feet)	x Factor	=	Pounds of nails
6d		x .00600	=	
8d		x .00700	=	
10d		x .01000	=	

Panel siding

Nail size	Wall area (square feet)	x Factor	=	Pounds of nails
6d		x .01700	=	
8d		x .02100	=	
10d		x .03000	=	

Cedar shake siding

Nail size	Wall area (square feet)	x Factor	=	Pounds of nails
6d		x .01000	=	
8d		x .01500	=	

Soffit and porch ceiling

Nail size	Ceiling area (square feet)	x Factor	=	Pounds of nails
4d		x .01000	=	
6d		x .01250	=	

Cornice

Nail size	Cornice length (linear feet)	x Factor	=	Pounds of nails
6d or 8d		x .01000	=	

Interior Wall and Ceiling Finish Worksheets

Wall and Ceiling Area

Room	Size	Ceiling height
_____	_____	_____

Perimeter of walls: _____width + _____ length x 2 = _____linear feet

Walls:_____LF (perimeter) x _____(ceiling height) = _____SF

Ceiling: _____width x _____length = _____SF

Total square feet of walls and ceiling _____SF*

_____square feet divided by 9 = _____square yards

*If openings are to be deducted, deduct them from this total.

Wallboard Fastener Quantities

1⅜'' annular ring nails				Adhesive			
Total surface area (square feet)	x	Factor	=	Pounds of nails			
	x	.00500	=				

Adhesive			
Total surface area (square feet)	x	Factor	= Number of tubes
	x	.00200	=

Finishing Materials Quantities

Rolls of tape

Total surface area (square feet) x	Factor	=	Number of rolls
x	.00167	=	

Cans of joint compound

Total surface area (square feet) x	Factor	=	Number of cans
x	.00100	=	

Joint compound for textured ceilings

Total surface area (square feet) x	Factor	=	Number of cans
x	.00250	=	

Wallboard Panel Quantities

4' x 8' wallboard

Total surface area (square feet) x	Factor	=	Number of panels
x	.03125	=	

4' x 12' wallboard

Total surface area (square feet) x	Factor	=	Number of panels
x	.02083	=	

Interior Trim Worksheets

Paneling Quantities (4 x 8 sheets)

Room perimeter (linear feet)	x	Factor	=	Number of panels
	x	.25000	=	

Paneling or Floor Underlayment Quantities

Panel size	Net wall or floor area (square feet)	x Factor	=	Number of panels
4' x 8'		x .03125	=	

Paneling Fastener Quantities

1⅝'' colored nails

Paneling area (square feet)	x	Factor	=	Boxes of colored nails
	x	.01000	=	

4d finish nails

Paneling area (square feet)	x	Factor	=	Pounds of finish nails
	x	.01000	=	

Adhesive

Paneling area (square feet)	x	Factor	=	Number of tubes
	x	.01000	=	

Trim Fastener Quantities

Floor underlayment

Floor area (square feet)	x	Factor	=	Pounds of nails
	x	.02000	=	

Baseboard

Baseboard length (linear feet)	x	Factor	=	Pounds of nails
	x	.01000	=	

Baseshoe

Baseshoe length (linear feet)	x	Factor	=	Pounds of nails
	x	.00500	=	

Weekly Timesheet

Page____of____pages

For period ending _____   _____ **job**

	Name	Exemptions	M	T	W	T	F	S	Rate	Reg.	Over-time	Total earnings
					Days						**Hours worked**	
1												
2												
3												
4												
5												
6												
7												
8												
9												
10												
11												
12												
13												
14												
15												
16												
17												
18												
19												
20												

Daily Log

Monday _____

Tuesday _____

Wednesday _____

Thursday _____

Friday _____

Saturday _____

National Estimator Quick Start

Use the Quick Start on the next ten pages to get familiar with National Estimator. In less than an hour you'll be printing labor and material cost estimates for your jobs.

To install National Estimator, put the National Estimator disk in a disk drive (such as A:). Start Windows™.

In Windows 3.1 or 3.11
go to the Program Manager.

1. Click on File.
2. Click on Run . . .
3. Type A:SETUP
4. Press [Enter ↵].

In Windows 95,

1. Click on [Start]
2. Click on Run . . .
3. Type A:SETUP
4. Press [Enter ↵].

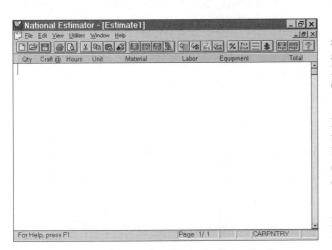

National Estimator Icon

Click on File. Click on Run.

Type A:SETUP in Windows 95.

Then follow instructions on the screen. Installation should take about two minutes. We recommend installing all National Estimator files to the NATIONAL directory. If you have trouble installing National Estimator, call 619-438-7828.

The installation program will create a Construction Estimating group and put the National Estimator Icon in that group. When installation is complete, click on OK to begin using National Estimator. In a few seconds your electronic estimating form will be ready to begin the first estimate.

On the title bar at the top of the screen you see the program name, National Estimator, and [Estimate1], showing that Estimate1 is on the screen. Let's take a closer look at other information at the top of your screen.

Your estimating form ready to begin the first estimate.

The Menu Bar

Below the title bar you see the menu bar. Every option in National Estimator is available on the menu bar. Click with your left mouse button on any item on the menu to open a list of available commands.

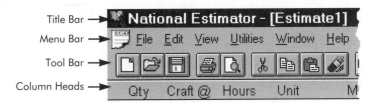

Title Bar →
Menu Bar →
Tool Bar →
Column Heads →

The National Estimator title bar, menu bar, tool bar and column heads.

Buttons on the Tool Bar

Below the menu bar you see 24 buttons that make up the tool bar. The options you use most in National Estimator are only a mouse click away on the tool bar.

Column Headings

Below the tool bar you'll see column headings for your estimate form:

- **Qty** for quantity
- **Craft@Hours** for craft (the crew doing the work) and manhours (to complete the task)
- **Unit** for unit of measure, such as per linear foot or per square foot
- **Material** for material cost
- **Labor** for labor cost
- **Equipment** for equipment cost
- **Total** for the total of all cost columns

The Status Bar

The bottom line on your screen is the status bar. Here you'll find helpful information about the choices available. Notice "Page 1/ 1" near the right end of the status line. That's a clue that you're looking at page 1 of a one-page estimate.

For Help, press F1	Page 1/ 1	CARPNTRY

Check the status bar occasionally for helpful tips and explanations of what you see on screen.

Beginning an Estimate

	The Blinking Cursor (insert point)
⮰	Mouse Pointer
I	Mouse Pointer

Let's start by putting a heading on this estimate.

1. Press [Enter ⏎] once to space down one line.
2. Press [Tab] four times (or hold the space bar down) to move the Blinking Cursor (the insert point) near the middle of the line.
3. Type "Estimate One" and press [Enter ⏎]. That's the title of this estimate, "Estimate One."

4. Press [Enter ⏎] again to move the cursor down a line. That opens up a little space below the title.

The Costbook

Let's leave your estimating form for a moment to take a look at estimates stored in the costbook. To switch to the costbook, either:

- Click on the [📖] button, -Or-
- Click on View on the menu bar. Then click on Costbook Window, -Or-
- Tap the [Alt] key, tap the letter V (for View) and tap the letter C (for Costbook Window), -Or-
- Press [Esc]. Press the [↓] key to highlight Costbook Window. Then press [Enter ⏎].

Begin by putting a title on your estimate, such as "Estimate One."

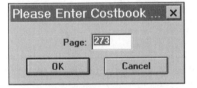

The costbook window has all the manhours in Chapter 12 of Carpentry Estimating.

All the manhour estimates in Chapter 12 of *Carpentry Estimating* are available in the Costbook Window. Notice the words *Page 273 Estimating Manhours for Carpentry* at the left side of the screen just below the tool bar. That's your clue that the table on page 273 is on the screen. To turn to the next page, either:

■ Press [PgDn] (with Num Lock off), -Or-

■ Click on the lower half of the scroll bar at the right edge of the screen.

To move down one line at a time, either:

■ Press the [↓] key (with Num Lock off), -Or-

■ Click on the arrow on the down scroll bar at the lower right corner of the screen.

Press [PgDn] about 40 times and you'll page through all the manhour estimating tables in Chapter 12. Obviously, there's a better way. To turn quickly to any page, either:

■ Click on the [ ] button near the right end of the tool bar, -Or-

■ Click on View on the menu bar. Then click on Turn to Costbook Page, -Or-

■ Press [Esc]. Press the [↓] key to highlight Turn to Costbook Page. Then press [Enter←].

Please Enter Costbook ...

Page: 273

OK   Cancel

Type the page number you want to see.

Drag the square to see any page.

Type the number of the page you want to see and press [Enter←]. National Estimator will turn to the top of the page you requested.

An Even Better Way

Find the small square in the slide bar at the right side of the Costbook Window. Click and hold on that square while rolling the mouse up or down. Keep dragging the square until you see the page you want in the Page: box. Release the mouse button to turn to the top of that page.

A Still Better Way: Keyword Search

To find any cost estimate in seconds, search by keyword in the index. To go to the index, either:

■ Click on the [ ] button near the center of the tool bar, -Or-

■ Press [Esc]. Press [Enter←], -Or-

■ Click on View on the menu bar. Then press [Enter←].

Notice that the cursor is blinking in the Enter Keyword to Locate box at the right of the screen. Obviously, the index is ready to begin a search.

Accessories, bathroom, manhours: 289
  Adding items to National Estimator
    cost: 321-322
    overhead and profit: 323
    text: 321
  Asphalt shingles, manhours: 282
  Baseboard, manhours: 288
  Bathroom accessories, manhours: 289
  Bituminous coating, manhours: 276
  Blanket insulation, manhours: 283
  Block flooring, manhours: 292
  Broom closet, manhours: 287
  Built-up girders, manhours: 278
  Cabinet setting, manhours: 287
  Carpentry, rough, manhours: 277-281
  Cedar closet lining, manhours: 290
  Cedar shakes, manhours: 281
  Ceiling panels, manhours: 291
  Cementitious dampproofing, manhours: 276

Use the electronic index to find cost estimates for any item.

Your First Estimate

Enter Keyword to Locate:

`trim`

Enter keyword to locate.

Suppose we're estimating the cost of exterior trim. Let's put the index to work with a search for trim. In the box under Enter Keyword to Locate, type *trim*. The index jumps to the heading *Trim, manhours.*

The first item under trim, manhours is *exterior: 284, 288*. Either:

■ Click once on that line and press [Enter ↵], -Or-

■ Double click on that line, -Or-

■ Press [Tab] and the [↓] key to move the highlight to *exterior: 284, 288*. Then press [Enter ↵].

Trim, manhours
exterior: 284, 288
interior: 288

The index jumps to Trim, manhours.

Choose One Page: [X]

Select desired page for exterior.   [Cancel]

[284]   [288]

If costs appear on several pages, click on the page you prefer.

To select the page you want to see (page 288 in this case), either:

■ Click on number 288, -Or-

■ Press [Tab] to highlight 288. Then press [Enter ↵].

National Estimator turns to the top of page 288. See the screen at the left below. Notice that estimates at the top of this page are for finish carpentry. You can scroll down the page by pressing the [↓] key or the [PgDn] key.

Splitting the Screen

Most of the time you'll want to see what's in both the costbook and your estimate. To split the screen into two halves, either:

■ Click on the [⊞] button near the center of the tool bar, -Or-

■ Press [Esc] and the [↓] key to move the selection bar to Split Window, -Or-

■ Tap the [Alt] key, tap the letter V (for View), tap the letter S (for Split Window).

Your screen should look like the example at the right below.

Costs for finish carpentry on page 288.

The split window: Costbook above and estimate below.

Notice that eight lines of the costbook are at the top of the screen and your estimate is at the bottom. You should recognize "Estimate One." It's your title for this estimate. Column headings are at the top of the costbook and across the middle of the screen (for your estimate).

To Switch from Window to Window

■ Click in the window of your choice, -Or-

■ Hold the [Ctrl] key down and press [Tab].

Notice that a window title bar turns dark when that window is selected. The selected window is where keystrokes appear as you type.

Copying Costs to Your Estimate

Next, we'll estimate the cost of 120 linear feet of fascia. Click on the [⊞] button on the tool bar to be sure you're in the split window. Click on the line that begins, "Corner boards, verge, fascia":

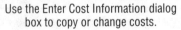

| Corner boards, verge, fascia | BC@4.00 | CLF | 0.00 | 104.00 | 104.00 |

To copy this line to your estimate:

1. Click on the line.

2. Click on the [⊟] button.

3. Click on the [⊟] button to open the Enter Cost Information dialog box. See the dialog box at the left.

Enter Cost Information

Title:	Finish exterior trim		OK
Description:	Corner boards, verge, fascia		Cancel
Quantity:	1.00		Paste *Title* ☑
Unit of Measure:	CLF		
Craft Code:	BC	1 carpenter	
Hourly Wage:	26.08		

	Unit Costs	Extended Costs
Hours:	4.000	4.00
Material Cost:	0.00	0.00
Labor Cost:	104.00	104.00
Equipment Cost:	0.00	0.00
Total Cost:	104.00	104.00

Use the Enter Cost Information dialog box to copy or change costs.

Enter Cost Information

Title:	Finish exterior trim		OK
Description:	Corner boards, verge, fascia		Cancel
Quantity:	1.20		Paste *Title* ☑
Unit of Measure:	CLF		
Craft Code:	BC	1 carpenter	
Hourly Wage:	26.08		

	Unit Costs	Extended Costs
Hours:	4.000	4.80
Material Cost:	150.00	180.00
Labor Cost:	104.00	124.80
Equipment Cost:	0.00	0.00
Total Cost:	254.00	304.80

Costs for the 120 linear feet (extended costs) are on the right.

Notice that the blinking cursor is in the Quantity box:

1. Type a quantity of 1.2 because the fascia is 120 feet long and the unit of measure is CLF for 100 linear feet.

2. Press [Tab] five times until the highlight is in the Material Cost box.

3. Type 150.00 because you estimate that 2" x 8" fascia material will cost $150.00 per CLF (100 linear feet). That's the same as $1.50 per linear foot.

4. Check the accuracy of your estimate. See the box at the left below.

5. Notice that the column headed Unit Costs shows cost per unit, CLF (for 100 linear feet) in this case.

6. The column headed Extended Costs shows costs for the entire 120 linear feet.

7. The lines opposite Title and Description show what's getting installed. You can change the words in either of these boxes. Just click on what you want to change and start typing or deleting. For practice, click after the word *fascia* in the Description box and type *2" x 8" redwood.*

8. You can also change the wage rate, hours, craft code, or equipment cost. Just click and start typing.

9. When the words and costs are exactly right, press [Enter ↵] or click on OK to copy these figures to the end of your estimate.

The new line at the bottom of your estimate shows:

Finish exterior trim						
Corner boards, verge, fascia, 2" x 8" redwood						
1.20	BC@4.800	CLF	180.00	124.80	0.00	304.80

Extended costs for Fascia as they appear on your estimate form.

1.20 is the quantity of fascia in hundreds of linear feet
BC is the recommended crew, a carpenter
@4.800 shows the manhours required for the work
CLF is the unit of measure, hundreds of linear feet
180.00 is the material cost (the 2" x 8" redwood)
124.80 is the labor cost for the job
0.00 shows there is no equipment cost
304.80 is the total of material, labor and equipment columns

Copy Anything to Anywhere in Your Estimate

Anything in the costbook can be copied to your estimate. Just click on the line (or select the words) you want to copy and press the F8 key. It's copied to the last line of your estimating form. If your selection includes costs, you'll have a chance to enter the quantity. To copy to the middle of your estimate:

1. Select what you want to copy.
2. Click on the 📋 button.
3. Click in the estimate where you want to paste.
4. Click on the 📋 button.

Your Own Wage Rates

The labor cost in the example above is based on a carpenter at a cost of $26.08 per hour. Suppose $26.08 per hour isn't right for your estimate. What then? No problem! It's easy to use your own wage rate for any crew or even make up your own crew codes. To get more information on setting wage rates, press F1. At National Estimator Help Contents, click on the Search button. Type "setting" and press Enter↵ to see how to set wage rates. To return to your estimate, click on File on the National Estimator Help menu bar. Then click on Exit.

Search for information on setting wage rates.

Changing Cost Estimates

With Num Lock off, use the ↑ or ↓ key to move the cursor to the line you want to change (or click on that line). In this case, move to the line that begins with a quantity of 1.20. To open the Enter Cost Information Dialog box, either:

- Press Enter↵, -Or-
- Click on the 💲 button on the tool bar.

To make a change, either

- Click on what you want to change, -Or-
- Press Tab until the cursor advances to what you want to change.

Then type the correct figure. In this case, change the equipment cost to 20.00.

Press Tab and check the Extended Costs column. If it looks OK, press Enter↵ and the change is made on your estimating form.

Unit Costs	
Hours:	4.000
Material Cost:	150.00
Labor Cost:	104.00
Equipment Cost:	20.00
Total Cost:	274.00

Change the equipment cost to 20.00.

Changing Text (Descriptions)

Click on the ▦ button on the tool bar to be sure you're in the estimate. With Num Lock off, use the ⬆ or ⬇ key or click the mouse button to put the cursor where you want to make a change. In this case, we're going to make a change on the line that begins "Corner boards."

To make a change, click where the change is needed. Then either:

■ Press the ⬚Del⬚ or ⬚←Bksp⬚ key to erase what needs deleting, -Or-

■ Select what needs deleting and click on the ✂ button on the tool bar.

■ Type what needs to be added.

```
Finish exterior trim
Corner boards, verge, fascia, 2" x
   1.20    BC@4.800      CLF
```

To select, click and hold the mouse button while dragging the mouse.

In this case, click just before "Corner boards." Then hold the left mouse button down and drag the mouse to the right until you've put a dark background behind "Corner boards, verge." The dark background shows that these words are selected and ready for editing.

Press the ⬚Del⬚ key (or click on the ✂ button on the tool bar), and the selection is cut from the estimate. If that's not what you wanted, click on the ▨ button and the words "Corner boards, verge" are back again.

Adding Text (Descriptions)

Some of your estimates will require descriptions (text) and costs that can't be found in *Carpentry Estimating*. What then? With National Estimator it's easy to add descriptions and costs of your choice anywhere in the estimate. For practice, let's add an estimate for four reinforced corners to Estimate One.

```
Finish exterior trim
Corner boards, verge, fascia, 2" x 8" redwood
   1.20    BC@4.800      CLF         180.00
Reinforced corners
_____

Total Manhours, Material, Labor, and Equipment:
```

Adding "Reinforced corners."

Click on the ▦ button to be sure the estimate window is maximized. We can add lines anywhere on the estimate. But in this case, let's make the addition at the end. Press the ⬇ key to move the cursor down until it's just above the horizontal line that separates estimate detail lines from estimate totals. To open a blank line, either:

■ Press ⬚Enter ↵⬚, -Or-

■ Click on the ▦ button on the tool bar.

Type "Reinforced corners" and press ⬚Enter ↵⬚.

Adding a Cost Estimate Line

Now let's add a cost for "Reinforced corners" to your estimate. Begin by opening the Enter Cost Information dialog box. Either:

■ Click on ⬚$ button on the tool bar, -Or-

■ Click on Edit on the menu bar. Then click on Insert a Cost Line.

1. The cursor is in the Quantity box. Type the number of units (4 in this case) and press ⬚Tab⬚.

2. The cursor moves to the next box, Unit of Measure.

Enter Cost Information		✕
		OK
		Cancel
Quantity:	4.00	
Unit of Measure:		
Craft Code:		
Hourly Wage:	0.00	

	Unit Costs	Extended Costs
Hours:	0.000	0.00
Material Cost:	0.00	0.00
Labor Cost:	0.00	0.00
Equipment Cost:	0.00	0.00
Total Cost:	0.00	0.00

Adding a cost line with the Enter Cost Information dialog box.

Enter Cost Information

	Unit Costs	Extended Costs
Quantity:	4.00	
Unit of Measure:	Each	
Craft Code:		
Hourly Wage:	0.00	
Hours:	0.000	0.00
Material Cost:	0.00	0.00
Labor Cost:	0.00	0.00
Equipment Cost:	0.00	0.00
Total Cost:	20.00	80.00

Unit and extended costs for four reinforced corners.

3. In the Unit of Measure box, type *Each* and press Tab.

4. Press Tab twice to leave the Craft Code blank and Hourly Wage at zero.

5. Since these corners will be installed by a subcontractor, there's no material, labor or equipment cost. So press Tab four times to skip over the Hours, Material Cost, Labor Cost and Equipment Cost boxes.

6. In the Total Cost box, type 20.00. That's the cost per corner quoted by your sub.

7. Press Tab once more to advance to OK.

8. Press Enter and the cost of four reinforced corners is written to your estimate.

Note: The sum of material, labor, and equipment costs appears automatically in the Total Cost box. If there's no cost entered in the Material Cost, Labor Cost or Equipment Cost boxes (such as for a subcontracted item), you can enter any figure in the Total Cost box.

Adding Lines to the Costbook

Add lines or make changes in the costbook the same way you add lines or make changes in an estimate. The additions and changes you make become part of the user costbook attached to *Carpentry Estimating*. You may want to create several user costbooks, one for each type of work you handle. For more information on user costbooks, press F1. Click on Search. Type "user" and press Enter twice.

Adding Tax

Enter Tax Rates

Tax on Materials:	7.25 %
Tax on Labor:	0. %
Tax on Equipment:	0. %
Tax on Total Only Costs:	0. %
Tax on the Contract Price:	0. %

Type the tax rate that applies.

To include sales tax in your estimate:

1. Click on Edit.

2. Click on Tax Rates.

3. Type the tax rate in the appropriate box.

4. Press Tab to advance to the next box.

5. Press Enter or click on OK when done.

In this case, the tax rate is 7.25% on materials only. Tax will appear near the last line of the estimate.

Adding Overhead and Profit

Set markup percentages in the Add for Overhead & Profit dialog box. To open the box, either:

■ Click on the $ button on the tool bar, -Or-

■ Click on Edit on the menu bar. Then click on Markup.

Add for Overhead & Profit

Overhead	15. %
Profit	10. %

Adding overhead & profit.

Type the percentages you want to add for overhead. For this estimate:

1. Type 15 on the Overhead line.

2. Press Tab to advance to Profit.

3. Type 10 on the Profit line.

4. Press Enter.

Markup percentages can be changed at any time. Just reopen the Add for Overhead & Profit Dialog box and type the correct figure.

```
File Name:  Estimate 1              Construction Estimate              Page 1
   Qty     Craft @ Hours  Unit    Material    Labor    Equipment       Total

                                Estimate One

Finish exterior trim
Corner boards, verge, fascia, 2" x 8" redwood
  1.20     BC@ .4000    CLF       180.00     124.80      24.00        328.80
Reinforced corners
  4.00        --@ .0000    --        0.00       0.00       0.00         80.00

Total Manhours, Material, Labor, and Equipment:
            4.8                    180.00     124.80      24.00        328.80
Total Only (Subcontract) Costs:                                        80.00

                            Subtotal:                                 408.80

                            15.00% Overhead:                           61.32
                            10.00% Profit:                             47.01

                            Estimate Total:                           517.13

                            Tax on Materials:                          13.05

                            Grand Total:                              530.18
```

A preview of Estimate One.

Preview Your Estimate

You can display an estimate on screen just the way it will look when printed on paper. To preview your estimate, either:

- Click on the [ ] button on the tool bar, -Or-
- Click on File on the menu bar. Then click on Print Preview.

In print preview:

- Click on Next Page or Prev. Page to turn pages.
- Click on Two Page to see two estimate pages side by side.
- Click on Zoom In to get a closer look.
- Click on Close when you've seen enough.

National Estimator - Estimate1

| Print... | Next Page | Prev Page | Two Page | Zoom In | Zoom Out | Close |

Use buttons on Print Preview to see your estimate as it will look when printed.

Printing Your Estimate

When you're ready to print the estimate, either:

- Click on the [ ] button on the tool bar, -Or-
- Click on File on the menu bar. Then click on Print, -Or-
- Hold the Ctrl key down and type the letter P.

Press Enter↵ or click on OK to begin printing.

Print dialog — Printer: Default Printer; Print Range: All / Pages From: 1 To: 1; Print Quality: 600 dpi; Copies: 1; Collate Copies; OK, Cancel, Setup..., Help.

Options available depend on the printer you're using.

Save Your Estimate to Disk

To store your estimate on the hard disk where it can be re-opened and changed at any time, either:

- Click on the [ ] button on the tool bar, -Or-
- Click on File on the menu bar. Then click on Save, -Or-
- Hold the Ctrl key down and type the letter S.

The cursor is in the File Name box. Type the name you want to give this estimate, such as FIRST. The name can be up to eight letters and numbers, but don't use symbols or spaces. Press Enter↵ or click on OK and the estimate is written to disk.

File Save As dialog — File name: FIRST; Folders: c:\national; Save file as type: Estimates (*.est); Drives: c: ms-dos_6; OK, Cancel, Help, Network...

Type the estimate name in the File Name box to assign a file name.

Opening Other Costbooks

Many construction cost estimating databases are available for the National Estimator program. For example, a National Estimator costbook comes with each of these estimating manuals:

- *National Construction Estimator*
- *National Repair & Remodeling Estimator*
- *National Electrical Estimator*
- *National Plumbing & HVAC Estimator*
- *National Painting Cost Estimator*
- *National Renovation & Insurance Repair Estimator*

Open the costbook of your choice.

To open any of the other National Estimator costbooks installed on your computer:

- Click on File.
- Click on Open Costbook.
- Be sure the drive and directory are correct, usually c:\national.
- Double click on the costbook of your choice.

To see a list of the costbooks open, click on Window. The name of the current costbook will be checked. Click on any other costbook or estimate name to display that costbook or estimate. Click on Window, then click on Tile to display all open costbooks and estimates.

Click to switch costbooks.

Select Your Default Costbook

Your default costbook opens automatically every time you begin using National Estimator. Save time by making the costbook you use most your default costbook.

To change your default costbook, click on Utilities on the menu bar. Then click on Options. Next, click on Select Default Costbook. Click on the costbook of your choice. Click on OK. Then click on OK again.

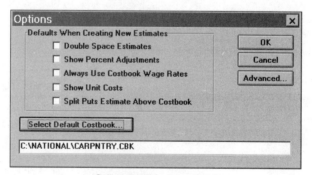

Select the default costbook.

Use National Estimator Help

Click on Print All Topics to print the entire Guide to National Estimator (28 pages).

That completes the basics of National Estimator. You've learned enough to complete most estimates. When you need more information about the fine points, use National Estimator Help. Click on [?] to see Help Contents. Then click on the menu selection of your choice. To print 28 pages of instructions for National Estimator, go to Help Contents. Click on Print All Topics (at the bottom of Help Contents). Click on File on the Help menu bar. Then click on Print Topic. Click on OK.

Click on File and then Print Topic.

Index

Other Practical References

Basic Engineering for Builders

If you've ever been stumped by an engineering problem on the job, yet wanted to avoid the expense of hiring a qualified engineer, you should have this book. Here you'll find engineering principles explained in non-technical language and practical methods for applying them on the job. With the help of this book you'll be able to understand engineering functions in the plans and how to meet the requirements, how to get permits issued without the help of an engineer, and anticipate requirements for concrete, steel, wood and masonry. See why you sometimes have to hire an engineer and what you can undertake yourself: surveying, concrete, lumber loads and stresses, steel, masonry, plumbing, and HVAC systems. This book is designed to help the builder save money by understanding engineering principles that you can incorporate into the jobs you bid. **400 pages, 8½ x 11, $34.00**

The Contractor's Legal Kit

Stop "eating" the costs of bad designs, hidden conditions, and job surprises. Set ground rules that assign those costs to the rightful party ahead of time. And it's all in plain English, not "legalese." For less than the cost of an hour with a lawyer you'll learn the exclusions to put in your agreements, why your insurance company may pay for your legal defense, how to avoid liability for injuries to your sub and his employees or damages they cause, how to collect on lawsuits you win, and much more. It also includes a FREE computer disk with contracts and forms you can customize for your own use. **352 pages, 8½ x 11, $59.95**

Handbook of Construction Contracting

Volume 1: Everything you need to know to start and run your construction business; the pros and cons of each type of contracting, the records you'll need to keep, and how to read and understand house plans and specs so you find any problems before the actual work begins. All aspects of construction are covered in detail, including all-weather wood foundations, practical math for the job site, and elementary surveying. **416 pages, 8½ x 11, $28.75**

Volume 2: Everything you need to know to keep your construction business profitable; different methods of estimating, keeping and controlling costs, estimating excavation, concrete, masonry, rough carpentry, roof covering, insulation, doors and windows, exterior finishes, specialty finishes, scheduling work flow, managing workers, advertising and sales, spec building and land development, and selecting the best legal structure for your business. **320 pages, 8½ x 11, $30.75**

National Building Cost Manual

Square foot costs for residential, commercial, industrial, and farm buildings. Quickly work up a reliable budget estimate based on actual materials and design features, area, shape, wall height, number of floors, and support requirements. Includes all the important variables that can make any building unique from a cost standpoint. **240 pages, 8½ x 11, $23.00. Revised annually**

Residential Steel Framing Guide

Steel is stronger and lighter than wood — straight walls are guaranteed — steel framing will not wrap, shrink, split, swell, bow, or rot. Here you'll find full page schematics and details that show how steel is connected in just about all residential framing work. You won't find lengthy explanations here on how to run your business, or even how to do the work. What you will find are over 150 easy-to-ready full-page details on how to construct steel-framed floors, roofs, interior and exterior walls, bridging, blocking, and reinforcing for all residential construction. Also includes recommended fasteners and their applications, and fastening schedules for attaching every type of steel framing member to steel as well as wood. **170 pages, 8½ x 11, $38.80**

Construction Estimating Reference Data

Provides the 300 most useful manhour tables for practically every item of construction. Labor requirements are listed for sitework, concrete work, masonry, steel, carpentry, thermal and moisture protection, door and windows, finishes, mechanical and electrical. Each section details the work being estimated and gives appropriate crew size and equipment needed. Includes an electronic version of the book on computer disk with a stand-alone *Windows* estimating program FREE on a 3½" disk. **432 pages, 8½ x 11, $39.50**

Finish Carpenter's Manual

Everything you need to know to be a finish carpenter: assessing a job before you begin, and tricks of the trade from a master finish carpenter. Easy-to-follow instructions for installing doors and windows, ceiling treatments (including fancy beams, corbels, cornices and moldings), wall treatments (including wainscoting and sheet paneling), and the finishing touches of chair, picture, and plate rails. Specialized interior work includes cabinetry and built-ins, stair finish work, and closets. Also covers exterior trims and porches. Includes manhour tables for finish work, and hundreds of illustrations and photos. **208 pages, 8½ x 11, $22.50**

Estimating Tables for Home Building

Produce accurate estimates for nearly any residence in just minutes. This handy manual has tables you need to find the quantity of materials and labor for most residential construction. Includes overhead and profit, how to develop unit costs for labor and materials, and how to be sure you've considered every cost in the job. **336 pages, 8½ x 11, $21.50**

Running Your Remodeling Business

All about operating a remodeling business, from making your first sale to ensuring your profits: how to advertise, write up a contract, estimate, schedule your jobs, arrange financing (for both you and your customers), and when and how to expand your business. Explains insurance, bonds, and liens, and how to collect the money you've earned. Includes sample business forms. **272 pages, 8½ x 11, $21.00**

Wood-Frame House Construction

Step-by-step construction details, from the layout of the outer walls, excavation and formwork, to finish carpentry and painting. Contains all new, clear illustrations and explanations updated for construction in the '90s. Everything you need to know about framing, roofing, siding, interior finishings, floor covering and stairs — your complete book of wood-frame homebuilding. **320 pages, 8½ x 11, $25.50. Revised edition**

Home Inspection Handbook

Every area you need to check in a home inspection ¾ especially in older homes. Twenty complete inspection checklists: building site, foundation and basement, structural, bathrooms, chimneys and flues, ceilings, interior & exterior finishes, electrical, plumbing, HVAC, insects, vermin and decay, and more. Also includes information on starting and running your own home inspection business. **324 pages, 5½ x 8½, $24.95**

Rough Framing Carpentry

If you'd like to make good money working outdoors as a framer, this is the book for you. Here you'll find shortcuts to laying out studs; speed cutting blocks, trimmers and plates by eye; quickly building and blocking rake walls; installing ceiling backing, ceiling joists, and truss joists; cutting and assembling hip trusses and California fills; arches and drop ceilings — all with production line procedures that save you time and help you make more money. Over 100 on-the-job photos of how to do it right and what can go wrong. **304 pages, 8½ x 11, $26.50**

How to Succeed With Your Own Construction Business

Everything you need to start your own construction business: setting up the paperwork, finding the work, advertising, using contracts, dealing with lenders, estimating, scheduling, finding and keeping good employees, keeping the books, and coping with success. If you're considering starting your own construction business, all the knowledge, tips, and blank forms you need are here. **336 pages, 8½ x 11, $24.25**

Managing the Small Construction Business

You can lead a crew of carpenters, but can you run a business? This book lets 50 successful builders tell you how to negotiate contracts, estimate and schedule jobs, keep accurate accounts, and manage relationships with employees, subs, and most of all, customers. You'll find the information you need on: bidding strategies, unit pricing, contract clauses, preconstruction meetings, bookkeeping basics, quality control, computers, overhead & markup, managing subs, scheduling systems, cost-plus contracts, personnel policies, pricing small jobs, insurance repair, and conflict resolution. **243 pages, 8½ x 11, 27.95**

Stair Builders Handbook

If you know the floor-to-floor rise, this handbook gives you everything else: number and dimension of treads and risers, total run, correct well hole opening, angle of incline, and quantity of materials and settings for your framing square for over 3,500 code-approved rise and run combinations — several for every 1/8-inch interval from a 3 foot to a 12 foot floor-to-floor rise. **416 pages, 5½ x 8½, $15.50**

Glass Block Handbook

Usage and interest in glass block construction has sky-rocketed during the past decade. Find out what you need to enter this lucrative field of glass block construction: installation methods, uses and applications, specifications and standards, details and finishes, design and selection. Includes step-by-step installation methods, reinforcing techniques, mortaring methods, and many photos showing how glass block construction can enhance any remodel or new construction project. **206 pages, 8½ x 11, $39.95**

Contractor's Growth and Profit Guide

Step-by-step instructions for planning growth and prosperity in a construction contracting or subcontracting company. Explains how to prepare a business plan: select reasonable goals, draft a market expansion plan, make income forecasts and expense budgets, and project cash flow. You'll learn everything that most lenders and investors require, as well as the best way to organize your business. **336 pages, 5½ x 8½, $19.00**

Drywall Contracting

How to start and keep your drywall business thriving and do professional quality drywall work. Covers the eight essential steps in making any drywall estimate. Shows how to achieve the six most commonly-used surface treatments, how to work with metal studs, and how to solve and prevent most common drywall problems. **288 pages, 5½ x 8½, $18.25**

Estimating Home Building Costs

Estimate every phase of residential construction from site costs to the profit margin you include in your bid. Shows how to keep track of manhours and make accurate labor cost estimates for footings, foundations, framing and sheathing finishes, electrical, plumbing, and more. Provides and explains sample cost estimate worksheets with complete instructions for each job phase. **320 pages, 5½ x 8½, $17.00**

Roof Framing

Shows how to frame any type of roof in common use today, even if you've never framed a roof before. Includes using a pocket calculator to figure any common, hip, valley, or jack rafter length in seconds. Over 400 illustrations cover every measurement and every cut on each type of roof: gable, hip, Dutch, Tudor, gambrel, shed, gazebo, and more. **480 pages, 5½ x 8½, $22.00**

National Electrical Estimator

This year's prices for installation of all common electrical work: conduit, wire, boxes, fixtures, switches, outlets, loadcenters, panelboards, raceway, duct, signal systems, and more. Provides material costs, manhours per unit, and total installed cost. Explains what you should know to estimate each part of an electrical system. Includes an electronic version of the book on computer disk with a stand-alone *Windows* estimating program FREE on a 3½" disk. **512 pages, 8½ x 11, $37.75. Revised annually**

Roof Framer's Bible

68 different pitch combinations of "bastard" hip roofs at your fingertips. Don't curse the architect — let this book make you an accomplished master of irregular pitched roof systems. You'll be the envy of your crew, and irregular or "bastard" roofs will be under your command. This rare pocket-sized book comes hardbound with a cloth marker like a true bible. **216 pages, 3¾ x 7½, $24.00**

How to Hire and Supervise Subcontractors

Here are the secrets to selecting, evaluating, and motivating subcontractors. You get effective strategies to work with subs — not against them; find subs who can do the job right; improve scheduling, maintain quality, control costs, and more. **60 pages, 8½ x 11, $15.00**

Drafting House Plans

Here you'll find step-by-step instructions for drawing a complete set of home plans for a one-story house, an addition to an existing house, or a remodeling project. This book shows how to visualize spatial relationships, use architectural scales and symbols, sketch preliminary drawings, develop detailed floor plans and exterior elevations, and prepare a final plot plan. It even includes code-approved joist and rafter spans and how to make sure that drawings meet code requirements. **192 pages, 8½ x 11, $27.50**

Fences & Retaining Walls

Everything you need to know to run a profitable business in fence and retaining wall contracting. Takes you through layout and design, construction techniques for wood, masonry, and chain link fences, gates and entries, including finishing and electrical details. How to build retaining and rock walls. How to get your business off to the right start, keep the books, and estimate accurately. The book even includes a chapter on contractor's math. **400 pages, 8½ x 11, $23.25**

National Construction Estimator

Current building costs for residential, commercial, and industrial construction. Estimated prices for every common building material. Manhours, recommended crew, and labor cost for installation. Includes an electronic version of the book on computer disk with a stand-alone *Windows* estimating program FREE on a 3½" disk. **560 pages, 8½ x 11, $37.50. Revised annually**

Blueprint Reading for the Building Trades

How to read and understand construction documents, blueprints, and schedules. Includes layouts of structural, mechanical, HVAC and electrical drawings. Shows how to interpret sectional views, follow diagrams and schematics, and covers common problems with construction specifications. **192 pages, 5½ x 8½, $14.75**

National Renovation & Insurance Repair Estimator

Current prices in dollars and cents for hard-to-find items needed on most insurance, repair, remodeling, and renovation jobs. All price items include labor, material, and equipment breakouts, plus special charts that tell you exactly how these costs are calculated. Includes an electronic version of the book on computer disk with a stand-alone *Windows* estimating program FREE on a 3½" disk. **560 pages, 8½ x 11, $39.50. Revised annually**

Scheduling Residential Construction for Builders and Remodelers

Successful builders organize staff, coordinate, monitor, and control what is taking place at one or more jobsites. Too often this involves a lot of stress and sixteen-hour days. Learn scheduling techniques that take relatively little time to implement and streamline your workload. These techniques include manual and computerized scheduling. **116 pages, 8½ x 11, $29.00**

Land Development

The industry's bible. Nine chapters cover everything you need to know about land development from initial market studies to site selection and analysis. New and innovative design ideas for streets, houses, and neighborhoods are included. Whether you're developing a whole neighborhood or just one site, you shouldn't be without this essential reference. **360 pages, 5½ x 8½, $37.00**

Roof Framing — The Video

Made-to-order for any carpenter, remodeler or builder who wants to become a master roof cutter. Marshall Gross, author of the popular book Roof Framing, shows how to cut gable, hip, Dutch, Tudor, gambrel, shed, and even gazebo roofs. After watching these videos and reading the companion book Roof Framing, you'll be ready to take on just about any type of roof cutting job, even an irregular roof with a non-centered ridge.

These two videos, and the 480-page book, are a complete training system designed to teach you the art of roof cutting. Running time for each videotape is approximately 90 minutes. Video 1 covers the basics: calculating rise, run and pitch, and laying out and cutting common rafters. Video 2 covers more difficult work: framing a hip or irregular roof and making tie-ins to an existing roof. **$80.00 each**

Renovating & Restyling Vintage Homes

Any builder can turn a run-down old house into a showcase of perfection — if the customer has unlimited funds to spend. Unfortunately, most customers are on a tight budget. They usually want more improvements than they can afford — and they expect you to deliver. This book shows how to add economical improvements that can increase the property value by two, five or even ten times the cost of the remodel. Sound impossible? Here you'll find the secrets of a builder who has been putting these techniques to work on Victorian and Craftsman-style houses for twenty years. You'll see what to repair, what to replace and what to leave, so you can remodel or restyle older homes for the least amount of money and the greatest increase in value. **416 pages, 8½ x 11, $33.50**

Profits in Building Spec Homes

If you've ever wanted to make big profits in building spec homes yet were held back by the risks involved, you should have this book. Here you'll learn how to do a market study and feasibility analysis to make sure your finished home will sell quickly, and for a good profit. You'll find tips that can save you thousands in negotiating for land, learn how to impress bankers and get the financing package you want, how to nail down cost estimating, schedule realistically, work effectively yet harmoniously with subcontractors so they'll come back for your next home, and finally, what to look for in the agent you choose to sell your finished home. Includes forms, checklists, worksheets, and step-by-step instructions. **208 pages, 8½ x 11, $27.25**

Basic Construction Management: The Superintendent's Job, 3rd Edition

Today's construction projects are more complex than ever. Managing these projects has also become more complex. This perennial NAHB bestseller, now in its third edition, addresses the issues facing today's construction manager. New managers can use this as a great training tool. More experienced superintendents can brush up on the latest techniques and technologies. **87 pages, 8½ x 11, $27.50**

Contractor's Guide to the Building Code Revised

This completely revised edition explains in plain English exactly what the Uniform Building Code requires. Based on the newly-expanded 1994 code, it explains many of the changes made. Also covers the Uniform Mechanical Code and the Uniform Plumbing Code. Shows how to design and construct residential and light commercial buildings that'll pass inspection the first time. Suggests how to work with an inspector to minimize construction costs, what common building shortcuts are likely to be cited, and where exceptions are granted. **384 pages, 8½ x 11, $39.00**

Builder's Guide to Accounting Revised

Step-by-step, easy-to-follow guidelines for setting up and maintaining records for your building business. This practical, newly-revised guide to all accounting methods shows how to meet state and federal accounting requirements, explains the new depreciation rules, and describes how the Tax Reform Act can affect the way you keep records. Full of charts, diagrams, simple directions and examples, to help you keep track of where your money is going. Recommended reading for many state contractor's exams. **320 pages, 8½ x 11, $26.50**

Rafter Length Manual

Complete rafter length tables and the "how to" of roof framing. Shows how to use the tables to find the actual length of common, hip, valley, and jack rafters. Explains how to measure, mark, cut and erect the rafters; find the drop of the hip; shorten jack rafters; mark the ridge and much more. Loaded with explanations and illustrations. **369 pages, 5½ x 8½, $15.75**

National Repair & Remodeling Estimator

The complete pricing guide for dwelling reconstruction costs. Reliable, specific data you can apply on every repair and remodeling job. Up-to-date material costs and labor figures based on thousands of jobs across the country. Provides recommended crew sizes; average production rates; exact material, equipment, and labor costs; a total unit cost and a total price including overhead and profit. Separate listings for high- and low-volume builders, so prices shown are specific for any size business. Estimating tips specific to repair and remodeling work to make your bids complete, realistic, and profitable. Includes an electronic version of the book on computer disk with a stand-alone *Windows* estimating program FREE on a 3½" disk. **416 pages, 8½ x 11, $38.50. Revised annually**

Contractor's Survival Manual

How to survive hard times and succeed during the up cycles. Shows what to do when the bills can't be paid, finding money and buying time, transferring debt, and all the alternatives to bankruptcy. Explains how to build profits, avoid problems in zoning and permits, taxes, time-keeping, and payroll. Unconventional advice on how to invest in inflation, get high appraisals, trade and postpone income, and stay hip-deep in profitable work. **160 pages, 8½ x 11, $22.25**

Builder's Guide to Room Additions

How to tackle problems that are unique to additions, such as requirements for basement conversions, reinforcing ceiling joists for second-story conversions, handling problems in attic conversions, what's required for footings, foundations, and slabs, how to design the best bathroom for the space, and much more. Besides actual construction methods, you'll also find help in designing, planning and estimating your room-addition jobs. **352 pages, 8½ x 11, $27.25**

Craftsman's Illustrated Dictionary of Construction Terms

Almost everything you could possibly want to know about any word or technique in construction. Hundreds of up-to-date construction terms, materials, drawings and pictures with detailed, illustrated articles describing equipment and methods. Terms and techniques are explained or illustrated in vivid detail. Use this valuable reference to check spelling, find clear, concise definitions of construction terms used on plans and construction documents, or learn about little-known tools, equipment, tests and methods used in the building industry. It's all here. **416 pages, 8½ x 11, $36.00**

Building Contractor's Exam Preparation Guide

Passing today's contractor's exams can be a major task. This book shows you how to study, how questions are likely to be worded, and the kinds of choices usually given for answers. Includes sample questions from actual state, county, and city examinations, plus a sample exam to practice on. This book isn't a substitute for the study material that your testing board recommends, but it will help prepare you for the types of questions — and their correct answers — that are likely to appear on the actual exam. Knowing how to answer these questions, as well as what to expect from the exam, can greatly increase your chances of passing. **320 pages, 8½ x 11, $35.00**

Construction Forms & Contracts

125 forms you can copy and use — or load into your computer (from the FREE disk enclosed). Then you can customize the forms to fit your company, fill them out, and print. Loads into Word for *Windows*, Lotus 1-2-3, WordPerfect, or Excel programs. You'll find forms covering accounting, estimating, fieldwork, contracts, and general office. Each form comes with complete instructions on when to use it and how to fill it out. These forms were designed, tested and used by contractors, and will help keep your business organized, profitable and out of legal, accounting and collection troubles. Includes a 3½" disk for your PC. For Macintosh disks, add $15. **432 pages, 8½ x 11, $39.75**

Roofing Construction & Estimating

Installation, repair and estimating for nearly every type of roof covering available today in residential and commercial structures: asphalt shingles, roll roofing, wood shingles and shakes, clay tile, slate, metal, built-up, and elastometric. Covers sheathing and underlayment techniques, as well as secrets for installing leakproof valleys. Many estimating tips help you minimize waste, as well as insure a profit on every job. Troubleshooting techniques help you identify the true source of most leaks. Over 300 large, clear illustrations help you find the answer to just about all your roofing questions. **432 pages, 8½ x 11, $35.00**

Bookkeeping for Builders

Shows simple, practical instructions for setting up and keeping accurate records — with a minimum of effort and frustration. Explains the essentials of a record-keeping system: the payment, income, and general journals, and records for fixed assets, accounts receivable, payables and purchases, petty cash, and job costs. Shows how to keep I.R.S. records, and accurate, organized business records for your own use. **208 pages, 8½ x 11, $19.75**

Contractor's Year-Round Tax Guide Revised

How to set up and run your construction business to minimize taxes: corporate tax strategy and how to use it to your advantage, and what you should be aware of in contracts with others. Covers tax shelters for builders, write-offs and investments that will reduce your taxes, accounting methods that are best for contractors, and what the I.R.S. allows and what it often questions. **192 pages, 8½ x 11, $26.50**

CD Estimator

If your computer has *Windows*™ and a CD-ROM drive, CD Estimator puts at your fingertips 85,000 construction costs for new construction, remodeling, renovation & insurance repair, electrical, plumbing, HVAC and painting. You'll also have the National Estimator program — a stand-alone estimating program for *Windows* that *Remodeling* magazine called a "computer wiz." Quarterly cost updates are available at no charge on the Internet. To help you create professional-looking estimates, the disk includes over 40 construction estimating and bidding forms in a format that's perfect for nearly any word processing or spreadsheet program for *Windows*. And to top it off, a 70-minute interactive video teaches you how to use this CD-ROM to estimate construction costs. **CD Estimator is $59.00**

CD Estimator — Heavy

CD Estimator — Heavy has a complete 630-page heavy construction cost estimating volume for each of the 50 states. Select the cost database for the state where the work will be done. Includes thousands of cost estimates you won't find anywhere else, and in-depth coverage of demolition, hazardous materials remediation, tunneling, site utilities, precast concrete, structural framing, heavy timber construction, membrane waterproofing, industrial windows and doors, specialty finishes, built-in commercial and industrial equipment, and HVAC and electrical systems for commercial and industrial buildings. **CD Estimator — Heavy is $69.00**

Troubleshooting Guide to Residential Construction

How to solve practically every construction problem — before it happens to you! With this book you'll learn from the mistakes other builders made as they faced 63 typical residential construction problems. Filled with clear photos and drawings that explain how to enhance your reputation as well as your bottom line by avoiding problems that plague most builders. Shows how to avoid, or fix, problems ranging from defective slabs, walls and ceilings, through roofing, plumbing & HVAC, to paint. **304 pages, 8½ x 11, $32.50**

Simplified Guide to Construction Law

Here you'll find easy-to-read, paragraphed-sized samples of how the courts have viewed common areas of disagreement — and litigation — in the building industry. You'll read about legal problems that real builders have faced, and how the court ruled. Why pay lawyers' fees and spend your own time when the answer is probably already in this book? You'll find what you need to know about contracts and contract changes, torts, fraud, misrepresentation, warranty and strict liability, construction defects, indemnity, insurance, mechanics liens, bonds and bonding, statutes of limitation, arbitration, and more. These are simplified examples that illustrate not necessarily who is right and who is wrong - but who the law has sided with. **298 pages, 5½ x 8½, $29.95**

Bar Chart Scheduling for Residential Construction

How to use bar charts to schedule every aspect of homebuilding — from bidding and materials to the actual work. Includes plenty of easy-to-understand instructions, along with sample charts that you can copy and use. Includes a FREE computer disk with sample template files for bar chart formats in Microsoft Excel. **56 pages, 8½ x 11, $30.00**

Plumbing & HVAC Manhour Estimates

Hundreds of tested and proven manhours for installing just about any plumbing and HVAC component you're likely to use in residential, commercial, and industrial work. You'll find manhours for installing piping systems, specialties, fixtures and accessories, ducting systems, and HVAC equipment. If you estimate the price of plumbing, you shouldn't be without the reliable, proven manhours in this unique book. **224 pages, 5½ x 8½, $28.25**

Planning Drain, Waste & Vent Systems

How to design plumbing systems in residential, commercial, and industrial buildings. Covers designing systems that meet code requirements for homes, commercial buildings, private sewage disposal systems, and even mobile home parks. Includes relevant code sections and many illustrations to guide you through what the code requires in designing drainage, waste, and vent systems. **192 pages, 8½ x 11, $19.25**

Basic Plumbing with Illustrations, Revised

This completely-revised edition brings this comprehensive manual fully up-to-date with all the latest plumbing codes. It is the journeyman's and apprentice's guide to installing plumbing, piping, and fixtures in residential and light commercial buildings: how to select the right materials, lay out the job and do professional-quality plumbing work, use essential tools and materials, make repairs, maintain plumbing systems, install fixtures, and add to existing systems. Includes extensive study questions at the end of each chapter, and a section with all the correct answers. **384 pages, 8½ x 11, $33.00**

Concrete & Formwork

This practical manual has all the information you need to select and pour the right mix for the job, lay out the structure, choose the right form materials, design and build the forms, and finish and cure the concrete, Nearly 100 pages of step-by-step instructions show how to construct and erect most types of site-fabricated wood forms used in residential construction. **176 pages, 8½ x 11, $17.75**

Concrete Construction & Estimating

Explains how to estimate the quantity of labor and materials needed, plan the job, erect fiberglass, steel, or prefabricated forms, install shores and scaffolding, handle the concrete into place, set joints, finish and cure the concrete. Full of practical reference data, cost estimates, and examples. **571 pages, 5½ x 8½, $25.00**

Construction Surveying & Layout

A practical guide to simplified construction surveying. How to divide land, use a transit and tape to find a known point, draw an accurate survey map from your field notes, use topographic surveys, and the right way to level and set grade. You'll learn how to make a survey for any residential or commercial lot, driveway, road, or bridge — including how to figure cuts and fills and calculate excavation quantities. Use this guide to make your own surveys, or just read and verify the accuracy of surveys made by others. **256 pages, 5½ x 8½, $19.25**

Building Layout

Shows how to use a transit to locate a building correctly on the lot, plan proper grades with minimum excavation, find utility lines and easements, establish correct elevations, lay out accurate foundations, and set correct floor heights. Explains how to plan sewer connections, level a foundation that's out of level, use a story pole and batterboards, work on steep sites, and minimize excavation costs. **240 pages, 5½ x 8½, $15.00**

Paint Contractor's Manual

How to start and run a profitable paint contracting company: getting set up and organized to handle volume work, avoiding mistakes, squeezing top production from your crews and the most value from your advertising dollar. Shows how to estimate all prep and painting. Loaded with manhour estimates, sample forms, contracts, charts, tables and examples you can use. **224 pages, 8½ x 11, $24.00**

Painter's Handbook

Loaded with "how-to" information you'll use every day to get professional results on any job: the best way to prepare a surface for painting or repainting; selecting and using the right materials and tools (including airless spray); tips for repainting kitchens, bathrooms, cabinets, eaves and porches; how to match and blend colors; why coatings fail and what to do about it. Lists 30 profitable specialties in the painting business. **320 pages, 8½ x 11, $21.25**

Illustrated Guide to the 1996 National Electrical Code

This fully-illustrated guide offers a quick and easy visual reference for installing electrical systems. Whether you're installing a new system or repairing an old one, you'll appreciate the simple explanations written by a code expert, and the detailed, intricately-drawn and labeled diagrams. A real time-saver when it comes to deciphering the current *NEC*. **384 pages, 8½ x 11, $34.75**

Order Today! Money-Back Guarantee!

Craftsman Book Company
6058 Corte del Cedro, P.O. Box 6500
Carlsbad, CA 92018

☎ 24 hour order line ☎
1-800-829-8123
Fax (619) 438-0398

Order online
http://www.craftsman-book.com

In A Hurry?
We accept phone orders charged to your
Visa, MasterCard, Discover or American Express

Name
_____

Company
_____

Address
_____

City/State/Zip

Total enclosed_____(In California add 7.25% tax)

We pay shipping when your check covers your order in full.
If you prefer, use your

❑Visa ❑MasterCard ❑Discover or ❑American Express

Card#_____

Expiration date_____Initials_____

Tax Deductible: Treasury regulations make these references tax deductible
when used in your work. Save the canceled check or charge card statement
as your receipt.

10-Day Money Back Guarantee

- ❑ 30.00 Bar Chart Scheduling for Residential Construction
- ❑ 27.50 Basic Construction Management: The Superintendent's Job, 3rd Ed.
- ❑ 33.00 Basic Plumbing with Illustrations, Revised
- ❑ 15.50 Stair Builder's Handbook
- ❑ 14.75 Blueprint Reading for Building Trades
- ❑ 19.75 Bookkeeping for Builders
- ❑ 26.50 Builder's Guide to Accounting Revised
- ❑ 27.25 Builder's Guide to Room Additions
- ❑ 35.00 Building Contractor's Exam Preparation Guide
- ❑ 15.00 Building Layout
- ❑ 59.00 CD Estimator
- ❑ 69.00 CD Estimator — Heavy
- ❑ 17.75 Concrete & Formwork
- ❑ 25.00 Concrete Construction & Estimating
- ❑ 39.50 Construction Estimating Reference Data with FREE stand-alone Windows estimating program on a 3½" disk.
- ❑ 39.75 Construction Forms & Contracts with a 3½" disk. Add $15.00 if you need ❑ Macintosh disks.
- ❑ 19.25 Construction Surveying & Layout
- ❑ 19.00 Contractor's Growth & Profit Guide
- ❑ 39.00 Contractor's Guide to Building Code Revised
- ❑ 59.95 Contractor's Legal Kit
- ❑ 22.25 Contractor's Survival Manual
- ❑ 26.50 Contractor's Year-Round Tax Guide Revised
- ❑ 36.00 Craftsman's Illustrated Dictionary of Construction Terms
- ❑ 27.50 Drafting House Plans
- ❑ 18.25 Drywall Contracting
- ❑ 17.00 Estimating Home Building Costs
- ❑ 21.50 Estimating Tables for Home Building
- ❑ 23.25 Fences and Retaining Walls
- ❑ 22.50 Finish Carpenter's Manual
- ❑ 39.95 Glass Block Handbook
- ❑ 28.75 Handbook of Construction Contracting Volume 1
- ❑ 30.75 Handbook of Construction Contracting Volume 2
- ❑ 24.95 Home Inspection Handbook
- ❑ 15.00 How to Hire and Supervise Subcontractors
- ❑ 24.25 How to Succeed w/Your Own Construction Business

- ❑ 34.75 Illustrated Guide to the 1996 National Electrical Code
- ❑ 37.00 Land Development
- ❑ 27.95 Managing the Small Construction Business
- ❑ 23.00 National Building Cost Manual
- ❑ 37.50 National Construction Estimator with FREE stand-alone Windows estimating program on a 3½" disk
- ❑ 37.75 National Electrical Estimator with FREE stand-alone Windows estimating program on a 3½" disk.
- ❑ 39.50 National Renovation & Insurance Repair Estimator with FREE stand-alone Windows estimating program on a 3½" disk.
- ❑ 38.50 National Repair & Remodeling Estimator with FREE stand-alone Windows estimating program on a 3½" disk.
- ❑ 24.00 Paint Contractor's Manual
- ❑ 21.25 Painter's Handbook
- ❑ 19.25 Planning Drain, Waste & Vent Systems
- ❑ 28.25 Plumbing & HVAC Manhour Estimates
- ❑ 27.25 Profits in Building Spec Homes
- ❑ 15.75 Rafter Length Manual
- ❑ 33.50 Renovating & Restyling Vintage Homes
- ❑ 38.80 Residential Steel Framing Guide
- ❑ 22.00 Roof Framing
- ❑ 24 00 Roof Framer's Bible
- ❑ 35.00 Roofing Construction & Estimating
- ❑ 26.50 Rough Framing Carpentry
- ❑ 21.00 Running Your Remodeling Business
- ❑ 29.00 Scheduling Residential Construction for Builders and Remodelers
- ❑ 15.50 Stair Builder's Handbook
- ❑ 29.95 Simplified Guide to Construction Law
- ❑ 32.50 Troubleshooting Guide to Residential Construction
- ❑ 80.00 Video: Roof Framing, 1
- ❑ 80.00 Video: Roof Framing, 2
- ❑ 25.50 Wood-Frame House Construction
- ❑ 35.50 Carpentry Estimating with FREE National Estimator carpentry estimating program on a 3½" disk.
- ❑ FREE Full Color Catalog

Prices subject to change without notice